THE WORK OF KINGS

THE WORK OF KINGS

The New Buddhism in Sri Lanka

H. L. SENEVIRATNE

THE
UNIVERSITY
of CHICAGO PRESS
CHICAGO *and*
LONDON

H. L. SENEVIRATNE is associate professor of anthropology at the University of Virginia and the author of *Rituals of the Kandyan State.*

The University of Chicago Press, Chicago 60637
The University of Chicago Press, Ltd., London
© 1999 by The University of Chicago
All rights reserved. Published 1999

08 07 06 05 04 03 02 01 00 99   5 4 3 2 1

ISBN (cloth): 0-226-74865-0
ISBN (paper): 0-226-74866-9

Library of Congress Cataloging-in-Publication Data

Seneviratne, H. L.
    The work of kings : the new Buddhism in Sri Lanka / H. L. Seneviratne.
       p.   cm.
    Includes index.
    ISBN 0-226-74865-0. — ISBN 0-226-74866-9 (pbk.)
    1. Buddhism—Sri Lanka—History—20th century. 2. Buddhism and politics—
Sri Lanka—History—20th century. 3. Buddhism—Social aspects—Sri Lanka—
History—20th century. I. Title.
BQ376.S46   1999
294.3'095493'0904—dc21   99-34713
                                                                         CIP

FOR

Bryce Ryan, Murray Strauss, S. J. Tambiah, Gananath Obeyesekere

AND THE MEMORY OF

Ralph Pieris

Founders of Sociology in Sri Lanka

". . . So, your majesty, it is the business of the princes of this earth to know all about elephants, horses, chariots, bows, edicts, and seals, to be well versed in the textbooks of statecraft, in its tradition and custom, and to lead people into battle. . . . The Tathagata therefore urged the monks to devote themselves to their own work, and not that of others . . ."

The Questions of Milinda

"[The monk] neither constructs in his mind, nor wills in order to produce, a state of mind or body or the destruction of any such state. By not so willing anything in the world, he grasps after nothing; by not grasping, he is not anxious; he is therefore fully calmed within."

Majjhima Nikaya

"While this [Buddhist] Sangha, based on the ancient Sangha, has democracy [as its base] it has neither special country nor nation nor caste. To such a society which has no special country, nation, or caste, every human being is the same. . . .

If a given Buddhist is moral, wise, and just, that Buddhist can commit no crime for country, language, or nation. If a Buddhist commits a crime for whatever reason, that Buddhist is no Buddhist. Those who fight against the Tamils are not Buddhists."

Naravila Dhammaratana, Buddhist monk, in
Buddhagama navata soyaganima *(Rediscovering Buddhism)*

CONTENTS

A gallery of photographs follows page 188

PREFACE

This book is based on fieldwork conducted in Sri Lanka during 1990–91, followed up with shorter visits between then and 1995. In 1995–96 I spent another continuous period of eleven months during which I wrote a draft of the work. Fieldwork consisted of interviews (with monks, Buddhist leaders, and ordinary laymen and laywomen), participation in public activities related to the project, and work at the libraries of the Peradeniya and Colombo universities, the National Archives, the Colombo Museum Library, and the private library of the late Venerable Kalukondayave Pannasekhara at the Sugatabimbaramaya monastery at Navagamuva, on the Kelani river, thirty kilometres east of Colombo. Part of this library is now housed at the Colombo Museum Library.

My scholarly interest in the Buddhist monkhood of Sri Lanka goes back many years. Beginning in the mid 1970s I intermittently collected field data on the Asgiriya and Malvatta hierarchies, and it was my intention to publish a book on these medievally based cultures as well as on the larger monastic social organization in which they were embedded. However, as I became increasingly familiar with the gulf that separates the activities of the monkhood from its ideals, I was convinced that such a study could wait until a differently conceived work, namely an exploration of the origin and nature of what appears to be (and is widely believed to be) the monk's dynamic social role, is published first. My interest in the original project remains, and I hope to publish the material arising from that at some future date.

In this work, I contend that the conception of the role of the monk as social activism, widely believed by contemporary elite monks and the Sinhala Buddhist middle class to go back to two millennia, is in fact more convincingly traceable to the written and spoken words of Anagarika Dharmapala in the early decades of the twentieth century. Dharmapala's definition of the monastic role as dedication for national and moral renewal during the dark era of imperial domination went through rapid goal displacement

within a short period of about three decades, giving birth to a worldly individualism in the monastery unprecedented in the history of South and Southeast Asian Buddhism. I use a body of historical and contemporary ethnogra-
phy to show how the potential for the rationalization of institutions dormant
in the economic ethic of nineteenth-century reformist Buddhism failed to
materialize, channelling it instead in anomic and disruptive directions.

Among the many members of the Buddhist Sangha (Monkhood) who gave
me generously of their time are the Venerable monks Madoluvave Sobhita,
Akuratiye Amaravamsa, Akuratiye Nanda, Horana Vajiragnana and the late
Venerable Walpola Rahula. The Venerable Varakave Dhammaloka's support
of my work goes well beyond the period of the present research. I owe a
special debt of gratitude to the Venerable monks Madana Jinaratana of the
Sugatabimbaramaya at Navagamuva, Hinatiyana Nanda of the Hinatiyana
Potgul Vihara Dharmaduta Pirivena at Hinatiyana, and Henegedara Siddharta of the Purana Gallen Viharaya at Ratmulukanda for giving me access
to the papers of their renowned teachers, Kalukondayave Pannasekhara,
Hinatiyana Dhammaloka, and Hendiyagala Silaratana respectively, the three
"hero-giants" discussed at length in this work. Many young monks, most of
them of Colombo University, shared with me their thoughts about themselves and the Sangha, which greatly helped me to contemplate and articulate my own understandings of this historic Buddhist institution.

I received more encouragement and support than I can acknowledge
from Professors Stanley Tambiah, Gananath Obeyeskere, and Nur Yalman.
All three of these anthropologists of Theravada Buddhism read this work
laboriously and made valuable comments. I also received thoughtful and perceptive comments from Professors Charles Hallisey and Anne Blackburn.
Frequent discussions with my friend Rex Casinader during the later phases of
writing helped me broaden my perspectives regarding many of the issues dealt
with in this work. Lalitha Gunawardena carefully read the first draft of the
manuscript, and my conversations with her on the broader issues of society,
politics, and culture significantly affected my thinking about the material discussed here. Lise McKean read the manuscript painstakingly and helped me
vastly improve its coherence. I however take full responsibility for the views
expressed here, in particular considering their potential for controversy.

Numerous friends in Sri Lanka gave me their unstinting support during
my extended stays in the island. I wish to make special mention of the support and affection I have received from Sarath and Palika Amunugama and
their daughter Varuni, Senerat and Padmini Pilapitiya, W. D. and Pushpa
Ailapperuma, Dhammika Amarasinghe, Lalitha Gunawardena, Tissa Jayati-
leka, G. D. Wijayawardhana, and Nihal Seneviratne. I am grateful to Siri

Hettige, Professor of Sociology, Colombo University, for conferring on me the honor of an affiliation with his department, which gave me access to many faculty privileges. I am also grateful to Director Radhika Coomaraswamy and the staff of the International Centre for Ethnic Studies (ICES) for their support, in particular the use of space in their library. Ajit Serasundera worked with enthusiasm and ability as my primary research assistant. Kala Sommerville helped out with many chores including typing and the preparation of the pictures. My nephew Chandrasiri Wijeratne and niece Dhammi are invaluable sources of continuing support.

I wish to thank the Associated Newspapers of Ceylon Limited (ANCL), The Upali Group of Newspapers, the Sunday *Times,* and photographers Sriyantha Walpola, Denzil Pathiraja, Ajit Seneviratne, Cyril Vimalasurendra, and Sudath Malaweera for their assistance in obtaining photographs.

I wish to thank Phil McEldowney and Sajjad Yusuf of the Alderman Library, University of Virginia, for their unrivalled professionalism and courtesy in responding to my numerous bibliographical requests. Valuable bibliographic assistance was also provided by the LEO service of the Alderman Library. David Brent and Richard Allen guided the progress of this work through the press with care, interest, and the highest standards of editorial expertise. I would also like to record my appreciation of the enthusiastic work of Betsy Solaro.

I wish to thank the Fulbright Faculty Research program and the Wenner-Gren Foundation for Anthropological Research for providing funds that enabled me to take leave from normal duties for purposes of extended fieldwork.

Parts of this work were presented at various academic fora including the ICES, the Association for the Advancement of Science, the Department of Sociology, Colombo University, all in Colombo, Sri Lanka, and in the U.S., at Harvard and Johns Hopkins Universities and the University of Virginia. I wish to acknowledge the useful comments I received from participants.

In conclusion, I wish to mention the support of my family, which alone enabled the completion of this work at this time. During all our life together, my wife Indrani did two full-time jobs without ever complaining, with the sole purpose of enabling me to concentrate on the one full-time job of mine. My son Rajiva was unfailing in his eagerness to help the progress of this work in numerous ways, including his expertise as a professional editor, often giving priority to my work over his own. Besides, he has cheerfully taken on the unenviable role of permanent tutor for a pupil destined never to master the ways of the personal computer, going so far as to buy me a copy of *The Complete Idiot's Guide.*

NOTE ON USAGE

As a general rule, I italicize the first occurrence of Sinhala, Pali, or Sanskrit terms, leaving the subsequent occurrences in roman script. No diacritical marks are used in the text. In the index, which also functions as a glossary, I italicize these terms and use diacritical marks. I use the English plural marker "s" to pluralize Sinhala, Pali, and Sanskrit terms. In transcription I use the generaly accepted orthography which admits minor variations.

A monk has a personal name, prefixed by a village name. Monks, especially well-known monks, are often referred to by the latter, although this is by no means a general rule. I use my judgment as to what I consider to be the more common indigenous usage when choosing to use the one or the other or both in relation to a particular monk. I follow the same rule regarding lay names.

It is customary to prefix a monk's name with the honorific "The Venerable." Since the names of monks occur profusely in this work, the invariable use of this prefix would mar the reader's smooth progress. For this reason I do not use it except very rarely. This does not mean any disrespect to the monks mentioned. They are all venerable men.

BUDDHISM, CIVIL SOCIETY, AND THE PRESENT STUDY

In his celebrated essay on the social psychology of world religions,[1] Max Weber emphasized that his concerns were not the ethical theories of theological compendia but the imperatives of such theories for action. In this Weber was expressing a basic tenet of the sociology of religion—that its concerns are more with how people act in terms of what they believe than with what they believe per se. Weber exemplified this in much of his work, but in the vast range of his comparative religion, in particular in areas exotic to him, his choices were limited, and he failed to adhere strictly to this principle. The inventor of the ideal type in sociology, Weber sometimes put his guard down and let ideal typification become a habit of mind; in such instances he moved back and forth freely between the ideal and mundane worlds, treating the ideal type as if it were the reality. His model of "ancient Buddhism" was such an ideal type, which he intermittently mistook for its much more complex earthly representation.[2] Weber's "ancient Buddhism" was more an extrapolation from an essentialized Buddhist doctrine than an abstract of monastic life as it was actually lived, as far as we are able to reconstruct the latter. His typology of world religions needed an "otherworldly mysticism," and he invented one in his conception of "ancient Buddhism." In Weber's work, "ancient Buddhism," logically meant to be an ideal type, expresses itself as an empirical reality. This indeed is the general prob-

1. Max Weber, "The Social Psychology of World Religions," in *Max Weber: Essays in Sociology*, ed. H. H. Gerth and C. Wright Mills (New York: Oxford University Press, 1958), 267–301. The original German version of this paper served as the Introduction to a series of studies that Weber published on "The Economic Ethic of World religions" in *Archiv für Sozialforschung*, written in 1922–23.

2. On "ancient Buddhism" see Max Weber, *The Religion of India* (Glencoe: The Free Press, 1958), 204–30.

lem with the ideal type as an analytical construct: those who work with ideal types sometimes proceed as if they were real. Weber's "Ancient Buddhism" conceived of the Buddhist goal in very highly focused terms, and then worked backwards to invent a super-humanly goal-oriented system of behavior to achieve it. To state this differently, Weber failed to invest his construction of "ancient Buddhism" with the meticulous attention to detail by means of which he traced ingeniously, through a series of functional relations, the linkage between Calvinism and capitalism.[3]

Weber was not alone in this. His French contemporary Durkheim so essentialized Buddhism that he disagreed with Tyler's "minimum definition" of religion as "belief in spirit beings" by saying that Buddhism has no belief in such beings.[4] The footnotes of both Weber and Durkheim show that their view of Buddhism was derived from the same source, Indology as it was practiced in Europe in the late-nineteenth century. Indologists invented what might be called a Euro-Buddhist canon by portraying a rationalized and sanitized Buddhism in keeping with the imperatives of the sociology of their own intellectual life.[5] It is, ironically, this Euro-Buddhist canon that came to dominate and guide the religio-nationalist resurgence in the homelands of Buddhism colonized by western powers, in particular the Theravada societies of South and Southeast Asia.[6] In the present work I shall try to unravel some of the recent ramifications of this Euro-Buddhist canon in one South Asian colonial setting, the island of Sri Lanka. Thus, this work carries further the study of Buddhism in its dynamic and modernizing aspect that has been a major focus and trajectory of advancement in contemporary Buddhist studies.[7]

For these early western interpreters of Buddhism, there was no question or ambiguity as to the object and focus of their study, which was a select corpus of Buddhist texts. To them any material that did not conform to the

---

3. Max Weber, *The Protestant Ethic and the Spirit of Capitalism,* Trans. Talcott Parsons (New York: Charles Scribner's Sons, 1958).

4. Emile Durkheim, *The Elementary Forms of the Religious Life* (London: George Allen and Unwin, 1915; rpt., New York: The Free Press, 1965), 45.

5. These are a galaxy of scholars who, among other work, translated into the major European languages the "sacred books" of the orient. Among the best known of those who worked with the Buddhist texts are Hermann Oldenberg and T. W. Rhys Davids.

6. In this work by "Buddhism" I mean Theravada, unless specified otherwise.

7. We have a large number of studies in this area. Among these are Richard Gombrich and Gananath Obeyesekere, *Buddhism Transformed* (Princeton, N.J.: Princeton University Press, 1988); Richard Gombrich, *Theravada Buddhism* (London: Routledge and Kegan Paul, 1988); George Bond, *The Buddhist Revival in Sri Lanka* (Columbia: University of South Carolina Press, 1988); K. Malalgoda, *Buddhism in Sinhalese Society 1750–1900* (Berkeley: University of California Press, 1976).

imagined Buddhism of this Euro-Buddhist canon was outside Buddhism. Such material were labeled and classified away as pagan cults, animism, folk supernaturalism, idolatry, and so forth. By the process of biblification in the form of printed translations into western languages, they fixed and placed boundaries on this canon, paving the way for a new Buddhist scripturalism. The label "Buddhism" itself symbolized this process of fixing, cleansing, and establishing boundaries, for "Buddhism" had no such indigenous label,[8] and existed only as a "total social phenomenon" of pluralistic and unbounded beliefs and practices, a system with an "open boundary" that allowed free movement of belief and practice between the total system's center and periphery. Living Buddhism constituted a picture different from the essentialized, sanitized, cleansed, scripturalized, and objectified Buddhism of these texts. In living Buddhism these texts functioned in two ways: as a spiritual and ethical corpus and guide to life conduct somewhat resembling what they were wholly presumed to be in this new Euro-Buddhist canon, and more commonly as a chant of magical value, revived from the dead language of Pali.

In the western codification of the texts, an essentialized high Buddhism was made into a relic and was polarized from the folk religion. We see here the beginning of what Tambiah has termed the fetishization of Buddhism,[9] which made it a powerful item in the nationalist rhetoric of the Buddhist states of South and Southeast Asia in the twentieth century, while submerging its ethical content and values of pluralism and tolerance. This need not have been the only or necessary outcome of codification. It could instead have so enlivened the ethical and socio-political values of Buddhism as to enable their generalization to the social order, leading to an encompassing rationalization and ethicization life and the evolution of a tolerant, pluralistic

8. It was in the beginning of the twentieth century that Western scholars labeled great religions as "isms." The term "religion" originally had two meanings: the existence of a power outside man to whom he was obligated and the feeling of piety towards that power. Early Christianity added other meanings, such as a sense of community (church) and faith as integral to religion. Early Christianity also developed the notions of true and false religion, which was carried further in the Middle Ages by St. Augustine in his claim regarding Christianity as the only true religion. St. Augustine also emphasized the believer's personal relation to the one true God, as he did "faith" as opposed to "religion," which by then had come to mean monastic life. Religion in Calvin meant no such relation to the church, but a personal inner orientation to the transcendental. The conception of religion as a cognitive system with doctrine and dogma was a product of the Enlightenment, and since the seventeenth century, leaders of European thought used the term religion to refer to a system of thought. By the nineteenth century, this trend was taken further by the inclusion in religion of the study of religious history. Thus religion was substantialized and became an object of study where scholars could compare the histories of different religions. Hence the labeling of newly discovered religions as "isms." See Wilfred Cantwell Smith, *The Meaning and the End of Religion* (San Francisco: Harper and Row, 1978).

9. S. J. Tambiah, *Buddhism Betrayed?* (Chicago: University of Chicago Press, 1992).

civil society. But in the case we are examining, Sri Lanka, it did not. It did inspire, and continues to do sporadically, individuals and groups to universalist sentiment, but it fails to animate the society as a whole. I shall explore why this is so by using some of Max Weber's insights into the sociology of religion, in particular his idea of functional links between variables that he put so effectively to use in his studies of the relation between religion and capitalism.[10]

BUDDHISMS
One and Many

There certainly is what is often considered a "core" of Buddhism, such as the doctrines of Karma, No-Soul, the Four Noble Truths, and the Noble Eightfold path. This "core" is generally believed to be held in common at least by the Theravada Buddhists of different countries. If this is so, what lies outside this core is much more problematic. These aspects outside the core appear to be widely divergent, not only in the different cultural traditions of Theravada Buddhism such as Burma, Thailand, or Sri Lanka, but in the different regional and local traditions within each of these societies. Yet, the conceptualization of these systems as separate but as constituting a whole within each locale is one of the more useful developments in the sociology of Buddhism, articulated specifically in a series of anthropological writings beginning about the 1950s. Work on the three major Theravada traditions—Thailand, Burma, and Sri Lanka—conducted during this period converged on the view that each of these represents a unique variant of the expression of Theravada's open boundary policy.[11]

While this way of conceptualizing Buddhism accorded more with the empirical reality of a living religion by including the folk ritualistic practices as integral to the system, it failed to encompass many other aspects of that reality. One such aspect of major consequence is religio-nationalist ideology. This failure is partly attributable to the fact that the effect of such ideology

---

10. See Weber, *Protestant Ethic.*

11. These works articulated the view that Buddhism in different societies does not constitute discrete strata of belief and practice but a logically coherent and integrated whole. Excellent representative works are Manning Nash et al., *Anthropological Studies in Theravada Buddhism,* Cultural Report Series no. 13, Yale University Southeast Asia Studies, 1966, and S. J. Tambiah, *Buddhism and the Spirit Cults in North-East Thailand* (Cambridge: Cambridge University Press, 1970). While these studies broadly subscribe to this conceptualization, they still constitute different ways of understanding the phenomena. For example, whereas Obeyesekere, in the Nash volume, sees logical coherence in the Sri Lankan material, Tambiah sees a "tapestry" in the Thai material.

was still in incubation when the writers just mentioned were making their investigations and arriving at their conclusions. It is no accident that the theory of "the Buddhist State" was articulated, most eloquently by writers like Ling, Bechert, and Tambiah,[12] only in the period following the Sri Lankan general election of 1956, considered a watershed in the rise of religio-nationalist ideology in the modern history of the island. In this work I attempt to broaden the sociological conception of Buddhism to embrace a range of empirically existing and significant phenomena not included in existing frameworks.

The rise of ideology in turn has led Buddhist scholarship to the technically retrograde step of conceptualizing Buddhism stratificationally. This time around, the object of stigmatization and relegation to lowliness in this stratification is not the cultism and supernaturalism of the folk, but the ideology-driven intolerance and imposition of inequality, oppression, and violence on ethnic and other minorities within a given Theravada system. Thus Tambiah writes about two Buddhisms: the one compassionate and ethically sublime, the other with a dark underside that betrays the former.[13]

ANTHROPOLOGY AND THE QUESTION OF VALUE

This re-stratification of Buddhism also introduces a new element of value which stands in opposition to the standard anthropological view that anthropologists are impartial observers who, if ever they were to take a stand, should do so to defend the culture against outside dominations: by a big foreign power, big technology, big business, big irrigation systems, or some other big affair. This new element of value, however, brings into question one of the sacred dogmas of anthropology, the idea of cultural relativity. Cultural relativity came into being as a moral and intellectual reaction to the extreme ethnocentrism of Europe during the period of its expansion and the founding of its far flung empires. In that era and under the shadow of

12. S. J. Tambiah, *World Conquerer and World Renouncer* (Cambridge: Cambridge University Press, 1976); Trevor Ling, *The Buddha* (London: Temple Smith, 1973); Heinz Bechert, "The Beginnings of Buddhist Historiography: Mahavamsa and Political Thinking," in Bardwell Smith, ed., *Religion and Legitimation of Power in Sri Lanka* (Chambersburg, Penn.: Anima Books, 1978). Bechert's argument is conceivably more developed in his *Buddhismus, Staat und Gesellschaft in den Ländern des Theravāda Buddhismus,* vol. 1 (Frankfurt: A. Metzner), vols. 2 and 3 (Wiesbaden: Otto Harrassowitz, 1966 and 1973), available only in German.

13. S. J. Tambiah, *Ethnic Fratricide and the Dismantling of Democracy* (Chicago: University of Chicago Press, 1986); and *Buddhism Betrayed?* See also, Bruce Kapferer, *Legends of People, Myths of State* (Washington, D.C.: Smithsonian Institution Press, 1988).

unilinear evolutionary theory, subject peoples were designated "savages" or at best "natives" of inferior culture and genetic make-up. The persecution of the Jews also played a part in the acceptance of cultural relativity as a morally and intellectually laudable stand in the study of society. Accordingly, the idea became sanctified in functionalism, the dominant theory and method of the time.

Today however, with the decline of both colonialism and functionalism and the rise of conceptions of human rights, it has become increasingly difficult to analyze such classical anthropological phenomena as head hunting, infanticide, and genital mutilation with alleged scientific detachment, and merely for the sake of such classical anthropological exercises as symbolic interpretation. The rise of new nation-states upon the eclipse of empires has given rise to new nationalisms which have developed hegemonies over ethnic and other minorities that are no less oppressive than colonial hegemony. A host of other subjects have emerged as important social issues, such as religious fundamentalism and intolerance, ethnic cleansing, violence on women, drug dealing, corruption in governments, and environmental degradation to name a few, which demand the anthropologist's involvement, not merely as allegedly objective and impartial analyst or culture writer agonizing about how to write culture, but as a participant in unraveling social ills with a view to contributing towards their amelioration. The anthropologist's role has changed from participant observer to observing participant. This calls for the replacement of cultural relativity with notions of universal human values and human rights in increasingly more areas of inquiry.[14] This is neither to discard the idea of cultural relativity nor to devalue its achievements in anthropology, but only to re-assign it a legitimate place in what might be called a liberation anthropology.

This is a task easier said than done for the typical anthropologist, who is an outsider who often sees himself as a long-term guest among "his" people. It is also difficult because taking an evaluative position often involves explicitly or implicitly challenging the powers or groups who claim that a specific custom, for example genital mutilation, is "our culture." The native anthropologist is in an easier position, because it is his or her culture as well that he or she is writing about and if necessary questioning. It is therefore incum-

---

14. The question of human rights and anthropology is a difficult one, arising from the idea that cultures need to be treated on their own terms. This could condone the infringement of human rights as universalistically conceived, for example, as understood in international charters. But true to standard anthropological perspectives, some argue that human rights should be looked at in their cultural form, which does not help the conundrum. For discussions and an extensive bibliography, see Theodore E. Downing and Gilbert Kushner, eds., *Human Rights and Anthropology,* Cultural Survival Report 24 (Cambridge, Mass.: Cultural Survival, Inc., 1988).

bent on native anthropologists to take up for study, with a view to amelioration in the shorter or longer term, directly or indirectly, those subjects they consider deleterious to the happiness and well-being of the members of their societies. This explains the degree of involvement with which I have tried, as native anthropologist, to chronicle what I consider to be a crucially important chapter in the contemporary sociology of my culture.

Developments in academic social science fields have functioned to erase our memory regarding the origins of these fields in the work of those who endeavored to improve the quality of human social life, either in general or specifically in their own societies. This tradition of social concern characterized the work of the three greatest sociological thinkers of our time, Karl Marx, Max Weber, and Emile Durkheim. Societal concern dominated the minds of many other sociological thinkers as well, until the rise of the research universities especially in the U.S., and the institutionalization of funding for academic or "pure" research. In the present work, my purpose is not merely to analyze but to follow this tradition of social concern. I contend that the definition of a new role for the Buddhist monk, which was one aspect of the movement to modernize Sri Lankan Theravada Buddhism in the twentieth century, has been detrimental to the happiness and well-being of the people of Sri Lanka.

Stated differently, I contend that the anthropological categories such as "Thai Buddhism," "Burmese Buddhism," and "Sinhalese Buddhism" need to be expanded beyond their present connotation of a syncretism between doctrinal Buddhism and folk Buddhism, great or little traditions of mystical belief and practices and so forth, to embrace the broader array of religiously grounded phenomena like "fundamentalism" and "ideology." Such an expanded definition would cover the political, economic, and cultural activities of diverse religious personalities—monks and lay virtuosi, mystagogues, apologists, champions, and various other propagandists. Whereas we can approach in a more or less value-neutral way the different syncretistic Buddhisms on which anthropological focus has been so far nearly exclusive, it would be difficult to do so when it comes to the ideological actors and movements covered by our expanded definition.

BUDDHIST MODERNISM

Typologies of the sociology of religion identify religious modernization as a major area of research. An enduring framework for understanding change, of which modernization is part, is that of evolution, despite the stigmatization of evolutionary theory in early and mid-twentieth-century anthropology. Major modern sociological thinkers such as Comte, Marx, Weber, and Durkheim thought about social change, which included religious modernization, in broadly evolutionary terms. A contemporary sociologist, Robert Bellah, followed these thinkers when he formulated a scheme of "religious evolution" consisting of five ideal typical stages—primitive, archaic, historic, early modern, and modern.[15] This scheme conceptualizes religious evolution as a process of internalization of ethical and spiritual values in which religion increasingly becomes a private matter. "At each stage" says Bellah, "the freedom of personality and society has increased relative to the environing conditions."[16]

For Bellah, the first distinctive feature of modern religion is the idea that salvation is unmediated. This contrasts with the mediator/mediated duality of premodern religion. Bellah cites the examples of Christian monks, Sufi shaykhs, or Buddhist ascetics who could "through their pure acts and personal charisma store up a fund of grace that could be shared with the less worthy."[17] The achievement of the Reformation was "to break through the whole mediated system of salvation and declare salvation potentially available to any man no matter what his station or calling might be."[18]

Bellah's second feature of modern religion is an ever-present internal state of faith and ethicization rather than an intermittent religiosity of specific and discrete religious acts. It is a devaluation of ritual because internalization and ethicization render ritual superfluous. This eventually led modern religion, with its association with greater literacy, to tinge ritual with a rusticity that is inconsistent with its self-representation. The third distinctive feature of modern religion is its inner-worldliness. By proclaiming that the world was "the theater of god's glory and the place to fulfil his command, the Reformation reinforced positive autonomous action in the world instead of a relatively passive acceptance of it."[19] Salvation is not to be found in any kind of withdrawal from the world but in the midst of worldly activities. The world was accepted as an arena in which to work out the divine command. This undermined the idea of renunciatory world rejection characteristic of the historic religions.

---

15. Robert Bellah, "Religious Evolution," *American Sociological Review* 29 (1964): 358–74. Rpt. in William A. Lessa and Evon Z. Vogt, *Reader in Comparative Religion*, 2d ed. (New York: Harper and Row, 1965), 73–87. For the purposes of this discussion, I am treating Bellah's "early modern" and "modern" as a single category.
16. Ibid., 86.
17. Ibid., 82.
18. Ibid.
19. Ibid., 82–83.

Bellah cautions that his ideal type of modern religion is empirically derived from a single cluster of cultures, those that embraced Protestantism. Subsequent research has demonstrated that such caution was salutary, because religious modernism elsewhere is by no means identical with that of the Protestant world. It is nevertheless remarkable that numerous religious movements belonging to different religions have produced modernisms that exhibit several features of this ideal type. This may be partially explicable in terms of the influence wielded by missionary Protestantism in different parts of the world in the nineteenth and twentieth centuries. Roman Catholic Christianity itself has been influenced by Protestant Christianity. Missionary activity, as well as the general fact of colonialism or non-colonial western contact,[20] has brought about modernist developments wherever these contacts were established. Typically such contact becomes the stimulus for nationalist adaptation, reform, and resurgence. Movements for such modernization are typically led by persuasive and charismatic leaders who inspire diverse strata, but in particular the urban middle classes, to religio-nationalist action.

REFORM MOVEMENTS

The reform movements of nineteenth- and twentieth-century Hinduism and Islam provide excellent examples of religious modernism. The Brahmo Samaj, the oldest such movement in India, was founded in Calcutta by Ram Mohan Roy (1772–1833) and had at its core a group of westernized Bengali intellectuals.[21] Its aim was to establish a form of Hinduism cleansed of rituals and image worship, an eminently "modernist" tendency as understood by Bellah and others.

The Brahmo followers primarily came from a few specific castes and families that had risen to prominence through employment in the Mughal administration and later the British East India Company. Thus they were an urban-based wealthy class. We have here the familiar association between urban wealth and religious reformism. This is an association that echoes the ancient connection between urban wealth and Buddhism, the first great anti-ritualist and universalist religious reform movement in India.

---

20. Japan and Thailand provide us with good examples of non-colonial western contact. Thailand is of particular interest because of its greater comparability with our case study, Sri Lanka.

21. See David Kopf, *The Brahmo Samaj and the Shaping of the Modern Indian Mind* (Princeton University Press, 1979).

In other expressions of modernism, Brahmo leader Roy understood his movement as a rationalist and ethical reinterpretation of vedantic monotheism. He rejected priestly mediation, paving the way for a new type of religious leader—secular, radical, and reformist like himself—who typically came from castes, known as non-*kulina,* who, unlike the *kulina* or "high caste" were less concerned with purity and were willing to work for both Muslim and British rulers. Debendranath Tagore (1817–1905) and Keshab Chandra Sen (1838–84), who succeeded Roy as Brahmo Samaj leaders, codified the Samaj's teachings and campaigned against Christian missionary activity. Both leaders reinforced the view that religious authority rests not on caste but on reason. Thus they were using western influences to strengthen Hinduism by adapting it to modernity. Rejection of mediation and ritualism in this movement correlates perfectly with Bellah's model of modern religion.

The Arya Samaj,[22] founded by Dayananda Sarasvati (1824–83) in 1875, was based on a theory of return to the vedic religion by way of rejecting puranic ritualism. Sarasvati's vedic religion was, however, a reformist and modernist construction. For example, vedic knowledge, traditionally denied to women and low *(sudra)* castes, should in his view be accessible to all. Further, the performance of vedic rituals needed neither a brahmin nor his caste. They could be performed by anyone. It was the dharma of all to work for the well-being of all. These views were rejected by the Hindu orthodoxy, but they found acceptance in the merchant castes of Bombay, which brings us back to the affinity between urban wealth and religious reformism. Similar merchant groups in Lahore formed a second chapter of the organization in 1877. Such chapters were formed later in almost every Indian city, making the Arya Samaj a major nationalist and reformist force. Like all such organizations, it used western ideas and models of organization to combat missionary and imperialist forces.

There were other reformist groups, some of them breakaways from Brahmo Samaj and Arya Samaj. One such deserves mention here, the movement founded by Narendranath Datta (1863–1902), better known as Vivekananda.[23] Originally a Brahmo Samajist, Vivekananda accepted its reformist doctrines and programs, but not its rejection of the path of renunciation.

22. See Kenneth Jones, *Arya Dharm: Hindu Consciousness in Nineteenth-Century Punjab* (Berkeley: University of California Press, 1976); and idem, "The Arya Samaj in British India," in Robert D. Baird, ed., *Religion in Modern India* (New Delhi: Manohar, 1981); J. T. F. Jordens, *Dayananda Sarasvati, His Life and Ideas* (Delhi: Oxford University Press, 1978).

23. See George M. Williams, *The Quest for Meaning of Swami Vivekananda* (Chicago, Calif.: New Horizons Press, 1974); and idem, "Swami Vivekananda: Archetypal Hero and Doubting Saint?" and "The Ramakrishna Movement: A Study in Religious Change," both in Baird, ed., *Religion in Modern India.*

Visiting the Parliament of Religions in Chicago in 1893, Vivekananda apparently made a good impression, which attracted to him a group of western followers. With that he laid the foundations for a worldwide Hindu movement. More relevant for our purposes, his reinterpretation of renunciation as a mission to work for the welfare of others exemplifies the pattern of religious modernism. In 1897 he founded the Ramakrishna Mission on the basis of a new and universal Hinduism, which he termed "practical Vedanta," that combined devotion with work in the world.

The suffusion of mundane work with religiosity, which Bellah considers to be one of the distinctive features of religious modernism, also characterizes the message of Anagarika Dharmapala of Sri Lanka, the central figure of the present study, who shared the spotlight with Vivekananda at the Chicago Parliament. We shall focus on the ambiguities and dissonances in the ideology of Dharmapala and endeavor to unravel the vividly manifested chasm between the utopia Dharmapala envisaged and the reality that has come to pass. Dharmapala also exemplifies the pattern of religious reform on the model of western ideas and social forms while ideologically rejecting the west. This creative synthesis, meeting the western challenge by learning from the west and fighting it with its own weapons, is a characteristic feature of all situations of rational indigenous response to colonialism. The result is invariably the invention of a new religion which tallies well with the indices of religious modernity that Bellah enumerates, though entirely lacking in the latter's universalizing and liberating essence. Such newly invented religions are typically portrayed as dating back to immemorial times, and they are used by their carrier strata for political purposes, first as anti-colonial activity, and after independence to internally colonize the minorities and bring them under their hegemony.

Like the label "Buddhism," "Hinduism" is an orientalist construction which, according to Thapar, is no older than 200 years.[24] She also draws attention to the important feature of religious reformism and modernism, the imposition of uniformity on a body of divergent beliefs and practices, which then becomes the basis for the development of a group identity. This sense of identity in the Hindu case, which Thapar terms "Hindu communalism," ultimately led to the rise of Hindu fanaticism.[25]

Thapar describes the newly constructed Hinduism as follows:

---

24. Romila Thapar, "Imagined Religious Communities?" *Modern Asian Studies* 23 (1989): 209–31.

25. For a lively account of the fundamentalist, nationalist, and commercial ramifications of the Hindu reformist movements discussed here, see Lise McKean, *Divine Enterprise: Gurus and the Hindu Nationalist Movement* (Chicago: University of Chicago Press, 1996).

The modern description of Hinduism has been largely that of a *brahmana-*
dominated religion which gathered to itself in a somewhat paternalistic pattern a variety of sects drawing on a range of Buddhists, Jainas, Vaisnavas,
Saivas and Saktas. The texts and the tradition were viewed as inspirational,
initially orally preserved, with multiple manifestations of deities, priests but
no church, a plurality of doctrines with a seeming absence of controversies
and all this somehow integrated into a single religious fabric. Differences
with Semitic religions were recognized and were seen as true absence of a
prophet, of a revealed book regarded as sacred, of a monotheistic God, of
ecclesiastical organization, of theological debates on orthodoxy and heresy
and, even more important, the absence of conversion. But somehow the
logic of these differences was not built into the construction of the history of
the religion.[26]

While the imagined Hinduism of modernist reformism thus hegemonistically glossed over the variations, Thapar draws a different and pluralistic
picture of the religious scene in India, especially regarding what she calls
"Brahmanism" and "Sramanism." Sramanism refers to rivals of Brahmanism,
primary of which are the Buddhists, Jainas, and Ajivakas. These sects denounced the fundamentals of Brahmanism, such as the vedic *sruti* and *smrti*.
They were also opposed to sacrificial ritual because of their disagreement
with the efficacy of this ritual as well as their opposition to violence against
animals. These sects, unlike the Brahmanic religion, were open to all castes,
which implied openness to conversion. While in the beginning sects like
Buddhism attracted large numbers of recruits from upper castes, there was
no restriction on lower caste recruitment. The founders of Sramanic sects
were not divine incarnations. Both the Buddhists and the Jainas had an ecclesiastical organization and a concern with historicity, which were never part
of Brahmanism. Buddhism and Jainism, unlike Brahmanism but more like
Islam and Christianity, "see themselves as part of the historical process of
the unfolding and interpreting of the single religion and sects are based on
variant interpretations of the original teaching. They build their strength on
a structure of ecclesiastical organization."[27] In contrast to this, Hindu sects
often had distinct and independent origins. Even though there was "structural similarity" in the ritual practiced in different regions, this similarity,
argues Thapar, is "different from a shared creed, catechism, theology and
ecclesiastical organization."[28]

---

26. Thapar, "Imagined Religious Communities?" 210–11. Sarvepalli Radhakrishnan illustrates the
hegemonic articulation of Hinduism Thapar refers to here. See Radhakrishnan and Charles A. Moore,
eds., *A Sourcebook in Indian Philosophy* (New Jersey: Princeton University Press, 1957).

27. Thapar, 218.

28. Ibid.

Hinduism until about two hundred years ago was an extremely diverse set of beliefs and practices which did not constitute the basis for a Hindu religious community in the sense it is now widely understood to exist. Thapar lists three factors that went into producing the new definition of Hinduism: Christian missionary activity's view of such an amorphous body of belief as Hinduism's as primitive, the orientalist eagerness to fit the "Hindu" religion to a known model by means of a "comprehensible whole," and the attempts of Indian reform movements to cleanse Indian religion of "what they regarded as negative encrustations and trying to find parallels with the semitic model."[29] Thus, while the conception of community was not absent, precolonial India consisted of multiple communities identified by locality, language, caste, occupation, and sect. There was no notion of a uniform religious community readily identified as Hindu.

The rise of Sikhism as the basis for a community identity provides us with another Indic example of religious modernity taking the typical form of reformism with its distinctive features of scripturalism, de-ritualization, and homogenization. Premodern Sikhism included "sectarian conflicts, nature worship, witchcraft, sorcery, spirits, magical healing, omens, wizards, miracle saints, goddesses, ancestral spirits, festivals, exorcism, astrology, divination, and villages deities."[30] Among the leaders of the reformist and modernist movement was Sant Sunder Singh (1883–1930), who used his exegetical skills to purge diversity in Sikh doctrine, ritual, and practice. This led to the notion of a homogeneous community and eventually to a movement for a separate Sikh utopia where non-Sikhs had no place.[31]

Thailand provides a particularly interesting case because, besides exemplifying the general process of modernist religious reformism, it expresses specificities of a Theravada Buddhist society in many ways comparable to our focus in this study, Sri Lanka. As a country that was not colonized by a modern European power, Thailand also reveals with great clarity the fact that modernist religious reformism is more than simply a byproduct of colonial domination. Thailand's reformism is part of a general process of modernization that came into being as a result of non-colonial contact with the western world. Tambiah identifies three "spurts" of modernist, reformist "revitalization."[32] The first took place in the 1850s and represents the response to contact with western powers led by Mongkut, first as monk and later as king.

29. Ibid.

30. Harjot Oberoi, *The Construction of Religious Boundaries* (Chicago: University of Chicago Press, 1994), 30.

31. Harjot Oberoi, "Sikh Fundamentalism: Translating History into Theory," in Martin E. Marty and R. Scott Appleby, eds., *Fundamentalisms and the State* (Chicago: University of Chicago Press, 1993), 267.

32. Tambiah, *World Conquerer and World Renouncer*, 406–23.

These consisted of (a) a return to the true canon ("scripturalism"), (b) an emphasis on doctrinal ideas and abstract concepts accompanied by a devaluation of superstitious ritualism ("intellectualism"), (c) an attempt to translate the pantheon of gods and demons into a metaphorical idiom ("euhemerism"), (d) an attempt to correlate or reconcile Buddhist doctrines with western scientific ideas ("rationalism"), and (e) an attempt to train a new breed of orthodox monks, which resulted in an incipient sectarianism.

The second spurt is signified by an attempt to uphold the validity of Buddhist doctrine, ethics, and beliefs in relation to modern western scientific and other knowledge. This was articulated in the 1930s by the European monk Bhikkhu Khemo Navayansit and later by the Thai monk Pramaha Thong Su'p. This spurt included the denunciation of ceremonial and other practices and an advocacy of positive this-worldly activity for the monk. Paralleling Dharmapala's activities in Sri Lanka, this-worldly activity for monks was articulated more fervently by the laity than the monks themselves. The monk's role in national development became a central issue in relation to the idea that Buddhist ethical tenets were integral to the worldly task of national development.

The third spurt, which began in the 1970s, marks the appearance on the religio-political scene of the renowned forest monk Buddhadasa Bhikkhu, who combined orthodoxy with a doctrine of the relevance of Buddhism for the here and now. He stimulated worldly action by locating Buddhist cosmology within the individual and by denying fatalism and inaction. Monks like Phra Maha Sathenpong Punnavnno and Phra Sri Visudhimoli argued that monks must return the support that the laity gives them by (1) imparting education, (2) propagating dhamma and its practice, and (3) giving mundane assistance to the laity (for example, moral advice relating to mundane problems, performing rituals to give laymen moral support, and providing advice and leadership in social welfare and development work in the rural areas). Tambiah points out that what is striking here is not the idea of a return gift, but that such a gift is mundane in general and starkly economic in particular. These views were reiterated by other monks who added a further perspective by suggesting that the laity must not only be rationally active in the world but must also cultivate detachment. Tambiah points out that this is an idea reminiscent of the inner-worldly asceticism of Max Weber. This scene exhibits many of the ingredients of religious modernism and reformism described above and strikingly parallels the developments in Sri Lanka that I shall unfold in the following pages.

MODERNIZATION AND FUNDAMENTALISM

As mentioned above, Bellah's ideal type of religious modernity was admittedly based on one empirical case, the related cultures of the Protestant Reformation. His source for this ideal type is Max Weber's sociology of religion, in particular Weber's identification of a series of functional relations between Calvinistic theology and what he called the spirit of capitalism. In this analysis, the validity of the priest/layman duality is denied, and the impersonal principle of relentless mundane work in the glory of God is enthroned. The monastery as the dispenser of piecemeal absolution and the arena of intermittent religiosity is replaced by each individual's full-time work in the glory of God, converting the world into a monastery. This left no room for any other activity, in particular any kind of ritual or cultic activity, or any activity that gave anything like pleasure. The world was rid of magic and merriment, giving birth to an asceticism that, as Weber puts it, "descended like a frost on the life of 'merrie olde England.'" The resulting emotional poverty was compensated by a plenitude of rationality which embraced all spheres of life, not just the economic, political, intellectual, and organizational fields, but also religion, art, architecture, and music. The picture here is one of total social transformation, not a piecemeal one where specific institutions are transformed. The rationalization of economic thought and activity in particular led to a triumph of the economic over the ideological, constituting a calming of the ideological impulse, allowing its creative expression but swiftly clipping its excesses, which in turn aided the foundation of a civil society.[33]

Wherever conditions were unripe for such total transformation, the path of religious modernization was far from smooth. As a rule, in new nations emerging from colonial rule, religious modernization was allied with nationalist resurgence. Far from being the cradle of a systemic rationality that embraced all institutions, religious modernity in these and similar cases became an ideological force that, in the extreme, as in some instances of Islamic resurgence, took fundamentalist and fanatical forms. Scripturalism, which could have under favorable circumstances channeled the society in the direction of rationalization and civility, here opened the path to the fetishization of religion, making it part of the arsenal of hegemonization.

---

33. On the centrality of economic thought to modern western society, see Louis Dumont, *From Mandeville to Marx: The Genesis and Triumph of Economic Ideology* (Chicago: University of Chicago Press, 1977). On civil society, see Ernest Gellner, *Conditions of Liberty: Civil Society and Its Rivals* (New York: Penguin, 1994).

Bellah notes that unmediated salvation was not the exclusive prerogative of Protestantism. It was implicit in such other traditions as Shinran Shonin's version of Pure Land Buddhism and in certain tendencies in other forms of Buddhism, Islam, Taoism, and Confucianism. But in none of these was it institutionalized.[34] That is, the potential for religious modernism need not necessarily reach fruition, and, alternatively, it might meander in imperfect, irregular, or piecemeal fashion, reaching different fruitions. One such possible fruition is fundamentalism, which we might view as an aberrant form of religious modernization dysfunctional for societal harmony.

BUDDHISM AND CIVIL SOCIETY

Separated from India by only a twenty-mile expanse of shallow sea, Sri Lanka cannot be adequately comprehended except as one more regional culture of the Indic civilization. While the geographical and political separation has certainly left its stamp, so has the fact of belongingness to the Indic totality, a fact easily forgotten in the Sinhala Buddhist hysteria of today but not lost on perceptive observers. Ananda Coomaraswamy for example emphasized the critical significance of India for Sri Lankan art and culture, and numerous other Sri Lankan writers, artists, and musicians, one of the most colorful among whom is George Keyt, exemplified Indian inspiration in their work. The pattern of belongingness to an Indic totality applies to other regions peripheral to India as well, such as Nepal and Bhutan and the different localities of the nation-states of Pakistan and Bangladesh. Within this pattern of broad civilizational estampage, regional factors have influenced sociocultural developments, for example the impact of South India on Sri Lanka.

However, unlike any other culture in the Indic civilization with the exception of Nepal and Bhutan, which are predominantly Hinduized, Sri Lanka is Buddhist. Since the introduction of Buddhism in the third century B.C.E., its hold has been strong and continuous. The Buddhist Sangha, the order of monks, was historically well supported by the state. A system of monasteries is scattered throughout the island, with practically one in every village.

Buddhism's hold on Sri Lanka is discernible at two levels. At the macro level the "Buddhist state" exhibits a historical tendency for the identification of Buddhism with the state, kingship, and the people.[35] At the micro level,

---

34. Bellah, "Religious Evolution," 82.
35. This view is held by several scholars coming from different disciplines. It is best articulated by Trevor Ling, a student of religion, and S. J. Tambiah, an anthropologist. See Ling, *The Buddha,* and

the Buddhist monastery has played a role as a center of education and culture.[36] Thus "Sinhalese Buddhism," in addition to being a syncretism of Buddhist and folk beliefs and a hierarchy of mystical beings, constitutes a socially
and culturally significant monastic presence in daily life. Hinduism has had
no comparable priesthood, and the Hindu monastery *(math)* has played no
comparable role in the village.

The monk/village nexus was local in the precolonial era, but as colonial
rule advanced, a supra-local Sangha came into being, enabled by colonial
technologies, especially the print media. While there were certain supra-
local Sangha formations in precolonial times, as reflected, for example, in
the enunciation of *katikavat* rules, these were initiated by royal support and
had no autonomous existence. Contrary to opinion fearfully held by politicians and popularly by the Sinhala middle class, the Sangha has no overarching and unifying social structures that would make it into a powerful elite
endowed with a gnawing class consciousness. That is, the supra-locality of
the Sangha does not make it a power. It only confers on the Sangha a ceremonial and symbolic status. On very rare occasions, as in the general elections
of 1956, the Sangha could influence the voter, but the reasons for that are
not anything inherent in an objectified entity called the Sangha. By its very
nature the Sangha cannot be a power. It can only be a handmaid of power.
This is well understood by perceptive members of the culture who call the
Sangha a "tool of politics" *(despalana atakolu)*.

The cultural influence of Buddhism is a different matter, and there can
be little doubt that Buddhism did make a difference to the socio-cultural
institutions of Sri Lanka. Bechert has suggested that it was not by accident
but by conscious Theravada design that the Hindu epic *Ramayana* is blacked
out in Sri Lanka.[37] According to Amartya Sen, there is a religious elitism in

---

Tambiah, *World Conqueror and World Renouncer,* cited above. Textualists Heinz Bechert and B. G. Gokhale
share this view. See Bechert, the works cited in note 12, and Gokhale, "Early Buddhist Kingship," *The
Journal of Asian Studies* 26:15–22. These works refer to Sri Lanka and Thailand, two of the three "classical" Buddhist states. For the third, Burma, see anthropologist E. Michael Mendelson's *Sangha and State
in Burma* (Ithaca: Cornell University Press, 1975) and sociologist E. Sarkisyanz, *Buddhist Backgrounds of
the Burmese Revolution* (The Hague: M. Nijhoff, 1965). A political scientist, Donald. E. Smith, has expressed the same view using material from Sri Lanka and drawing comparison with Burma. See his
South Asian Politics and Religion (Princeton, N.J.: Princeton University Press, 1966).

36. See S. J. Tambiah, "Literacy in a Buddhist Village in North-east Thailand," in Jack Goody, ed.,
Literacy in Traditional Societies (Cambridge: Cambridge University Press, 1970); Wilhelm Geiger, *Culture
of Ceylon in Mediaeval Times* (Wiesbaden: Otto Harrassowitz, 1960). The central cultural role of the
Buddhist monastery is documented in numerous studies.

37. Heinz Bechert, "The Beginnings of Buddhist Historiography." We must note however that the
attempt to keep out the *Ramayana,* if indeed it was the case, is not shared by all Theravada systems. On
the contrary Thailand seems to have willingly embraced it. The Chakri kings of Thailand styled them-

Hinduism and Islam, with their respective reliance on Brahmin priests and powerful Mullahs, in contrast to the egalitarian and populist traditions of Buddhism, which encouraged the high levels of literacy that we know were actively and democratically facilitated by the monks.[38] Buddhism is possibly the best explanation of the relatively greater societal liberalism in Sri Lanka when compared with both Hindu and Muslim India. For example, while there is caste in Sri Lanka, it assumes a mild form even when compared to the caste system of the Hindu Tamils of Sri Lanka, let alone the extreme inequalities of untouchablility in India. Dumont's famous study of caste does not accord to the Sri Lankan system even the status of true caste.[39] Other observers such as Ryan and Yalman agree.[40]

A second area of greater social liberalism in Sri Lanka relative to India is gender. The gender inequalities in Buddhist Sri Lanka, while substantial, are not anywhere as extreme as those in India, and even in the southern region where bilateral kinship is associated with relatively greater liberalism. Buddhism survived in South India until the fifteenth century, and we thus have in Buddhism a rival or additional explanation of the phenomenon of greater liberalism there. Further, the dowry system of Sri Lanka is also mild when compared to Indian practices. Bride burning, female infanticide, and the use of amniocentesis to abort female fetuses are customs unknown in Sri Lanka. The Indian preference for male children and the discriminatory malnourishment of female children are rare in Sri Lanka if not altogether absent. Women in classical Buddhism enjoyed spiritual equality with men, although the monastic orthodoxy's prejudices are canonical and no secret. The earliest extant poetry written by Indian women consists of the *therigatha* of Buddhist nuns.[41] Despite the official denial of ordination to women, there is in

---

selves Ramas, and their empire a kind of "Ramrajya." Ramayana motifs were also freely integrated into Buddhist art and architecture. The difference between Thailand and Sri Lanka is the latter's historical vulnerability to Hindu invasions that typically demolished monuments, which might explain the Sri Lankan Theravada attempt to keep out the *Ramayana*. This is complemented by the Mahavamsa's perspective that "protection of religion" was their main concern.

38. Amartya Sen, "Radical needs and moderate reforms," in Jean Dreze and Amartya Sen, eds., *Indian Development* (London: Oxford University Press, 1997), 14–19. See also Amartya Sen, *India: Economic Development and Social Opportunity* (London: Oxford University Press, 1995).

39. Louis Dumont, *Homo Hierarchicus* (Paris: Editions Gallimard, 1966); trans. George Weidenfeld (Chicago: University of Chicago Press, 1970).

40. Bryce Ryan, *Caste in Modern Ceylon* (New Brunswick, N.J: Rutgers University Press, 1953); Nur Yalman, "On Royalty, Caste and Temples in Sri Lanka and South India," In H. L. Seneviratne, ed., *Identity, Consciousness and the Past* (New Delhi, Oxford University Press, 1997). Hocart's theory of caste, based on Sri Lankan material, implies a non-rigid system as well. See A. M. Hocart, *Caste: A Comparative Study* (London: Methuen, 1950).

41. See Susie Tharu and K. Lalita, eds., *Women Writing in India,* vol. 1 (New York: The Feminist Press, 1991), 65–70.

Sri Lanka a vibrant institution of female renunciants.[42] Recently, a breakaway group of monks gave confirmation to the ordination of a group of nuns.[43] Thus a de facto order of nuns, a *bhiksuni sasana,* now exists in Sri Lanka.

Finally, the question of property rights. Women in Sri Lanka enjoy a greater range of property rights than do their counterparts in northern India.[44] Here again, we must pay due attention to the complexity of the context: as just discussed in relation to gender, bilaterality is a significant variable in property relations, but equally clearly, we must give Buddhism its due share of credit. These observations do not by any means constitute a denial of the existing gender inequalities or violence against women in Sri Lanka. All I wish to say here is that the gender inequalities in Sri Lanka are less severe than those in India, and Buddhism must be considered the best explanation.[45]

SANGHA AND CIVILITY

Liberalism regarding parochial social formations like caste and gender oppression expresses Buddhism's potential for achieving a civil society, not only relative to Hinduism or any other specific religion, but in absolute terms. Such liberalism reflects greater acceptance of the values of human freedom, equality, pluralism, and tolerance that characterize civil society. What other kinds of evidence do we possess to further illuminate the question of the affinity of Buddhism to the genesis of liberal and universalist ideas? Here we can look into the all-important area of politics, in which

42. Tessa Bartholomeusz. *Women Under the Bo-Tree* (Cambridge: Cambridge University Press, 1994).

43. The ordination of 21 Sinhala Theravada nuns was carried out at Saranath, India, by a quorum of Chinese and Korean Mahayana nuns on 8 December 1996. It was confirmed by the Dambulla monks, a recent breakaway subsect of the Asgiriya Chapter. The heads of the Asgiriya and Malvatta hierarchies opposed it. See D. Amarasiri Weeraratne, "Maha na himivaru ha meheni sasna," *Ravaya,* 17 May 1998, 9.

44. Bina Agrawal, *A Field of One's Own: Gender and Land Rights in South Asia* (Cambridge: Cambridge University Press, 1994).

45. In Agrawal's view what matters in attitudes towards gender is not "India" or "Sri Lanka" but the regions. Thus she considers the South Indian region which includes Sri Lanka to be more liberal regarding women's rights than North India. I contend that within this region, Sri Lanka stands out as still more liberal regarding women's rights, with the exception of the classical matrilineal system of Kerala and its echo in Sri Lanka among the matrilineal *Mukkuvas* of Batticaloa. With the establishment of British rule, changes were introduced in keeping with British notions of morality and property. "Traditional Sinhalese customs of polyandry, polygamy *(sic),* easy divorce, several marriages in a lifetime, and the liberal definition of legitimate heirs, conflicted with the British notion of marriage as a monogamous, lifelong union sanctioned by the Church and the State, with clear lines separating legitimate and illegitimate heirs" (*Field of One's Own,* 182). It is this new western-derived morality that Dharmapala foisted on the Sinhala people as their two thousand year old morality. These changes affected women's property and other rights adversely.

we have one brilliant example, the Asokan Buddhist state. We must first acknowledge that there is a difference of opinion as to how Buddhist the Asokan state was. Was it Buddhism that made it possible for the Asokan state to become such a unique experiment in political civility and rationality, or was it something else, such as a secularly derived theory or interpretation of politics and diplomacy? Because, we have also in India a brilliant example of a *non*-Buddhist polity that exemplifies liberal and universalist values especially in the area of religious tolerance, the Mughal empire of Akbar. Thus the question is debatable, but what is undeniable is that there is no evidence of any other *religious* source than Buddhism that encouraged tolerance, pluralism, nonviolence, and so forth in the Asokan system. Tambiah has graphically described how the Buddhist conception of chakkavatti kingship became the model for the pluralistic ordering of relations between the emperor and the rulers of the kingdoms that constituted Asoka's center-oriented but non-centralized mega-empire.[46]

Does this translate into Buddhism being a sufficient precondition for the growth of a civil society, or, to put it once more in Bellah's terms, do these examples of Buddhism's liberalism, tolerance, and pluralism necessarily indicate effective and interlinked underlying social processes that can bring about a total social transformation? There is no easy answer, but we can approach the question differently, by looking at the subsequent historical developments in Buddhism in India and in South and Southeast Asia.

The Asokan Buddhist state ceased to exist, and although there were later Buddhist kings on the subcontinent, the Buddhist state did not take root in India. It is in Sri Lanka, and subsequently in Burma and Thailand, that it found its flowering. One aspect of this "flowering" is the gradual rise of the Sangha as an economically independent and culturally influential stratum, which enabled its members, according the monastic chronicles, to make and unmake kings. We have no independent collaboration of this unrealistic and hyperbolic sounding claim, and we must be aware that this is a claim not of the Sangha as a whole but rather of the particular faction that managed to prevail over all others. This faction had a monopoly over writing propagandist books and could prevent them from being consigned to flames by hostile factions, thus controlling the sole "mass medium" of the time. But some of the Sangha members did try to wield power over their colleagues and over the political order whenever they could, which adversely affected the development of the tolerance and pluralism that would have set the society on the path to civility.

46. Tambiah, *World Conquerer*.

The main chronicle, the *Mahavamsa*,[47] is a hegemonic text built around the saga of King Dutthagamani. This work makes Dutthagamani a hero by virtue of his militant defense of Buddhism, and it confers on the imagined Sinhala ethnic community exclusive rights to inhabit the island. The victorious Dutthagamani, anxious about the karmic consequences of his violent activity, is assured by the monks that he need not worry because the thousands killed in the war were nonbelievers who are therefore nonhuman; killing them causes no retribution to the king. This contrasts with Asoka's remorse in his bloody and crowning Kalinga campaign, which became a turning point in his personal and imperial life. In fairness to Dutthagamani, we must remember that, while we know of Asoka from his own inscriptions, we know about Dutthagamani only from the monks. They wrote from their own point of view, which may not necessarily be the king's, and, in addition, the entire story is probably fictional. Whether fictional or true, what the story reflects on the Sangha is clear: its culture did not have effective mechanisms for imbuing itself with the universalist values of tolerance, nonviolence, and pluralism that we readily infer from the ethical theories of Buddhist compendia and celebrate as the achievement of the Asokan Buddhist state. Thus, in the Sangha or at least in a decisive section of its membership in the Buddhist state as it blossomed in early medieval Sri Lanka, we are able to isolate a crucial variable inhibitive of the development of civility.

The activities of the Sangha in Burma and Thailand, historically and in more recent times, only confirm this, although there are obvious differences, especially relative to the Thai case. Differently stated, the much-written-about cultural role of the Sangha in Buddhist kingdoms involved, amidst many positive contributions, a parochializing and hegemonizing tendency which could only have had a chilling effect on the possibility of working out effective cultural linkages in the arduous task of constructing a civil society. In the present work, I shall explore how, under conditions of colonial-era and post-colonial nationalism, the Sangha's perspectives in this respect have only worsened. Just as the politico-ethical potential that was realized in Asokan Buddhism failed to suffuse the medieval flowering of Buddhism in Sri Lanka with the golden glow of its civility, reformist Buddhism of modern times failed to take the path that would have ultimately led to a civil society. Instead, it launched itself on a trajectory that has plunged the society in darkness.

A logical question now emerges: given Buddhism's universalism, which

---

47. *The Mahavamsa, or the Great Chronicle of Ceylon*, trans. Wilhelm Geiger (London: The Pali Text Society, 1912; rpt. Colombo: The Government of Ceylon, 1960).

gives it an unprecedented initial push to enable the building of a civil society, is it possible to imagine a Buddhist state in which the Sangha reverts to the profile it enjoyed in the proto-Buddhist Asokan state? This certainly seems to be the case in the imagined Buddhism of the Indian Buddhist leader Bhimrao Ramji Ambedkar. Buddhism to Ambedkar was primarily a liberating ideology for the here and now, whatever eschatological meanings it may have had for him personally. The assumption was that Buddhism's ideal ethical structure was robust and usable for the task at hand. For Ambedkar, liberation from Hindu oppression was possible only through a total rejection of Hinduism and its discriminatory social formations.[48] This necessitated conversion to a non-caste religion. As a nationalist, Ambedkar found it problematic to accept Islam and Christianity, both of which originated in non-Indic cultures. Two of the indigenous alternatives, Sikhism and Jainism, were too Hinduistic and lacked the dynamism Ambedkar needed. Buddhism on the other hand repudiated caste with an intellectual and ethical vigor and confidence as no other Indian religion did. Further, Anagarika Dharmapala had, in the founding and activities of the Maha Bodhi Society, laid the foundations for an Indian Buddhist renaissance.[49] Thus Ambedkar was left with a clear choice. However, in Ambedkar's ideal social order based on Buddhist ethical ideas, there was no room for a Sangha of the type that was historically instituted in the classical Buddhist states of South and Southeast Asia. In this sense the social order of Ambedkar's imagination, like the Asokan polity, is proto-Buddhist. The Asokan and Ambedkarist systems, which we can label "Indian Buddhism," must be distinguished from the "classical Buddhism" of the South and Southeast Asian model best exemplified by Sri Lanka, Thailand, and Burma. In addition to these two models we can posit logically though not empirically a third model, that imagined in the work of the orientalists and sociologically extrapolated upon by Max Weber and his followers. Here not only is the Sangha politically absent altogether but, in characteristically Weberian typological form, that absence is construed as part of the mutual repellency between religion and all aspects of mundaneity, such as the economic, the intellectual, the aesthetic, and the erotic.

In conclusion, we can make an observation on the distinction we have made between the two social formations—proto-Buddhist or Indian, and

48. On Ambedkar and his Buddhism-inspired activism, see Gail Omvedt, *Dalits and the Democratic Revolution* (New Delhi: Sage Publications, 1994). For an excellent general account of Ambedkar's work in the context of a worldwide Buddhist movement, see Heinz Bechert, "The Buddhist Revival in East and West" in Heinz Bechert and Richard Gombrich, eds., *The World of Buddhism* (London: Thames and Hudson, 1984), 274–85.

49. Bechert, "The Buddhist Revival."

Classical or South and Southeast Asian. One area of consensus in the scholarship on religious movements is that they are rebel movements whose popular appeal is to a great extent dependent on the charisma of the founders or "prophets," as Weber generically calls them.[50] The social origin of such founders is typically an oppressed group or stratum. The founders of Buddhism and Jainism, the Buddha and Mahavira, were exceptions, but it is noteworthy that they both came from the Ksatriya caste which, though "royal," is ranked lower than the priestly Brahmin caste in the Hindu hierarchy. Both Buddhism and Jainism were, in other words, rebel movements against the dominance of Brahmanism. In the imagined social order of Ambedkar this is much more so: his Buddhist movement is a defiant rejection of Hinduism, in particular the *varnasrama dharma* or the theory of castes. Therefore, neither in the Asokan nor the Ambedkarist versions is Buddhism an "establishment."

In contrast, the classical Buddhism of South and Southeast Asia as institutionalized in Sri Lanka, Burma, and Thailand are historic establishments. The Sri Lankan Buddhist establishment in particular is closely associated with the state, although the precise nature of this association is unclear: as we noted above, in the books of the dominant monastic faction, there is an unambiguous ideology of the Sangha's precedence over the king. This echoes what Ananda Coomaraswamy has cogently shown to be the precedence of spiritual authority over temporal power, the Brahmin over the king, in Hindu political theory;[51] and Hocart's assigning of precedence to the sacred ("law king") over the secular ("executive king").[52] In South and Southeast Asia, Buddhism had become an establishment not only in religious but also in economic terms. In Sri Lanka, monastic establishments were the recipients of vast endowments, and monks had become landlords.[53] The Sangha's charisma in these lands of classical Buddhism was routinized. Thus we have a dichotomy between the free, propertyless, and charismatic Sangha of the proto-Buddhist or Indian Buddhist system, and the established, landed, and

50. Max Weber, "Social Psychology of World Religions," 291. In terms of Weber's analytical usage, the Buddha is an "exemplary prophet" although in ordinary usage the Buddha is emphatically not a prophet. See also *The Sociology of Religion* (Boston: Beacon Press, 1963), 55. This is an English translation of the original, published under the title "Religionssoziologie" in *Wirtschaft und Gesellschaft* in 1922.

51. Ananda Coomaraswamy, *Spiritual Authority and Temporal Power in the Indian Theory of Government*, American Oriental Series, vol. 22, ed. Zellig Harris (New Haven, Conn., 1942).

52. A. M. Hocart, *Kings and Councillors* (Cairo: The Printing Office Paul Barbey, 1936); rpt. Rodney Needham, ed. (Chicago: University of Chicago Press, 1970), chap. 12.

53. See R. A. L. H. Gunawardana, *Robe and Plough: Monasticism and Economic Interest in Early Medieval Sri Lanka* (Tucson: University of Arizona Press, 1979); Michael Carrithers, "'They will be Lords Upon the Island': Buddhism in Sri Lanka," in Bechert and Gombrich, eds., *World of Buddhism*, chap. 5.

routinized Sangha of the classical or South and Southeast Asian systems. The first, while in fact highly conscious of group belongingness especially arising out of charismatic devotion to the founder, professes openness and tolerance and stands for ideals which are always articulated in universalist terms. The second, ensconced in privilege and bounty and committed to their perpetuation, is allied in mutual interest with a dominant linguistic, regional, ethnic, or other parochial group.

While the Sri Lankan Sangha was "established," there were always rebels who expressed their dissent in the form of ascetic movements. Whatever their deeper motivations were, these movements were always overtly articulated in universalist terms. If there were any universalist secular movements led by breakaway Sangha factions in precolonial times, we do not hear of them, but when we come to the colonial era, we do have examples.[54] Socialist and anti-imperialist Sangha rebels expressed themselves as spokesmen for freedom and social justice, and some in the late colonial era allied themselves with Marxists. Thus, in this broad distinction between Buddhism as orthodoxy and Buddhism as rebellion, we have an important clue. It is the latter that embraced universalism while the former remained tethered to the parochial interests of a dominant group, functioning as a legitimizer of that group's hegemony. These categories are greatly simplified, and we must be aware of the constant threat that routinization poses for the universalism of rebel movements. Such movements can also be quite misleading and could sometimes be parochial and sectional though disguised in the garb of universalism. The broad Sangha movement described in the following pages provides us with a case of such disguise. Originally allied with Marxist universalism, it soon embraced a narrow ethnic, linguistic, and religious chauvinism that represented the interests of the Sinhala Buddhist elite and its hegemonic dreams.

54. Kumari Jayawardena, "Bhikkhus in Revolt," *Lanka Guardian,* May 15, June 15, July 1, and July 15, 1979.

DHARMAPALA AND
THE DEFINITION OF THE
MONK'S MISSION

A new role for the monks came into being in Sri Lankan Buddhism in the twentieth century. The broad framework of the definition of this role is the rise of Buddhist modernism, an aspect of the momentous changes brought about by contact with the western world. The island was first exposed to the West at the beginning of the sixteenth century with the arrival of the Portuguese. While the Portuguese and later the Dutch controlled the coastal regions of the island, and thereby exerted socio-economic and cultural influence, the most sustained and significant influences were those brought about by the conquest of the island by the British, who exercised a systematic and centralized rule over the entire island for one and a quarter centuries. How these vast influences affected the society is the subject of most of the contemporary historiography. From their own particular points of view, sociologists and anthropologists also have written a good deal about these changes, religion being an area of special anthropological focus. Changes in that area were primarily the result of attempts by the emerging new classes to modernize Buddhism.

The definition of a new role for the monks was part of this creative process of modernizing Buddhism. We can refer to this process or phenomenon as "Buddhist modernism" or "Neo-Buddhism." It is in effect a new religion that the classes that successfully adapted to the changes wrought by colonialism needed and invented. They had accepted the politics, the economics, and the culture of the colonial master and inevitably had to do the same in religion.[1]

---

1. Strictly speaking, two paths were available to do this. First, they could accept the religion of the conqueror which had "modern" attributes that were congruent with the already accepted modernity in

While rejecting Christianity as a faith, the modernizing or "new" Buddhists consciously or unconsciously modeled their religion on it. Supported by the energetic and economically capable new classes, these adaptations prospered, transforming the traditional Buddhism of Sri Lanka into this new religion. The movement for fashioning it cannot be regarded anything less than a Buddhist reformation. It is largely for this reason that Gananath Obeyesekere, who first identified the process, called it "Protestant Buddhism."[2]

The new Buddhists themselves did not see their invention quite that way. In their view, what they were doing was reviving the true Buddhism and Buddhist Sinhala culture that had been corrupted by various outside influences and by the ritualism of the peasantry. Thus, for them it was not a reformation but a renaissance. It is the imagery of renaissance, not of reformation, that pervades the movement from its inception in the late nineteenth century to its culmination in the mid-twentieth century. The tension between renaissance and reformation is the most striking feature and the source of the inner conflict and ambivalence of the entire nationalist movement. The failure to face candidly the reformative force in its totality and logical purity, and allowing it instead to be diluted and reversed by mistakenly perceiving the process involved as a renaissance, constitute the tragic flaw of the nationalist movement of the nineteenth and twentieth centuries. When we reach the movement's climax, the meaning of "renaissance" was broadened to include not just rebirth but also repossession of what was considered to be originally Buddhist but to have subsequently fallen into non-Buddhist hands. Early in the movement, Sinhala ethnicity was integrated into the new conception of Buddhism, so that an affirmation made on behalf of Buddhism became an affirmation of Sinhala ethnicity as well. This powerful merging of religious and ethnic identities held sway until very recently, when the ethnic crisis brought the Sinhala Christians and Buddhists somewhat closer together in the same way as it did the Tamil Hindus and Christians.[3] This whole story is

---

politics, economy, and culture. Second, they could redefine and reorganize the traditional religion to conform to modernity. A minority took the first alternative and embraced Christianity. The majority opted for the latter.

One more expression of this is the attempt by Buddhist intellectuals to make Buddhism compatible with science on the one hand and Marxism on the other.

2. Richard Gombrich and Gananath Obeyesekere, *Buddhism Transformed.* For an appraisal of the concept see, John Holt, "Protestant Buddhism?" *Religious Studies Review* 17, no. 4 (1991): 307–12. Continental writers have preferred the usage "Buddhist modernism," for example Bechert in Bechert and Gombrich, *World of Buddhism;* Alexandra David, *Le Modernisme Bouddhiste* (Paris: Librairie Felix Alcan, 1911).

3. What Dharmapala disliked about Christianity is not its doctrine, but its social organization, which he thought was allied with rapacious and concupiscent imperialism. Dharmapala wanted Sinhala

a very broad and complex one, and our focus here is limited to how the new Buddhism defined the role of the monk and to how that definition affected both the monk and the society.

The widely held conception of the central role of the monk in precolonial Sinhala society is a myth that was invented by Anagarika Dharmapala, the founder of Buddhist modernism, and fostered by later advocates, both monk and lay. Monks did play a social role in precolonial times, and that role changed within a pattern of broad continuity, but it is nothing like the one that Dharmapala invented. The model for that newly invented role was the Christian priest ministering to his flock. The monk of Dharmapala's paradigm is a personality in whom a complex of traits—methodism, punctuality, cleanliness, orderliness, time-consciousness, dedication, and "non-sensuousness" (to use Dharmapala's own term)—was rationally integrated. Such a personality was derived from the model of the Christian missionary, as Dharmapala sometimes makes it very easy to infer.[4] Monks who exhibited these traits had substantial exposure in their early life to Christianity or its culture directly or indirectly. They are not the product of precolonial Buddhist culture but of a neo-Buddhist culture whose neo-ness was derived from contact with Christianity, its organizational structure, its social teachings and, above all, its idea of ministering to a flock. The amelioration of the living conditions in Sri Lanka, especially of the peasants who constitute the vast majority of the population, was indispensable for the revival of the imagined past glory of the Sinhala Buddhists. In Dharmapala's conception, that mission needed a missionary, and the monk was the obvious choice. By inventing a new type of sermon, among other means, Dharmapala made the monk a caretaker of the flock and a social worker. Once this initial change was effected, the flood-gates were opened for further changes. The monk came to think of himself as an empowered political activist and an entrepreneur, in addition to being a caretaker of the flock. In recent times this

---

Buddhists and Christians to unite and get rid of foreign bishops. At one level at least, he had no problem with Christianity; his problem was its priesthood. He urged Christians to elect a Sinhala bishop and work together as Sinhalese. Ananda Guruge, ed., *Dharmapala Lipi* (Colombo: Government Press, 1991), 145.

Dharmapala also disliked what he considered the "folklore stories" of the Old Testament. He expressed the need to sift "the pure teachings of the gentle Nazarene" from "later theological accretions." Thus his scripturalism was not confined to Buddhism; it extended to Christianity. See Ananda Guruge ed., *Return to Righteousness* (Colombo: Government Press, 1965, rpt. 1991).

4. This comes through in numerous contexts where Dharmapala admires the work and social commitment of Christian priests. His attacks on the power and influence of Christian priests are often inverted admirations and calls for appropriating these for Buddhists. See Guruge, ed. *Dharmapala Lipi,* 3–31.

redefinition received a boost socially from the changes brought about by an "open economy" and individually by the breakdown in the traditional system of monastic authority and the rise of a new monastic individualism.[5]

ANAGARIKA DHARMAPALA, THE FOUNDER OF BUDDHIST MODERNISM

It is not possible to talk meaningfully about any area of social and cultural life and particularly about aspects of social change in contemporary Sri Lanka without discussing the reformer Anagarika Dharmapala (1864–1933). Dharmapala's writings and fiery speeches held audiences spellbound and inspired both his contemporaries and the generations to follow. To talk about the political and social developments in Sri Lanka since his time up to now without reference to his work is to ignore the spring of these developments. No major Sinhala thinker or writer after him has escaped his influence, directly or indirectly. That he has by and large attracted only passing attention in the mainstream history of the island is a commentary on its unidimensionality and on the alienation of the elites who set the agenda for that historiography. The westernized elite who were Dharmapala's contemporaries, and on whom he poured scorn, were in the center of the evolving politico-administrative machinery of the then British colony, but it was Dharmapala who was at the center of the society on which that machinery was an imposition. He was like a powerful and cascading river, whereas the politico-administrative machinery was at best a stagnant pool.

Dharmapala forcefully articulated the new religion (which in his mind was only a revival of the true traditional religion) and in turn became the inspiration for its further development. He was the son of a furniture producer who, through dedication and hard work, acquired considerable wealth. He was sent to Christian schools, where he felt a great sense of humiliation at the hands of teachers who were Christian priests, presumably due to their denigration of Buddhism as a primitive and idolatrous religion. It would seem appropriate, then, that he would grow up to be someone who would show the world that Buddhism had all the nobility and modernity a religion could offer and that it was in fact Christianity and other theistic religions that were primitive and deficient. The family habit of hard work was the

---

5. At ordination the monk ideally becomes an individual although in fact he becomes a member of a monastic "family." By "new individualism" I refer to a new assertiveness in the monastery correlatable with the breakdown of the traditional socialization of the monk.

other important factor that he wove into the new religion. He changed his foreign name "David" to "Dharmapala," meaning "Guardian of Dharma" which was his own evocative definition of his destiny and mission. The first part of his name, Anagarika, meaning "homeless," further defined his task: the renunciation of the world but also being in it for the purpose of regenerating his country on the basis of Buddhist morality and of carrying the mission of Buddhism to the rest of the world. Like a renouncer, he wore ocher, but, like a layman, he made his apparel a tailored one, an ensemble that exteriorized his inner state of part monk and part layman.[6] He exhorted the Buddhists to give up the ritualism characteristic of rural peasant Buddhism and, instead, to cultivate morality and to infuse themselves with methodical and incessant productive activity rather than be content with the mere subsistence characteristic of peasant life. By making the peasantry embrace the new religion, he was trying to elevate the quality of life of the ordinary people.

UTOPIA, AS DHARMAPALA SAW IT

In numerous writings and speeches starting from about the last decade of the nineteenth century, especially the column prosaically entitled *Danagatayutu karunu* ("Facts that one should know") in *Sinhala Bauddhaya,* the weekly newspaper he founded and edited, Dharmapala gradually unveiled, mostly by means of his critique of the existing state, an ideal Sinhala Buddhist society that existed until the end of the Sinhala monarchy in 1815, and which now needed to be revived.

His image of the past society is based on the *Mahavamsa,* although it is likely that the writings of British colonial authors, like Tennent whom he cites, gave him his first inklings into that society, as well as into the *Mahavamsa* itself. The central political feature of that ideal past society was righteous and paternalistic kingship. The basis of the social order was Buddhist morality or righteousness. That morality was also magically powerful: so long as it existed—and it always did when there was righteous kingship—the nation prospered and no foreigner could overpower it. The present state of kinglessness, in contrast, has caused a decline in Buddhist morality, which has resulted in the acceptance of foreign customs and mores, keeping the

6. For a perceptive analysis of Dharmapala's self-definition, see Gananath Obeyesekere, "Personal Identity and Cultural Crisis: The Case of Anagarika Dharmapala of Sri Lanka," in Frank E. Reynolds and Donald Capps, eds., *The Biographical process: Studies in the History and Psychology or Religion* (The Hague, Mouton, 1976), 221–52.

society in subjugation to alien rule. Whatever the present depths are to
which the society has descended, morality can throw off the foreign yoke
and restore society to its former ideal state. What is needed therefore is a
return to righteousness. It does not take much: living in accordance with
Buddhist morality for a mere five years would restore Lanka to its former
glory, but a glory that so accommodates and conforms to modernity that,
except for its unique cultural stamp, it would appear no different from a
prosperous, developed, and modern nation. That is, Dharmapala is envisag-
ing here a society that is technologically advanced yet uncompromisingly
moored within the moral and cultural frameworks of tradition. From some
of his remarks it is clear that the models that he has in mind are Japan and
the United States.[7]

The great culprit that has caused the society's decline is the loss of purity
brought about by the incorporation of foreign political, physical, and moral
structures and substances, which corrupt and make unwholesome the individual body as well as the body politic. Foreign customs and mores corrupt
the moral life, and foreign foods, especially meat and alcohol, corrupt the
physical. Dharmapala expresses the idea in his *History of an Ancient Civilization:*

> This bright beautiful island was made into a Paradise by the Aryan Sinhalese
> before its destruction was brought about by the barbaric vandals. Its people
> did not know irreligion. The pagan beliefs of monotheism and diabolic poly-
> theism were unknown to the people. Christianity and polytheism are respon-
> sible for the vulgar practices of killing animals, stealing, prostitution, licen-
> tiousness, lying and drunkenness. Read the "History of Ceylon," by Sir
> Emerson Tennent, and the "Records of the Western World," by Fa Hian and
> Hwen Thsang, for they have written what they observed. This ancient, his-
> toric, refined people, under the diabolism of vicious paganism introduced
> by the British administrators, are now declining and slowly dying away. The
> bureaucratic administrators, ignorant of the first principles of the natural
> laws of evolution, have cut down primeval forests to plant tea; have intro-

7. For example: Dharmapala's statement that "although we belong to Hinayana we can accomplish
much work as in Japan" (Guruge, ed., *Lipi,* 5); and his high praise for the American system of education,
which he thought is the best in the world, because of its pragmatic approach. This contrasts with the
local elite's idealization of the liberal-humanist and intellectualist education epitomized by Oxford and
Cambridge. Dharmapala was impressed with the weaving of patriotism into the training of children in
the American system by means of having them learn and recite the Pledge of Allegiance, and with how
research was geared to agricultural and industrial productivity rather than being an expression of pure
intellectualism (Guruge, ed., *Righteousness,* 530, 854–55). This pragmatic approach of Dharmapala's
stands in sharp contrast to the strident anti-Americanism of those who today consider themselves his
progeny.

duced opium, ganja, whisky, arrack and other alcoholic poisons; have opened saloons and drinking taverns in every village; have killed all industries and made the people indolent.[8]

The following extracts from the same work express further Dharmapala's conception of Buddhism and what we might call his paradigm of Sinhala society. In that paradigm "kings were not absolute rulers; they were elected, by the people, and the people had the power to depose any sovereign who went against the wishes of the people."[9] In addition, "Buddhism is absolutely ethical and psychological. Its fundamental principles advocate mercy, charity, strict temperance, perfect purity of mind and body, and complete submission to truth" (530). Consequently, "the Buddhist kings never gave the Aryan Sinhalese opium, arrack, whisky, and from the revenues of the land the people derived manifold advantages. . . . Arts and crafts flourished . . . trade was in the hands of the people, education was an appendage of every Sinhalese child, and the great Buddhist Church was supported by the kings and Buddhism was the state religion of the land." The British administration brought "drunkenness, poverty, increase of crime and increase of insanity." The Sinhalese people do not want "political self government" because "their most noble religion is spiritual self government, transcending the political principles of selfish statesmen and adventurous politicians. The Buddha taught the essentials of a higher form of self government of an individualistic type" (530–31). Moreover, "Higher Buddhism is pure science. It has no place for theology. . . . It is the religion of absolute freedom, which is to be gained avoiding all evil, doing all good and purifying the heart. It is against alcoholism, and killing animals for food and sport. . . . It is the friend of enlightened progress, and preaches the sublimest truths of meritorious activity" (658–59).

This paradigm conveys to the Buddhist and his antagonists, namely the British colonial government and Christian missionary, the idea that Buddhism has everything necessary to build a prosperous, peaceful, and cultured modern society. Underlying this is the answer to some of the criticisms generally leveled against Buddhism and the Sinhalas, namely that Buddhism is other-worldly and provides no basis for a progressive society, that Buddhism is selfish, and that the Sinhalas are lazy. These are Dharmapala's own criticisms of the Sinhalas, but only of the modern-day Sinhalas, not the true

---

8. Dharmapala, *History of an Ancient Civilization* (Los Angeles, 1902), in Guruge, ed., *Righteousness*, 482.

9. Ibid., 529.

Sinhalas of old. The moderns are so now precisely because they in their stupidity embrace the customs of the foreigner and eat the foreigner's foods.

Foreign domination or even intimate relations like intermarriage with foreigners leads to dissention and loss of unity within the social order. Thus purity, morality, and unity are different manifestations of the same wholesome state. With a return to the righteous Buddhist way of life, progress will occur, and the country will be prosperous. For this, effort is necessary to convert the rural people to true Buddhism and to the norms of economic conduct based on it. Besides, the world would benefit from Buddhism, and it is therefore the duty of the Sinhalas to propagate Buddhism. For this dual task of propagating Buddhism locally and overseas, missionaries are needed.

In the Dharmapalite paradigm of Sinhala society and Buddhism, no person plays a more significant and crucial role than the monk. In that paradigm, society is indeed a nonpolitical ethico-moral system where conformity comes through internal discipline and not through external coercion or the threat of such coercion.[10] In the absence of a king, no central authority emerges, and the polity seems to consist of conglomerations of innumerable village theocracies, where the monk, though not a ruler, is still the most important and benevolent leader, a little king. It is the monk who has the duty and the capacity to teach the villagers the now eclipsed true Buddhist way of life. He should instruct the villagers to abide by the five precepts, and to stay away from the ten sinful activities, and where possible try to cultivate mental concentration *(bhavana)*.[11] With that as the non-negotiable moral base, the monk must instruct the people in good habits—health, manners, cleanliness, activeness, diligence, prudence, punctuality, and guidance in everything such as how to get the proper scientific knowledge necessary for productive agriculture, crafts, and commercial activity, in short in all ingredients of a prosperous, healthy, peaceful, and happy civic life. The knowledge necessary for this is found in Buddhism and the Pali language, and therefore it is essential for monks to learn Pali thoroughly. Instead of somehow gaining an empty scholastic medal and a smattering of Sanskrit after which they establish a rural *pirivena* (college) and lead a false life, monks should translate Pali into Sinhala for the benefit of others.[12]

While the "victory" in the first century B.C.E. of the *dhammakathika* (village dwelling, ministerial) over the *pamsukulika* (forest dwelling, ascetic)

10. "Buddhism is spiritual self-government." The central government is not explicitly defined in Dharmapala's social theory but can be inferred to exist as a perfunctory epiphenomenon.

11. Dharmapala, *History*, in Guruge, ed., *Righteousness*, 530–31.

12. Guruge, ed., *Righteousness*, 160.

monks led to closer interaction between the monks and the laity, the emphasis in that relationship was on the monk's needs rather than the laity's, expressed in the conception of the four requisites the laity must provide for the monks. This is further expressed in the special relation the monks have with their "village of focus" *(gocaragama)*, which in Sinhala also has the meaning "village of prey" *(godurugama)*, an image that brings out this fact, namely it was the monk's needs that the monk-lay relation was concerned with. What and whether the laity received was non-material and immaterial respectively. The kind of mundane service a priesthood provided for the laity was performed not by monks but by the priests of the folk cults. Strictly speaking, even the merit received for providing the monk's requisites did not need to be given by the monks, because it was an automatic moral result of the laity's generosity. In ritualized giving however, the monks formally did give the laity merit, or at least verbalized formulaically and stylistically so that the grant of merit assumed a performative form with a religio-emotional content. The other gift of the monks to the laity was the *dhamma* (preaching the Buddhist doctrine), which was itself highly ritualized, the aesthetic and religio-emotional elements dominating over the moral, as the traditional sermon or *dharmadesana* (discussed below) indicates. The most important source of moral instruction were the Jataka stories, which were encapsulated in the dharmadesana. The major purpose both of the acceptance of the four requisites *(dana)* and of doctrinal instruction *(bana)*, which constituted most of the monk's service to the laity, was the facilitation of the next world, and not this world. The role of the monk was certainly not giving the laity advice regarding household economy, about which the monks were not supposed to know a great deal in the first place, marital problems, which were plainly out of bounds, and cleanliness, hard work, and so forth, which are defined as the central features of the monk's role in the Dharmapalite paradigm of society.

While the victory of the *dhammakathikas* enabled monks to move closer to the laity, the monk-lay relation was always hedged with suspicion and tension. Despite compromises with mundane life that often took away all semblances of asceticism, the ascetic ideal constantly reasserted itself. Even when the ideal lost ground to established monasticism, the cultural view that defined the monk rather than the laity as the focus of attention was never abandoned. The lay fantasy that the monk was a potential ascetic remained intact, preventing the growth of the idea of ministering to a flock, or of a material return gift. This and the recurrent appearance of attempts to boost monastic morality by "purifications" *(sasana sodhana)* and *katikavat* (colloquia) point to the tension between the monks and the laity and to the sensitivity that characterized the border between the two. Even in the eighteenth century, when the "decline" in Buddhism led to the emergence of a secularized monkhood known as the *ganinnanse* institution, the monk-lay relation never included functions such as advising the laity on household economy, cleanliness, and so forth. A recent correspondent in a national daily newspaper, *The Island,* expressed shock at a monk conducting on television the new year ceremony of applying oil in which he ritually touched a woman's hair with his fingertips.

While giving advice on household economy is a different exercise, this nevertheless illustrates the extent to which domestic involvements were outside the boundaries of the monk's services to the laity. In fact, monks are explicitly asked to limit their relations with the laity, an excess of which is an offense known as *kula dusanaya* (abuse of the privilege of associating with the laity). Some individual monks, who may have had kinship or other social relations with the royal family, may have had considerable political influence, a pattern that may have been repeated locally on a lesser scale. But the monkhood as a whole did not wield that power. Such a monkhood in fact did not exist.[13] Furthermore, if any such power was wielded, it is quite different from the worldly role as minister and mundane advisor that is the cornerstone of the monk's activity imagined in the Dharmapalite paradigm. Writing on the role of the monk, the Pali and Buddhist scholar Y. Karunadasa says, "The monk is a path shower, a philosopher and friend of the layman, but it is not his task to institute a pattern of activity about the worldly affairs of laymen."[14] Dharmapala's plan was precisely to institute such a pattern of activity.

The puritan values of discipline, hard work, punctuality, and so forth had been already accepted by the rising middle classes. Dharmapala knew that they were inextricably bound with worldly success, like his family's. And his truly patriotic dream was to make every Sinhala Buddhist family as affluent as his own. He constantly talked about the Sinhalas not having any crafts or industries, which his family did. And he knew the hard work, methodism, and dynamism (that was the opposite of laziness which he attributed to the ordinary Sinhalas) that it took to be successful in business. Thus it is not surprising that he wanted these values cast far and wide in the countryside,

13. A supra-local Sangha, or "the Sangha as a whole" in the socio-political system as understood today, came into being only recently, after the proliferation of the print media in the late nineteenth and early twentieth centuries.

14. Y. Karunadasa, "The Social Philosophy and Responsibility of the Contemporary Monk," *Divayina,* Nov 11, 1990. Abstracted from a lecture at the Vidyalankara Pirivena, Paliyagoda, on Vidyalankara Day, 1990, the centenary of the college.

using the monk as his agent. The role in that task Dharmapala attributed to the monk in traditional Sri Lankan society, and which he wanted the monks to regain, was more a need of his paradigm and project than a fact of history.

Reviving Buddhist society, according to Dharmapala, involves educating the society in Buddhist social and religious morality by means of propagating true Buddhism among the people. The Sinhalas as the bearers of Buddhism also have a moral duty to propagate Buddhism overseas, especially in India, and to wrest for the Buddhists, from the Hindu priests, the custody of the sacred Buddhist sites. Buddhism and the Sinhala nation need monks to propagate Buddhism domestically and overseas, and the laity to help that project financially. In the present state of moral decay the Sinhalas are mired in selfishness,[15] which in turn is a result of their acceptance of foreign ways. This is a vicious circle and it can only be broken by waking up the Sinhalas. Thus in Dharmapala's writings and speeches he did what it takes to wake up deepsleeping people, namely some not too gentle nudging. Images of sleeping and closed eyes abound in the relevant writings, and roars of anger and condemnation of the Sinhala sloth, stupidity, and inefficiency erupt every now and then. The Sinhalas are unfavorably compared with every other ethnic group in the island, each of which is said to be intelligent, committed, hardworking, and true to its own customs.

Thus the Sinhalas alone have neither industries nor commerce, and, in the rare instances they do, such as graphite mining, as soon as some wealth is accumulated, the successful families adopt foreign names and take to foreign food, dress, and customs. Dharmapala derides such people endlessly as beefeating, trouser-, coat-, tie-, shirt-, and shoe-wearing, whisky-drinking, language- and custom-abandoning males; and pudding-eating, straw-hat-, high-heel-, and short-dress-wearing, "this erotic thing called novels" reading women. The commonest compliments the Sinhalas get for their imitation of foreign ways are "stupid," "idiotic," "dumb," "buffalo," "wild elephant," and so forth. The Sinhalas are frequently called lazy, time-wasting, slothful, unable to make (or conserve) money, given to pleasure and superstition, and ignorant of Buddhism: "The Sinhalas have the stupidity that enables them to loose all their wealth. . . . The Sinhalas started to act like idiots three generations ago."[16] And: "Let the Sinhala idiots who fill their bellies with ham, bacon, stuffed meat, soup, sausages, beefsteak, mutton chops, pudding, and cutlets, and drink whisky, brandy, wine, beer, and poteral *(sic)* make an effort to gain

15. This echoes the Christian critique of Buddhism.
16. Guruge, ed., *Dharmapala Lipi,* 149. From here to the end of the chapter, intratextual citations are to this work.

some wisdom" (183). And: "There are [other] dark skinned people in Lanka. They do not adopt English customs. Only the Sinhala fool adopted them, and declined. . . . Foreigners who land in Lanka to earn a livelihood see the stupidities of the Sinhalas and call them 'the dumb Sinhalas'. . . . Other groups do not waste their money like the dumb Sinhala does" (73).

The villages are in a particularly deplorable state of poverty, ignorance, lack of cleanliness and health habits, all of it the result of accepting foreign items, foods, customs, names, and ways of thought. But in addition there is also decline caused by the superstitious ritualism of ignorant villagers. Pervasive reform in habits and thoughtways is necessary to bring about the regeneration that would make Sri Lanka a modern nation like any in the West, at the same time making it what it was in its pristine glory—a Buddhist state where Sinhala customs and manners, language, thoughtways, dress, and food were the norm. Dharmapala's vision is twofold, first, economic and pragmatic; and second, political and ideological. Different groups appropriated and combined these two elements differently during the ensuing period of nearly a century, with fateful consequences for the nation.

MONKS
Soldiers of the Dhamma

Who must perform this great national and religious task of reviving the nation and how? In Dharmapala's vision it is the duty of the monks to accomplish that task and of the laity to support it. The pattern of unity and cooperation in a common task by different yet complementary and compatible groups is a recurrent theme in Dharmapala's model of society. His diagnosis of the problem of cooperation between the monks and laity involves a vicious circle: monks commit immoral acts because they do not have lay support, and the laity does not support the monks because they commit such acts. How are they immoral? They are immoral because they engage in beastly arts *(garhita vidya, tirascina vidya)* such as the practice or teaching of medicine and astrology, and they get too involved with the laity in inappropriate ways. They are also immoral because they seek gainful employment. Dharmapala cites, without mentioning names, monks who violate Buddhist morality by either borrowing from or lending money to the laymen. "You must understand that monks who accept gold and silver *(jata, rupa, rajata)* are impure" (57). "In Lanka now adharma (non-righteousness) has come to power. Immoral monks are too many" (81).

Dharmapala also attacks the monk's traditionalism, which makes the monk a partner with the peasant in traditional ritualism, which to him is vulgar and non-Buddhist. The monk, like the villager, is relentlessly accused of being lazy and confined to sleepy monasteries. They must first go out and learn proper Buddhism, and then preach it to the people. They must convert rural Buddhists to proper moral Buddhism free of theistic and other supernatural ritualism. Spreading true Buddhism in the villages includes the task of telling rural Buddhists about the Buddhist guide to life conduct which would bring them not only a higher morality but a higher standard of living. While Dharmapala considered this guide to be Buddhist, many of its rules are in fact derived from his experience with missionaries and other representatives of western culture. In emphasizing the need to work for others, Dharmapala primarily meant to raise the moral and physical life of the people, but it also is possible that he may have been trying to counter the Christian criticism that Buddhism is selfish.

The task of the Buddhists was not only to spread true Buddhism locally but also to propagate it internationally. Particularly after his visit to the World Parliament of Religions in Chicago in 1893, Dharmapala was convinced that the western world was ready to accept the enlightened message of Buddhism. Referring to his successful speech at the Parliament, he states: "I saw the great desire they [the Americans] showed to learn about Buddhism. I understood clearly that if we can send knowledgeable monks it is possible for us to propagate Buddhism there" (7). Again, "There are in western countries more intelligent people than the Sinhalas. If one were to go those countries and preach the dharma of the Buddha, they will be able to easily understand the truth of it" (284). This readiness of the West to receive Buddhism made it a matter of the greater urgency that monks come out of their cobwebbed monasteries and learn proper Buddhism as well as the foreign languages and other skills necessary to propagate Buddhism overseas. For establishing a mission in England he was even willing to revise his view of the otherwise irremediable incompatibility between the English and Sinhalas. Here he also abandons his idea of Sinhala superiority and shows remarkable tolerance to borrowed cultural items. However, this tolerance is temporary and contextual: it is related to his keenness to establish a monastic residence *(avasa)* in England: "In the future the two parties Sinhala and English must live in amity. The Sinhalas have borrowed from the English various things like clothing, music and dance and foods. The Sinhalas do not have the intelligence to give the English anything worldly. The only wealth the Sinhalas can give the English is the noble dharma. We must build a *vihara* (monastery) to give [the British] the gift of the dharma. Time has come to built a vihara in London, the capital" (286). Besides, a vihara in London will help dispel false views about Buddhism and Sri Lanka: "Many false rumours about Ceylon have been spread in England. If there is a permanent Buddhist residence in London, it is possible to fully eliminate these wrong views" (284). He urges Buddhists to help the project by cutting down on alcohol and donating that money, adding that "any person who does not contribute is truly a slave" (285).

Dharmapala was devoutly committed to the establishment of Buddhism in the land of its birth, and he alternated between using polite language and his normal language to express his frustration with the monks for their poor cooperation: "If the good monks take to heart we can spread Buddhism in India as was done before" (5). And: "It is possible to say with definiteness that if there are virtuous monks today it is possible to propagate Buddhism in diverse foreign lands as was done before. Many padres from England and America leave their country and their loved ones and go to Africa where there are very fierce and uncivilized people, and to Australia which is situated far to the south, to propagate the Christian dharma. But it is greatly saddening to find our monks practicing indifference,[17] and have no intention of propagating Buddhism in the provinces" (5). Moreover: "It is clear that the noble people of the past have given their lives going out to propagate the dharma of the Buddha. Therefore may the contemporary Sangha ignore suffering and try to propagate Buddhism" (5). And: "It is sad to note that our Sangha now does not follow the instructions of the Buddha [to propagate the doctrine]. [When asked to go and work in India] what the *unnanses*[18] ask is, if we go to India will we get our *dana* (food) and other requisites? . . . Christian missionaries leave their loved ones and go overseas to work, out of generosity to others, willing to sacrifice their lives" (5–6).

In keeping with his principle that unity is necessary for progress and, at the same time, placing himself in early Buddhism, Dharmapala criticizes monks for their sectarian and other divisions. He says there are different *nikaya*s (sects, fraternities) but no *Bhiksu sasana* ("Buddhist Church") that pursues dharma. He satirizes the divisions among the monks:

> Today in Lanka there are monks who cover one shoulder, both shoulders, and neither; who shave and do not shave eyebrows; who wear belts; who carry silk umbrellas; who have short hair and shave their beards; barrister monks who carry leather bags; who eat from plates; who eat from bowls; immoral

17. The Sinhala term glossed here as "indifference" is *upeksa*, which is an ironic usage, because *upeksa* (equanimity) is a basic Buddhist virtue, here missed by the monks.

18. *Unnanse* is a disrespectful term to refer to a monk when used by a layman.

monks who hang around restaurants and courthouses; immoral monks who practice medicine and astrology; immoral monks who teach sciences like medicine to young laymen; immoral monks who have taken to socialising, immoral monks who associate people unworthy of doing so; monks who pompously use the letter "sri" (before their names) and who practice "sri" more than they adhere to morality *(sila);* monks who do editorships of magazines for the sake of money with a layman as the frontman; and monks who deposit Rs. 4000 in the bank account of their acolytes. . . . It is easy to make the sasana of Lanka shine if five virtuous monks get together and work in a dedicated manner for the progress of the sasana. . . . Monks have become immoral *(dussila)* because of their [desire for] worldly things, instead of annihilating the *prapancas* [obstacles to spiritual progress], *tanha, mana, viparita,* and *ditthi.* (114)

Dharmapala criticizes monks for living in luxury surrounded by material goods, without performing the proper (monastic) rites, for squandering wisdom, for enjoying books of Sanskrit poetry, and for failing to behave according to the noble Aryan (i.e., Vinaya) customs. A few monks have established colleges *(sastrasala)*[19] and are teaching medicine, astrology and poetics to a few. This to Dharmapala is behaving like the Chabbaggiya monks (134).[20] "Let those monks who spend a false life by having learnt a little Sanskrit, by some means or other have obtained the empty title *pandita* ("doctor"), and established a pirivena in a village, realize that translating a Pali book is a great act of merit, and [that they must try to] do so for the sake of others" (160).

Dharmapala refers to pirivena principals as "shameless, virtueless card-

19. *Sastrasala,* literally "science hall," is the term Dharmapala uses to refer to *pirivenas,* the newly revived monastic colleges. Vidyalankara was originally known as a *sastrasala.* The English term "university" was glossed by the early-twentieth-century monk scholars as "samastha sastrasala." The present term "visva vidyalaya" has survived the parochial attempt to gloss the term as "sarasaviya."

20. *Chabbaggiya* were a group of rebel monks during the Buddha's time who advocated lax behavior. Here Dharmapala quotes a Pali passage to make his point about the parallel between the monks he criticizes and the Chabbaggiyas: *Tena kho pana samayena chabbaggiya bhikkhu mamcam pitham pi kulu navam karapenti. Manussa vihara carikam abhimdanta passitva ujjhayanti khiyanti vapacenti "katham hi nama samana sakyaputtiya mamcampi pithampi tulonaddham karapessanti seyyathapi gihikamabhoginoti"* (At that time, the gang of six monks were making couches and chairs by tying cotton. People touring the monastery saw that and grumbled, took offense, and were annoyed. "How can ascetics who are the sons of the Sakyan [the Buddha] make couches and chairs? They are like laymen, who enjoy the pleasures of the senses.") I wish to thank Charles Hallisey for this translation of the relevant passaage in Hermann Oldenberg's edition of the Books of Discipline, *Vinaya Pitakam* (London: Pali Text Society, 1977), 2:150. Professor Hallisey notes that in Dharmapala's quotation, the Pali words are "broken at bizarre places" (Personal Communication, November 17, 1998). It is possible that Dharmapala was quoting from memory and that, in contrast with his impressive English, his Pali was folksy, like that of some rural monks.

board monks" (54). They are immoral monks who teach beastly sciences like medicine and astrology, and the secular subject of poetics to young laymen. They are classed among the monks who live in mansions surrounded by material goods, enjoy poetry *(kavyalankara)*, and fail to observe monastic rites. Here he is referring to some of the most respected scholarly monks of the time, who have also later been hailed as the leaders of the revivalist movement. But he spares none who deviate from what he holds to be proper monastic conduct. It is obvious that these relentless attacks would have antagonized some monks, but the idealism would have appealed to the younger monks. In fact some of the most ardent of his followers were young students at these same *pirivenas* at the time. For example, Kalukondayave (see below) was sixteen years old and had just enrolled at Vidyodaya in 1911, when the earlier of these exhortations was written. The idea of missionary work gradually gained greater currency even though not every convinced monk actually took to it, and in the 1930s there was increasing elite interest in improving the life of the villagers, as discussed below. Monks involved in missionary activity attracted the respect and attention of these elites, providing the monks an acceptance and a centrality that they historically never enjoyed, despite frequent claims today to that effect.

The idea of the mission is central to Dharmapala's entire agenda. If the mission can be established and monks trained and motivated, the project of restoring Lanka to its pristine state can be accomplished within the estimated five years. It is a project that involves the reestablishment of purity in the land by enthroning a society and traditional custom based on Buddhist morality. It is necessary to instruct the people in the truth, or "facts that one should know," as Dharmapala had been propagating from his column in his newspaper *Sinhala Bauddhaya*. The project is one of "development" from a state of poverty and servility, to prosperity and national dignity, guided by and based on Buddhist morality. Thus the missionary project united the socio-economic and the religio-cultural.[21] The two spheres were one and inseparable, and the ideal missionary embodied in him that unity and inseparability. The missionary's work consisted of trying to persuade the rural peasantry to put into practice the "facts that one should know."

The majority of the population during the period of Dharmapala's exhortations (from the end of the nineteenth century and up to the 1930s) were

---

21. While for Dharmapala these two were inseparable, he provided no mechanism to prevent the one dominating the other. In emphasizing the religio-cultural, Dharmapala's aim was more to ensure that morality did not leave economics, than that linguistic nationalism or anti-minority feelings should triumph. A sober union of the two was possible, as Vidyodaya demonstrated.

either illiterate or barely literate. Thus a newspaper column like Dharmapala's could not have reached them. Besides, there was no habit of reading, the rectification of which indeed is one of the tasks the missions were trying to accomplish. It was therefore imperative that human agents roam the countryside to teach the people how to achieve development and morality. As observed already, as in the case of the assumed "Buddhist rules of behavior," the underlying model for this was not Buddhism but Christian missionarism with its idea of service to others bound together with religious and moral development. In addition to "learning to do everything the Reformed Church way" (140) Dharmapala writes about his exposure to the Salvation Army:

> In 1883 a preacher of the Salvation Army named Gladwin landed in Colombo with his wife and children, rented a house on Kaiser Street in Pettah, and started work in a corrugated metal roofed hall. On many occasions I went to that corrugated metal roofed hall and listened to the speeches made there. The army that started very humbly has now reached fullness. Buddhists should [take this lesson and] resolve to establish [an army of their own known as] a Roar of Liberation Army *(Vimukti Ghosaka Samudava)*. Buddhism is a philosophy of liberation wisdom. The final goal in the Buddhist teaching is liberation. It is known as liberation wisdom *(vimukti gnana)*. The Buddhists are under orders to sound the drums of the dhamma. Buddhists are under orders to blow the conch of the dhamma, to raise the flag of the dhamma. Why aren't there hero-giants *(yodhavirayan)* pleased to preach the doctrine of liberation, sounding the drum of the dhamma, blowing the conch of the dhamma and raising the flag of the dhamma? . . . Obeying the Buddha's word I went to America and preached the dhamma, and many [Americans] embraced it. Having heard that dhamma, a lady by the name of Foster of the Honolulu country became a convert *(upasika)*. Preachers of various creeds come to Lanka and mislead the Buddhist public. A delegation of Buddhist preachers should go to preach in foreign countries. Buddhists are under orders to teach the dhamma to those who commit sinful acts and to place them in virtue. (201)

The military analogy that runs through this passage is remarkable. Clearly the idea of the Salvation Army generated in Dharmapala's mind a counter army, identical to the enemy's except for the message. It is noteworthy, however, that the army is legitimized in relation to the "orders" that the Buddha himself gave, and Dharmapala Buddhisizes the military regalia—the drum, the flag, and the conch, which recall the Buddhist "regalia" like the relic and the monk himself militarized in the *Mahavamsa* account of the campaign of Duttagamani, giving us a clue to the thin line in religion between piety and warriordom, and the easy transferability of the drums of the doctrine to the drums of war. He is careful to also Buddhisize "Salvation" into "Liberation." The early Sangha is also militarized: "The Bhikkhu Sangha was a spiritual army, and they were expected to travel nine months in the year from country to country, village to village preaching and exhorting the people."[22]

While the immediate inspiration for Dharmapala is Christian missionary work, the mission is an idea central to Buddhism, the Buddha himself exemplifying it, and even more, creating the first core of missionaries (sixty disciples) whom he instructed to wander the countryside and preach the doctrine for the comfort and happiness of the many. That is how Dharmapala thought of it and legitimized it. Frustrated after many attempts to recruit monks, but never giving up, he referred over and over again to this exhortation and called it the Buddha's "order" *(agnava),* not failing to point out that similar orders given by Christ were being faithfully carried out. He found the vital instrument of the mission, the sermon, lost in a jungle of ritualism which he considered to be part of the non-Buddhist superstitions of illiterate villagers. Successful missionary activity required a succinct and carefully crafted statement (a sermon), and it was necessary to salvage suitable items from this jungle and fashion such a message. That is, the traditional sermon known as dharmadesana would not do, and a new one had to be invented. The denigration of village monks and their performatively elaborate dharmadesana as well as their other ritualisms was a theme energetically taken up by such lieutenants of Dharmapala's missionary army as Kalukondayave Pannasekhara, Hendiyagala Silaratana, and Hinatiyana Dhammaloka, and others under his influence, such as Walpola Rahula, as elaborated below.

DHARMADESANA
Old and New

The idea of dharamadesana is as old as Buddhism, though the particular form it took and its content changed with place and time. The greater the monk's association with the laity, the more popular the form and content of dharmadesana had to be, a trend which is reflected throughout the history of the almost exclusively religious Sinhala literature.[23] When we come to the era immediately before the conquest of the island by the British, the dharma-

22. Guruge, ed., *Righteousness,* 428.

23. Martin Wickramasinghe, *Sinhala Sahityaye Nagima* (Colombo: Gunasena, 1946; 11th ed. Dehivala: Tisara, 1991). See also J. B. Disanayaka, *Sinhala Buddhagama* (Colombo: Government Printing Corporation, 1991).

desana had been thoroughly adapted to its largely rural audience. It had grown in emotion and performative appeal but had lost in intellectual content and sobriety of presentation. Even at the most sophisticated level it consisted of the preacher first reciting the text and later the commentary which was also a text. The following account, by Hendiyagala Silaratana,[24] illustrates the genre:

> To cultivate this method of dharmadesana, the preacher must be good at learning from memory. Should have a sweet voice. Must be a person of good memory power. Should be a healthy person capable of being seated on the same seat for an entire night. Above all he must be a person able to withstand the irritations *(karadara)* issued by the congregation.
>
> First of all awnings are tied in the entire hall and the preaching pavilion *(dharma mandapaya)* is decorated in great beauty by hanging lotus flowers and coconut fronds. In the middle of the pavilion a traditional preacher's seat *(purana dharmasana)* is made by placing cushions so that the orator of the dhamma *(dharmakathika,* i.e., preacher) can comfortably sit in the lotus posture *(baddha paryankayen),* with curtains *(vatatira)* drawn in a circle around it. About twenty to thirty coconut-oil-fuelled brass lamps are lit and hung all over the preaching hall *(dharma sala).* There is no objection to electric lights if available. No later than 9:00 in the night the venerable orator of the dhamma is placed on a chair and carried up to the preacher's seat with great honor and love by two strong and pure men, amidst exclamations of "Sadhu." The venerable dhamma orator [preacher], dressed in a robe of Benares silk, stands near the preacher's seat and, leaning against it and holding with both hands the great fan, chants the grant of merit for the preacher's seat *(dharmasana pin dima).* He is helped to the preacher's seat only after this grant of merit. Some preachers take about fifteen minutes to deliver this entirely melodious grant of merit for [providing him with] the preacher's seat.
>
> After the preacher is helped to ascend the seat, the encircling curtain is raised so that only his upper body becomes visible. Only the front of this circle is open, and the other three sides are decorated with colorful cloth, similar to traditional *somanas.* Now the venerable orator is seated in serene glory on the dharmasana.
>
> Now preparations are made to perform the invitation to preach *(bana aradhanava)* by offering and placing popped rice *(vilanda),* the fivefold flowers *(lada pas mal),*[25] incense, and sandalwood water in the area surrounding the preacher's seat everywhere on the pavilion, and by playing the drums of the

24. Hendiyagala Silaratana, *Mage Jivita Kathava,* vol. 1 (Kuliyapitiya: Sastrodaya Press, 1971), 85–90. My translation.

25. These are not really flowers, but buds or popped grain.

first watch. One or two beautifully dressed handsome boys kneel down in worshipping posture and, facing the direction of the preacher's seat, chant verses, *gathas* and *prasas* inviting the preacher to deliver his sermon. This may also be done by grown ups. But it is beautiful only when a child does it. On this occasion the parents and kin of the boy give him presents. Now the preacher administers the five precepts and chants the invitation to the gods *(devataradhanaya)*. This consists of a long *prasa* as well. Next the preacher chants in a beautiful meter *(vratta)* three or four verses of worship *(namaskara gatha)* and in a lullabic voice chants a *prasa* that extols the good effects of worshipping the Triple Gem. I think it is amidst the deities' exclamations of "Sadhu" that the sound of these *prasas* delivered in a melodious voice by preachers of the past rose and echoed in the surrounding sky, filling and spilling over the preaching hall and pleasing the ears of listeners, even though there were in those days no loudspeakers as exist today.

Next, the preacher chants the benefits of [hearing] the dharma *(dharma-nismsa)*, preaches a considerable portion of the sutra that is the subject of the sermon, and explains it drawing out the explanations in the commentary. The dawn portion of the sermon is concluded with the chantings of the Extolling of Maitreya *(maitri varnanava)* and the Donation of Merit *(pindima)*. Sometimes the preacher descends from the preacher's seat only after the sunrise. During the entire threefold watches of the night the hearers of the doctrine hear it, without leaving the hall and with great piety *(sraddhava)*. About once in two hours, the venerable preacher takes a break of about thirty minutes, giving also a break to the congregation. He takes refreshments and a chew of betel. At appropriate times the drums of the watches are played, incense and gifts *(pirikara)* offered. The collection is the preacher's. The donors [supporters of the monastery] do not take it even for the use of the monastery. In some places yards and yards of white cloth are offered.

At one location where I preached in 1928, due to the heap of gifts that the assembled lay and monastic noblemen offered, I could not even get off the preacher's seat. It is the habit of the listeners to offer whatever they bring along, like wristwatches, pocket watches, umbrellas, robes, silk kerchiefs, bedsheets, towels and so forth. . . .

I mostly preached from the *Paticcasamuppada* or the *Alavaka sutra*. I had memorized *bana* [the sermon] for the Paticcasamuppada completely. It was not from memory that I preached a section of the *Alavaka sutra*. Later on, gradually, I designed *bana* from the *Samacittapariyaya sutra, Dhammacakka sutra, Satipatthana sutra,* and so forth. I learnt from memory all that was needed, such as verses of worship *(namaskara gatha)*, donations of merit *(pindim)*, *prasa,* and Extolling of Maitreya *(maitri varnana)*. By the end of 1928, I could manage to preach a *bana* by myself. I performed *(pavatvimi)* three or four all night sermons while I was still a novice *(samanera)*.. . . .

I memorized new sutras, about one a month, and crafted *bana* for preaching. I trained to preach from the *Mahamangala, Vasala,* and *Parabhava sutras* as well. Now I know from memory everything I need to perform [all] night sermons. Even if I had to preach several consecutive days at the same place, I could do so without repetition, by alternating among about five or six *sutras*. Because I have memorized the *Paticcasamuppada*, I could preach from it for about two hours. Because the *Alavaka sutra* is prefaced by a long *nidhana katha* (preamble),[26] I can manage to preach *bana* for a couple of hours from that. Because the *Samacittapariyaya sutra* has a similarly long, beautiful story, that is also a bana I liked. By joining the biography of Visakha and the story of offering the Purvarama Vihara, I fashioned a *bana* of about three hours. Because Merit Givings for the Seat, the Invitations to the deities and their meanings, Verses of Worship and their meanings and narratives of the benefits of hearing dharma needed to be preached before the sermon, and, Extolling of Maitreya and gifts of merit had to be chanted after, I could manage to spend about five hours [on those].

This account makes it clear that the dharmadesana was an all-night performance. The author candidly admits how he "managed to" fill the time, which is one whole long night, and how the excessive greed of the pious to accumulate and hoard merit could actually be irritating. Second, the doctrinal content was insignificant. The dharmadesana consists of the following sequence.

1. The arrival of the preacher.
2. Giving merit for the *dharmasana,* first time.
3. The invitation to preach, in *gatha* and *prasa* (verses).
4. Giving merit for the *dharmasana,* second time.
5. Invitation to the gods.
6. Verses of *namaskara.*
7. *Prasa* on benefits of hearing *bana,* lullabically.
8. Benefits of *bana,* second time, in a different literary mode.
9. The sutra.
10. Commentary.
11. *Maitrivarnana.*
12. Giving of merit.
13. Gift giving to the preacher.

A look at this sequence makes it clear that the doctrinal content is limited to the core of the sutra and the commentary. Even there the sutra is not understood, because it is in Pali. Even the commentary may well be another text, in Pali or Sinhala, which is also memorized by the preacher and chanted. The appeal of this was more poetic or musical within an overall structure of religious emotion. It is possible that some preachers improvised

26. The story of the context in which it was preached.

and got across to the more educated or more intellectually inclined listeners
some of the doctrinal content. But for the majority the sound was the message, the act of hearing itself being understood as generative of merit. This
is brought out by the emphasis made in the quoted passage to the importance
of the voice, its melodic quality, and the lullabic element. Third, there is the
great emphasis on the giving and receiving of merit. Several of the elements
of the sequence above has to do with merit making. There is a surge of religious emotion from time to time, generated by the different elements in the
program. The whole scene is reminiscent of the descriptions of the Buddha
preaching, seated in the lotus position on a bejewelled dharma throne, surrounded by his disciples and such model Buddhist supporters as King Kosala
or Visakha, the banker's daughter, so familiar in the tradition of medieval
Sinhala literature. Fourth, there is the idea of performance. Several elements
of the sequence of events are dramatic. We have dramatic personae, the primary or the heroic being the monk costumed in Benares silk, hoisted on a
chair, and carried to the pavilion, which itself has characteristics of the stage.
There are the costumed boys playing the role of implorers to preach. There
is drumming, incense, and lighting. The author uses the term *pavatvanava* to
mean delivery of the sermon, a term suggestive more of a performance than
an exposition of doctrinal concepts. What we see here is the kind of elementary rendering of the religion into aesthetic performance which was encouraged and which did achieve its fullest development in Hinduism (music and
dance), but which was discouraged by the Theravada orthodoxy. The evolution of dramatic forms was more successful in the folk healing rituals where
the orthodoxy had no say.[27] For ordinary people, however, this ceremonial-
ism, and not any abstruse doctrines, constituted the essence of religion.

In some examples the traditional dharmadesana was even more inte-
grative of folk elements. For example, after the commentary was chanted,
stories were told for their narrative interest, although they were perfuncto-
rily connected to the sutra's theme. There were other dramatic segments,
for example, *Alavaka damanaya* (The Taming of Alavaka, the story of the Buddha's taming the "demon" Alavaka) and *Milindaprasnaya* (Questions of Milinda, the dialogue between king Milinda and the monk Nagasena), where lay
actors acted out the respective lay roles with the monk representing the
Buddha and Arahant Nagasena respectively. In others such as *Revati vilapaya*
the preacher himself acted as the character Revati, gesticulating histrioni-

27. This subject is discussed in Ediriweera Sarathchandra, *The Sinhalese Folk Play* (Colombo: Lake
House, 1953); rev. ed., under the title *Folk Drama of Ceylon* (Colombo: Ministry of Cultural Affairs,
Government of Ceylon, 1966).

cally and crying melodramatically. Another example consisted of the logical idea of employing two preachers. In this, known as the sermon of the double seat *(asana deke bana),* one preacher recited the text and the other the commentary, everything else remaining the same. Further, sometimes, money collecting devices, such as auctioning basketfuls of flowers *(malvatti vendesi)*[28] were tagged on to the event. While in the sutra a subject existed, its exploration was highly diffused and diluted. This sequence of events was also often preceded by the further peripheral activities such as processions *(perahara),* bazaars *(salpil),* fireworks *(malvedi)* and dances *(natum).*

We have here an example of rural Buddhism. Primarily motivated by a desire to accumulate and horde merit, the performance had a strong component of entertainment.[29] Such a grand performance, which required planning and extensive cooperation, could not have been frequent and probably was held about once a year, hence the great desire to make all the merit one could when the opportunity arose. Further contributing to its infrequency was the fact that it had to be coordinated so that it did not conflict with the harvesting and cultivating cycles that demanded all the community's labor.

Dharmapala's view of folk religion is one he shared with the missionaries. To restore the Sinhala people to their pristine glory while bringing them into modernity, it was necessary to get rid of rural superstition and ritualism, as exemplified by this performance of dharmadesana. To achieve this, Buddhist practice needed to be organized rationally, in keeping with the "pure psychology" of textual Buddhism.

As mentioned above, Dharmapala spoke about the Buddha's exhortations as commandments *(agnava).* Buddhists, like Christians, must engage in religious activity once every week, instead of following the traditional practice of doing so on full moon days. (Even that was not a commandment.) He also spoke about the generosity of the Bodhisattvas in terms that recall the Christian idea of a savior doing good to others. Indeed one of the strongest ideas of Dharmapalite Buddhism is charity. The Buddha himself is described as having suffered for the benefit of others, which Dharmapala expresses in words highly reminiscent of Christ's suffering for the good of others.

Within this broad framework of thought, it is not surprising that Dharmapala wanted the dharmadesana to be a sermon analogous to the Christian one, a combination of moral instruction with practical guidance for mun-

28. The idea of auction, and the term *vendesi* with its Latin root and Portuguese origin, suggests that this is an innovation, although it is possible that there were precolonial forms that are similar to this.

29. While it might be argued that other types of dharmadesana existed, they were not qualitatively different: they were merely variations of this.

dane living and covering a vast range of topics from economic productivity
and cleanliness to personal and family problems. What he wanted in the
dharmadesana was not a ritual but an instrument of regeneration, a time-
framed and thematically focused address that would get across a message
succinctly and effectively. A traditional dharmadesana was also unlikely to
appeal to educated urbanites, who in any case had regular work schedules in
full-time clerical, professional, or other jobs, which would prevent them
from considering an all-night performance to be their routine religious experience. They preferred succinctly presented doctrinal ideas and moral instruction for which their appetites had been whetted by late-nineteenth-
century Buddhist-Christian debates and by the activities of the Buddhist
Theosophical society, both of which signified a new scripturalism. Their
general acquaintance with modern knowledge and ideas prompted them further in the direction of a short modernized sermon. As a folk performance
the rural dharmadesana was too long and too rustic for the city audiences to
constitute any kind of entertainment either.

Thus there was at the beginning of the twentieth century a convergence
of interest between the urban laity and the newly emerging missionary
monks of the city who were inspired by Dharmapala for a time-framed,
thematic, non-ritualist dharmadesana that was doctrinal in content, morally
and socio-economically didactic, and largely devoid of emotion. Given the
processes of radical change the society was going through, a sermon suitable
for that changing environment would have evolved anyway, but Dharmapala's
vision of social and religious amelioration and of the restoration of a Sinhala
Buddhist society expedited its emergence and gave it its particular structure
and content. Early modern dharmadesana thus wove social issues specifically
related to the conditions under colonial rule into itself, i.e., issues articulated by Dharmapala. Its ardor and style owed something to Mohottivatte
Gunananda's (1823–90) debates and to the Christian pulpit (to which Gunananda himself owed a debt). There was also the shining example of the "sermon" of Dharmapala which he perfected as he traversed the country, and
which he committed to written form in his "Facts One Should Know." The
younger and more dynamic monks of the city, especially those associated
with the newly established Vidyodaya Pirivena, were quick to see the potential and adaptive possibilities of that sermon. For these monks, who were
also increasingly under the spell of Dharmapala, a dharmadesana that appealed to an elite constituted an attractive status prospect as well, for it
would reunite them with the elite from whom colonial domination and the
ensuing cultural differentiation had separated them. Thus from Dharmapala's zealous message and from the needs of the monastic and lay urban
religiosi arose an entirely new dharmadesana.

DHARMADESANA
For the City Elites

This new dharmadesana was a radical departure from the traditional. It was confined to about one hour, a remarkable shrinkage into one twelfth of its original duration. Next, it was free of the elaborate ritualism that conferred on the traditional dharmadesana most of its length. It was not a performance in the same sense as the traditional one was, and it lacked the dramatic elements we noted in it. Above all it focused on a theme, a feature structurally integrated to the sermon in the form of a Pali verse that the preacher chanted, explicitly recognizing it as the theme *(matrka)*. While there are some precedents for this in the medieval Sinhala literary works which were essentially dharmadesana in written form, the new dharmadesana in its succinctness and unity resembled more the sermon that emanated from the Christian pulpit, like the ones which the young Dharmapala heard over and over again at the corrugated-metal-roofed hall on Keyser Street.

The late nineteenth and early twentieth centuries comprised a period of great enthusiasm in Buddhism. This enthusiasm arose out of the Buddhist response to the missionary threat, which received the unacknowledged backing of the colonial government. The five great Buddhist-Christian debates at Baddegama (1865), Varagoda (1865), Udanvita (1866), Gampola (1871), and Panadura (1873) were both an expression of that enthusiasm and a stimulus for its further intensification. The controversies that took place within the dominant Siyam Nikaya as well the establishment of the Ramanna Nikaya in 1864 provide further evidence of ferment and new vigor.[30] All this was part of a general resurgence of Buddhism and Buddhist nationalism that was slowly building up since about mid-nineteenth century.

An important aspect of this enthusiasm was the heightened interest in Buddhist doctrine on the part of the western-educated professional and business laity in the urban areas, most notably the capital Colombo. The establishment of the Vidyodaya Pirivena in 1873, the same year as the culminating and the most memorable of the debates, showed the coming into being of a community of scholarly monks in the city of Colombo who were as keen to feed the new educated urban lay interest in Buddhist doctrine and morality as that urban laity was hungry for it. This was the first time after the establishment of British rule that an opportunity opened up for the monks, at least the educated Colombo monastic elite, to establish social contact with the western-educated elite. It was not the case that the monks "lost power" at the advent of colonial rule, as is often assumed: what really happened was

---

30. See K. Malalgoda, *Buddhism in Sinhalese Society, 1750–1900*.

that the elite split into western-educated and indigenous sections, and that the monks lost contact with the western-educated and therefore more powerful section. During this period, beginning about the last quarter of the nineteenth century, we see an attempt at detente on the part of the urban elite monks and the urban lay elites, a telling expression of which is the interest among the scholarly monks to learn English and among a section of the laity to learn Buddhism, and to a lesser extent Pali and Sinhala.

This interest of the laity is part of the larger interest in Buddhism that was generated by the debates, which were themselves the expression of a broader movement, spurred by the Christian critique, at rediscovering, systematizing, and streamlining Buddhism. The Buddhist elites were interested in finding the answers to the critique as much for their own intellectual reconciliation as for the need to respond to it by showing that Buddhism was in fact more moral and ethical, more conducive to progress, more systematic and philosophical, more compatible with modern science, more free of ritual than Christianity. In their Preface to the 1903 edition of the Panadura debate the editors write of this new interest in Buddhism: "It is a widely accepted fact that the Panadura debate was the incomparable reason . . . for [the existence today of] a pious enthusiasm about Buddhism among the Buddhist public of Lanka unknown thirty years ago."[31] Similarly, P. Arunachalam, a civil servant who was to later become one of the leaders of constitutional agitation, made the following observation: "Previously it was considered among Sinhalese rather fashionable to be thought Christian, and I have, in my judicial experience, known Buddhists taking [the] oath on the Bible as a matter of course. This is no longer the case. They are rather proud of their religion, and have even become aggressive to Christianity."[32]

The scene in Colombo in 1873, the year of the Pandura debate, is captured by John Capper, the editor of the oldest colonial newspaper, the *Times of Ceylon,* as follows:

> There is no doubt that whilst we [Christians] are congratulating ourselves on the successful work of our missionary and educational establishments, the Buddhists are stimulated by the same success to fresh efforts in behalf of their own faith. Not only have one or two of the most educated men amongst them, priests and laymen, put forward pamphlets and periodicals in the vernacular, in defense and illustration of their creed, but there is a greater activity amongst the Buddhist priesthood, with the object of awakening in the

31. T. S. Dharmabandu, ed., *Panca Maha Vadaya* (Colombo: Gunasena, 1992), 60.
32. *Census Report,* 1901, Quoted in Arnold Wright, ed., *Twentieth-century Impressions of Ceylon* (London: Lloyds Greater Britain Publishing Co. Ltd., 1907), 224.

minds of the people a more lively feeling towards their faith. Religious services are now being held every Sunday, as the appointed day of rest amongst nearly all classes, whereas it was the wont of the priesthood some few years ago to call their congregation together only on the occasion of some day memorable in their calendar for its sanctity. Temples are in course of construction, and where such work is not immediately practicable, temporary structures have been erected in which the people may assemble, and seated on benches listen to the recital of "Bana" and the exhortations, and illustrations of the ministering priest.

One such structure of rather large size we entered on a recent Sunday. The service was conducted by Sipkadua *(sic)* Sumangalabhidana, High Priest of Adam's Peak, the most accomplished Pali scholar in the island. . . . He stated that Buddha's doctrines may be divided into two parts—one the philosophical portion, containing sublime truths which only the eminently learned can understand, and the other, the plain discourses, embodying great truths, but couched in homely language. The homely language used, the priest went on to say, often conveyed false ideas with it, but such language was made the medium of conveying facts, with the view of adapting himself to the capacities of the common people, and he would particularly remind them that they were not to suppose that the "Great High Buddha" meant to countenance the superficial meaning which those words implied.

After speaking of the importance of works, of the necessity of personal merit, he enlarged upon Sowan, Skradagami, Anagami, and Arhat, the four paths of virtues prescribed by the Buddha to obtain Nirvana (at the mention of which all the assembled crowd cried Sadu); he concluded a learned sermon of some two hours duration by exhorting the congregation to exercise patience, and to follow Buddha's command of not even so much as thinking evil of those who cruelly used and persecuted them. . . .

Attached to the temple, which is to be erected on the ground now occupied by the temporary building, will be a college for priests and laymen, in which Pali alone will be taught to such students as may frequent it for secular education only, and the High Priest stated how gladly he would give instruction to any English gentleman desiring to learn the Pali language.[33]

This eyewitness account, albeit from the point of view of a Christian, is explicit on the new enthusiasm about Buddhism in the city of Colombo. It mentions the importance of the debates and the effect of the Christian missionaries' very successes in stimulating that enthusiasm. Various publications in Sinhala dealing with religious issues were proliferating, and after a

33. Introduction by John Capper to Controversy at Panadura or *Pandura Vadaya,* ed. Pranith Abhayasundara (Colombo: The State Printing Corporation. 1990), 3–6.

period of withdrawal as if in shock, monks are suddenly stimulated into activity, and into learning the ways of the new social order which they had
shunned so far. Capper lists some of these activities: "Services" (i.e., sermons) are performed every Sunday rather than on some calendrical sacred
day, which were probably confined to the more important full moon days.
Temples are being built in the city, and until they are ready groups of people
assemble in temporary structures, as if responding in kind to the "loose no
time" attitude reflected in the Salvation Army's corrugated iron roofed structure. Some of what was said in the "service" itself indicates the atmosphere
of activity, for example, the reference to the "false ideas" that have crept
into the "homely" language, is probably a reference to some of the common
missionary criticisms of Buddhism as superstition, and it illustrates the
"scripturalism" that was emerging in the environment of modernist reformism. The Buddhist heroic debater Mohottivatte Gunananda consulted this
preacher (Hikkaduve Sumangala, the Pali scholar whose sermon Capper describes), on some of these commonly raised missionary critiques just before
the Panadura debate, which indicates Sumangala's full awareness of this kind
of critique and which also makes it probable that the people he meant when
he referred to those who misunderstood the "homely language" were Christian missionaries. Finally, we have what would appear very likely as part of
the same general enthusiasm: a hint of the emphasis laid by the monks on
the availability of Pali to anybody willing to learn. Pali, the language of Buddhism, will not only help Buddhist resurgence but also will help people to
advance beyond the "homely language" and to understand Buddhism properly. Let us also recall that in Dharmapala's view Pali contained all the knowledge necessary for rebuilding a modern version of the glorious society of
the past, and that he urged monks to learn it rather than gain a smattering
of Sanskrit. This great interest in facilitating access to "proper Buddhism"
both to local Buddhists, peasant as well as elite, and to the outside world
was a central motif in the ideology and activities of Dharmapala, and it represents the scripturalism that we have already encountered in the movement
and in our comparative material.

   This facilitation was just as well because the laity in traditional times had
no access to "proper Buddhism," which was in Pali, with which even among
the monks only a minority were adequately conversant. So with the increasing demand for a knowledge of Buddhism, due to the general atmosphere
of the missionary challenge as well as to the personal religious and ethical
needs of urban elites, and above all because of Dharmapala's constant refrain
to all classes, especially those who are capable, namely the elites, to learn
Buddhism and thereafter serve the people's needs, groups formed to seek

that knowledge. One group met at a place explicitly called "Dharma Sala," or "Hall of the Doctrine," located on the present Vajira Road in Bambalapitiya, Colombo. In 1901 this group, apparently consisting of upper-class professionals, approached Hikkaduve Sumangala, the principal of the Vidyodaya monastic college (and the scholar in Capper's account) and asked him if he would provide the group with an appropriately qualified monk to reside at Dharma Sala. Hikkaduve suggested Palane Vajiragnana, the best student of the graduating class and winner of the prestigious King of Thailand Prize. Palane took up residence at Dharma Sala, which was subsequently known as Vajirarama.

The Vajirarama monks claim the new dharmadesana—short, devoid of ritual, well-integrated and focused on a theme, and above all relating religion to daily life—to be the invention of their "founding superior," Palane Vajiragnana. Such a dharmadesana would on each of the above criteria be the opposite of the traditional. While Palane undoubtedly deserves some credit for this—he was probably the first monk to do this—it is equally without doubt that the broader current of inspiration for the invention came from Dharmapala. The idea of consciously applying "Buddhism" to daily life is Dharmapala's; it is probably one more thing he learnt from the Reformed Church. And Dharmapala, as a layman, was already preaching this kind of sermon. As part of his general critique of the illiterate village monks, Dharmapala had launched an attack on their ritualism, specifically citing some of the elements of the all-night dharmadesana held in the villages, such as drumming and dancing, processions and fireworks, all of which became targets of the critique of ritualism by Dharmapala's soldiers and hero-giants, as we shall see below.

The other current of inspiration for Palane to design a new dharmadesana came from his urban clients, which as noted above suited the status aspirations of his own and other educated Colombo monks. We find a clue to the nature of the new dharmadesana and the new religiosity to which it appealed in the subjects they chose, for example, in the striking popularity of the *Vyaghrapadya* sutra with Palane, Kalukondayave, and later with Hendiyagala. All the major preachers of the time found it to be a popular sutra or were under some constraint to come up with a sutra like it. The contents of the sutra explain why. It extols the virtues of honesty, hard work, austerity and savings, all of which suited the rising urban bourgeoisie.

Palane Vajiragnana (1878–1955) was, as his renowned pupil Piyadassi put it, the "founding superior" of Vajirarama. Ordained in 1893 under the tutelage of Veragmpita Siri Revata of the Devagiri vihara, Kamburugamuva, Valigama, and admitted to higher ordination in 1900, he joined Vidyodaya in

1897. Hikkaduve Sumangala, the founder of Vidyodaya, was his mentor. Palane was the son of the Sinhala scholar, Don Andris Tudave Panditaguna-wardena. Proctor R. G. L. Perera, father of well-known lawyer R. L. Per-era, held private English classes for him and several other monks, and he improved his knowledge of English through further self-study.[34] Among his pupils were well-known monks: Narada, who became a favorite preacher, Mahanama, Sumanasiri, Metteyya, Piyadassi, Madihe Pannasiha, Ampitiye Rahula, and Panvila Vipassi. According to Piyadassi, Palane revolutionized the dharmadesana by doing two things. First he confined it to one hour, and second, he "applied to modern life, both to the individual and the society" the theme or the moral that was being discussed in the sermon. It is relevant to quote Palane himself:

> A sermon should be preached according to times and circumstances. Since in these days men do not have more than an hour to devote even to listen to a sermon, it is inappropriate to preach a sermon for longer than an hour. It is better to listen [to a sermon] for fifteen minutes per two or three days than to preach for two or three hours each day. . . . What is preached should be intelligible to even a child. . . . [C]ollections, auctions, music, dancing and fireworks . . . should not be allowed during a sermon. A sermon is meant to teach ethical conduct and improve virtue and [worldly] wisdom and not to collect money by swaying the people by means of music, dancing, gymnas-tics, invitations to preach, fireworks and so forth. Such brief sermons will help the development or virtue and [worldly] wisdom, and the decline of crime, theft, bad manners in the villages, and promote harmony.[35]

It is clear that this is Dharmapala from top to toe. Palane ridicules the tradi-tional dharmadesana and extols the virtues of the new, time-framed one. He makes particular mention of the unacceptability of activities like music and dancing, collections, fireworks, and performances which accompanied the traditional sermon. He specifically refers to the uses of the sermon to im-prove the state of the person and society. The traditional dharmadesana, to quote Piyadassi again, "did not teach the audience the art of applying this dharma to life and to society. . . . They [the preachers] would read gathas and sutras and people would listen . . . [i.e., gain merit, but] they didn't understand, they fell asleep. Palane was popular because even people who

---

34. R. G. L. Perera built the Maitreya hall and started a school for monks in Bambalapitiya to teach them English. Suriyagoda Sumangala, who went to Oxford and later was the subject of a scandal, was a student of this school. Personal communication, Mr. N. P. Kumaratunga, 12 August 1996.

35. Madihe Pannasiha, ed. *Sri Vajragnana Sahityaya* (Colombo: Bhasa Press, 1967), 1:36.

were not very interested in dhamma got something out of it, even non-Buddhists [because his sermons represented the application of the dhamma to everyday life]."[36] The contrast between this and the traditional dharmadesana could not be more pronounced. Among other details of contrast noted already, it is striking that the sermon had application in day-to-day life, for individuals and for society; that is, there was an acceptance of social and personal problems as legitimately falling within the framework of the religious sphere, and hence there was a devaluing of the preoccupation with gaining merit for the sake of better future worlds. The inspiration for this is clear: it is Dharmapala's yoking together as one and inseparable material and spiritual progress by means of locating both in Buddhist morality. Thus amelioration in the areas of crime and temperance as well as economic rationality and civic responsibility are ultimately moored in religion and are legitimate topics for a sermon.

The introduction of radio sermons in the 1940s made the time frame even more important and served to consolidate the image of the new dharmadesana as a crisp, well-focused affair. Palane also went out to preach in provincial towns although not in rural areas, as did some others whose work is discussed below. Piyadassi described Palane as "*dharmaduta* (missionary) within the country,"[37] a description pregnant with the meaning, on the one hand, that the people were being converted to a new urban Buddhism and, on the other, that literacy and urbanization were spreading rapidly and hence diminishing interest in the traditional dharmadesana. It indicates that the new scripturalism was spreading and creating an ideologically and self-consciously new Buddhist middle class that would suffuse their religion with resurgent Sinhala nationalism, with disastrous results to the nation. More telling for our concerns, namely the evolution of a new role for the monk, "dharmaduta within the country" heralds the appearance of the monk of Dharmapala's imagination and solemn prayer. In Palane, the first hero-giant and soldier of the Roar of Liberation Army is born, and he and others like him would sound the drums, blow the conch, and raise the flag of the dhamma.

36. Interview with Piyadassi (1995).
37. Interview with Piyadassi.

THE ECONOMIC STAGE: VIDYODAYA AND RURAL DEVELOPMENT

The previous chapter described how the ideal society of Dharmapala was expressed in economic and cultural frameworks.[1] While the living conditions of the people needed urgent and radical improvement, that project had to be based within a specific cultural framework, that of Buddhist morality. This amounts to nothing less than a revival of the traditional Sinhala social order in all respects except kingship (only because the royal line was extinct). An important ingredient of the revival is the restoration of the Sinhala language and of Buddhism to their former status as "state language" and "state religion" respectively. How these two aspects, economic and cultural, of the Dharmapalite agenda were pursued, and the reverberating consequences of that pursuit, constitute much of the history of the Sangha (monkhood), indeed of the nation, in the twentieth century. The sequence of events was as follows:[2] (1) Dharmapala's words caused the first stirrings in the sleeping monkhood at about the beginning of the new century. (2) The realization of the economic part of the message was attempted in the 1930s and the 1940s. (3) The cultural part was in a great ferment during the 1940s and continued to be dominant until the late 1970s. (4) At present the monkhood is facing the consequences of the extraordinary turbulence brought about by these attempts. In this chapter we are concerned with the

---

1. "Cultural" is used here in the broad sense to include religion.
2. This is not to suggest a rigid periodization. There were monks in the economic era who had political interests and vice versa. However, the broad outlines are clear as to a predominantly "economic" stage to be followed by a predominantly "political" stage.

economic agenda for an ideal society, and in the next we will examine the cultural agenda. The consequences of these will be discussed in later chapters.

Starting at about the turn of the century, Dharmapala's writings and speeches inspired his audiences, especially the younger generation, by their forcefulness, freshness, and nationalist sentiment. Let us recall that the main agent in Dharmapala's attempt at regenerating the society would be the monk. The basis of the message is Buddhist morality, with a socio-economic content integrated into that primary message. It is therefore not surprising that some of the more sensitive and socially conscious young monks would have responded to these calls with fervor, commitment, and enthusiasm. Among such enthusiasts several stand out, and in this chapter we shall focus on the work of three of the best known of them.

The two seats of monastic learning in the city of Colombo were the Vidyodaya pirivena and the Vidyalankara pirivena, founded in 1873 and 1875 respectively. The two were identical in their curricula and overall organization, and both were the offspring of the same intellectual ancestry. The typical student in each was an able and hardworking young monk who came from the village and adapted with great success to the busy political and commercial capital Colombo. Yet in their political and ideological orientations they turned out to be quite unlike each other. Vidyodaya evolved in a conservative and pro-establishment direction and Vidyalankara became rebellious, foreshadowing the youth violence that became a pervasive factor of the national life since the 1970s. Of the two agendas of Dharmapala, Vidyodaya embraced the sober and pragmatic economic one, and Vidyalankara the ideological and uncompromisingly cultural one which by definition was nationalist.

Dharmapala's economic program centered on the concept of rural regeneration. Briefly, it meant a self-sufficient and predominantly agricultural economy modeled on the imagined economy of precolonial Sri Lanka. Within agriculture, primacy was to be given to rice cultivation, with the cultivation of vegetables and fruit trees and the building of rural crafts and industries constituting the rest of the economy. The main organizing mechanism of agriculture, as of all other rural activity, was to be a rural association, to be founded in every village, called a Gramaraksaka (Village Protection) or a Maha Bodhi (Great Bodhi) society. Here is how Dharmapala proposed the idea:

1. The residents of every village should form a Gramaraksaka or Maha Bodhi Society.

2. The members of the village should try to work for the development of the village.
3. They must teach knowledge *(sastra)* to boys and girls, and if the village has some craft or industry it had been engaged in, such craft or industry should be promoted further.
4. The society must let those who lazily waste time know the cruel consequences of laziness, and must provide them work and get them employed in that work.
5. A leading monk of the village should be appointed to the position of Patron/Advisor to the society.
6. Measures should be taken to make all men and women, including village headmen, observe the eight precepts on full moon days and hear a sermon at least once every week.
7. The monks and the village headmen must strive hard to keep the members of the society away from killing, stealing, adultery, lying, using harsh language, tale-carrying, drinking alcohol like toddy and arrack, hatred, jealousy and so forth.
8. The society should do the following: keeping the houses of villagers clean, clearing the overgrown yards, acting with unity regarding the dangers that come from enemy populations of other *jatis* (ethnic groups), and resurrect ancient customs that have lapsed.[3]

What is envisaged here is an idyllic community that is close to the "village communities" idea that has fascinated such western writers as Sir Henry Maine and B. H. Baden-Powell and that has been earnestly proposed by Indian reformers such as Gandhi and his disciple Jay Prakash Narayan.[4] The only difference is the Buddhist moral basis of this one, symbolized by the preeminent position accorded to the monk, who along with the headman holds power. The ideal village is a self-sufficient, self-governing, democratic community that is responsible for educating its young in academic knowledge as well as the crafts. Most of the above guidelines have a moral character, and there is a noticeable preoccupation with laziness as the enemy of progress, the combating of which along with combating other vices consti-

---

3. *Gihi dinacariyava,* "Daily schedule for laymen," first published in 1898, nineteenth printing in 1958. Reproduced in Ananda Guruge, ed., *Dharmapala Lipi,* 40–41.

4. Maine, for example, considered Indian village communities to be self–sufficient, independent, closed entities. As Sir Charles Metcalf, an East India Company official, put it, the communities were "little Republics, having nearly everything they want within themselves, and almost independent of any foreign relations." Quoted in Vijaya Samaraweera, "Litigation, Sir Henry Maine's writings and the Ceylon Village Communities Ordinance of 1871," in *Senarat Paranavitana Commemoration Volume,* edited by L. Prematilleke, K. Indrapala, and J. E. van Lohuizen-deLeeuw (Leiden: E. J. Brill, 1978). See also, Henry S. Maine, *Village Communities in East and West* (New York: Henry Holt, 1876).

tutes a major responsibility of the association. There is also a preoccupation with cleanliness and neatness, both of persons and houses, and a corresponding inner purity that is maintained by means of good social and ethical behavior, and by the observance of religious precepts as well as listening to sermons. These guidelines indicate what in fact the village is not: hence the need to endeavor to endow it with these habits and values. While in Dharmapala's view—and that of his followers, some of whom we shall discuss below—these are Buddhist values, they are in fact urban, middle-class values ultimately derived from "learning to do everything the Reformed Church way."

In this chapter we discuss how this concern with the improvement in the conditions of village life, the economic part of Dharmapala's twofold approach, was put into practice by some members of the younger generation of monks of Dharmapala's time who were inspired by him. Dharmapala's campaign to spread his ideas started about the turn of the century, but it was not until about the thirties that an attempt was made to put them into practice. By then, it had been forgotten that the whole idea was Dharmapala's, at least by the general public, though not by these workers themselves. Kalukondayave Pannasekhara, the most prominent among them, explicitly says that in this area he considers Dharmapala to be his teacher, and he regrets that he was not born ten years before, when he could have actually worked with the reformer.[5] The ideas of reformers often get translated into practice only if conditions that precipitate a society to do so are available. Hence the dormancy of Dharmapala's ideas for about thirty years, until two such conditions emerge on the Sri Lankan scene.

First, in 1931, as part of the Donoughmore proposals, universal franchise was introduced to the island. This suddenly made "the people" a force to reckon with. The politicians needed a mechanism of establishing rapport with the masses of voters. While a genuine interest in the peasantry cannot be altogether denied, the sudden burst of enthusiasm for rural development cannot be explained except with reference to the need for politicians to woo voters. The politicians belonged to the urban, culturally alienated elite who were not proficient enough in Sinhala, the language of the electorate, to make rousing speeches. The educated Colombo monk, with his knowledge of Sinhala, Pali, and Buddhism, and as an erstwhile villager, was ideally suited to bridge the gap between the rural voters and the urban politicians.

---

5. Kalukondayave Pannasekhara, *Svyamlikhita Sri Pragnasekhara Caritapadanaya* (Megodakolonnava [Colombo]: Sri Press, 1970), 118–19. Parenthetical citations in the text, for references relating to Kalukondayave, are to this, his autobiography.

For the monk, it was an undreamed of opportunity to regain his relevance in the village where, although the rural culture remained, the tentacles of a modern economy and government had diminished his role and prestige. The second factor that favored the translation into practice of the ideas of Dharmapala is the severe malaria epidemic in the mid-thirties that swept through the island, taking a heavy toll of life and causing a great deal of suffering in many areas (some, like the Kegalla and Kurunagala districts, were more affected than others). These two factors suddenly focused attention on the village as never before and provided an opportunity for the young enthusiastic monks to put into action the plan of rural regeneration impressed on them by Dharmapala. The symbiosis between monk and politician was salutary at the time, or at worst harmless. It broadly represented a consensus of economic interest despite the politics of suffrage. It was free of ideology. In two decades this was to change. By the 1940s the soberly economic was pushed out to accommodate the grossly political. Ideology was enthroned. After 1956, the monk-politician relation, once benign, led to a series of developments that ultimately turned the nation into a land of corruption, murder, and war.

It is not the case that the movement only started after the politicians got interested in rural life. Contrarily, it was the politicians who jumped on the bandwagon when the monks, inspired by Dharmapala, had already launched the program. In exhorting the monks to give up their ritual-infested, lazy monastic life and instead work compassionately and in earnest for the people, Dharmapala actually gave them a role in society that was altogether new and revolutionary, contrary to claims that they always played that role. This claim, originating in Dharmapala, was best articulated by the Vidyalankara monks in their effort to justify political activity.

Our interest is in the evolution of this role, of which the project for rural regeneration is the first and finest expression, and our interest is in the monks. Nevertheless it is difficult to talk about rural regeneration without referring briefly to a lay activist in whose work we have its first expression. This is the philanthropist Wilmot A. Perera. It is not clear whether Dharmapala's ideas were the driving force behind Wilmot's activities. He was a cosmopolitan intellectual who would have found Dharmapala's nationalism too narrow, and he was clearly influenced by western socialist ideas as well as by Indian ideas such as Gandhi's on rural society and Tagore's on education. But there cannot be any doubt that he was also influenced by Dharmapala. In fact, he may well be the most discerning of the Dharmapala disciples in the sense that he accepted the good part of Dharmapala and discarded the bad. That Wilmot's family were benefactors of Dharmapala's work is a further reason why he could well have been influenced by Dharmapala.

MONKS AND RURAL DEVELOPMENT
The Gramasamvardhana Movement

Gramasamvardhana means "village development" and refers to the movement that came into being in the thirties for that purpose. This movement is of great interest to us because of the role it played in providing an opportunity for the monks to make themselves relevant in a changing society, which alone would ensure them satisfactory acceptance in the emerging new social order. Gramasamvardhana was the launching pad for monks to take off into "social service" and into the resulting limelight. We must remember that the monks who came to study at Vidyodaya and Vidyalankara came from the countryside and were the cream of the crop of rural monks, and while they were stimulated and thrilled by the city, they were nostalgic about the village and were interested in its welfare. By virtue of their rural experience, perceptiveness, and now their detachment and widened horizons, they knew the village, intellectually and experientially, better than anyone. The city politicians and philanthropists who were involved in Gramasamvardhana needed experts on village life for the efficient planning and organization of their work. No one better suited that expert role than these monks. Thus, since the monks were looking for exactly the role the city elites were looking for someone to fill, both embraced the Gramasamvardhana idea with enthusiasm and vigor.

The first Gramasamvardhana organization was founded in Horana by Wilmot A. Perera in 1932 and was called "The Rayigam Korale Village Life Protection Society" *(Rayigam Korale grama jivita samraksana samitiya)*. Wilmot was the son of Abraham Perera, a wealthy agriculturist whose specialty was growing rubber, having built up his early wealth through arrack renting.[6] Thanks to a long-term contract with a British company that gave him pre-negotiated high prices even after the market prices slumped, Abraham Perera's wealth grew immensely, as did his rubber empire, appropriately earning him the folk title "Rubber King," or we might say "Rubber Baron." Wilmot's mother, Lilian Phoelicia Dias, came from another family whose wealth was built on arrack renting. She was the sister of Arthur V. Dias, a philanthropist, who spent on the Temperance Movement the fortunes his father made from dealing in alcohol. After his early education at Royal Col-

---

6. Arrack is a hard liquor made by tapping the budding coconut inflorescence while it is still in its unopened sheath and distilling the sap. "Arrack renting" is British colonial and Sri Lankan English; it refers to running taverns that sold arrack, "renting" referring to the licensing fee paid to the government. The source for information on Wilmot A. Perera is Gunadasa Liyanage, *Sirikita ha Vilmat* (Nugegoda: Janajana Publishers. 1985).

lege, Colombo, Wilmot planned to go to England to study accountancy. His father did not think much of accountancy, although there were only a handful of Chartered Accountants on the island at the time. Wilmot then decided to study archaeology. He applied to Cambridge and was accepted. However, on the eve of his departure to England his father died, and he had to abandon archaeology for the sake of managing the family fortunes. Returning from Colombo to the countryside where the plantations were located was a turning point in Wilmot's life. An avid reader and lover of the arts, the young agriculturist, perhaps influenced by English authors who sang of the countryside and the peasantry, was greatly attracted both to the beauty of the village and the simplicity and charm of the rural people. At the same time he saw first hand the poverty and the need of the people, and he resolved to do what he could.

This interest as well as his thoughtfulness on the subject is reflected in a series of articles he published in the major daily, *The Ceylon Daily News*, in 1932 or shortly before that. These essays were later published in book form, its Preface promising "the net proceeds of the sale of this booklet . . . towards Rural Reconstruction work."[7] In retrospect and with the benefit of the knowledge we have of the dishonesty, profiteering, and colossal corruption of politicians of later decades, Wilmot's interests appear genuinely altruistic, his ideas informed, and his commitment and approach inspired. His personal library, which he later donated to Sri Palee,[8] the unique school he founded in Horana, reflects wide and sophisticated interests. Indicating both his aesthetic sensibility and his romantic vision of rural society, that library included a numbered copy of the first edition, limited to 425 copies, of

---

7. Wilmot A. Perera, *Problems of Rural Ceylon* (Colombo: Associated Newspapers of Ceylon. 1932).

8. Sri Palee was a total school. Its curriculum consisted of the regular arts and science subjects and arts and crafts including textiles and pottery. It was modeled on Shantiniketan of Ravindranath Tagore who, on Wilmot's invitation, laid the foundation stone for the school buildings (1934) and named it "Sri Palee," the Abode of the Goddess. Music, dance, and art teachers were sent to India for training. Indian artist and critic Mukul Dey, the author of *My Pilgrimages to Ajanta and Bagh,* painted the murals and was probably a resident art teacher in the early days of the school. Tagore's visit, which included a performance of his dance drama *Saap Mochan* in Colombo, and his appreciation of Kandyan dance, which led him to take with him to Shantiniketan a drummer and a dancer, gave a fillip to the movement for forging a national dance and music and encouraged talented young men and women to go to Shatiniketan and Bhatkande for training in these two subjects. The search for an indigenous theater, which culminated in Sarachchandra's Maname (1956), while deriving from a different stream, the tradition of the folk theater, was fertilized by the events that can be traced to Tagore's visit; for example, some of the stylized movements in Maname were composed by the Indian-trained Vasanta Kumar. The nationalization of private schools in the 1960s destroyed this unique experiment and reduced Sri Palee to a normal school, ultimately resulting in the government's appropriation of its magnificent campus, which is now home to a part of the aesthetic education program of Colombo University.

Ananda Coomaraswamy's *Mediaeval Sinhalese Art.*[9] It is a measure of the regard in which he held this rhapsody of the peasant's way of life that, when he took office as the first Sri Lankan ambassador to China, one of the gifts Wilmot presented to Premier Chou En Lai was a copy of the work. Wilmot was interested in improving the totality of the peasant life—health, economy, education, leisure, aesthetic discernment, and outlook. This further suggests the influence of Coomaraswamy, who conceptualized peasant life as an organic whole. But as *Problems of Rural Ceylon* amply demonstrates, Wilmot was no mere romantic dreamer. He displayed both a mastery of the facts of rural life and an understanding of what needed to be done if the life of the peasant was to be truly improved, and he pragmatically gave prominence to the economic sphere. He talked about free education in 1933, ten years before it became a reality, peasant agriculture in 1934, cotton cultivation in 1936, and he founded the first trade union on the island in 1938. He advocated better health facilities, nutrition, a midday meal for school children, and the development of rural handicrafts. Besides, both his library and his writings show his affinity to socialist thought, and on the basis of some of the statements he makes it is fair to describe him as an Owenite socialist.

This interest, derived from human concern and romantic and nationalistic idealism for a vigorous peasantry, combined with universal suffrage and the malaria epidemic, gave rise to a concept of improving the lot of the peasantry, variously termed "rural reconstruction," "rural uplift," "protection of rural life," and so forth. In this work, following the usage that subsequently became the common one, we shall call it *gramasamvardhana* or its English gloss, Rural Development. A remarkable feature of this concept, despite its underlying motivation of electoral gain, was its non-ideological nature and its multipartisan support base. "Multipartisan" is used here to mean a sense of general consensus: political parties in the contemporary sense were not in existence in the thirties in Sri Lanka. In other words, the cause of rural development was taken up by politicians of varying political views, broadly "capitalist" or broadly "socialist." Philanthropists, intellectuals, and bureaucrats were involved in it in different ways. Upper-class urban women founded Women's Associations *(Mahila Samiti)* to help foster and promote rural arts and crafts. Most relevant for our purposes, urban monks who had

9. This edition was printed at the Essex House Press in the Norman Chapel at Broad Campden, Gloucestershire, England, under the author's care, begun September 1907 and completed December 1908. Twenty five more copies were printed on handmade paper. Personal note: My own introduction to this book as a high school student was this particular numbered copy.

comprehended the momentous nature of the social changes that were oc-
curring before their eyes saw in Rural Development an opportunity to become meaningful and relevant to contemporary society.[10]

The gramasamvardhana concept was also non-ideological in the following
sense. First, it did not blame colonial rule for the state of the peasant. In fact
blaming was not a major part of the dialogue of gramasamvardhana. Whatever blame was talked about was placed not on colonialism but on the precolonial feudal system and its abuses.[11] Second, it was understood as an activity of the economic sphere that was independent of the political. In a
colonial setup, the elites who are comfortable can afford to talk about political freedom, rights, and so forth, but these do not mean much to the impoverished majority whose concerns are predominantly economic. Rural Development therefore need not necessarily get involved with any political
struggle for such things as freedom, rights, and culture. Wilmot A. Perera
quotes Gangulee approvingly: "While the administration of a country by an
alien government brings about a psychological state of mind resulting in
excessive political preoccupations of the educated classes, it must be realized
that for a vast population, living as they do bound in economic fetters, mere
freedom to vote cannot gain for them bread and butter."[12] It is as if these
pioneers separated the ideological from the pragmatic, which were united
in Dharmapala's thinking, and tossed out the former and hung on the latter.

Let us now examine in some detail the careers of the three monks who
figure prominently in the Rural Development movement—Kalukondayave

10. As I discuss below, Kalukondayave, following Dharmapala, emphasized the monk's duty to be
of worldly service. Other-worldly service often has an ambivalent ritual status refracted from Hindu
ideas relating to priesthood. For example, concerning the monk in his ritual capacity (as opposed to
being a social worker), despite the Buddhist idea that seeing monks *(samananam ca dassanam)* is auspicious *(mangala)*, there is also in village Buddhism the belief that the monk is inauspicious. Thus, it was,
and sometimes still is believed that it is not a good thing to see a monk first thing in the morning, and
monks were structurally and functionally separated from marriage ceremonial. Significantly, educated
modern monks, like Elle Gunavamsa and Kananke Dhammadinna, those who have now inherited the
idea of social service as the monk's primary and proper duty, are trying to erase this inauspicious image.
A dramatic way to do this is precisely to demand to participate in the marriage ceremony, the auspicious
ceremony par excellence. Thus Elle Gunavamsa argues that monks should have the licensed right to
consecrate marriages (interview with Elle Gunavamsa, 1993). This idea in particular illustrates another
interesting sociological process in the upper rungs of the new monkhood, namely the influence of travel
abroad or close association with monks who live abroad, especially in the West, where some monks
have obtained the authorization to perform marriages and function as marriage registrars, itself an
adaptation by monks residing in these countries to Christian practices. Some monks resident in foreign,
especially western, countries have adopted a new style of naming themselves, with the village name as
a surname, connotative of high status.

11. Wilmot A. Perera, *Problems of Rural Ceylon,* 7.

12. Ibid., 26.

Pannasekhara (1895–1977), Hinatiyana Dhammaloka (1900–1981), and Hendiyagala Silaratana (1913–1982).

DHARMAPALITE MISSIONARIES (1)
Kalukondayave Pannasekhara

Kalukondayave Pannasekhara, the greatest preacher of modern times, started preaching in 1911, at the age of 16, though he "apprenticed" at age nine, as noted below.[13] Starting two years later, he kept a diary of which some parts, those between 1913 and 1933, were destroyed by time and pests. Those from 1934 to 1965 are intact. All are written in clear, graceful, leisurely handwriting, though he had been told at some stage in his early career that his handwriting was bad. The son of Liyanage Don Romanis Appuhamy and Malavipatirage Dona Docco Hamine, Kalukondayave was named, according to astrological determination, Don Ingonis, a name whose origin he says is at best baffling. He had five older brothers and one younger sister. His first schooling was in a Baptist school in Dekatana, the village adjoining his. At this school he excelled in studies, including Christianity. He first preached several years before he even entered the Order, when he was only eight or nine years old. Sitting on a high seat amidst elderly men and women who had observed *sil* (the eight precepts), he read from books such as *Pujavaliya, Milindaprasnaya,* and *Jataka Pota,* which his father explained to the congregation. Kalukondayave was admitted to the Order on February 23, 1911 under the tutelage of Mulleriyave Gunaratana, incumbent of Sunandarama of Ganegodalla. He spent only three months in the Sugatabimbaramaya (formerly Sri Sudarsanaramaya) as an acolyte *(pandupalasa),* which is less than the normally accepted period but fully justified by his preparation at home and his extraordinary sincerity and socio-religious sensitivity. When Kalukondayave was about ten years old, a young monk named Kitalagama Dhammaratana (formerly Sumedhamkara) came to reside at the Lenagampola vihara at Malvana. This monk was instrumental in building a bridge across a stream that enabled traffic between the villages Kalukondayave and Malvana. Prior to this the two villages were connected only by a log, from which, as a child, Kalukondayave fell into the water twice and was nearly drowned. In addition, this monk organized children's societies in the two

---

13. The sources for this discussion are the diaries of Kalukondayave located in his library at Navagamuva, interviews with his pupil Madana Jinaratana, and Kalukondayave's autobiography, *Svyamlikhita Sri Pragnasekhara Caritapadanaya,* cited in note 5 above.

villages. He also organized a ten-day dharmadesana series, all of which Kalukondayave attended with enthusiasm. Clearly, these activities must have
impressed the young Kalukondayave. They represent everything that he was
to later pursue with such tenacity and assiduity, namely rural reconstruction, self-help, and dharmadesana. These early influences probably received
a strong boost and their driving force from his contact with the writings of
Dharmapala. These early experiences indeed may have made the difference
between mere doctrinaire compassion and the dedicated activism he was to
later exhibit in extraordinary measure.

Kalukondayave conducted his first religious service in 1913, at age eighteen. It consisted of inviting a congregation, leading a collective offering of
flowers and lamps, and delivering a short sermon. What is of significance to
us in this event is his reason for doing so, which he describes as follows:
"How good it would be for me to motivate in righteous conduct the people
of the village who so generously treat the monastery with its needs?" (90).
Here is the seed of an idea which defined his mission in life: working for
others, motivating them in good conduct which he considered to be the basis
of gaining a good life in this world, without either denying or paying much
attention to the other world. It foreshadows his later achievement in bringing together two traditionally and apparently disparate activities, gramasamvardhana and dharmadesana, which he molded into a single whole.
Philosophically, it reinterprets Buddhism, an "other worldly" doctrine, as a
blueprint for action in this world, echoing the idea of *loka nibbana* (liberation
in this world) that arose in Burma.[14] Further, it expresses his sense of gratitude and obligation to the laity, which is the germ of the idea now emerging
in the Sangha but still weak and inconsistent, that it must pay some attention
to the mundane problems of the laity.

Early in his monastic life Kalukondayave started reading the *Sinhala Bauddhaya,* the weekly nationalist newspaper started and edited by Dharmapala.
A regular feature in it was the column *Danagatyutu Karunu* ("Facts that one
should know"), and Kalukondayave found the column to be immensely appealing. In particular he was inspired by the following statement of Dharmapala: "If a person is born in this land, that person, whether he be monk
or layman, must do something for the benefit of the people." Kalukondayave
writes, "My ideas changed completely by reading that. Every man born in
the Sinhala country, whether monk or layman, must do some service in the
name of the country, religion, or the people. . . . Reading these writings

---

14. On *loka nibbana,* see E. Sarkisianz, *Buddhist Backgrounds of the Burmese Revolution* (The Hague:
Martinus Nijhoff, 1965), 169–71.

made me very enthusiastic [about doing some national or religious ser-
vice]. . . . Therefore I must say that in this, Dharmapala was my teacher"
(118–19). This is the origin of the slogan *rata, jatiya, agama* (country, nation,
religion), which has now become the refuge of scoundrels.

Erasing the difference between monk and layman when it comes to service is the most important clue to the changes in the the monastic order
towards modernity which we are concerned with in this study. Throughout
the entire history of Theravada Buddhism, monks had thought of themselves
as recipients of economic support. Dharmapala's message and project was
to reverse this and make the monks contributors to the economic welfare of
the people as a whole. This is the crucial breakthrough that led to a new
definition of the role of the monk. By taking to "social service," the monk
has defined his role as no different from that of the layman. Although the
aim is ideally altruistic, we shall see how it was taken to its extremes by
young educated monks in directions that would please neither Kalukondayave nor his "teacher" Dharmapala. For what has now happened is that "service" has become an excuse, a justification, for erasing the differences between monk and layman for purposes of personal gain, rendering "erasing"
and not "service" the concern. In articulating the notion that there should
be no distinction between monk and layman when it comes to service, Kalukondayave was not alone. He gave voice to the consensus of the monks who
were becoming urbanized, especially those in the metropolis, Colombo.

Kalukondayave stated that a monk's life involves three kinds of work, relating to *sasana* (religion), *sastra* (knowledge), and *samaja* (society). We are
interested in the third, but insofar as the three are intertwined we shall make
some reference to the other two as appropriate. In 1916, at age 21, Kalukondayave was invited to participate in, and a year later to be deputy patron *(upa
anusasaka)* of, an association called the Saddharmamrtadana Society (Society
for Donating the Ambrosia of the Doctrine). The Patron was Madaduve
Vipula Senasabha, principal of Sri Lanka Vidyalaya, Maradana. In two years
Kalukondayave became the patron. This society started a free, bilingual
night school, a boon to children from poor families. Kalukondayave taught
three nights a week at this school, preached frequently, participated in
the proceedings of the society, did other work for the school, taught elocu-
tion and wrote speeches for students, and still was first in his class at Vidyodaya.

This was the start of Kalukondayave's long, involved association with numerous societies in different parts of the country. He held offices of some
kind in about 275 societies between 1917 and 1970. Of these the Sri Samb-
hasavardhana Bhiksu Samitiya (The Noble Association of Monks for the

Improvement of Language [Skills]) was explicitly organized to encourage
and train young novices to be better orators and moral personalities. Its
unstated function was to increase the relevance of monks in the rapidly
changing society by organizing activities that qualified them better to work
with people and that made them more acceptable as a stratum of useful social
leaders (132). Membership the first year was 30, which increased to 44 the
next. During the first year the Samitiya organized 206 talks, of which 25
were religious lectures *(dharma katha)* and the rest academic, which repeats
the theme of greater attention paid to secular matters (133). About 25 special prizes were awarded to members. In the second year a competition was
held in the two areas, oratory and progress in morality *(pratipattivardhana)*.
In the latter category the competitors were examined on their knowledge
of vinaya (discipline), a recurrent motif in Sri Lankan monastic history that
equates knowledge of the rules with adherence to them and that echoes
the "victory" in the first century B.C.E. of the scholars or village dwellers
(dhammakathika) over the meditators or forest dwellers *(pamsukulika)*.

Kalukondayave's uncompromising addiction to work reminds us of the
"work ethic" that some writers trace to the Protestant, and especially Calvinistic, Reformation. In this too he probably was influenced by Dharmapala's
exhortations to shake off laziness and work with dedication. There is in Kalukondayave an explicit awareness of time that surpasses Dharmapala's, with
all his vigorous condemnations of laziness and idleness. Kalukondayave's own
early education, as noted already, was in a missionary school, a rural Baptist
school at Dekatana near his own native village. His brother, who converted
to Baptism, was a teacher there, earning Rs. 9.00 per month (5–6).

He expressed his addiction in one area of his work as follows: "While my
handwriting was not good, my desire for writing was not the least affected.
Therefore I wrote, wrote, wrote incessantly, wrote useful things, wrote useless things" (34). We have confirmation of this extraordinary productivity in
the arrangements he made for it: he designed furniture for writing when
sitting down, standing, lying down, and traveling. Besides, looking back to
his early career where he thought there were some wasted moments, he had
devised methods to rectify that. For example, when presiding at meetings,
he did his writing while the speakers were holding forth, especially, he said,
because they did not say anything worth listening to anyway. Later, he
learned to do this even at funerals.

The same spirit pervaded all his activity. For example he did not preach
"to fill the time" but prepared for it earnestly. "I learnt from memory the
entire *sutra* that was the subject of the sermon. I memorized the *arthakatha*
(commentary) as well, unless it was very long in which case I learnt the parts

relevant to the sermon" (72–73). With all this exertion his rest was well earned and sleep was not one of his problems, despite his not having the luxury of sleeping in one place for any length of time due to his endless preaching engagements in distant parts of the country. "People might think that my preaching prevented me from getting much sleep. But it is inappropriate to think so. Change of bed or place of sleep was not enough to affect my sleep adversely. I could [no doubt] sleep on a bed. I also could sleep on a chair, a train or a car. I have also gone to sleep while standing, and on two occasions, while preaching," he wrote, adding that on the second of these occasions he slept through the mild tremors of the 1913 earthquake (77–79). This is a record that outperforms Socrates, because although we hear of the Greek philosopher having fallen asleep while standing, there is no evidence that he fell asleep while corrupting the youth.

The following brings out Kalukondayave's methodism and the value he attached to performance. In April 1924 Kalukondayave was elected executive committee member and assistant secretary of his sub-fraternity (which we shall here call "sect"), and he lost no time in putting the house into order:

In the earlier times an executive committee meeting was held only once in a few years, when an ordination had to be held. . . . Since it was a meeting held after three or four years, those who spoke at the previous meeting did not remember whether they did so or not. There were no records. Therefore during the session various opinions came into being. Because of that time was wasted. I had noticed these before I was elected to the committee. After my election I made arrangements to rectify all those.

Now an agenda is drawn prior to the meeting. The proceedings of the previous meetings get recorded. At an appropriate time it gets presented to the assembly and gets adopted after being so proposed and seconded. . . . Gradually the rules were changed so that instead of meeting ad hoc once every few years, regular general meetings of the sect and the committee were scheduled. In this manner I converted our sect into a body that conducted its business methodically and in keeping with parliamentary procedure. (206–207)

Kalukondayave's literary output was prodigious, especially considering his total involvement in social work and dharmadesana. It includes a large number of commentaries on various texts which were later published as a 816–page, one volume work, *Sutrarthasekhara* (1967), and the multi-volume *Puvatpat sangara itihasaya* (History of Newspapers and Journals), which, at over 4,000 pages, is the longest book in the Sinhala language. The

latter is an extremely valuable account of all the newspapers and magazines
ever published in Sinhala that he could find.

KALUKONDAYAVE'S ACHIEVEMENT
The Sober Application of Dharmapala

By the time Kalukondayave became a preacher, the new dharmadesana inno-
vated by the Vajirarama monks under the influence of Dharmapala had been
enthusiastically accepted by urban audiences. It was the achievement of Kalukondayave to accomplish the same task for the countryside. Dharmapala's
influence on Kalukondayave is pervasive. As noted above, he considered
Dharmapala to be his "teacher" in the area of social work. This is the more
remarkable because it was at that time rare for a monk to admit a layman to
be his "teacher," even in the extended sense in which he uses the term. He
recalls with awed respect the occasion when as a young monk he met the
reformer to whom he showed some of his youthful writings. Dharmapala
showed his appreciation of the work but in a characteristic mode told him
not to be overtaken by pride that he had done something big, but to work
hard, "because it looks like the little monk was the kind of person who could
do some useful work." To come from Dharmapala, this was an extraordinary
compliment and encouragement. This incident may have enhanced the relentless impact the writings of Dharmapala had on the young Kalukondayave.
Kalukondayave's writing reflects this. His literary mannerisms—for example, the frequent use of the term *adbhuta* (awesome, mysterious)—is
reminiscent of Dharmapala's own style.[15] Further, Kalukondayave's writings
often mimic, as if in ritual union with his "teacher," the words of some of
Dharmapala's castigations which spared no group. But the rage that often
came through such statements of Dharmapala's is entirely absent. As a po-
lemicist of Sinhala Buddhism, Kalukondayave is unconvincing at best. While
instances of Sinhala Buddhist sentiment are present in Kalukondayave's writing, it is completely absent from his social program, and as we shall see
below, he worked with people of all communities. This freedom from ideology that Kalukondayave's perspectives represent also agrees with the generally conservative outlook he adopted in politics and other areas. This contrasts him with the anti-imperialism and nationalist activism of Dharmapala,

---

15. Martin Wikramasinghe, the greatest Sinhala writer of modern times, also used the term frequently, bringing out the pervasive nature of Dharmapala's influence among the major national and
cultural figures.

which made him a suspect in the eyes of the colonial authorities and which led to his arrest and imprisonment in India. What we have in Kalukondayave is a loyal and determined attempt to put into practice the plan for regeneration outlined in the Dharmapalite project. In him we have a conscious selection of the economic and the pragmatic part of Dharmapala's project to the exclusion of its political and the ideological part. Thus Kalukondayave, though highly influenced by Dharmapala, represents a remarkable reformation of the latter into the sober and civilized dialectic of Buddhist texts and thought.

Kalukondayave, in keeping with the exhortation of Dharmapala to the monks, the soldiers of his army of liberation, undertook the task of helping the people regain their lost greatness by doing three things: rural development, crime eradication, and temperance. Actually these were one, united under the rubric of gramasamvardhana, rural development. For purposes of organization, rural development primarily meant the economic uplift of the people. But it was a total concept that included motivation, ethical conduct, cleanliness, activeness, punctuality, conflict resolution, and of course everything to do with economic activity. Its goal was a harmonious and prosperous village community. In short it was no less than an attempt to recreate the idyllic rural community that Dharmapala alleged was the foundation of ancient Sinhala social life.

Kalukondayave's interest in social amelioration received a boost from the anti-crime *(aparadha mardana)* movement that came into prominence in about 1931–32 (236). Throughout the island anti-crime societies had been founded in the hundreds. The movement was led by M. T. Akbar, a Muslim judge of the supreme court. In 1933 Kalukondayave was asked to speak at a meeting held at Ananda College. This was the premier Buddhist school founded by the theosophist Henry Olcott in Colombo, which had become the venue for numerous such meetings. By then Kalukondayave had "understood that a lot of work can be done in the villages to very easily raise the standard of living of the people, to make them more fortunate and to quell the restlessness that is brought about in the villages due to minor disputes." Accordingly he thought he would in his speech "briefly mention a few facts on that subject" (242). He made a long speech. Judge Akbar thanked him, saying that the speech was the best support he ever got for his anti-crime movement, and asked Kalukondayave whether he would agree to publishing the talk in the form of a booklet. Kalukondayave gave him a revised version, which was serialized in the major Sunday Sinhala newspaper, the *Silumina,* starting the very next week, under the title *Gramapratisamskaranaya ha Aparadhamardanaya,* (Rural Development and Crime Prevention). One thousand copies of the booklet were printed and soon after, due to great demand, another five thousand and then another one thousand. Later under the patronage of the Inspector General of the Police S. W. Osmund de Silva, a further ten thousand copies were printed (243–44). The thirty-five-page document is now available in his autobiography.

Gramapratisamskaranaya ha Aparadhamardanaya is a critique of society, a guide to action, and the portrait of an ideal society. It seeks change but not revolution. We could call it a "Manifesto of Rural Development." It defines a new pastoralism for the monk. The work consists of ninety-nine points, though he refers to it as consisting of one-hundred points (282), perhaps taking into account the introduction. First, he defines the problem: "To reflect soberly on the state of our country today is to break one's heart, is to fall unconscious. Morality declines daily. Crime prospers daily. There is none to save the villages. There are thousands to kill the villages. This fall is frightening. It is appropriate at this stage to meditate with sadness that our villagers are on the lowest step of the ladder of decline. A disaster will happen if a powerful movement is not organized to help men to the step above or at least to keep them where they are. Because to fall further is to fall into a fearful bottomless abyss. Therefore, it is well to contemplate making use of our human status. It is well to contemplate that it is not human nature, but beastly nature to think only of oneself. It is good to open one's eyes and look at the calamity that is gradually enveloping one's flock. It is well to tarry not even a bit" (245).

The intention here is to draw attention to the urgency of the problem. Thus the appeal is emotional. But this is only the first paragraph. As he gets down to the ninety-nine points, he is practical and specific. Two facts stand out. First, he evokes "our human status" as the reason why we should not be selfish, only beasts being selfish. The underlying Buddhist meaning is that human life is one of the four most rare things in the world, which is a metaphor for the urgency with which we must accomplish what only humans can. Traditionally this refers to disciplining the mind and setting oneself firmly on the path to liberation, because no birth other than human, be it divine or superdivine (brahmic), will provide that opportunity. Here Kalukondayave is transferring this otherworldly urgency to matters of immediate interest here and now. This theme recurs in Kalukondayave, namely, the equation of this-worldly amelioration with other-worldly amelioration: it is not possible to help a person progress towards the ultimate goal (of Nirvana) unless that person is first helped with his mundane needs. Plainly put, without food, clothing, shelter, medication, i.e., a generally acceptable standard of living, there is no sense in preaching to the people the path to salvation. The second fact that stands out is the specific audience Kalukondayave is addressing, namely the monks. He is of course addressing all. But he is specially appealing to the monks to "open their eyes" and look at the problem. While it is an appeal to monks for help, it will also help monks, because gramasamvardhana is social work which is practically meaningful, which will bring them in touch with people who matter, and which will thereby bring them back to significant social status. To do work in the area of ameliorating the living standards of the people is to relegate to the background the ritual services of *dana* (accepting alms), *bana* (delivering sermons), and *pirit* (chanting texts for magical purposes) which have not done much to give them status in a changing society. As we shall see later, the noble ideal of helping others that Kalukondayave expresses here was soon made subservient to seeking status and personal benefit.

The ninety-nine points constitute a critique of society that is in fact an elaboration of the Dharmapalite critique. It is specifically addressed to the monks, who Dharmapala wanted to be the soldiers of his army of regeneration and who earned his ire for their sloppy response. After devoting the first eight points to expose an entrenched fabric of false values, a breakdown of responsibility between parents and children, teacher and pupil, and monk and layman, and the breakdown in the system of education, the document goes on to make suggestions as to how to get about the task of rural development. The very first of these is about the instrument of development, the dharmadesana. He says that in every village, once every week, there should be a dharmadesana, one of the tasks laid down by Dharmapala in his instructions for the *Gramaraksaka Samagama* (Village Protection Society), the prototype of the Rural Development Society.

Other points include suggestions to establish parent-teacher associations; reading rooms; sports facilities; volunteer groups; homes for beggars; free pharmacies; cooperative stores and societies; small industries; instructions as to how to establish and conduct meetings; to observe health habits; and condemnations of drinking, smoking, ostentatious ceremonies, and public meetings where the virtueless rich and corrupt politicians are welcomed as heroes and leaders of men; superstitious activities, which include consulting astrologers, enacting exorcisms, and other folk rituals; staging plays, auctioning flowers, and having firework competitions on religious occasions; seeing films and plays; employing children and women in domestic slavery; bribery; and non-punctuality.

The document urges the use of local foods, drinks, crafts, and manufactured items in preference to their imported counterparts. Foods that are "packaged" in the broad sense of being transformed in order to extend their shelf life and which thus represent the tentacles of the market are discouraged, and terms that evoke disgust are used to describe them; for example, bottled drinks are referred to as "stagnant water" *(pal vatura)*, tinned biscuits as "stale" *(parani vu,* lit. "ancient"), and dried or salted fish and Maldive fish as "rotting and stinking dirt" *(kumbala rodu, kunu jadi)*. Traditional yams and roots are encouraged as rice substitutes, reflecting on the one hand Kalukondayave's sensitivity to shortages of rice, the staple, and on the other his loyal citizenship under the colonial regime that officially encouraged the habit of rice substitution. Local decorations derived from plants, such as coconut fronds and moss, are advocated for ceremonial occasions in preference to imported, manufactured material like colored paper. All of the above are based on Dharmapalite ideas, sometimes in their pristine form, sometimes slightly amended or elaborated. While the material advocated here—foods, craft items, decorations, and so forth—are local, the organization and driving ideas, as we know, are derived from the culture of the Protestant churches, which by the turn of the century had trickled down to sections of the urban middle classes.

The society envisaged here is the perfectly harmonious recreation of the idyllic rural community of the past glorious civilization. But since, in the idyllic community, parents and grand parents are venerated and the aged and the destitute cared for by their families, the homes for the aged and beggar shelters recommended here stand out as rather superfluous and give away the imagined nature of that idyllic community. It is also striking that, despite the sincerest adherence to Dharmapalite ideas, Kalukondayave as well as the other monks whose work we discuss below are simplistic in their understanding of Dharmapala. They are oblivious to the economic cosmopolitanism of the Dharmapalite utopia, in which business and industry play a dominant role. This dimension is completely absent in the work of these monks whose experience, with all their good intentions, remains strictly bound within the confines of idyllic pastoralism, which, originating in their reading of Dharmapala, blended resonantly with their own now-idealized experience of growing up in rural surroundings.

PURSUING A DREAM
Rural Development

As we noted above, there are conflicting claims as to who founded the Rural Development Movement. Kalukondayave's answer to this question is unambiguous: he claims that he is the founder *(adi kartr)* of the movement (238–

39). There is an explanation of this uncharacteristic self-assessment, namely that here Kalukondayave is really expressing his disillusionment with the party system which he thinks has ravaged the social order. He hints at some personal attacks on him and attributes them to the system of party politics. The opposition to the party system, held by many monks, is derived from two sources: first, the traditional conception of a society centering on kingship in which opposition would be equal to treason; and second, the culturally derived divisiveness in the working of the party system which does not allow compromise and the rational accommodation of dissent, which is the essence of the system.

The favorable public reception the booklet *Gramasamvardhanaya ha Aparadhamardanaya* received led Kalukondayave to ponder the idea that "if rural development and crime eradication were to take place simultaneously, all or most of the hundred points mentioned in my booklet should be put into practice." And hence he suggested that "it is good if, for experimentation purposes, such a movement is launched in a limited area" (289). Thus Kalukondayave, not content with writing and preaching alone, resolved to put into practice the 99-point program. He selected a place convenient for travel, an area not too far from Colombo where he worked, and the place where his own native monastery was located, namely Hevagam Korale (the Division of Hevagam, of the Colombo District). He solicited the support of R. P. Ruberu, the Mudaliyar (chief) of the Korale, "a religious man who sat respectfully on the floor even when he heard *bana* on the radio" but who was nonetheless "not entirely free of the habits and weaknesses of Mudaliyars of the time" (282), a choice that reflects the ideological neutrality and pragmatism that Kalukondayave brought to his work. The Mudaliyar's first request was "to give primary place to dharmadesana." This was easy because Kalukondayave's own belief was that "a dharmadesana not confined to otherworldly matters was essential to the country" (283). He then gave all his time, except for teaching duties, to rural work, visiting every village and soliciting the support of key rural figures like the headmen, physicians, and teachers.

Kalukondayave then pursued the matter with two higher authorities, Judge M. T. Akbar, already mentioned, and the member of the State Council for the area, F. A. Obeyesekere. The movement was launched on April 30, 1933 at his monastery, the Sugatabimbaramaya at Navagamuva. The meeting was presided over by M. Chinniah, District Judge, Avissavella. Kalukondayave's aim of establishing branch associations in every village did not succeed largely due to an emergency that arose, the spread of the malaria epidemic in the area. Although this broader program met with only limited success,

Kalukondayave stated that the large number of congratulatory messages and invitations he received asking him to help in rural development activity made him redefine his task: instead of focusing and working intensively in one region, he would travel to areas far and wide in the island wherever there was interest, explain his ideas about the movement through dharmadesana, and help the local communities to establish societies to deal with rural development and crime eradication (284). Thus, despite his travels, he became more of a theorist and an inspiration, much like his "teacher" Dharmapala (that is, Dharmapala in his capacity as rural revivalist, propagator of Buddhism and claimant of the Buddhist sites in India for the Buddhists). But he never ceased to be an activist. Dharmadesana became his sole task, which undoubtedly tipped the balance of its contents even more than before towards concerns in this world, and he became even more of a "hero-giant" in the Dharmapalite sense than he already was.

These facts illustrate the details of the launching of Kalukondayave's movement and support the observation made before that, although we certainly find in Kalukondayave's writings some specimens of the harsh language characteristic of the Dharmapalite critique of borrowed foreign customs, foods, and so forth, and although there is reference to the Sinhala culture and language, such comments sound more like obligatory and ritual acknowledgements of the general Dharmapalite ideology than like expressions of rigidly held ethnic or other sectional prejudices. In practice, Kalukondayave's work reflects pragmatism and a freedom from the kind of imprisonment in ideology that beset the monks at Vidyalankara. In founding the association at Hevagam Korale, for example, Kalukondayave worked cordially with judges Akbar and Chinniah, a Muslim and a Tamil respectively, which shows an ability to gloss over parochial divisions for the attainment of goals with national significance and common benefit. This ethnic blindness resonates with the general attitude of his sedate college, whose ceremonies were attended by the colonial Governor and by the Tamil-elite politicians Ponnambalam Ramanathan and Ponnambalam Arunachalam.[16]

16. In the same vein, three eminent Tamil members of the State Council, Periannan Sundaram, S. Natesan, and A. Mahadeva, spoke in support of a bill introduced in the State Council to regain the control of Buddha Gaya by the Buddhists, a favorite Dharmapalite project. See Hansard, State Council of Ceylon, 28 March 1935, cols. 1124–26. Mahadeva hoped that when Hindus supported the Buddhists "in their predicament," the Buddhists would "likewise use every ounce of their influence" to see similar treatment afforded to the Hindus and to see that [the Kataragama] shrine is brought as speedily as possible under control acceptable to the Hindus. The Buddhists however failed to respond in kind. Instead, Kataragama was increasingly Sinhalized. See Richard Gombrich and Gananath Obeyesekere, *Buddhism Transformed*, 411–44.

V. Nalliah, a Tamil member of the State Council, in his speech in the Council supporting the Free Education Bill, credited the success of the bill to the work done by "the politically conscious section of

The monks at Vidyalankara represent a contrast: they took over Dharma-pala's ideologically charged and exclusivist dark side, ignoring his eco-nomic message.

While there was some interest on the part of the government to help the people suffering under the malaria epidemic of 1934, Kalukondayave real-ized that the government was not capable of providing the necessary relief, nor was it just to expect the government to do so, which again reflects an unusual sense of civic responsibility and initiative. He therefore resolved to solicit support from individuals. As before, he first met the member of the State Council for the area, F. A. Obeyesekere, and walked the villages in the Hevagam Korale on a fact-finding mission. The facts he found were deeply disturbing. He met Muhandiram D. H. T. D. Gunawardene and solicited his support to send the needed supplies and medication to the villages.

Kalukondayave describes movingly the efforts made to deal with the ma-laria epidemic. He had successfully collected enough material and medica-tions to deal with the problem in his own area, Hevagam Korale. But the news from Kegalla was bad. He then joined the All Ceylon Buddhist Con-gress in an effort to collect and transport the needed supplies. He preached in the night to solicit help for the sick and used his radio sermons for the same purpose. "Before these sermons there was no adequate knowledge in the country about this tragedy. . . . [Afterwards] some wrote to me to say that the sermons brought tears to the country's eyes. Since then help poured in. Many carried the needed supplies to the villages themselves. It is as if Bodhisattvas had appeared all over the land" (304–307).

Kalukondayave was interested in temperance from the inception of the movement in 1912. Demonstrating his tolerant and pragmatic attitude, he defined the aim of the Temperance Movement not as the prohibition of li-quor so that no one ever can get a drop of alcoholic drink, which he says would not be practicable, but rather as an attempt to discourage drinking with a view to eventually achieving successful temperance by introducing a system of permits to those who are addicted to it, and thereby protecting the younger generation. He cites the system of regulating opium by this means about half a century earlier, which led to a successful eradication of the drug.

Kalukondayave's specific active participation in temperance, apart from

---

the Buddhist clergy" and remarked that the bill "marks the first great indication of political awareness, of an awakening, among the masses of this country." Nalliah was thinking of the "masses" as one un-differentiated category of Sinhala Buddhists and Tamil Hindus. He referred to the "Buddhists and Hin-dus who have a record of wide tolerance towards other faiths." He censored Christian missionaries for demanding the right to educate "our children—to educate Buddhist children and Hindu children—in a Christian atmosphere." Hansard, State Council of Ceylon, 15 May 1947, cols. 1664–70.

his sermons, was in 1933 when he was involved with his Rural Development movement in the Hevagam Korale. A fellow monk, Dehipe Dhammaratana, asked his help to stop the opening of a tavern in a neighboring village, Valivita. The opening of the tavern had to be ratified by a vote of the people of the affected area, and Kalukondayave started a campaign to stop it (287). He canvassed personally, held public dharmadesanas, and, on the day of the vote, organized a sit-in of monks at the entrance to the polling booth, which discouraged voters and prevented the proponents of the tavern from getting the required votes.

With that success Kalukondayave realized the value of inaugurating a movement to close down existing taverns and prevent the reopening of closed ones, by persuading voters (288). He resolved to work closely with the Temperance Association *(Amadyapa Sabhava)* and attended its meetings at Ananda College. Often the five members needed for the quorum were not present, but undaunted, Kalukondayave campaigned nationally through his travels and dharmadesana, sometimes accompanied by the nationalist novelist Piyadasa Sirisena (289). Kalukondayave recalls proudly how the British rulers underestimated the Sinhalas when they laid down the rule requiring 75 percent of the registered vote to close down a tavern because he succeeded in getting 98. He mentions that in the beginning many Buddhists accumulated fortunes from arrack renting but later gave it up as a business contrary to Buddhist business ethics. These Buddhists concentrated on other businesses such as plantation agriculture and prospered. This led non-Sinhala and non-Buddhist business interests to step into the alcohol business and to campaign to reopen taverns. As Patron and later President of the Temperance Association, Kalukondayave traveled to every locality that was holding a vote to reopen taverns. His tactic was to first talk to the voters and on polling day to stage a sit-in near the entrance to the booth. Kalukondayave outwitted opponents who had planned to bring voters to the booth during lunch, which monks are required to take before noon. He broke up the vigilants into two groups so that they could take lunch by turn and continue the vigil uninterrupted (291).

We may note, in conclusion, the following: First, the strong motivation Kalukondayave's writings and activities express regarding temperance. While the Buddhist five precepts include abstention from alcohol, that never gave rise to any organized temperance activity. The strength of drive and the evangelism with which Kalukondayave invested temperance work had to come from somewhere. That source is Dharmapala, for whom alcohol was one of the greatest of all evils. Second, in Kalukondayave's adaptation of the dharmadesana to rural conditions, we have a further stage of evolution in the dharmadesana, which the Colombo monks transformed from a traditional all-night performance to an exposition suited to urban, middle-class audiences. Third, in the process of ruralization, the Colombo dharmadesana carried into the village, as part of its cultural baggage, the values and instructions for behavior of the urban middle classes, such as the conceptions of how females should dress,[17] which were ultimately derived from Dharmapala, who in turn actually derived them from the culture of Protestant Christianity, while believing and insisting that they were Aryan and immemorial.

CRIME ERADICATION

This program is actually inseparable from the broader project of rural development. Yet the rubric was used particularly in those instances when Kalukondayave worked in the villages with the cooperation of the Police Department. The most successful of these efforts was the meeting in 1940 of Kalukondayave and a young police officer, Osmund de Silva, who was Assistant Superintendent of Police for the Kegalla District.

Kalukondayave was delighted at the deep interest de Silva had in village reconstruction. What de Silva expected of Kalukondayave is something he had tried hard to achieve and failed, namely to establish trust between the people and the police.[18] For this purpose Kalukondayave started a series of "sermon classes," a term that tells us again of an idea basic to Kalukondayave, that of yoking together the religious and the mundane.

The sermons consisted of advice relating to economics, health, and civic conduct. To put this into practice, Village Protection Societies were organized in every village of the police district. In many villages rural development centers were built. Kalukondayave talks with delight about the success of this, citing the village of Pallepamunuva as an example. He reports that there was not even a square yard of unutilized land and the whole village turned into a garden full of fruit trees, vegetables, and yams.

17. See note 50 below.

18. President Premadasa's (1988–93) activities show Dharmapalite influence either directly or mediated through a soldier like Kalukondayave. Premadasa considered the police to be an important agent of social service, hence his elevation of the police as one of the trinity of institutions, along with the school and the monastery, to a place of eminence in the village. See Josine van der Horst, *Who is He, What is He Doing?* (Amsterdam: VU University Press, 1995). It is also no coincidence that Premadasa appropriated the term *sucarita* (good character, morality), a favorite term of Dharmapala's (and Kalukondayave's), but for purposes, it is believed, far from moral.

In peasant Buddhism, the source of a better next world and ultimately Nirvana is not morality but ritualism and ritualized good works. In Dharmapala's theory, unlike in peasant Buddhism, the promise of a good next birth was causally connected to worldly moral action. Further, whereas in peasant Buddhism moral action was understood in ritualized terms, in Dharmapala it was based on ethical conduct as prescribed in Buddhism, namely living according to the five precepts, avoiding the tenfold impure or "sinful" activities *(dasa akusal)*, following the tenfold pure activities *(dasa kusal)*, all of which added up to the conception of Right Livelihood of the Noble Eightfold Path. Thus the task of the monk is not to preach high doctrinal matters but to teach people to work for an acceptable standard of living within the bounds of the moral framework of Buddhism. Dharmapala repeatedly talked about the Buddha's "order" to the monks, to wander the countryside for the happiness and comfort of the many. It is with this exhortation of Dharmapala in mind that a new dharmadesana providing Buddhist answers to day-to-day problems was invented in Colombo.

It was the achievement of Kalukondayave to tirelessly traverse the land with a rural version of that new sermon, as if embodying in his person the Buddha's exhortation, made into an "order" and reinterpreted by Dharmapala. The amelioration of the poor according to Buddhist principles was undoubtedly supreme in the project of Dharmapala, but we must not forget that it consisted of precisely a confrontation of the Christian missionary critique of Buddhism as selfish and superstitious. Thus the Dharmapalite project, while ameliorating the peasantry's condition, was also a rebuttal of the Christian critique of Buddhism. It was at the same time an assertion of not only Buddhism's adequacy but superiority in dealing with the human condition, as Dharmapala's many descriptions of Buddhism illustrate.

Following this Dharmapalite formulation, Kalukondayave's emphasis was on *ubhayalokarthsadhanaya*, "ensuring the success of both worlds." People try to achieve a heavenly existence, says Kalukondayave, which is not a difficult thing for a Buddhist. But the proper way to do this—this is what *ubhayalokartha* means—is by perfecting oneself in this world through moral living, and achieving *dhana* (wealth), *guna* (virtue), *gnana* (wisdom), and *bala* (power). It is of no use to be born like a man and to die like a beast (i.e., without having achieved anything) while hoping to reach heaven in the next birth (332). To expect no happiness and comfort in this world in the expectation of a comfortable existence in the next is madness: "There are fools who say that every act of merit is done for comfort in the next world. Such people are sure not to get a next world in which this could happen. Because they did the same in the previous world" (333).

In driving home this point, Kalukondayave comes up with a satirical list of the contents of the traditional dharmadesana in which preachers portrayed fanciful pictures of the divine worlds and fearsome pictures of hell (229–30). What he, Kalukondayave, would include were "not the length of divine abodes, the number of divine beings in it, the extent of gold, silver, pearls, gems found there, the length of the thorns of the thorny *imbul* tree of hell [that adulterers have to climb], the size of its molten iron pot, or how people lived in the Benares of king Brahmadatta once upon a time." It is not that Kalukondayave is denying these worlds. "But we must preach sermons in such a way as to help people design their lives so that they will avoid hell and go to heaven. It is true that we must learn about how people lived in Benares once upon a time, but that is not how our village people live today. The first function of listening to the dharma is to purify character. To have pure character, people must earn a livelihood. In sum, the function of a religion is moulding people's lives. To do that we must find out the reasons why people do wrong, and try to eliminate those." These reasons are primarily economic, as he illustrates with the following story (230).

A good, honest, hardworking villager falls ill with a fever. For some time he manages to get medication and to feed his wife and children through his meager savings, but these were soon gone. There is a prospering Rural Development society in the village. The crops are abundant, and the convalescing good man sends his child to get some cassava from the forty–acre cassava garden of the headman. The child is refused, and the desperate father steals some. "Can a father resist when his two little children are withering of starvation while there is food within sight, even if stealing would send him to hell straight away?" asks Kalukondayave. The Rural Development society learns of the theft, accuses the man and finds him guilty. Kalukondayave adds: "It is true that stealing is a sin. It is true that monks should explain to their flocks the consequences of stealing. But this helpless fellow is not a thief. He is the most virtuous man in the village. He was tempted to steal because of the love of his children. For satisfactory results what should be treated is not the act of doing wrong, which is only the symptom, but its cause" (233). What the Rural Development society should do in an instance like this is to give the man a modest loan at a just rate of interest. He should be found a job and asked to pay the loan back in fair installments. "When that is done, the man could care for his family in peace, refrain from theft, and be grateful to the [Rural Development] society for life." Kalukondayave comments on the story further:

What I intended in this little story is to show that treatment without first locating the cause does not produce a proper result. In particular, the monks who preach to the rural people must understand this. In my series of dhar-

madesana I was not trying to drive these people up to heaven instantly, but
to teach them how to earn qualifications for that in this world, i.e., how to
lead a happy and healthy life in this world. (234)

Kalukondayave's story is a perfect blending of the economic and the religious, following the Dharmapalite formulation but giving the economic
sphere an autonomy that would make it the foundation for the building of
morality. His emphasis is that it is no use treating the symptoms of immorality. What needs treatment is its cause, in the present case, for example, the
cause of the theft, which is poverty. In other words, morality is not made an
abstraction but a possibility and an eminently rational one in day-to-day life.
Morality need not be a bitter medicine people are compelled to take but a
matter of self-interest, especially interest in a happy and prosperous this
world and a blissful next world, realizable through hard work. A further
implication of this is that there is no sense in preaching morality abstractly
to the people: instead, people should be given the wherewithal to practice
and sustain that morality, namely motivation and opportunities for productive work. That is, they should be told that morality is the same as earning
an honest livelihood. The principles of an honest livelihood are elaborated
over and over again in Dharmapala's writings and are repeated by Kalukondayave and his other disciples. These reformers are convinced that the path
of progress for the now-impoverished rural population is a Buddhist one,
the "Protestant" basis of which they either do not realize or do not admit.

Kalukondayave's formulation in this story, as elsewhere, is anti-ritualist.
Heaven is ensured not by ritual activity by a good life here and now, which
can be done with honest and hard work. This goes against much of traditional rural Buddhism, in which heaven is the reward for ritualized good
works. Since prosperity in this life is the basis for heaven in the hereafter,
there is in this theory an encouragement of rational economic behavior, such
as hard work, saving, and reinvestment. But the rural masses have by and
large been unable to respond to this liberating doctrine.

Finally in Kalukondayave's story there is a critique of the Rural Development project itself of which he was such an indomitable champion, which
hints at his own premonition of its non-durability. The rural development
activity in the village of the above story is clearly successful in terms of its
productivity. Forty acres of cassava are waiting to be harvested. But there is
a suggestion of corruption and inequality. The crop belongs to just one person, the headman. In keeping with the Dharmapalite strictures, the monk is
the patron of the society and is the judge in the case against the good man
whom poverty turns into a thief. It is the monk who returns the cold verdict

on the good man. The insinuation is that the monk who is the patron and the headman who is the chairman of the society have evolved into a corrupt village-level oligarchy devoid of compassion. Together, they represent the destruction of the spirit of the Rural Development project. This may not be entirely imaginary. Kalukondayave, with as wide an experience in rural development as anybody, must have known well the gap between the theory of rural development and how, after festive inauguration and a period of pristine glory, society after society, village after village succumbed, one by one, to the very sloth, laziness, and lack of alertness and commitment that the project was to combat in the first place, rendering the entire island-wide project, after barely more than a decade, into a mere memory. The processes that underlie such robust propensity to enthusiasm and abandonment, to ignition and extinguishment, are part of the cultural genetics of the Sinhalas. This trait is immortalized in the culture's own persistent self-critique, which nevertheless fails to vanquish that same process of self-annulment, rendering that critique itself a fetish or dinner-party talk rather than a source of inner questioning and reform. It is this mysterious illness that explains much of the failure of the culture, a failure that has led to all the easily avoidable errors and left the dream villages of the reformers, not dotted with flour-ishing gardens, but littered with gunfire.

Having infinite trust in the Dharmapalite theory of the idyllic village community and of a nation consisting of such communities, Kalukondayave shared a view that is commonly expressed among traditionalists, the need for consensus and unity rather than for differences of opinion that can coex-ist with orderly conduct. Hence his distrust of the party system (239). He even opposed universal suffrage or at least considered it premature to have been introduced in 1931, little realizing that most of the political support he got for his Rural Development project was the result of it. He also rejected Marxism. Kalukondayave considered monkhood to be national and above parties and that monks should not have any political affiliations. These views are derived from his own traditionalism and that of the political leadership with whom he was mostly associated. It was the view of that leadership that monks should stay away from politics, a question to which we shall return in the next chapter. He also firmly believed that the advent of party politics was behind the breakdown of the rural authority structure. Thus in Dhar-mapalite terms "politics" is one more "foreign" item (though not officially listed as one) that had entered the indigenous culture much to its detriment.

Kalukondayave took the view that Marxism destroyed the traditional or-der and the mosaic of deference that in his view sustained the idyllic harmony of the village community. This view is, on the one hand, one more instance of the many visions of the unspoiled village that have come up again and again in Sri Lanka in the nineteenth and twentieth centuries. On the other, it is a remarkably restrained view of colonialism and western impact especially when compared to the rhetoric that led to the "revolution" of 1956 and the events thereafter. The blame is placed not on imperialist exploitation or decadence brought about by western culture. It is placed rather on the introduction of party politics, and even universal franchise, into a semi-literate society ill-equipped to exercise that responsibility. It is clear, however, that the underlying gloss for what he calls the party system or politics is Marxism. For the Marxist parties are the first viable political parties to come into being in the island (in 1935), and the rightist United National Party (UNP) was a reactive formation that came into being in opposition to the Marxist parties. Kalukondayave was right about the breakdown of the rural authority structure but not about its cause, which was not Marxism but the new social changes.

The conception of indigenous society that underlies Kalukondayave's thought here is actually not very different from that of certain nationalists and more recently of Jatika Cintanaya.[19] This is the conception of a highly unified, integrated, and harmonious social order the main enemy of which is the outside world. Yet Kalukondayave's view must be distinguished from that of the nationalists and xenophobes to the extent that in his system of ideas the imaginarily self-sufficient and organic isolationism of xenophobia remains a passing thought that forms no part of his program of action. His efforts to bring about village harmony, which were remarkable, did not conflict with the status quo: he accepted the framework of colonial authority as a part of the landscape, and he also accepted the conservative indigenous political leadership of the day that ruled the country in collaboration with the colonialist power as the legitimate authority which could restore to the village its unity and prosperity. He considered the damage that had been done to the village, the objective referents of which are crime, alcoholism, disharmony and poverty, as eminently rectifiable through Rural Development. It is this belief which can explain the astonishing energy he put into traversing the length and breadth of the land, and using to the maximum of his capability the eloquence of the spoken and written word he was gifted

19. Jatika Cintanaya, or National Way of Thought movement, came into being in the mid-1970s. It is broadly an anti-foreign, specifically anti-western, inward looking movement which posits and advocates a uniquely nationalistic way of thinking, planning, and carrying out policy. Its leaders are Gunadasa Amarasekera and Nalin de Silva, a dentist-novelist and a professor of mathematics respectively. The theory is still vague and general and yet to formulate any concrete measures that would bring it within the realm of practice.

with. It is to this end that he utilized the sermon, carrying further its changes for rapt audiences oblivious to the innovative nature of this homiletic technique. Writing in his autobiography about his experience of growing up in a sedate village about seventy years before, he could gloss over the imperfections and imagine an idyllic society, relatively speaking, and be convinced that a revival of that is possible through rural development.

Given Dharmapala's emphasis on a good life to be built in this world on the basis of Buddhist morality, and his repeated references to Buddhist texts that contain exhortations towards a healthy and successful organization of lay life, it is not surprising that the young and educated monks who were inspired by him would seek out particular canonical texts that are relevant for this purpose. It is in this context that we can explain the scholarly and homiletic interest taken, for example, in the *Mangala,* the *Sigalovada,* and the *Vyaghrapadya sutras* by these new preacher-monks.[20] Indeed it is possible to explain the popularity these particular sutras enjoyed in these terms: they were popular for the same reason as the new dharmadesanas were popular, namely providing Buddhist guidance for the conduct of a successful and ethical life.

DHARMAPALITE MISSIONARIES (2)
Hinatiyana Dhammaloka

Hinatiyana Dhammaloka (1900–81), the Mahanayaka (head, lit., Great Chief) of the Amarapura Nikaya,[21] was involved for fifty years in activities related to rural development: health, especially dealing with the thirties epidemic of malaria, crime prevention, self-help, and teaching. He was also in a significant way involved with missionary work known as Dharmaduta, messengers of the dharma.

Born on 23 September 1900, Hinatiyana was the second son of Kalinga

20. See, for example, on the *Vyaggapajja Sutta (Vyaghrapadya Sutra),* Palane Vajragnana, *Vajragnana Sahityaya,* ed. Madihe Pannasiha (Kottava: Moravaka Press), 2:20–26; and Kalukondayave, ed., *Vyaghrapadya Sutraya* (Maharagama: High Level Press, 1970). This and other laity-oriented sutras have continued to be published; see, for example, Valigepola Ratanasara, *Bauddha Samajaya* (Colombo: Gunasara, 1967); Bambarande Sivali, *Mangala-Parabhava dharma* (Kalaniya: Vidyalankara, 1966); Maho Sumedha, *Sigalakovada dharmaya hevat gihi sirit virit* (Kandy: Bauddha Grantha Prakasana Samitiya, 1964).

21. Sources for information on Hinatiyana are: (a) oral information provided by his pupil Hinatiyana Nanda and other informants; (b) Vijayapala Mendis, *Atipujya Hinatiyana Sri Dhammaloka Mahanayaka Svamindra Caritapadanaya* (Colombo: Government Printing Department, 1981); (c) Hinatiyana Nanda, ed., *Minis lovata seta salasamu* (Colombo: Samayavardhana, 1982); and (d) the newspaper *Sinhala Bauddhaya.*

Karolis de Silva and Manikkuge Maria Nona de Silva of Unnoruva, Pillavatta, of the Katana electorate. His lay name was Kalinga Piyasena de Silva. He was first educated at Pillavatta Girls School and later at the Andiambalama School. Later he was enrolled at the Roman Catholic School at Yatiyana. He studied English and went to Sunday school held at the Surammaramaya, Pillavatta, to learn Buddhism.

Hinatiyana was ordained in 1911, at age 11, by Hinatiyana Dhammak-khanda, at the Hinatiyana Potgul Vihara monastery and was given the monastic name Unnoruve Pannaloka. He returned to lay life three times before making a firm decision to stay in the monkhood. After the third derobement (at age 15), he went to the Methodist Church school of the Kurana-Katunayaka Methodist Diocese, to study English. He studied three years there, winning the best orator prize and the best biblical student prize twice. He was skilled in cricket, football, and boy scouting. Clearly he was excelling not in the spiritual but in the corporeal realm, and he is said to have lost interest in the monastic order, a speculation to which his multiple derobements bear some testimony. But his preceptor Hinatiyana Dhammakkhanda persuaded his mother to have a little talk with him, and it appears that under maternal pressure Hinatiyana was persuaded to return to the spiritual life. At 18 he was ordained once more, this time permanently, and given the monastic name Hinatiyana Dhammaloka. Hardly a decade after Hinatiyana's death there are conflicting hagiographic accounts of the basis of his attraction to the monastery. One recurring theme is his interest in preaching. As a fifth grade student, he was apparently greatly attracted to preaching, having heard a speech by Valisingha Harishchandra, a well-known disciple of Dharmapala. According to another story, the inspiring experience was a public speech by the monk Kotahene Jinananda of the Dipaduttarama monastery, Kotahena, at Price Park. Both these stories may well be fictional, but they are meaningful for their symbolic association with oratory. Both signify the use of oratory for social amelioration, and thus, as is the case with other hero-giants, yoke together the sermon and socio-economic activism.

At the monastery, Hinatiyana received primary monastic training from Pillevatte Ariyavamsa and Hinatiyana Dhammakkhanda, and his primary academic training from Kirimatiyane Sudharmalankara of the Vidyabandhu Pirvena, Kirimatiyana. He studied Pali, Sinhala, Sanskrit, Prakrit, grammar, poetics, logic, history, and Buddhism. For his secondary academic studies he was admitted to Vidyodaya in 1919, under Mahagoda Gnanesvara, principal. He was actively involved in social work, which sometimes interfered with his studies.

While there are anecdotes that confirm his proclivity for preaching, it was not until 1923 that he became a proper preacher, a *dharmakathika,* an orator of the dhamma. He became a regular preacher every Sunday at the newly founded Young Men's Buddhist Association (YMBA), then located at the Pavilion Hotel, Maradana. As a part of the service of religious propagation, 23,000 copies of Hinatiyana's sermon were published by the YMBA and distributed free in Colombo and its hinterland (up to Gampaha in the North and Kalutara in the South). Funds were provided by Mrs. Jeremias Dias (mother of the philanthropist Arthur V. Dias, mother-in-law of Wilmot A. Perera) of Panadura. The printed version of the sermon, the same as the one preached, was known as a *dharma patrika,* "dharma leaflet." Printing a sermon, which became quite common during this time among the major preachers, is one more example of Buddhist modernism. There is however another side to the story, as in so many other examples of "Protestant Buddhism." Printing the sermon evokes the medieval practice of writing books which were essentially sermons. Such books were read before illiterate peasant audiences by monks or lay literati.

It is significant that the printed versions were distributed in Colombo and its hinterland because these were also the target areas of the Christian missionaries. Thus the subtext of the dharma patrika was different from its overt meaning. It was the broader one of meeting the challenge of the Christian missionaries using their own weapons, the pulpit and the press. The dharma patrika had another underlying purpose, which was no less evangelical and probably more important for these monks. This was to convert rural Buddhists to urban Buddhism. It was a conversion from ritualism to ethical action and from other-worldly to ambi-worldly concerns.

Hinatiyana's greatest strength was his skill as a preacher. The sermon was to be his weapon in fighting social ills and defending and promoting social health, the union of dharmadesana and gramasamvardhana, the sermon and rural development, now familiar to us. The sermon was also his greatest pleasure. At this time he delivered about ten sermons a week, in about 65 regular preaching sites, traveling in a car donated by Mrs. Jeremias Dias.

With such energy, enthusiasm, and support, it is no surprise that he was to play a major role in the association founded in 1924 specifically for the promotion of Buddhism through the sermon, known as the Lanka Dharmaduta Sabhava (The Lanka Missionary Society). The office bearers suggest its powerful base and elite status. The Joint Secretaries were G. P. Malalasekera, the Buddhist leader and scholar, and R. S. S. Gunawardena, member of the State Council and later ambassador to the UN. The treasurer was D.C. Senanayake, a member of the most prominent political family of the time. Hinatiyana, then studying English and teaching Sinhala at Mahabodhi

College, was the Patron *(anusasaka)*. A sister organization, Lanka Dharma-duta Bhiksu Sangamaya (Lanka Missionary Monk's Society), was founded with Hinatiyana as the Secretary. These societies consisted of about 1,000 members. Financial support came from D.C. Senanayake and Mrs. Jeremias Dias.

At about this time, Hinatiyana was invited to preach at the Ubhayalokar-tha Sadhaka Samitiya at Alutkade, and also at the Santhagara Salava (rest house) at Foster Lane, Maradana, named after Mrs. Foster of Honolulu, Hawaii, supporter of Dharmapala, who called her his "Foster mother." The name Ubhaya Lokartha Sadhaka Samitiya means "The Society for Gaining Both Worlds." Thus it is candid and explicit about not losing this world in the process of ensuring the next. While this and similar movements of the time were fully aware of the threat of the Christian missionaries, it is important to understand that the real purpose of these Dharmaduta sermons was, as we just observed, internal conversion.

These preacher-monks were after the illiterate or barely literate poor urban and the rural Buddhists, two groups that subscribed to folk Buddhism, which sharply divided the two worlds, this and other. Magic and propitiation of the gods were for this world, and "Buddhism" for the next. "Buddhism" meant the ceremonial offering of food to the monks *(dana)* and rural religious ceremonial that had as its core a sermon *(bana)*. Both these, and especially the latter, were occasions for festivity and community entertainment. The religious core of the *bana* ceremony, the dharmadesana, was, as we know, an all night affair that consisted of religiously emotional and sometimes cathartic storytelling. From the point of view of the new reformist urban intellectuals, these were long and tedious performances which should be replaced by soberly presented moral teachings. While such sermons could have a certain spiritual content, they must, more importantly, promote the cultivation of disciplined, ethical, and productive worldly conduct that served the progress of individual and society. The aim of these elite new preachers was thus to convert the poor from their folk Buddhism to an urban Buddhism in which the distinction between this world and the other world was blurred. This new urban Buddhism contended that any act that did good to oneself and to others was a religious and merit generating act, a doctrine reminiscent of the moral efficacy of loving oneself and one's neighbors. Here is how Hinatiyana puts it:

> Illiterate Buddhists consider . . . offering flowers, giving food to the monks, and going on pilgrimage alone to be acts of merit. . . . Doing one's job properly, treating one's parents well and taking good care of them, helping the sick and the needy, getting on well with others are all acts of merit. The person who does his work diligently will gain this world and the next. . . .

If in a given land the people practice diligence, that land will prosper. . . . Not practicing diligence so valued in the *Appamadavagga* [of the Dhamma-pada] is a hindrance to the progress of Buddhists. In every house the children should be made to memorize the *Appamadavagga* and it should be recited every morning and evening. . . . The mind of an indiligent man who is not engaged in some useful work becomes the home for various sinful thoughts. . . . To practice diligence, people must learn to work according to a time table.

It would be very useful for every Buddhist monastery to design an appropriate timetable for the villagers, get it printed on good quality paper, hang it on the wall of every house, and arrange to work according to that. It gives pleasure to the Buddhists to remember that the Buddha worked according to a timetable. . . . It is time for the Village Committees to devise a method of putting the temple bells to their proper use. . . .

The Sinhala Buddhist has no specific time to wake up or to engage in worship. But in no religion has work according to a timetable more valued than in Buddhism. But Buddhist laymen and monks are lazy and live indiligent lives. In the Catholic church the 5:00 a.m. service starts exactly at 5:00 a.m. In many Buddhist temples the sermon scheduled for 9:00 does not start even at 10:00. In some places, because of the auctioning of flowers and the sale of sundry items *(salpil)*, the sermon does not start till 11:00 or 12:00. Postponing work and indiligence are obstacles to the progress of a country and nation. . . . The Lanka Dharmaduta Maha Sabhava now performs about 108 sermons a month. These start at various times: 8:00 and 9:00 a.m., 1:00, 2:00, 3:00, 4:00, and 4.30 p. m., and 6:00, 7:00, 8:00 in the night. It is obvious that some of these times are very inconvenient for some listeners. However difficult, hundreds and thousands attend these sermons punctually. The reason for this is that [we] the Dharmaduta monks begin and end the sermon on time. . . . If people act diligently, we can soon make this country a glittering Buddhist mansion. . . .[22]

This is not a total condemnation of Buddhist religious acts like food offerings *(dana)* and sermons *(bana, dharmadesana)*. In Hinatiyana's view such acts are well and good so long as they are focused on their core intent and activity and strictly motivated by moral and ethical considerations. They should be freed from the jungle of festivity, ritualism, and emotionalism with which folk Buddhism surrounds them. The effort here is to propagate among the peasantry the sanitized, moralistic, and ethical Buddhism of the urban elites.

Hinatiyana was employed at Nalanda College, one of the two best known Buddhist schools in Colombo. Hinatiyana's position was *dharmacarya*, instructor in Buddhism, a post previously held by Balangoda Ananda Maitreya,

22. *Sinhala Bauddhaya*, 19 October 1929.

who was to later achieve much fame. To better carry out his duties, Hinatiyana resided at the hostel. At this time, some other monks who were to gain
renown later, such as Walpola Rahula, Kalalalle Anandasagara, and Talpavila
Silavamsa, joined Dharmaduta. In 1933 Rahula wrote in catechistic form a
devastating critique of ritualism, entitled *Satyodaya* (The Dawn of Truth).
Dharmaduta was not just a specific message but also an attack on the system
of folk belief which to these monks was as heathen as it was for the Christian
missionaries. Folk ritualism was a corruption from which Buddhism should
be purified and saved. Dharmaduta thus was an attempt to proselytize and
convert folk Buddhists to urban elite Buddhism.

As the movement grew it needed more preachers. For this, a training
center *(Dharmaduta Asrama)* for preachers was established at Rajagiriya. This
was run by the Dharmaduta Society. Land for the Asrama was donated
by the Senanayake family. Supporters included such prominent persons as
D. L. Wijewardena, C. A. Hevavitarana, Raja Hevavitarana, Arthur V. Dias,
R. S. S. Gunawardena, G. P. Malalasekera, and P. de S. Kularatne. At about
this time, a Buddhist seminary (Samanera Vidyalaya) was founded by Anagarika Dharmapala in Kandy, near the Kandy Lake. Eight monks were trained
there to be sent as missionaries to India, after further training at Shantiniketan, India. Dharmapala selected Hinatiyana to be in charge of this delegation of young missionaries. Along with Davamottave Sasanasiri and the
young missionaries, and accompanied by two laymen, M. Piyadasa and Raja
Hevavitarana, Hinatiyana went to India in 1929. At Shantiniketan, along
with the young missionaries, Hinatiyana studied Mahayana, Hindi, Bengali,
Sanskrit and English.

Upon return to Ceylon in 1935 he resumed his position at Nalanda as
Dharmacarya. In that year he founded a society called the Janopakara Samitiya (Help the People Society), which launched the rural development
movement that, besides dharmaduta, became his other major activity. The
first task this society undertook was the development of a poor village in
Kuliyapitiya. In 1937 Hinatiyana started rural development activity at his
own village Hinatiyana, which became his model gramasamvardhana village.
This was supported by D. S. Senanayake, Minister of Agriculture, Arthur V.
Dias, and Ernest de Silva, Buddhist philanthropists. A body known as the
Hinatiyana Rural Development Society was formed under the presidency of
Kalinga Don Timon de Silva, probably a kinsman. Work was decentralized:
the village was divided into fourteen sections, with a male and a female
society for each section, a total of twenty-eight branch societies for the village. Monthly meetings were held where minutes of the branch societies
were presented. As one informant observes, the village of over one hundred

acres was made into a single farm. A 3½ mile length of road was constructed in the village by the branch societies. People were involved in the twin activities of hearing sermons and improving their village, of dharma and development. All was tranquil in the village. There were no police complaints, no court cases. Crime had fled, like an exorcised demon.

The news of the project's success reached Governor Andrew Caldecott, who wrote a congratulatory letter to the society and sent a gift. D. B. Jayatilake, Leader of the House, made a speech in the State Council praising the movement. During the malaria epidemic of 1935, Hinatiyana played a major role in caring for the afflicted. He established seventy temporary hospitals in the Kegalla district, one of the worst affected areas. In the same spirit he organized relief to drought victims in Anuradhapura in 1968, and to flood victims in the North Central Province a year later. He founded the Lakshmi Orphanage at Mutuvadiya, Valana, Katunayaka, funded by A. E. de Silva. He worked for the establishment of the Minuwangoda Nalanda Central School and organized relief for the Catholic village attacked by African soldiers stationed at a World War II military camp at Katunayaka.

From the early 1940s, Hinatiyana preached over the nationally owned radio; he was one of the pioneering radio preachers. In 1956, on the occasion of the Buddha Jayanti celebrations, he began giving an innovative series of short radio addresses, called Buddha Jayanti Adhistanaya, which continued for three years. In 1958, he was appointed the Sangha Nayaka (head, lit., chief monk) of Colombo of the Amarapura Nikaya (sect), a position without any real authority but paralleling Christian diocesan heads. In 1960 Hinatiyana was appointed the first Warden of the newly opened Sangharamaya, the hostel for undergraduate monks at Peradeniya University. He also worked in Germany as a delegate of another organization, the German Dharmaduta Society. Upon return to Sri Lanka he founded the International Buddhist Center at Wellawatta. He frequently contributed Poya Daham Pada, short essays on religious subjects written in simple language, which repeated the pattern of concise radio messages.

He was well known as a skilled fund raiser for social causes, such as the anti-malaria work he did in the thirties; his fund raising was even more effective later, after his fame had spread. According to some accounts he ventured into the ghettos, made lists of names, took them to merchants in different parts of the city, and persuaded them to support the families on the lists—a nonviolent form of Robinhoodism. Indeed his sermons, besides being concise, high on ethics and morality, and couched in simple language, were persuasive and not so subtle appeals for contributions to social causes. (While Hinatiyana did not even accept a salary for his teaching at Nalanda, a generation of monks was to come into being later, as we shall see, which copied this kind of monk in externals such as travel in foreign lands, but in fact amassed wealth for themselves.) In 1980 he was elevated to the status of Mahanayaka of the Amarapura Nikaya, the highest position in the Nikaya. He was a delegate for the Sixth Buddhist Council held in Burma in the 1950s. During his Nalanda days he taught Buddhism to prominent people such as the members of the Senanayake family, the well-known monk Piyadassi of Vajirarama, and a host of other members of the political, professional, and the administrative elite.

Two selected informants' statements regarding Hinatiyana illustrate further the nature of the monk's role as it evolved since its identification by Dharmapala as central to social life. The first is that of Hinatiyana Nanda, present incumbent of the Hinatiyana monastery and a student of Hinatiyana Dhammaloka, and the second by M. O. de Silva, a resident of the village Hinatiyana, and past secretary of the Hinatiyana Rural Development Society. At the time of the interviews in 1994, Hinatiyana Nanda was in his mid-forties, and M. O. de Silva was eighty-two.[23]

Hinatiyana Nanda: Working in the affected villages near Aranayaka, some fellow worker monks came and told Hinatiyana they cannot work because there is an Appuhamy [gentleman] on the mountain who is hostile. Hinatiyana went to meet him. He told those who went with him to stay at the gate and went in alone. The Appuhamy was in an *amude* (loincloth). He was Valipitiye Appuhamy. A well built man. He was not friendly. He was sweeping the compound with his *idala* (broom). He did not stop what he was doing, and Hinatiyana approached. He did not even look up. Kept sweeping. Hinatiyana got closer and closer until the Appuhamy's *idala* was near his feet. Then he stopped and looked at Hinatiyana from foot to head. Then he spoke. "What *vikara* (mad acts) are you doing? This is not work that *mahanunnanses* (you robed men) should be doing. This is the work of kings and princes, not your work. Go to a monastery and do a *bana pirita* (preaching, chanting texts). That is your work." Hinatiyana calmly said, "I am a prince," which startled the Appuhamy. He invited him into the house. He called his wife and daughter and had a discussion. He asked Hinatiyana whether he knew of any house where there was no malaria. He answered "no." The Appuhamy said there was one house, his. Why? They live according to what the Buddha said, following the five precepts. They don't kill. Their diet is vegetarian, not even Maldive fish [dehydrated fish used as a condiment in Sri Lankan cooking]. They do not steal, not for generations have their lineage stolen anything. This

23. Interviews on 8 July 1994.

is my wife, in her fifties. About ten years ago, I called my wife, "*Sondura* (Dear), we must enter into a *givisuma* (treaty, agreement) to live like siblings (i.e., let us give up sex). However sick I get, you must not touch me. However sick you get I will not touch you. We will of course see that we get the care we need. We must observe this *brahmacarya* (celibacy) thus." Look at how we look, young and healthy because of celibacy. We do not lie. We do not even know what a lie is. Alcohol? We have not even seen any. We do not even chew tobacco with our betel.

There was a French priest at the Kahalagoda church. He had refused to let his flock talk to Hinatiyana about starting gramasamvardhana there. Hinatiyana asked him why. The French priest said, the Sinhala people will start something, but will need somebody to push them from behind. If you are willing to do it, that's fine by me, you can start gramasamvardhana.

M. O. de Silva: Hinatiyana went to Kegalla to do malaria relief work. He took eight lorry loads of rice and 18 lorry loads of clothing. One man was not friendly. He didn't talk to Hinatiyana. He asked him why. He said this is not any of your business. This is the work of kings. Hinatiyana asked him, "Do we have a king?" The man was moved. He touched Hinatiyana's feet and said, "I have seen a Buddha."

The two statements narrate two different stories about Hinatiyana encountering a powerful opponent during his malaria relief work. When Hinatiyana approaches, the adversary in each of the stories is hostile and there is even the suggestion of danger. The Appuhamy keeps sweeping and the sweeping strokes are "Get out of here" statements. So is his stony silence and all other aspects of body language, which are reversals of ordinary polite behavior and more so when directed against a monk who is invariably treated with a very different body language, that of deference. But note Hinatiyana's undaunted march towards the adversary, in Nanda's story, right up to the broom strokes, expressing his defiance and indeed aggressive intrusion into another's territory. Hinatiyana is not defying the Appuhamy personally, but the idea that social service is not the work of monks, but of kings.

Hinatiyana on his part calls himself a king, explicitly in the first story, which startles the Appuhamy, and indirectly in the second when he rhetorically asks his adversary "Do we have a king?" (implying that, since he is de facto doing the work of kings, he is king: kingship is what kingship does). Here we also see a repetition of the monk's status-yearning, his desire to be king, and the symbolic superiority of the monk over the king in the Buddhist tradition, a superiority however that in reality becomes a caricature, which is in fact the problem of the monk, specially under conditions when, as in colonialism, ritual and symbolic superiority finds no place in the newly rearranged universe of power, and the monk's identity is in crisis and trauma. "Work of kings" has also the sense of noblesse oblige, which implicates the monk in nobility status. Metaphors of status-yearning more than the desire for power emerge even when the monk is involved in the most practical and beneficial of activities. "I am a prince" also evokes the Buddha's own royal status before his renunciation, a status with which a monk is symbolically identified in the ceremony or ordination, implying both a status claim and the accompanying sovereign power.

Thus when Hinatiyana tells the Appuhamy, "I am a prince," he is telling him as well as the rest of the world that he will jolly well do what he pleases. What he pleases here however is limited to social work. Hinatiyana desires no more, but more importantly, no less. He is going to stand his ground and tell anybody in his way that his work as a monk is social service. The Appuhamy's idea of a monk is that of a ritualist, a preacher of *bana* and *pirit,* and a recipient of food to cause merit for the giver. Hence his instruction to Hinatiyana to go home and do those things, which Hinatiyana firmly rejects. Thus this story condenses the definition of the role of the monk proposed by these new monks—a definition that is expressed in their missionary (dharmaduta) work of internal conversion, rooted in Dharmapala, and brilliantly articulated by Walpola Rahula (see chap. 4).

Further, the two stories, with their dramatic juxtaposition of Hinatiyana and his adversary, recall the Buddha's dramatic confrontations with fierce adversaries such as Angulimala and the inebriated elephant Nalagiri, narrated in the medieval Sinhala Buddhist texts with such popular emotional appeal.[24] In all these the adversary ends up converted. So is he in these two stories. It defines Hinatiyana's life's task, conversion of people from bad to good, from idleness to work, from crime to citizenship, from ritualist folk Buddhism to ethical middle-class Buddhism and above all from the idea that a monk's work is ritual to the idea that a monk's work is social service. Finally, in the Appuhamy's assertion that the work of *mahnunannses* is ritualism *(bana, dana,* and *pirit)* we have a statement of protest over boundaries that monks violate to enter into lay territory that has echoed and re-echoed since this time. It is much aggravated today and is a divisive issue that is disturbing to the orthodox, like the Appuhamy before his conversion experience.[25]

24. For example, *Butsarana.*
25. We cannot be sure whether Hinatiyana actually had this Appuhamy encounter. What we can be sure is that his pupil is telling us a story. Its contents reflect his (the pupil's) notions of the role of the monk, which he has derived as much from the work of his teacher as from Walpola Rahula's *The Heritage of the Bhikku* (see below).

We have quite an interesting episode in the Appuhamy's explanation of the mystery of his and his family's immunity to malaria. The secret is the moral rectitude of the family, as expressed in its observance of the five precepts, especially the nonconsumption of meat and alcohol and abstention from sex. In the case of the last we see here a reflection of the broad South Asian medical belief according to which semen is a distilled form of blood, and loss of semen which intercourse brings about is therefore precipitously unhealthy. It also resonates with another South Asian idea that celibacy (retention of semen) has salutary physical effects and is convertible into supernatural power. That some monks have supernormal powers is an enduring belief, held by pious believers or the monks themselves, all evidence to the contrary. The potent force in the health of the Appuhamy family is the rigid adherence to the five precepts, as opposed to their mere ritual recitation or to the prophylactic ritualism of the folk religion, which is the source of immunity to disease in ordinary peasant thought. Thus the Appuhamy becomes a model of the disinfected city Buddhism to which Hinatiyana is trying to convert ordinary Buddhists, whose immunities to disease are derived not from morality but from ritual. This completes the process of resolution of the tension between the two that started with the Appuhamy's acceptance, by backing off, of Hinatiyana's royal status and the ensuing prerogative, indeed the obligation, to help people. i.e., that a monk is entitled to do social service. In both stories, the ease with which Hinatiyana conquers the adversary recalls the supernatural powers the informants attribute to him. In reality, Appuhamys are a rare species if at all extant in the villages. Such a person, like the idyllic society centered around the reservoir, the stupa, and the rice field, is a fantasy born in the imagination of the urban middle class.

The comment of the French priest, that the Sinhala people lack the dynamism and the drive necessary for maintaining the momentum of any enterprise, and hence that they need constantly to be pushed, was a theme that was part of the critique of the people launched by Dharmapala and other nationalists in an effort to awaken them to sustained productive activity. This was also the view that the Europeans took of subject peoples in general, and directly or indirectly the nationalists owe this view to the colonial ruler. This same view appears in technical form in the literature of the sociology of underdevelopment. That Hinatiyana helped the French priest's flock to start a gramasamvardhana program of their own suggests his overt or tacit acceptance of this view. It is fashionable anthropology to condemn this view as Eurocentric. But in a world obsessed with the idea of market economy, cultures without the dynamism the French priest and the nationalists have in mind are going to stay in poverty. Reform-oriented monks like Hinatiyana saw this, and there is no doubt that, while they may have been acting to enhance their own status and prestige, they were also trying to uplift their fellow men.

It is part of this attempt, made first by laymen and later joined by monks, that the literature of anthropology labels Protestant Buddhism.[26] One aspect of "Protestant Buddhism" is the attempt by Buddhist middle classes to cultivate systematic work habits under the influence of a colonial and missionary culture of methodism in work and life. Having done so, these classes forgot that influence and imagined it to have come from Buddhist sources. That imagination was both possible and convincing to them precisely because "ancient Buddhism," which was dug up and shown to these classes by Western scholars, did contain precisely those imperatives that we associate with Protestant, especially Calvinist, Christianity. Buddhism was a reformation that constituted a rebellion against the ritualism of Hinduism as the Reformation was against the ritualism of Catholicism. Buddhism, however, soon re-embraced ritualism, especially as it changed from a religion of the urban elites to that of the rural masses. It is therefore as justifiable for anthropologists to think of urban elite Buddhists as "Protestant" as it is for these elites to believe their ideology is "true Buddhism" in contrast to the ritualism of the folk. Hinatiyana's work, inspired by Dharmapala, constitutes the yoking together of Buddhist values and social and economic progress, dharma and development, as we have seen in the case of Kalukondayave. Despite weaknesses in how it was understood and its ultimate failure, the economic aspect involving the mundane welfare of the people was the dominant theme. In the next phase, when we come to advocates like Rahula, this important and meaningful aspect, i.e. the economic, gets superseded by politics and ideology, paving the way for a national tragedy on a scale previously unknown.

DHARMAPALITE MISSIONARIES (3)
Hendiyagala Silaratana

Hendiyagala Silaratana (1913–82), our third hero-giant of Dharmapalite regeneration, was born in 1913, eighteen years after Kalukondayave.[27] That Silaratana was nearly a generation younger than Kalukondayave and the fact

26. See, for example, Richard Gombrich and Gananath Obeyesekere, *Buddhism Transformed,* 202–40; Kitsiri Malalgoda, *Buddhism in Sinhalese Society 1750–1900,* 246, 260–61.

27. The sources for this account are the autobiography of Hendiyagala Silaratana, *Mage Jivita Katava* (Kuliyapitiya: Sastrodaya Press, 1971), and his other works. Hendiyagala's students who at present reside at his Ratmulukanda monastery provided valuable oral evidence. Unless otherwise noted, intratextual page citations concerning Hendiyagala refer to this work (but see note 38). See also Premachandra Disanayaka, *Sadaham Piyuma* (Kuliyapitiya: Sastrodaya Press, 1982).

that he was a student at Vidyodaya make it very likely that Silaratana was as much inspired by Kalukondayave's activation of the Dharmapalite principles as by the principles themselves. Born to Sirisinha Mudalige Palis Appuhamy and Kandavala Patiranage Reginahamy, Hendiyagala attended the Roman Catholic school at Nalavalana, which then had an enrolment of about fifty students. The school was administered by a French priest, Fr. La Fabre. In contrast to the young Dharmapala under the tutelage of Catholic priests, Hendiyagala had the most positive of impressions of La Fabre. He describes him as a "kind priest [who] had a long white beard, a full tall figure, and a smiling face" (15). Also unlike Dharmapala, who felt personal and cultural humiliation, Hendiyagala had the freedom to go outside the classroom and play with other Buddhist children while the Catholic religious services were conducted. There was more to the springs of young Hendiyagala's admiration of the kindly father than this ideological fact of exemption from alien ritual and the father's saintly personality: he had a supply of candies which he regularly doled out to the children. In contrast to Dharmapala again, Hendiyagala explicitly says that he recalls no attempt on the part of the school to convert any Buddhist children to Catholicism. Further, Hendiyagala enjoyed participation in the extracurricular activities of the school such as fairs and firework displays. Altogether his school experience was pleasant, which perhaps explains his milder and more cosmopolitan attitude to other religions and the absence in his writings any indication of ethnic or religious exclusivism. That is, like Kalukondayave and Hinatiyana, Hendiyagala embraced the non-ideological, pragmatic, and moral-economic side of Dharmapala and ignored the ideological and the political.

After leaving the Nalavalana Roman Catholic School, Hendiyagala joined the Swabhasa Mixed Buddhist School at Hendiyagala. His mother gave him money for the vegetables he grew, a Dharmapalite idea which suggest that his parents were under the reformer's influence, widespread at this time. He was encouraged, after the Protestant and Dharmapalite fashion, to save money in a piggy bank. This early thrift enabled him to buy his own school books and supplies without parental help, a self-sufficiency that was a source of both happiness and pride. It was carried to lengths that foreboded his extraordinary commitment, ascetic bent of mind, and capacity for hard work.[28] Instead of asking his parents to buy him the books that his private income failed to buy, Hendiyagala borrowed the books from teachers and

---

28. On the "work ethic" of monks such as Hendiyagala, see the editorial in *Prabhasodaya,* December 1936. The editor describes how he toiled relentlessly despite ill health: *"davasin vadi kalayak adhyapana karyayanhi yedena apa lath svalpa visramaya pava sangarava pinisa yodanu labe"* (Because we devote most of the day to educational work, even the little break we get is used for work on this journal).

copied them wholesale by hand. He was to remember this; in 1942 he stocked the Sunanda library he founded with books for children. Further, he donated to this library the 1,200 books he received as gifts in appreciation of his work as a celebrated preacher, the library building itself having being financed with Rs. 15,000 worth of cash gifts he received for the same service.

His mother's deep religiosity had an impact on Hendiyagala, and he often observed *sil* (observance of the eight precepts) and participated in other forms of religious activity. Like Kalukondayave, as a boy he "preached" by reading a book to elderly devotees who had observed *sil*. Despite such potent signs of religiosity he was a reluctant acolyte, his horoscope also not indicating a "powerful renunciatory potential" *(balasampanna pavidi yoga)*.[29] He could not take life in the monastery, and, one day, in the midst of a chore, he pretended to swoon and went home. His plan was to become a teacher and to take good care of his mother, whom he dearly loved. Her own desire, however, was to make him a monk. The night he returned home he heard his mother sob out of grief that he left the monastery. She told him, "My golden son, you enter the monkhood. If I see you in robes that is like nirvana for me" (55). Even this moving display had only a temporary effect, for he fled three times before finally deciding, in 1928, at age fifteen, to stay in robes. In this last attribute his career resonates with that of Hinatiyana, who de-robed twice before he finally made up his mind at his third ordination to stay on. This time, however, the desire to become a preacher and the exemplary character of his teacher had made his decision firm. His "desire for monkhood *(pavidda)* grew every day" (144). He realized the purity of monastic life and, on 3 January 1934, went on *pindapata* (begging for alms). Like Kalukondayave and Hinatiyana, he excelled in studies, easily learning from memory the basic literature expected of a preacher, such as the *Bana Daham Pota, Paticcasamuppada, Namaskara Gatha,* and *Maitrivarnana.* Like Kalukondayave and Hinatiyana, and indeed Dharmapala, he had his early education in a Christian school.

His next educational step was to join, in 1929, the Sangharaja Pirivena, Malvatta Vihara, Kandy, where he skipped the entering class (*Varga* 9) because of his prior preparation. He excelled in his academic work. In a class

29. For a successful lay life, the "four centers" *(satara kendra)* of one's horoscope must be inhabited by planetary dieties, non-occupancy foreboding dire bad luck. One way of dealing with such a misfortune is to ordain the person, which effectively makes the monkhood a resort for holders of such horoscopes. Monks rationalize this by saying that such a horoscope is exceptionally auspicious for the monastic life.

of fourteen students, he stood first every year throughout his stay. (Palipane Chandananda, the present Mahanayake of Asgiriya, was second.) In 1937 he joined Vidyodaya under the tutelage of Kahave Sumangala, graduating in 1941. At Vidyodaya he was also tutored by several distinguished scholars including Devundara Vacissara, Valivitye Sorata, Kukulnape Devaraksita, and Baddegama Piyaratana. Most interestingly he was tutored by the two modernist monks, Kalukondayave Pannasekhara and Paravahara Vajiragnana in the task of internal conversion by training him in the new time-framed dharmadesana, radio preaching, and missionary work (dharmaduta). His mastery of the "new gospel" of urban, time-framed, non-ritualist, and moralist *bana* was reflected in his book on how to preach, entitled *Bana kiyana hati hevat dharma desana krama* (How to Preach, or, Methods of Dharmadesana), which earned him invitations to teach the subject to novices.[30] During a short stay between his graduation from Sangharaja and his entering Vidyodaya, he already showed his interest in training the young by organizing a *sil* for boys and girls during Vesak (May) 1936, providing the children with the requisite white cloth for free. He organized men's, women's, and youth associations in the Ratmulukanda area, where his monastery is located, indicating the inspiration of both Kalukondayave, Hinatiyana, and ultimately Dharmapala. Thus, even while he was still a student at Vidyodaya, he had mastered the existing theory of Rural Development and was trying his hand at implementing its main recommendations at the village level.

His series of short published sermons, *Dharma Patrika* (Dharma Papers), bear testimony to the influence on him of the modern urban dharmadesana. The work is written in simple, crisp, short sentences that are conspicuously lacking in the luxurious imagery, alliteration, narrativity, and the profusion of metaphor characteristic of traditional prose works, which, starting with the twelfth-century *Butsarana,* were traditional dharmadesana in written form.

An example can be given from his Dharma Patrika on *Vinnanaya* (consciousness). This is the first paragraph:

> A deep subject. But a term that should be well understood by Buddhists. A long and broad commentary exists. [But] shall explain briefly. Being is divided into two, name and form. Form refers to this body our eyes can see. Name refers to the mind and thoughts. Mind is a single aggregate. It is that we call the aggregate of the mind. There are fifty-two thoughts. These are catego-

30. Hendiyagala Silaratana, *Bana kiyana hati hevat dharma desana krama* (How to Preach, or, Methods of Dharmadesana) (Maradana: Ratna, n.d.).

rized under three aggregates, *vedana, sankhara, vinnana.* The aggregate of *ved-ana* refers to the chaitasika. Chaitasika means thought *(sitivili).* Thought means things that can come to mind.[31]

This is a lesson to long-winded preachers. Though written, this is actually a sermon, a modern, thematic one. It is this modernity that Hendiyagala and others like him applied also to social service. It is as if he is addressing an audience rather than writing on the subject of "Consciousness." The entire patrika is constructed this same way, in short simple sentences. This is conscious and has in view a specific audience that is clearly not the peasant, as the conclusion shows: 'It must be understood that the analysis of consciousness is very detailed, and this is not the place for it'.

Wilmot Herat Gunaratne's Foreword to Hendiyagala's autobiography correctly captures Hendiyagala's outlook on life: it emphasizes the privileged position of being born as a human, a homocentrism which is both reminiscent of early Buddhism and derived from contemporary western influences. To quote the Foreword: "In both this and other worldly terms, the noblest of all achievements is possible not for gods and *brahmas* but for man. If man, who has got such a valuable life, is to receive the highest and noblest benefit from his life, he must work for both this- and other-worldly benefit, for himself and others. Thus working for others is an integral part of one's self realization." This is exactly the philosophy of monasticism handed down by Dharmapala and held by Hendiyagala and other Buddhist modernist monks.

Like Kalukondayave, Hendiyagala kept a meticulous diary that runs to 1,280 pages on legal-sized paper. Also like the former, he drew on his diary to write his long autobiography, which records all kinds of events. For example, he notes the death of Thomas Edison, "a world renowned scientist in New Jersey in America aged 84," and further describes Edison as "a noble person who made 1500 inventions" (117). This admiration of science and progress was shared by Kalukondayave and Hinatiyana, and was ultimately derived from Dharmapala. Also like Kalukondayave, Hendiyagala gave away the gifts such as silk scarves, cloth lengths, bedsheets, and towels he received for his preaching, sometimes selling them to make money for the schools or the library he founded.

In 1939 Hendiyagala decided to give up his teaching position in Kandy and return to his home area at Ratmulukanda (near Hettipola, Kurunegala) to devote himself full time to the social service activities he had been trying to do since his graduation from the Sangharaja Pirivena (232). Having gone

31. Hendiyagala Silaratana, *Vinnanaya* (Kuliyapitiya: Sastrodaya Press, n.d.).

through training at Vidyodaya that broadened his vision, and enriched by his urban experience, he had no interest in traditional ritualism. The options for him were either to engage in a professional activity like teaching or to engage in social service. This intellectual and emotional need, with its ramifications of social acceptance especially by the middle and upper classes, is the obverse of the idealism, moralism, and dedication these monks exhibit in such abundance. In 1942, Hendiyagala founded the Henegedera Gramasamvardhana Society:

> I decided to enlist the help of D. D. Rupasinghe Appuhamy, who was a wealthy gentleman of the area. I got him elected as the president of the *samitiya* (society). For the other offices, I got elected appropriate individuals. I became patron and started work for the progress of the area. This was the end of World War II and there was a great food shortage. I created a feeling for self-sufficiency in the area by encouraging people to cultivate yams, vegetables, and so forth and getting as much help from the government to assist in agriculture, like implements and fertilizer. I started a dharmadesana series and preached continuously for two years once a week or once a fortnight. I preached in a new way. I ask for the company of a boy or a *dayaka* (donor) and, about 7 p. m., leave for the school first of all. On the way I tell everybody I meet, "come and listen to *bana*." I ask for mats from the neighbors and a chair, and chat with people till about fifty or sixty gather. I will preach to this crowd for a about an hour on how they can organize their lives. Often I ask that coconuts be brought and get them split and, after the *bana,* auction the coconut halves to support the Ambavagedara school. In 1942 alone I preached 12 *banas* at this school alone. I did not accept gifts for these. Nor money. Often bazaars were held where I sold the gifts I had deservedly received and used the proceeds for the school. (235–36)[32]

In 1935 Hendiyagala widened the *Daham Pasal* (Dhamma school, "Sunday school") service because he felt his native locality needed help more than the Kandy area, where he first taught. He taught children for the school-leaving

---

32. Hendiyagala mentions difficulties in working with villagers and organizing these activities, which contrasts with the idyllic pictures we get from the writings of and reports about Kalukondayave and Hinatiyana, and other enthusiasts. An exception to this is G. de Soyza, *Report on Rural Reconstruction in Ceylon,* Sessional Paper 23 (Colombo: The Government Press, 1944). These difficulties also contrast with contemporary idyllic pictures of rural harmony and project successes portrayed by fund-seeking NGOs. The difficulties often center around parochial conflicts in the village. For example, the case of Ambavagedara school. This school, started by a "professional," had neither permanent and certified teachers, nor buildings and equipment, nor ownership of the land on which it was situated. With great effort Hendiyagala accomplished all this. This however meant the original "founder" had to leave. According to Hendiyagala, he created problems that led to a division of the village. This went on till 1968, when the school was taken over by the government (236–39).

examination, holding classes in his monastery, often providing the books, and instructing the parents on the importance of giving their children an education. For four years he maintained a schedule of hopping tirelessly from school to school, often walking the two- to four-mile distance that separated the schools. In four years he had trained local students capable of doing the local teaching themselves. By 1971, the date of the autobiography, he notes with satisfaction that about 130 of these students had achieved distinction as teachers, university graduates, government employees, and workers in private enterprises. Some were principals of schools. A few of these were disciplined monks involved in useful work (243). As Hendiyagala puts it, "I did this work voluntarily to create out of the youth in the area a group of educated men who would provide service to the community." Working like a true Dharmapalite soldier, he organized periodic public meetings, inviting well-known figures from Colombo and elsewhere, and he held annual *pinkam* (merit-making ceremonies), all these for the sole purpose of waking up the people. By his own evaluation, his rate of success was 70 percent. "People woke up. Thought we must mould our children [to be successful]. Get them educated. [The people] got my help for numerous things. Progressed. At the same time, the majority quickly forgot my services. But that is the *loka dharma,* the way of the world" (244).

He was particularly interested in improving the conditions of women. "If a society is to achieve social and national awakening," he wrote, "it is necessary to improve the moral state of its mother party [i.e., women]" (245–46). He founded the Sri Ratnavali Kulangana Samitiya (Sri Ratnavali Women's Association) in 1943, and in 1971 (the date of his autobiography), this society, after 28 years, was still functioning well. By 1942, he had done 241 dharmadesanas and had published a series of gramasamvardhana patrika dealing with temperance, cattle slaughter, and Buddhist education. These were an innovation on the dharma patrikas of Hinatiyana and were of Dharmapalite origin, and as we know by now from the Dharmapalism of Kalukondayave and Hinatiyana, they combine the moral and the economic, dharma and development.

In 1944, Hendiyagala went to teach at the Vikramasila Vidarsana Pirivena at Pallevela for six months. This visit points to another dimension of gramasamvardhana that, like much else, is of Dharmapalite origin. This is meditation, which is, we recall, an ever present undercurrent in the Dharmapalite utopia. Vikramasila specialized in meditation, and Hendiyagala here also mentions Salgala and other meditation centers. With such admiration for Dharmapala, we also see him building into his youth programs an attempt to make children knowledgeable about the reformer. We have no evidence of any such conscious attempt to do so by either Kalukondayave or Hinatiyana, although it is unlikely that they would not have talked about him to their disciples. In contrast, Hendiyagala held a Dharmapala commemoration meeting in 1945. A large color portrait of Dharmapala was carried around the villages of his gramasamvardhana activity. This was consciously done "to give an idea of Dharmapala to our children" (289, 310). One explanation of this is possibly that it represents, twelve years after the reformer's death, the beginning of a hagiographic image, which in the case of the other two leaders was not possible because of their temporal proximity to him.

In his project of national regeneration Dharmapala envisaged his hero-giants and soldiers enlisting the help of the political and other elites. His problem with these elites was their deracination. Kalukondayave and Hinati-yana adopted a pragmatic approach and chose to ignore a good deal of this deracination so long as devout Buddhist and broadly nationalist lay elite members, especially of the political elite, could be enlisted to support their work. Underlying this is a factor of great sociological significance in the contemporary history of Buddhism in Sri Lanka: namely, the interest in the newly educated Sangha, the core of which was based in Vidyodaya and Vidya-lankara, to re-unite with the secular elite from which it was separated at the advent of colonialism, a separation which Dharmapala and his followers such as Rahula considered a conscious and devious colonialist method of weaken-ing the nationalist resistance to the colonial project. In Hendiyagala we see the pragmatic process of the Dharmapalite monk's alliance with the western-ized elite taken a step further: Hendiyagala was in touch with a larger num-ber of politicians and other elite members than were either Kalukondayave or Hinatiyana, and he brought into the midst of his gramasamvardhana proj-ect a greater variety of such elite figures. They included literary and cultural personalities who made strange bedfellows with their westernized counter-parts, as the following situation and events illustrate.

It was one of his Vidyodaya teachers, Kukulnape Devarakshita, who initi-ated Hendiyagala's relations with the political elite. One day Kukulnape unceremoniously walked in along with a stranger to the classroom where Hendiyagala was teaching and said to him, "Silaratana, do you know this *hamu mahattaya* (scion)? This is Dickie Hamu, Gothabhaya Senanayake, Mr. Samarakkody's brother-in-law, F. R. Senanayake's oldest son" (277). Kukul-nape instructed Hendiyagala to promptly stop the test he was administering in the classroom and go to Ratmulukanda with Gothabhaya (R. G.) Senanay-ake. They stopped at (later prime minister) Sir John Kotelawela's house and proceeded eventually to address a meeting in Ratmulukanda in support of R. G. Senanayake's candidacy for Parliament. The meeting was addressed by several other prominent monks, and R. G. Senanayake won the election with a majority of 13,000 votes. This propelled Hendiyagala into this elite political circle, whose good offices he used to gain support for his grama-samvardhana work. For example, he ensured that schools were registered, dispensaries and post offices opened, and wells constructed in the North-west provinces, where his gramasamvardhana activities were located (289, 295). When he obtained a Central School for the Seven Korales area,[33] the opening of the school was celebrated with a carnival *(sanakeliya)* code-named *Bingunaada* (The Bee's hum); the carnival included a seminar on literature with I.M.R.A. Iriyagolla, G. P. Malalasekera, G. H. Perera, and Minister of Agriculture (later Prime minister) D. S. Senanayake in the chair! (304).[34] Among other names whose support he enlisted in the propaganda meetings for gramasamvardhana were T. B. and Vincent Subasinghe, Kalalalle Anan-dasagara, Dharmasiri Kuruppu, Walpola Rahula, Cyrus W. Surendra, and Talpavila Silvamsa (312–13). These people represent an amazing gathering of the widest possible range in the political-ideological-cultural spectrum in Sri Lanka and an equally wide and incongruous assemblage of journalists, poets, scholars, and politicians. Such a creative tapping of national leadership resources in a common task is as sorely needed today as it is unimaginable. While one could see in it the germ of politicians using monks for political purposes, I think it is misleadingly reductive to think so.

It is rather the other way around: what we have are patriotic monks who are overlooking cultural and ideological differences among the lay leader-ship, astutely addressing their commonness rather than their differences, and "manipulating" them in the task of national regeneration. What stands out, in a proper understanding of these events, is a potential that was untapped, a journey on the right path that was derailed, and a benign symbiosis of ideological and cultural opposites and of monk and laymen in the face of national challenge that was aborted. It is an equilibrium that could have set Sri Lanka on the path to civility and development. It is the culmination of a healthy and realistic attitude towards western influences which the Vidyo-daya monks were able to creatively generate, as they bravely resisted the ethno-religious exclusivist impulse that constituted one half of their progen-

33. As a key instrument in free education adopted in 1947, Central Schools were established in different electorates to impart knowledge to rural children. These schools were modeled on the presti-gious private schools in Colombo. There was competition for establishing these schools and one way politicians could woo voters was to by getting a Central School for their electorate.

34. The first is a politician who started as a writer. The second is a scholar, and the third a poet. From the perspectives we have today, this kind of congregation is both ideologically unimaginable and incongruous.

itor Dharmapala's philosophy and activist project. But fate decreed that the hand of Vidyalankara, Vidyodaya's sister institution, rock the cradle of this delicate balance with violence, breaking it up into pieces, never to be put back together again.

Hendiyagala provides a fascinating picture of a village, Kohombana, in the Vavgam pattuva (district) of the Eastern Province, where he delivered a sermon. The schoolmaster had invited him to preach. The school had forty children. Since boys married at age thirteen or fourteen, after starting school when they were about ten, their total schooling lasted only for three to four years. This is how Hendiyagala describes his visit:

The extent of the Kohombana village that we saw that day was no more than 10 acres. The village was located at the foot of a tank. Right round the village is thick jungle. A circular area of about 10 acres had been cleared like a threshing floor and the houses built around it. The houses share the single compound [that faces each]. The people live in amazing unity. They commit no demerit other than hunting, and that to eke out a living, because there is no other livelihood. There is an *arachchi* (headman) and a *vattavidane*. They value the connections with the Tamils, and the *arachchi* was married to a Tamil woman from the coast. In their speech there are as many Sinhala words as there are Tamil.

Two or three times a year, a high-wheeled cart drawn by buffaloes arrives in the village from the coast, laden with salt, dry fish, textiles, and so forth. This is a Muslim trader who barters these items for the grain, deer and sambhur skin and horns, honey and so forth. The village is perpetually indebted to the Muslim trader. He determines the parities and the villagers get a raw deal.

That night, 16 July 1948, I preached at the Kohombana school for three full hours, between 9 and 12 in the night. This was my first and last sermon in the eastern province. What I said most that night, at the request of the schoolteacher, was that this country is Sinhalese, and is ruled by them, and this small crowd that lives inside a forest should not think that they are a minority living inside a Tamil Muslim country. An *anusasana* of this sort was made because it was learnt that these people believed they were a minority in a Tamil country. But I later learned from the teacher that the majority of them did not understand more than exactly half of what I said. But they heard the sermon with great devotion. It was said that that was the first *bana* some of them ever heard.

I went to the village at about 4 p. m. and left at about 8.00 the next morning. That night was a *mangala* (festive) night for the villagers. They expressed their joy by lighting firecrackers and playing the *rabana* drums [both signs of celebration].

Next morning, they wanted to bring the breakfast *dana* to the school. But I expressed the desire to have the food in one of the houses. They were so thrilled at the idea that they said that was a good fortune they never experienced in their whole life. Never had a monk, they said, visited and had a meal in their houses.

I, along with those who accompanied me, went to several of the houses. They did not have chairs to sit on, and at many places they turned the mortar upside down and spread a mat over it to make a seat. They made our lunch to take with us [on the long journey back] and, as we were leaving, many eyes were full of tears. (338–42)

This passage paints a picture of the harshness and need of life in an isolated village, exploited by an urban itinerant trader, that is in stark contrast to the middle-class fantasy of the idyllic village. It describes the cultural position of the villagers as a mixture of Sinhala and Tamil, their language an even mixture of the vocabulary of the two languages. This pattern is repeated in the marriage of the most important Sinhala man in the village to a Tamil woman. It constitutes an objectification of the commonness shared between ethnic groups to which extremists of all groups are blind, and expresses evocatively the adaptability of peoples as opposed to the rigidity of demagogues and liberator-murderers. Now Tamilized, the Kandyan Sinhala origins of these people are clear in their names, such as Dasanayake Mudiyanselage, Ratnayake Mudiyanselage, and Disanayaka Mudiyanselage. Lurking in the background is the schoolteacher, who brings from the outside Sinhala world the ethnic prejudices and notions of numerical superiority and other dominances derived from that, and on a civilizing mission. The monk, persuaded by the teacher, introduces the element of ethnicity which is otherwise absent from his work, indicative of the fragility of the monk's mission and its vulnerability to the dark side of the Dharmapalite teachings.[35]

35. As I have repeatedly observed, these monks themselves were well fortified against the kind of ethnic prejudice that plagues some contemporary monks. Hendiyagala, for example, learned Tamil, visited Jaffna, and wrote a booklet (80 pages) entitled *Uturudiga Lankava* (Northern Lanka) (Colombo: Mahabodhi Press, 1955), where he gives an admiring description of Tamil culture, especially when compared to the relatively more decadent (in the Dharmapalite westernization sense) Sinhala culture. For example, he mentions that, unlike in the Buddhist temples, rules apply to the high and low alike. He gives a dispassionate account of the caste basis of temple entry. He mentions appreciatively that Buddhist monks are accorded the unique privilege and courtesy of entry with upper body covered, the robe covering one or both shoulders (22–23). He describes the tasteful glitter of a Jaffna wedding ceremony and comments that while the Sinhalas with a mere smattering of English blindly imitate the West, the Jaffna citizens, however wealthy, however western-educated, are adept at despising western customs and protect with great love their traditional national customs (70). This contrast is taken over to another area that is a favorite with Dharmapala and his soldiers, the proper dress for women. The Jaffna women measure up commendably, being clad top to toe when compared to the Sinhala women,

The immunity of the villagers themselves in their elemental state, unexposed to the ethnicities and nationalisms of the cities and the elites, to the ethnic prejudices and even to the high moral part of the sermon is clear, as is their delight with the more ritualistic merit-making and celebratory aspects of the event. The mission of the Dharmapalite army is to replace this "merrie olde life" of the peasant with the colorless morality and bourgeois ethic of urban Buddhism.

Hendiyagala provides us with a parting scene of sorrow so reminiscent of the inevitable departure of the wanderer monks of ancient India as they left the villages in which they observed the rainy season, as depicted in the vinaya literature. He also makes the ironic comment that these jungle-living Sinhalas possess more nobility of character and greater virtue than the progressive and civilized (urban) Sinhalas, which recalls the Dharmapalite theory of an original state of nobility and virtue from which the Sinhalas deteriorated owing to the adoption of western foods, customs, habits, and thoughtways. Hendiyagala's higher evaluation of these people is based on his determination that they do not drink, gamble, lie, or commit sexual misconduct, a conclusion based on a mere one night's stay. On the basis of the theory of the Appuhamy of Hinatiyana's story described above, their style of life should give these villagers an incontrovertible measure of immunity to malaria.

True to his form, Hendiyagala did not simply remain sentimental. He wrote an article for the *Silumina* on "The Outer Communities of the Eastern Province" and sent a clipping to the Government Agent (GA), Batticaloa, requesting to him to pity the plight of these villagers and help them. That apparently had some effect because he received a thankful letter from the *vattavidane* informing him that the GA, District Revenue officer (DRO), and police officials had visited the village and established a cooperative store to free them to some extent from the visiting traders, and had given them some

---

as perceived by Dharmapala and his followers (65). It is particularly notable that Hendiyagala describes with the detachment of a scientist items of Jaffna culture that are often ethnically stereotyped.

Hendiyagala's interest in the Tamil language and culture is not isolated but represents a tradition that was severely weakened with the ethnic polarization of recent times. Hissalle Dhammaratana, Buddhist monk and scholar, was steeped in Tamil learning and read learned papers in Tamil at Tamil language and culture conferences. Literary sources of the fifteenth and sixteenth centuries regard learning Tamil as a worthy intellectual accomplishment. For example, Alagiyavanna's *Subhasitaya* lists Tamil along with Pali and Sanskrit as languages learned by the sophisticated. Many of learned monks of the Vidyodaya, Vidyalankara, and Sri Lanka Vidyalaya monastic colleges were learned in Tamil. That the tradition of Buddhist monks studying Tamil is not extinct is seen in a recent plea by a Buddhist monk for inter-ethnic harmony by the study by each ethnic group of the others' language. See "Bhasa adhyayanaya tulin jatin atara samagiyak" (Inter-ethnic harmony through the study of language), *Sambhasa* 1, no. 1 (May-August 1990).

other help as well. Hendiyagala adds, "I have preached over a thousand sermons in my career. But there is no sermon that touched me more, and that
I have thought about more afterwards, and none that benefited the audience
more" (341).

While Kalukondayave and Hinatiyana did talk about social service abstractly, neither expounded a systematic theory. In this respect Hendiyagala
stands out. Activism was central to Hendiyagala's work, but, among these
three, he alone came up with a broad and comprehensive theory.[36] In his
works dealing with social service he comes through entirely as a social
worker with genuine commitment in contrast to the impression we get from
Vidyalankara treatises dealing with social service as the monk's vocation,
which consciously drag in the spiritual dimension or "monkness" *(mahanakama)* as they call it, resulting in an unconvincing and contrived hybrid of a
social worker. In his treatises, as a social worker, Hendiyagala displays no
pretenses about high spirituality; he even explicitly says that, for all his love
of the forest, the mountains, and solitude, it should not be thought that he
has achieved any states of higher mystical power (341–53).[37] The result is
that Hendiyagala comes through as possessing of a monkness in a much more
convincing and greater measure than apparent in the self-proclaimed saints
of Vidyalankara. In this respect, as an active social service person, Hendiyagala's genuineness and lack of any profit motive, monetary or otherwise,
stands in contrast to the new social service monk that has now appeared in
the Sri Lanka scene primarily as the child of the pirivena universities and of
Walpola Rahula's *The Heritage of the Bhikkhu* (discussed in chapter 4). Hendiyagala, like Kalukondayave and Hinatiyana, was poor. This contrasts with the
huge resources, fund-raising acumen, and haughty academic tenures of some
of these new monks.

"To the Sinhala Buddhist," writes Hendiyagala in *Samaja Sevaya,* "*samaja
sevaya* (social service) is neither a subject that needs introduction nor a new
thing. If the Buddhist leads a truly Buddhist life, his whole life should be one
of social service."[38] It was the Buddha, he says, who for the first time in the

36. This theory is spelled out in different places in Hendiyagala's prolific writings. Special mention,
however, must be made of the following: *Gramasamvardhanaya,* 2 vols. (Kuliyapitiya: Sastrodaya Press,
1950, 1951); *Samaja Sevaya,* Dharma Pushpa, no. 2, Trincomalee District Local Government Association (Kuliyapitiya: Sastrodaya Press, 1968). Both Hendiyagala and Dharmapala extol the dedication of
Christian priests.

37. It is a heinous *(parajika,* "defeative") Vinaya offense for a monk to falsely claim supernatural
powers, which renders him a "no-monk" *(assamano)* and "no son of the Sakyas" *(asakkaputtiyo).*

38. Hendiyagala Silaratana, *Samaja Sevaya,* vi–viii. From this point until the start of the discussion
of *Gramasamvardhanaya* below, parenthetical page references are to this work.

world trained a group of people to be agents of social service, namely his disciples. The Buddhist emperor Asoka dedicated himself to social service and so did many ancient kings. The Sinhalas valued social service, and their religion and culture encouraged them in it. So, the explanation for the present lack of a sense of service to others is clear: it is the destruction of that noble culture by the advent of foreign rule. People who grew up according to European customs helped not to foster but to destroy these virtues. We have arrived at the pitiable state in which our own noble natal heritage has now to be reintroduced. This, it will be recalled is Dharmapala all over.

Hendiyagala then illustrates the Buddha's social service, and social service as it is depicted in Buddhist literature. Next, he provides examples of social service from Indian and Sri Lankan luminaries such as Nehru and Dharmapala. Piyadasa Sirisena and Tagore used literature to do social service, and what politicians properly should do is social service. Next, Hendiyagala comes to the point most relevant to us, namely the Dharmapalite idea that the monk is the ideal person, the soldier in the war against social problems. "There is in Lanka a person who more than anyone of these categories just mentioned has the leisure and the ability to engage in service to society, namely, the Buddhist monk" (8). This, as we noted before, was Dharmapala's profound realization. The monk, free of ordinary cares, dedicated to a moral life, having leisure, disciplined in a distinctive culture, and educated—who can be more suited to social service? For the more intelligent and dynamic monk, bored with the humdrum routine of rural monasticism, and lacking the recognition he craves from an urban middle-class society and officialdom, this was a tailor-made assignment. Hence the enthusiastic and easy acceptance of the role by the modern monk and his startling reinterpretation of the Buddha's exhortation to travel and preach the doctrine to mean an exhortation to travel and do social service, despite the disciplinary (vinaya) rules that prevent the monk both from engaging in the proximity that "social service" requires and from doing certain kinds of specific "social service" activity.

Hendiyagala says that in ancient India there were various ascetics and truth seekers but that they all were refugees from society. They were renouncers who did not want any social involvement. The Buddha alone, as soon as he had a core of sixty disciples, on the full moon day of 11 (November), told them to go and traverse the countryside, no two of them going in the same direction, and to preach, for the benefit and happiness of the many, the pure doctrine, meaningful and well composed, beautiful in the beginning, beautiful in the middle, and beautiful at the end. That was the beginning of the Buddhist monk's social service. During this period of 2,556 years, monks have left country and home and traveled thousands of miles and gone amidst different peoples. The social service thus accomplished is beyond description.[39] From the great Arahant Mahinda, who had overcome impurities, to the humblest monk with his impurities intact working today in poor monasteries in jungle villages, social service is what the monks rendered.

Monks, he continues, were in the forefront of the miraculous progress and development of the Sinhala society of the past. The service that is the monk's heritage is not to preach to the people and make them realize Nirvana. If the country is ridden with threats from enemies, if the people have sunk into poverty and are in darkness due to the decline of learning, if they have declined in health and are a sick people, if they are torn by caste and other divisions, of what use is it to preach to them *bana* that is meant for spiritual progress (*marga phala*, lit., paths and fruits)? Here Hendiyagala is echoing Dharmapala through two of his major interpreters, Rahula and Kalukondayave. He uses the term "heritage," a term first used by Rahula to discuss these matters, and he echoes Kalukondayave's doubts as to the use of preaching the *paramattha dhamma* (the essence of the doctrine, active effort towards liberation) to the poor.[40] It is the duty of *anusasakas* (preachers, advisors) to show the path of progress in this world before showing the path to heaven. Monks who live among such a (depressed, poverty-stricken) people, must stop for some time the practices of meditating in seclusion for seeking their own Nirvana and of giving merit to people for providing the fourfold requisites that they give with such hardship for themselves, so that they receive every wealth and fortune in the next world.

In sum, Hendiyagala's point is that monks should give up the selfish act of seeking their own salvation when all they do for the people is give merit while enjoying the food and other needs poor people give at the cost of depriving themselves. He is echoing the Christian critique that Buddhism is selfish, on the one hand, and advocating that something needs to be done about it, on the other. This heralds a profound and revolutionary change of monastic attitude that monks must do something that is of material and this-worldly benefit to the people who serve them so well and with such devotion. As we have seen, this is rooted in Dharmapala and was ably expressed

39. To describe the activities of these missionaries in Buddhist history, Hendiyagala here uses Dharmapala's language, which expresses admiration for the dedication of Christian missionaries, to whom the Buddhist monk compares unfavorably.

40. Dharmapala advocated *paramattha dhamma*, but that was to ask monks not to abandon it in preference to social service (Guruge, ed., *Dharmapala Lipi*, 10).

both in words and action by his soldiers. It is the challenge and the unconscious influence of Christian charity and care of the flock that drove Dharmapala to comprehend and advocate this. There is also a critique here of
the monk's involvement in ritualism and in merit giving, which all these
Dharmapalite monks articulated.

Hendiyagala goes a step further and argues against monks engaging even
in meditation. In his view, meditation in seclusion amounts to a depletion of
manpower that should properly be channeled into the urgent task of regeneration of the people by means of social service. There is also a subtext in
this critique: at this time, there was a great deal of interest in meditation,
both lay and monastic, and a major forest meditation center was Salgala,
located in the northwestern province which was the focus of Hendiyagala's
work. Too much attention to meditation would hinder and challenge the
worldly work he was advocating, not to mention the diversion of manpower.
Therefore Hendiyagala here has a message to these meditating monks, that
they should postpone the selfish act of meditation and come out and help.
An extension of the same subtext is that this is a critique of Vinayavardhana,
the reform movement that was challenging established monasticism for being too worldly. This interpretation is supported by Hendiyagala's emphasizing the point, as if he had the Salagala monks in mind, by giving historical
examples of how ascetics in forest hermitages actually responded to national
service when necessary. The following passage, which for Hendiyagala is a
true picture of what happened in the past, is in fact an expression of his
ideal of how the monk should act. It will be obvious that it is the role that
Dharmapala envisaged:

> [The monks of ancient times] advised the king to build reservoirs like the
> Kalavava. This made the land full in food supplies. They taught the people,
> considering this a service alone [and not for any reward], faultless crafts and
> industries and illuminated the country and nation with knowledge. When
> righteous kings appeared and the country [was] self-sufficient and united,
> they preached *bana* replete with noble ideas to that comfortable and con-
> tented people. To such free men who can let thoughts of liberty be born in
> their minds, they preached on Nirvana, the ultimate of enchanting liberties.
> They themselves, free [of worry] and relaxed, meditated in freedom and real-
> ized Nirvana. (11)

The idea that runs through this passage is the necessity to make a choice and
to relegate to a secondary place the striving for the Nibbanic liberation at
times like the present, when the nation is sunk into poverty and bondage, in

favor of doing work that will bring immediate this-worldly benefits in terms
of a higher standard of living for the people. In this example of the imagined
ancient society, the monks clearly establish priorities: first they advise the
king in the purely material area, the construction of irrigation works necessary to ensure adequate food supplies. That is the first priority. Next they
teach the people the arts and sciences that lie between the material and non-
material, because the applications of knowledge bring material results while
its history has a nonmaterial dimension. It is only as the third priority, when
the country is prosperous, relaxed, and free, that preoccupation with the
spiritual is justified, and the monks can then teach the Nibbanic path. Hendiyagala suggests here again what he explicitly states in a previous paragraph:
when the nation is suffering, even ascetic monks do not have the peace of
mind to meditate, much less teach others how to liberate themselves. Thus
the message for the contemporary monk is clear. They must forget about
meditation for now. They must instead motivate the people to work and
help raise their standards of living. It is only then that they may move on to
concerns with Nirvana. This, we know, is Dharmapala's message.

"Considered thus," says Hendiyagala, "the power a monk has as a social
worker is very great. The services he can do are equally great." But, he
warns, "if a monk is to engage himself in that service honestly and bravely,
he must remain fully free, unfettered by any salary, job, or obligation to the
government or any other institution. To the extent that a monk's life is light
and unburdened by anything, like a bird that flies from tree to tree with only
the weight of its wings, the monk can do honest service to society" (11).
This is a recurring contrast to the tortuous advocacy of salaries and other
mundane benefits for themselves made by the Vidyalankara monks (see
chap. 4).

Like Kalukondayave, Rahula, and of course Dharmapala, Hendiyagala dis-
tinguishes between ritualist observance and true morality. To him morality
is universal and transcends particular religions:

> What in every religion is called merit is what is done for the good of the
> world. That is what we mean by morality *(sila)*. . . . A cultured man is a man
> who lives without being a nuisance to others. That is the truly moral person.
> The criminal who goes to Anuradhapura and puts on white clothes and sits
> in a corner on full moon day but oppresses others during the rest of the week
> is hardly moral. Again the good man who, even if he never puts on white
> clothes (i.e. never observes the higher precepts) even for a day, but takes care
> of his family by means of a just livelihood, and if he conducts his job, whether
> it is trade, agriculture, or salaried employment, as a disciplined person who
> is not a nuisance to others is a truly a moral person. (13)

Hendiyagala comes up with a label to identify the ritualized morality, as opposed to true morality, of a person who puts on white clothes on full moon days while misbehaving during the rest of the month: he calls it *caritra sila,* "the morality of custom." While anti-ritualism is not new in Buddhism—in fact, it is the very hallmark of early Buddhism, which condemned Hindu ritualism—the distinction between morality and ritualism is one that had been forgotten in the process of Buddhism's adaptation to the world, in particular its ruralization. It is a distinction restated in recent times in the reformist writings of Dharmapala and articulated ably by his soldiers like Kalukondayave, Hendiyagala, Hinatiyana, and most brilliantly by the early Rahula.[41]

Hendiyagala includes in social service activity the contributory functions of animals and inanimate objects. He quotes a Sanskrit stanza "uttered by the rishis" which says that the sun, the moon, rain, trees, cows, and good men have been created by fate solely for the welfare of others. Trees by the roadside perform a great social service by giving shade to men standing in the sun. Giant trees like *nuga* and *asatu* do service by providing shelter to birds and venomous snakes like cobras and copperheads *(polanga)*. Dogs repay for the food they get by watching the house against intruders. And the cow, for the grass it eats, works with its entire strength as a work animal, performing a great social service. Here Hendiyagala is reaching towards a different climax: "But does not ungrateful man sell the cow to the butcher when it is no longer capable of work? Merit doers with a heart, can you imagine greater treachery that not even the great earth can bear?"

For the sake of social service, says Hendiyagala, people engage in selfless acts of exploration. His examples again illustrate his very wide definition of social service: climbing the Himalayas, descending into volcanoes, diving into the depths of the sea, exploring Antarctica, going into outer space, and being confined "for thirty or forty years" in laboratories to make discoveries about germs and medications. Not everyone can shine like the sun, but if an effort is made, everyone can shine like a firefly and not exist like a lump of charcoal. Everyone can place a container of water in his yard or on the edge of a wooded area so that animals and little creatures like ants and termites can quench their thirst. He then argues, typically reverting, like all true soldiers, to his Dharmapalite mode, that under the colonial government useless trees have been planted along streets, and he urges instead the planting of useful trees like margosa *(kohomba)* and tamarind *(siyambala)*. The ancient kings grew forests of useful trees like bitter olives *(aralu, bulu)*. These have

41. Walpola Rahula, *Satyodaya* (Colombo: Granthaprakasa, 1933–34; rpt. Colombo: Godage, 1992). Trans. H. L. Seneviratne, unpublished ms.

been cut down and now our forests are being destroyed. Instead, forests should be conserved.[42]

Here his critique is not of the government but the irresponsibility of the villagers who practice slash-and-burn cultivation, destructive of the forest: "It is a crime against the country and religion to cut down and burn these forests for cultivating a minor crop, with no respect to the pious people who establish forest hermitages, the meditators, the government, law, virtue, duty and human rights" (21). (We shall see later that this environmentalist social service was taken up by some monks, but not always in the same spirit as Hendiyagala's). Hendiyagala here is directly critical of the people, in a mild way compared to Dharmapala; also like Dharmapala at moments, he is somewhat admiring of the West: "Many people of our country do not understand what duty [in general] is, far from understanding social service. Some foolish, self-centered people think that obeying the law, respecting the law, and doing one's duty is below their dignity. This is a national weakness of ours. In this regard, the lessons we can learn from the West, especially the British, are very important" (21). He adds here that obeying the law, which children should be taught to do from early on, is a noble social service, because laws are enacted for the well-being of society. This brings out the benign conservatism of Hendiyagala and the rest of the social service monks associated with Vidyodaya. This conservatism enabled them to make their peace with imperial domination while maintaining a healthy attitude of trying to make the best of it for national advancement.

Social service for Hendiyagala is thus a very broad matter. In addition to the activities listed above, including the services rendered by plants and animals and the human activity of planting trees, we should mention a social service that anybody can do: simply to live in a responsible way, that is, by not engaging in activities like vandalism and by avoiding indiscipline in every activity including walking, driving, and riding bicycles. These are elaborations on Dharmapala's *Gihi Vinaya,* the code of conduct for the layman.

We shall now try to further understand Hendiyagala's work by looking at some specifically religio-moral topics on which he wrote. Here we again see

42. Forests should be conserved, among other reasons in a Theravada country, for the use of forest meditators. To facilitate such forest meditation grounds *(tapobhumi)* "suitable for the war against impurities" by establishing, maintaining, and administering them is a great social service. Note the modernized nature of such meditation areas connoted in the idea of maintenance and administration, the very structures the traditional renouncer flees. This emphasis on meditation, apparently contradictory with his anti-meditation stand, is in fact not. What we have here is a matter of priorities—economic and social development first, meditation next, which reverses Rahula's labored idea that monks who take to social service should be those who have attained high spiritual states (see chap. 4).

him in the context of the modernization of Buddhism, whose roots go back
to the nineteenth century, and in the company of Dharmapalite soldiers and
ideas. In particular we see him writing (i.e., preaching, in the print medium)
the new gospel of the thematically focused and modernized dharmadesana,
presented with precision.

In the printed sermon entitled *Atalo dahama* (Eightfold Way of Things),
directed to an urbanizing middle class and published in a series appropriately
called *Asala daham panduru* (Dharma gifts of August), Hendiyagala states how
the world maltreated the great thinkers of the world—the Buddha, Jesus,
Mohammed, Socrates, Aristotle, Plato, Gandhi, Dharmapala. This echoes
an article entitled "The harassments meted out to great people who served
the world" *(Loketa mehekala srestayanta labunu hirihara)* by Walpola Rahula.[43]
Social workers, says Hendiyagala, should be aware that great religious teachers and other thinkers (all of them "social workers") were venerated, but also
subjected to ridicule and harassment. Some who did not have this awareness
became so disillusioned that they went into the forest and never returned to
a human habitation. He quotes a *paccekabuddha* (Silent Buddha) in the *Sutta
nipata:* "It is only if it benefits them that men associate others. Friends who
associate others with no expectation of gain are rare. These impure men
always think of their own interest. Thus the reclusive lives alone like the
rhinoceros."[44]

Next, he gives his own modernist interpretation to the legendary story
of the Daughters of Death, in which they try to seduce the Buddha at the
time of his Enlightenment. In a patrika entitled *Mara Yuddhaya* (The War of
Mara), he explains that maras are not demons but merely sinful thoughts
that have resided in our minds for innumerable births. Warring with maras
is nothing more than fighting these. Since the beginning of the world the
forces of good and the forces of evil have been pitted against each other in a
fierce battlefield. "This is the battle between good men and bad men, virtuous and the virtueless, merit doers and demerit doers, dharma and adharma,
justice and injustice, law and lawlessness, truth and falsity, meritorious
thought and demeritorious thought. That is what the mara yuddha means."
He describes graphically the war-zone mind of the ascetic as he is crossing
the boundaries of a given state to a higher state, a scene of phantom figures
of various types, female figures clothed in luxurious material, same without
clothes, similar male figures, figures of demons *(yaksa),* fearsome figures like

43. *Kalaya,* March 21, 1946.
44. *bhajanti sevanti ca karanattha—nikkarana dullabha ajjamitta
atthattha pana asuci manussa—eko care caggavisanakappo*

leopard, bear, tiger and lion, foul smelling dirty *preta* (goblin) figures, figures of unclean beasts, all of which parade in front of the meditator "like in a cinema." He asks: "Do you think these are a play? No. They are the concretization of impurities that our minds had harbored for innumerable births." He gives glosses for these phantoms: the sensuous nude figures are our desires for pleasure; the fearsome animal figures are the anger and hatred in our minds; the disgusting *preta* figures are miserliness, jealousy, fraud, craftiness and ingratitude.

In the printed patrika entitled *Parabhava Dharma* (1978), there are twelve causes of decline *(parabhava)*. He adds, a thirteenth: "Among all of us is a fault that must be considered the thirteenth reason for *parabhava*. That is, while we have among us the priceless doctrine of the Buddha, we are not prepared to accept it. We only listen to it as custom *(caritra dharma)*. We only learn it. We only take examinations and receive degrees in it. While we complicate it with our own theories . . . we are not prepared to order our lives according to it."[45] This important observation is central to understanding both the state of crisis in Sri Lanka today and the cultural problem of Sri Lanka in general. It is the major point made by Tambiah in his *Buddhism Betrayed?*—the banning of which by the government of Sri Lanka paradoxically proves his (and Hendiyagala's) point.

Another patrika, *Mavpiya Upasthanaya* (Treating Parents, 1957), is about respect and taking care of parents, but it soon turns into a tirade against western customs, which is Dharmapalite almost verbatim. The use of western address terms for parents and kin leads to lessening of love. Indians and Ceylon Tamils were colonized but they never lost their cultural identity. Contrasting India and Ceylon, he states that, although India drove out foreign things as soon as they became free, when we gained our independence we embraced even more foreign customs. Ballroom dancing, rock and roll dancing, nude dancing, nude pictures and figures, obscene pictures and books—these, he states, are more prevalent now than in colonial times.[46] The link between improper care of parents and western customs is, presumably, as follows: women are the socializers of children. Women nowadays have accepted western customs that they bequeath to their children. Since according to western custom, parents are not cared for, the children learn that from their mothers.

Children grow up under the care of parents. Why then cannot they be molded according to parental wishes? . . . There is today a dangerous misfor-

45. Hendiyagala Silaratana, *Parabhava Dharma* (Kuliyapitiya: Sastrodaya, 1978), 28.
46. Hendiyagala Silaratana, *Mavpiya Upasthanaya* (Kurunegala: Rivirasa, 1957), 4.

tune that has befallen us. . . . This is the decline in virtue in our women. Shouldn't we say that it is the women who today more than men desire dancing, tomfoolery like rock and roll, and clothing that does not properly cover the body? Today in the homes of the so called upper classes, Sinhala customs have completely disappeared. Schools today support rather than discourage these tomfooleries. Would it be wrong to say that it is by imitating the teachers that girls of even very good parents get cultured into these bad customs?[47]

Among other monastic disseminators of this attitude were the monks at Vajirarama, the English-speaking elite monastery in Colombo. In the 1940s in his sermons to schoolgirls in Colombo, Narada, the well-known Vajirarama preacher, admonished them not to wear shorts and short dresses, and to make cakes without eggs.[48] They were also admonished not to engage in athletics and bicycling, presumably because of the threat these activities allegedly posed to virginity. This puritanical attitude toward the body, derived from the missionaries but imagined by Dharmapala to be "Aryan," is expressed in the instructions Dharmapala gave "Aryan Sinhala" women as to how they should be clothed: without exposing the navel, breasts and legs. "Aryans never exposed their limbs," Dharmapala wrote, and "black Sinhala [female] legs should not be exposed."[49] Dharmapala objected to the two-piece attire, consisting of a cloth *(redda)* wrapped casually around the waist and a top *(hatte)*, a sensible tropical ensemble universally favored by Sinhala and Kerala women. "It is not appropriate," he wrote, "for noble women to wear a half a cloth *(kamba kalla)* and a short blouse that exposes the midriff *(udaraya)*."[50]

47. Ibid., 5–6.
48. I owe this information to Lalitha (Adihetty) Gunawardena and some other high school students of the time.
49. Guruge, ed., *Dharmapala Lipi*, 33–34, 85.
50. Ibid., 89. Dharmapala's dress code for women is in effect an admission of the fact that what women actually wore was what the code was not. The gist of the code is that women should cover themselves fully except for hands, feet and face. Girls should be admonished to abandon short dresses (Guruge ed., *Dharmapala Lipi*, 85). Dharmapala adds, seemingly objectively and dispassionately, that it has been four-hundred years since the two-thousand-year-old Aryan customs have ceased to exist, and since women took to exposing their bodies.
This attitude to the body, until recently confined to the urban middle classes, has now become generalized to the wider society. The Palace of the Tooth Relic in Kandy, to which access was free, was brought under a dress code by Nissanka Wijeratne, a Colombo bureaucrat and neo-Buddhist, as soon as he was elected trustee (Diyavadana Nilame) of the Palace. The code barred female worshippers or tourists in shorts or short dresses. Further, imitating Christian and Islamic practice in places of worship in some parts of the world, cloth lengths were made available at the gate for rental by the prospective offenders, making a business out of the taboo. This taboo has now been adopted by neo-Buddhist monks such as Inamaluve Sumangala (for visitors to the Dambulla cave temple) and the incumbent of the Isurumuniya temple at Anuradhapura. This contrasts with the Hindu-Buddhist practice of baring the body as a mark of respect for the sacred and one's superiors. Thus an attitude to the body derived

RURAL DEVELOPMENT AS INNER DEVELOPMENT

We will now return to a consideration of Hendiyagala's work on rural development, *Gramasamvardhanaya.* The central thesis of the work is that gramasamvardhana is actually an internal, moral matter. It is not, as often supposed, building roads, bridges, wayside rests *(ambalama),* and playgrounds, or sinking wells in the villages, but the development of men and women who live in those villages. A basic ingredient of development is the ability and strength to accept with a smiling face when our weaknesses are pointed out to us. This is a favorite statement of the Dharmapalites, especially Kalukondayave. We have here a subtextual reference to Dharmapala, who did not mince his words when he talked about these "weaknesses." The blame for the state of underdevelopment of the people, says Hendiyagala, should go to monks and other rural elite members and not to the people. This again is a defense and reiteration of Dharmapala, who repeatedly mentions, in frustration and sadness, that monks in particular but lay elites as well are slow to heed his exhortations, and who contrasts this with the admirable nature of the commitment of Christian missionaries to their cause. Hendiyagala amplifies this by mentioning one heroic example, Livingstone, and by quoting from his diaries.[51]

Elaborating on the Dharmapalite idea that monks should be the soldiers of rural development, and placing development on a multi-religious basis, Hendiyagala further expounds his approach:

There are today in Lanka places of worship at the rate of one for every three or four villages, if not in every village. By places of worship I do not mean

from the Christian missionaries has been foisted on the Sinhala Buddhists on the theory that this is an immemorial Aryan custom. If the Aryan queens of the past were to mysteriously appear in these temples, they would either be barred from entry, or would have to go through the humiliation of renting a piece of cloth to conform to the present dress code. For a more objective description of how ancient Sinhala women dressed themselves, see Martin Wickramasinghe, *Purana Sinhala stringe anduma* (Maharagama: Saman Press, 1935; rpt. 1960).

51. Hendiyagala writes: "Lessons are many that noble people who are friends of gramasamvardhana and who are involved in it can derive from these words that the great social worker, the priest Dr. Livingstone, who, having left London in 1840, spent full 30 years endeavoring to civilize the jungle dwelling Negro people, while suffering their harassment, and died there, has written in his diary." Hendiyagala admiringly notes Livingstone's disappointments and hopes by quoting Livingstone's diary entries for the end of one year and the beginning of the next: "Now we have come to the end of 1866. That year was not a very fruitful or productive year. I will try in the year 1867 to work better, try harder and to be more kind and compassionate."

"May the Lord full of truth and kindness epitomize his character in me. May he cause to arise in me the desire to show kindness and compassion, truthfulness, honesty and respectfulness" (quoted in *Gramasamvardhanaya,* 1:3).

only Buddhist monasteries, but sacred places of all religious groups such as Roman Catholics, Hindus, and Muslims. In connection with rural or social development, the exemplary center for the village or cluster of villages should be the place of worship. A place of worship should be maintained in such a way as to provide lessons in rural development for the people of the area. First let us divide the development we are talking about into two parts, external and internal. And let us divide external development in turn into the three sections, economic development, health development, and behavioral development, and the internal development into two sections, intellectual and moral. A person who develops properly in all five areas, economic, health, behavioral, intellectual, and moral, is a person developed fully externally and internally. If a village is complete with men and women so developed, that village, by nature of the requirements of such development, will have all it needs. It is the place of worship of the village that must provide guidance for this fivefold development. It is only when such social needs are met *(siddhavana kalhi)* by the place of worship, that it will become one *(siddhastanaya)* in the literal sense. In my view, it is with that expectation that the ancient kings donated hundreds of acres of land and paddy fields to the old Buddhist places of worship. (1:5–6)

The following points are notable in this passage: (1) To begin with, this is a critique of established landlordist monasticism. (2) It depicts a theory of development which is holistic, with the central role played by factors interior to the individual. (3) It centralizes activity in the village place of worship, implicating the elites, especially the religious functionary, as a major role player. (4) Though located in the center of worship and otherwise structurally dominated by religious organization, religion covers only one fifth of the envisaged social and moral development at best. (5) Despite the obvious fact that the empirical basis of the imagined center is the Buddhist monastery, the concept consciously makes it universalistic and multi-religious. (6) In the statement that a place of worship becomes truly so solely by nature of its capacity as an instrument that fulfills social needs, it restates the Dharmapalite conception, elaborated by Kalukondayave and others, of the moral nature of economic activity, both based in morality and productive of moral worth. As we know, this econo-moral conduct involves looking after one's affairs efficiently and taking care of one's family. A further restatement of this is the idea that the ancient kings, by their endowment of the monasteries, placed on the monks an obligation to promote the economic, social, and moral well-being of the people, making their return gift to the laity both moral and material. The implicating of the king through endowments at once echoes and affirms the Dharmapalite theory of benign paternalistic kingship, with the monk playing a key role, and it confers on the monk a widely defined role in the personal and social life of the laity. With the central part of gramasamvardhana theory thus formulated, Hendiyagala takes up each of the aspects of development. I shall consider only one, the economic, to illustrate its ancestry in Dharmapala, and in particular to bring out, as I did in the case of Kalukondayave, the elevation of economic activity to the moral domain. This equation of success in this world with happiness and liberation in the next is the core of the theory of *ubhayalokartha,* the gaining of both worlds.

THE MORALITY OF THE ECONOMIC

Hendiyagala first defines economic development (1:6) as the increase in the goods and resources of a person. Consciously continuing to place his discussion beyond any particular religion, he says that all religions outline in their doctrines how men could improve themselves economically. For Buddhism he gives, as examples, (a) the *Parabhava sutta* (The Discourse on Decline), (b) the causes of destruction of wealth in the *Sigalovada sutta,* and (c) the *sapta aparihaniya dharma,* the sevenfold dharmas that prevent decline (sometimes known as the Buddha's advice to the Vajjis). He refers to folktales in which people pay a fee to experts to ask for economic advice but reassures that no such fee needs to be paid to religious specialists for giving that advice. Basing himself on the *Sigalovada,* but making adjustments suitable for modern society in Sri Lanka, Hendiyagala lists six factors that impoverish a man and make him "hellward bound" *(apayamukha),* thus connecting inextricably, as he did before and as did Dharmapala and Kalukondayave, prosperity in this world with a good rebirth in the next. The list clearly constitutes instructions for an inner-worldly asceticism in which time is measured in coffee spoons and idling, leisure, and enjoyment are banished:

1. Use of alcohol, ganja (marijuana), opium, and so forth.
2. Loitering in the streets and in the villages at all hours in the night.
3. Seeing films, plays, and *nadagam* (folk performances).
4. Gambling by means of betting on horses or card games.
5. Associating with false friends who do these things.
6. Laziness. (1:7)

Hendiyagala elaborates upon each of the above. For example, expressing great concern at the sums of money spent on seeing films, Hendiyagala says the film should be used to promote health, education, culture, and good behavior. And he is shocked at the time wasted the next day because of people staying awake to see films or other shows the previous night. In the category of gambling he includes all kinds of fraudulent trades and vending activities that deceive people into buying or participating. Besides, the gramasamvardhana system itself (by this time brought under a government department, the Department of Rural Development) has become a den of corruption. In discussing association with bad company, Hendiyagala enters into a long discussion of a subject which re-opens like a wound in his writings: namely, the harassment of the very people who selflessly engage in gramasamvardhana and other social work by means of anonymous letters and broadsides, petitions with false signatures, and false accusations.

Hendiyagala further charges that belief in karma, the worship of deities, and the practice of astrology make the Sinhala people lazy (1:15). The belief that if one's karma is good there is no need to exert, or that nothing will work because the astrological timing is bad—such are excuses for inaction. But Hendiyagala then uses the same ideas himself, although with a characteristically modernist interpretation: "It is easier to reap fruits of this world's karma than that of the next world's. . . . Even the deities and the planets help the man who is strong, persistent, and pure, and the deities and the good planets do not even look at the lazy man" (1:16). The topic of laziness then takes him back to aimless loitering and the all-important theme: time. "If someone were to ask me what the most noble and valuable thing in the world, my answer is 'time'. No one can ever make up for lost time in this entire samsara." We are reminded of Kalukondayave's preoccupation with time, and his determination not to waste even a second of it.

In the recent history of Sri Lanka, no one articulated the importance of work more forcefully than Dharmapala and, after him, his soldiers of regeneration like Kalukondayave, Hinatiyana, and Hendiyagala. What is even more striking and novel is their suffusion of work with morality and their promise that hard work, that is, the proper use of time without being lazy, will ensure not only prosperity in this world but a better situation in the next life and eventual liberation. Emphasis on time, work, and the dangers of sloth are too integral to Protestant Christianity to have been invented by Dharmapala independent of it, especially considering his early socialization at the hands of the missionaries and his own admission that he "learned to do everything the Reformed Church way." We should here remember that Kalukondayave, Hinatiyana, and Hendiyagala, in addition to being powerfully influenced by Dharmapala, also had their impressionable early schooling in missionary schools. Attributing these values to "ancient Buddhism" enabled their easy acceptance by those who transcended rural Buddhism and imbibed "ancient Buddhism."

In a program of national regeneration, it was natural to advocate these values, as opposed to ritualism, as the authentically Buddhist ones. This is what Hendiyagala does in *Gramasamvardhanaya*. He points out that a group of monks who exhibit these values has come into being. While monks have been, he continues, accused in the past of "filling spittoons" (i.e., doing nothing useful), this allegation does not apply to those monks who are industrious and who make proper use of time. And he is eager to point out that such new monks are doing proper social service by teaching the people (a) that development is less an economic than a moral matter and, therefore, interior to the individual and (b) that development involves the cultivation of morality and the rejection of ritualism and other traditional practices, including the building of religious edifices. As in the case of Kalukondayave, it is not a question of denying the other world, but one of the priorities. As Hendiyagala puts it, "It is true that there is for man a next world. It is also true that that next world should be made comfortable. What that needs is good character. What should be considered more important is the here and now" (1:20).

The theme here, repeated in the works of Kalukondayave, Rahula, Hinatiyana, and Hendiyagala, is that the other world is important but that it can wait until this world is won, which will automatically ensure the other world. "Let us imagine there is a monk in a certain monastery who has understood properly what Buddhism really is about. That educated, compassionate monk, who sees his *dayaka*s (donors, lay supporters) declining in morality, and their children declining in knowledge of the *dharmasastra*, knows that using the meager amount of money that the villagers have to build a monastery for him is not going to help. When he contemplates the path that the founder of his religion took, that monk realizes that the one service that is due from him to his dayakas is first to steer these dayakas away from immorality, and save his village from the terrible crime of not making available to the children an education with which they could better their lives, and next, if necessary, if the villagers still want to, build the monastery" (1:21). As we have seen repeatedly, the priorities are clear: this world comes first, and then the next, if all parties are still interested.

But here is the rub. If the monk goes ahead with that noble idea, the elite dayakas will accuse the monk of making the monastery desolate *(palu)* and of not undertaking building work. Why do they do this? Because they gain the honor if they get the building done, and, by diverting the monk's attention to building work, they also prevent the poor children getting from an education and improving themselves. Such motives indicate an ignorance of what Buddhism is: "As far as I have been able to judge, what the dayakas of most monasteries want to do is to get their monk to build more and more buildings in the monastery premises, by resort to whatever means possible. They do not care much about any guidance or advice the monk can give them. They expect neither morality nor education in their monk. Their pleasures come from the extent to which their monastery supersedes the one in the neighboring village in the number of buildings built, with their names publicized as being responsible" (1:21).

Hendiyagala goes on to describe how this affects the monk. He has to leave aside the knowledge he gained painfully, studying for examinations, which he planned to use to help the improvement of rural education levels, and get into the "business of construction." He must thenceforth do things that are unworthy of a monk. He has to enact rules to control the dayakas. He has to go from shop to shop buying building material. He has to forget the dignity of his monkness and go up to wealthy people of different religions and nationalities and pester them for donations, to lay foundation stones, to open and to auction flower baskets *(malvatti)*. This erodes the monk's nobility and self-respect. Thenceforth the monk can get no proper sleep. If the work that has been started is unfinished, it is a matter for embarrassment. The laborers pester the monk for wages. The freedom of being a monk is gone. The renouncer's life of unparalleled tranquillity becomes one of unparalleled troubles. It is perfectly acceptable if dayakas want to get together in piety, collect funds, and build buildings peacefully and happily. It is the monk's duty to give such a project his advice and guidance. But if the dayakas put the burden of building temples entirely on the monk, and thus destroy the monk's freedom, that is not a good thing (1:21–22).

Hendiyagala here disapproves in no uncertain terms the "business of construction" as an activity to which the monk should devote his time. But for many monks it is an important part of monastic life, explicitly termed "developing the place" *(sthane diyunu kirima)*. We shall see later how in their advocacy of secularism in the monkhood, the Vidyalankara monks tried to bring building works within what they called "monkness" *(mahanakama)*.

A monastery needs monks, continues Hendiyagala, not to build various structures but to guide the dayakas and to train their young in discipline and morality. This is not all. The laity also expect the monk, in addition to the ritualism of *dana, bana,* and *pansakula* (funeral ritual), to do meaningless things; they expect the monk to go to the next village's monastery in a procession, raise funds by going from place to place, and thank the laity for their donations for building construction. They come to the monastery, not for any moral guidance but to borrow money, rice, work animals, or a cart, or to get an auspicious moment determined and a horoscope cast. And they come drunk. When the monk accedes to these demands, his values are turned upside down, says Hendiyagala, and the blame lies squarely on the laity (1:22). Hendiyagala accuses the laity of not doing their part in advancing the goals of gramasamvardhana—honest, productive work in agriculture, husbandry, and the crafts, diligence, temperance, and morality, all part of the development of the inner individual.

DIET, HEALTH, AND NATIONAL CUSTOMS

Many of Hendiyagala's prescriptions concerning which foods are to be consumed or avoided restate advice previously given by Dharmapala. Thus, people must eat fruits and vegetables and avoid not only fish and meat, but also dried fish and sweet potatoes (both of which incidentally are the mainstay of the standard rural diet). While smoking and alcohol are obviously taboo, people must also keep away from drinking excessively sugared tea, although up to about three cups of moderately sweetened tea seem to be acceptable. Hendiyagala also condemns unclean food preparation, the unsanitary handling of food in eating places, and the unconscientious practice of making money by feeding unclean food to people under unclean conditions. He criticizes health inspectors for not doing anything about this. In addition, ayurvedic medicinal herbs are left exposed and dirty in stores. How much better, exclaims Hendiyagala, if they are kept clean and packed safely. Gramasamvardhana societies can help by taking an interest in food cleanliness and safety in their area.

Health is the indispensable basis of gramasamvardhana. The enemies here are the usual: imported foods, canned foods, dried fish, alcohol, and lack of sleep due to immoral nocturnal activities like seeing films and plays. Poor health standards are the result of eating the wrong foods: for example, people sell nutritious fruits and buy dried fish and other bad foods and drink tea derogatorily described as "a brew made of dry scraps" *(rodu vatura)*. People have no wells, so they drink unclean tank water. They eat boiled gram (chick peas) from vendors. Childhood diseases are not treated due to the ignorance of parents, which affect children's lives. People invite monks to unclean houses. People should eat healthy food like rice with bran, and vegetables, and drink healthy liquids like boiled water and king coconut water (i.e., "coconut milk" in English usage). They must inhale clean air by making houses airy and letting in germ-killing sunlight. All these improvements should be included in gramasamvardhana.

Gramasamvardhana is most of all *caritasamvardhana,* the development of behavior, i.e., civic behavior and courtesy. Like Dharmapala, Hendiyagala sees weaknesses in Sinhala businessmen; they lack of courtesy, for example, in contrast to those of other ethnic groups who are polite and courteous. Hendiyagala also follows Dharmapalite standards in describing how to behave in public places, bathing places, highways, bazaars, restaurants, trains, buses, airplanes, at home, at a wedding, at a funeral, at a monastery, at a church, at a shrine of the gods *(devale),* at a theater, a meeting, and even a palace. Proper eating habits are outlined through a critique of existing habits (1:52–53). Development involves respect towards other religions, and getting rid of folk performances *(kolam)* near temples. Gramasamvardhana also includes the cultivation of national customs *(jatika caritrasamvardhanaya).* This includes speaking one's own language (rather than English), using the oriental form of greeting (rather than shaking hands), and writing postal addresses in Sinhala. Ballroom and other forms of western dancing are to be avoided. Girls should not run, ride bicycles, drive, race, walk alone, wear short dresses, cut their hair short, or use nail polish. These are good habits now-a-days he grants, but not for Sinhala girls. People should not eat beef or drink alcohol during weddings. From these "national customs," Hendiyagala outlines "common social customs" *(podu samaja caritra).* For example, proper marriage: "If a man and a woman want to get married, there are accepted methods of doing so in the civilized world, by registering first and having a marriage next. Despite this, many village people ignore this respectable custom and live together for a year or so and separate, and they keep doing this."[52] "Who are responsible for the children?" asks Hendiyagala, and "How many more customs like this do we have that need improvement?" (1:60). Another example is coordinating agriculture.

Hendiyagala lists the work that should be done by a Gramasamvardhana Society. It is easy to see that the core concepts are Dharmapalist, although the list itself is more elaborate in some ways.

1. First, start a Gramasamvardhana Society in your village. Ask and expect the support of the village monk or the pastor of the local church, school teachers, the headman.

---

52. Hendiyagala is here again true to Dharmapalite form, which considers western Christian monogamous marriage as both civilized and indigenous. In fact the Sinhala people practiced both polygyny and polyandry. Registering marriage between a man and a woman, which Hendiyagala considers to be civilized, was unknown in precolonial society. Further, the sacrality of the monogamous union that underlies Hendiyagala's comments here was nowhere so in the Sinhala system. Temporary unions, known to the modern West as "living together," were socially accepted. See Bina Agrawal, *A Field of One's Own,* 182; Richard Gombrich and Gananath Obeyesekere, *Buddhism Transformed,* 255–73.

2. Then form also a Kulangana Samitiya (a women's association).
3. Start a dharma school (Sunday school) and hand over its management to the Kulangana Samitiya.
4. Build a meeting hall in the center of the village and have a free library and sports facility there.
5. If there is no school in your area, build one and hand it over to the government.
6. Open a free pharmacy.
7. Build a home for the aged and try to treat well the aged in your village and vicinity.
8. Try to build a common water source for the village.
9. Start a co-operative society and run it well without letting it deteriorate into an exploitative institution.
10. Start, through the women's association, on a co-operative basis, home-based industries like weaving bags, *vatti* (trays), *petti* (baskets), and embroidery *(renda getima)*.
11. Build a fleet of ox-drawn carts and take the local products for sale to markets.
12. Establish a health center.
13. Start a milk feeding center. (Feed the children local, and not imported milk.)
14. Organize a "house for mothers" for pregnant women.
15. Start a common farm while improving farming privately as well.
16. Start centers for carpentry, metal smithing, coir yarn making, and weaving, one of each kind for the village.
17. Try to resolve conflict within the village itself.
18. Work in the rice and *chena* ("slash and burn") fields co-operatively and in a coordinated manner.
19. Start a common fund in the village itself.
20. Lend money to villagers interest free and make them pay back.
21. Let the association as a whole take the responsibility of selling the produce of the village.
22. Meet once every week.
23. Arrange public talks twice a month on health, civility, crime prevention, and so forth.
24. Build roads in and for access to the village.
25. If the village cannot help itself, do not have much faith in outside help. (2:75–76)

This list conveys the substance of Hendiyagala's theory of rural development. It is in fact, not theory at all but a practical guide, although his book, *Grama-samvardhanaya,* begins with a theory interspersed with a social critique. The basic idea is self-help, and the conception of society underneath both "theory" and practical guide is one of numerous, decentralized, self-contained, and self-sufficient village communities—as were dreamt of by the colonial European writers and appropriated and imagined by Dharmapala to be the genuine Sinhala society of the past. Despite this mooring in the past, it is also a modern society making use of modern knowledge, industry, craft, and improvements in health, education, and so forth. These ideas were fervently put into action nationally by Kalukondayave, regionally by Hendiyagala, and locally by Hinatiyana, all three using the newly invented mode of preaching, the time-framed and thematically focused dharmadesana, to exhort people to work hard and gain both worlds in one stroke.

The most enduring activity of gramasamvardhana has been the co-operative society. In the 1970s, such co-operatives, now brought under the monolithic Co-operative Wholesale Establishment (CWE), more or less took over the entire wholesale and retail distribution of food and clothing, thereby demonstrating the vulnerability of village-based structures either to inner decay or to conglomeration. As they became national institutions, the co-operatives became part of a tentacular bureaucracy.

This brings us to the central weakness of the rural development project, namely its romantic and idyllic nature. It was Dharmapala's imagined village community, based on European conceptualizations, as the vital building block of a regenerated society that in the first place gave rise to the project. Dharmapala himself was well read in English, had traveled widely, in India, Europe, America and Japan, and had gained first-hand experience of industrial technological society and capitalist enterprise, an experience for which he also had preparation in growing up in an enterprising family, in a dynamic colonial commercial city, and in a Christian missionary school. His followers, the "soldiers" and "hero-giants" of his project, had none of this. While their early schooling was in Christian schools, this was elementary, and their broader education was confined to the doctrinal texts and Sinhala and Pali literature, which gave them no exposure to any kind of knowledge dealing with social and economic institutions. Their imagination could grasp only the idyllic and romantic part of the Dharmapalite vision, which even under the best conditions had no scope for accommodating a process of self-generating economic and social development. Their vision bore family resemblances to the village based, anti-industrial, anticapitalist system articulated by Gandhi and his disciples, including Jay Prakash Narayan and Vinobha Bhave. Their rural communities were vulnerable to numerous forces that could and did nullify them overnight, ranging from state control to incentive-based alternatives, and from the appeal of ideology to the very cultural conditions that the project was supposed to combat. They simply had neither the vision nor the qualifications to launch a meaningful activist project.[53]

But these monks had their hearts in the right place. Because they were convinced of the truth and feasibility of Dharmapala's message, they tried to do what he told them to do to the best of their capacity. They represent a pragmatic nationalism as opposed to a nationalist ideology with built-in propensities for degeneration into narrow ethnic and religious chauvinism. Their education and socialization was traditional as was their "monkness," about which the Vidyalankara monks made a loud, self-conscious, and futile defense, and which for these monks was unnecessary because they had nothing to hide. They did not explicitly talk about their monkness or have to define or defend it, because their lifestyle conformed to accepted rules of monkness, and they had no personal or ideological reason to change that lifestyle. They were patriots without being narrow nationalists, and they were able to conceptualize in principle a social order in which the economic was primary, with the potential for economic self-interest to triumph over ideology, aided by the inner-worldly asceticism they, after Dharmapala, were able to fashion. They made accommodations to a government that they knew fully well to be alien and imperial, but which they chose to interpret as representing the familiar notion of kingship to which obedience was due. In this too they represented a benevolent aspect of tradition. They were, however, nontraditional to the extent that they were influenced by both Dharmapala and the neo-Buddhist ethic of the urban atmosphere of the time, although both dovetailed with the "Protestant" spirit of ancient Buddhism.

These monks represent a conservative and nonideological approach to development that accepted ethnic and cultural diversity as a fact of Sri Lankan life. They represent a conservative as opposed to a radical socialism, and a specific path of ethnic harmony and national development which, had it not been undermined by the ideology brewing at Vidyalankara, had a fair chance of guiding the different ethnic groups that comprise Sri Lanka towards prosperity and harmonious nationhood. In this sense they represent a

53. G. de Soyza's *Report on Rural Reconstruction,* cited above, was very critical of the project. According this report, the work done by the police in Kegalla "suffered from an excessive showmanship" (16). It refers to the "undue sentimentality that the cry of Rural Reconstruction has come to acquire" and "the opportunity that private individuals have taken to trade on the cry" (53). "Rural Reconstruction is getting to be considerably overdone in the country. The gospel has suffered much through "hot gospelling" and is in danger of developing into what is vulgarly called a 'racket'" (53). While this is an unduly harsh critique, and reflects the arrogance of the colonized mentality towards anything indigenous—though not truly "indigenous"—there is no doubt that the movement failed to achieve its objectives and withered away.

continuity with the dominant current of history, which was inclusivist and accommodative as opposed to the alternative current of exclusion and hegemony which could and did exist only ideologically due to the inherent nature of the premodern polity. With the advent of British rule and de facto centralization, the path was cleared for the dormant exclusivist current to awaken with force and encompass the social order. In the next chapter I discuss the sociology of this project, with special reference to some monks who were at its forefront.

VIDYALANKARA: THE DESCENT INTO IDEOLOGY

With the approach of the mid 1940s, the rightist ruling elite that soon became the United National Party (UNP) was clearly showing signs of apprehension about the socialist movement, which had made its debut in the mid 1930s. The Lanka Sama Samaja Party (LSSP), the original socialist party and the first effective Sri Lankan political party, was founded in London in 1935. Upon return to Sri Lanka the young intellectuals of the LSSP launched themselves in the country, successfully and dramatically, by means of two activities. The first was their assumption of leadership of the Suriya Mal (Sunflower) movement. This movement came into being in 1936 due to the dissatisfaction of some ex-servicemen as to the apportionment of funds collected through the sale of poppies on Remembrance Day. In the hands of the LSSP the Suriya Mal movement was molded into a purely anti-imperialist campaign with no relation to the issue of the ex-servicemen. This campaign went on for the next four years until the outbreak of war in 1939.

The second springboard of the LSSP's successful launch was their swift response, under the banner of Suriya Mal, to the malaria epidemic of 1934–35, especially in the badly affected Kegalla district. In addition, the LSSP lost no time in taking advantage of the Bracegirdle incident—the attempt by the British colonial government in Ceylon to deport a young Australian Communist, M. A. Bracegirdle, for taking an interest in trade union activity and for speaking on LSSP platforms.[1] In June 1940 the leaders of the LSSP

1. The clever handling of this matter gave the LSSP the opportunity to define themselves as the only genuine anti-imperialist force, and it "brought the LSSP into the limelight on a national scale, and gave it substantial publicity and increased popularity" (*University of Ceylon History of Ceylon,* ed. K. M. de Silva [Peradeniya: The University of Ceylon, 1973], 513).

were arrested for detention without trial under the defense regulations, while the Communists who took their orders from Moscow remained free. During the war most of the leadership broke out of jail and escaped to India, and the party went underground. Thus there were two anti-imperialist forces in Sri Lanka at the time. The first, emanating from Dharmapala, was a broad nationalist movement led by the indigenous elite including some monks. The second was the LSSP. The Marxists, though "nationalist," came from the westernized elite. It is a measure of the sharp division between the westernized and indigenous elites that these two streams functioned independently of each other until brought together (for a short time) by a common connection with India. A group of monks who had followed Dharmapala to Calcutta and had been exposed to Indian nationalism there later made Vidyalankara the center of their intellectual and political activities.[2] By the mid 1940s these monks became openly associated with Marxism in general and the LSSP in particular. As later developments show, the Marxism of these monks was superficial. Their true connection with the LSSP was anti-imperialism, which in a deeper sense expressed their indigenous roots and connected them with Dharmapala. Thus Vidyalankara, from the infancy of its modern political activity, embraced the political, i.e., nationalist and ideological, agenda of Dharmapala to the diminution and later total exclusion of the more sober and beneficial economic agenda that was espoused by their counterparts at their sister college, Vidyodaya. The Vidyalankara monks continued to talk about socialism, but this has to be distinguished from the international socialism of the Marxists. Theirs was rather a "Buddhist Socialism." Increasingly it became more "Buddhist" than socialist, and by the mid 1950s it turned into a hegemonic Sinhala Buddhist chauvinism.

The contrast between the Marxist-dominated and anti-imperialist Vidyalankara and the conservative Vidyodaya could not be greater. The position of Vidyodaya can be illustrated by an incident, the occasion of the prize-giving on August 4, 1928, presided over by Governor J. Herbert Stanley. The governor was welcomed with the following felicitation, *stuti patra,* in a mixture of Pali, Sanskrit, and Sinhalese:

2. At the failure of his case to establish Buddhist control at Buddha Gaya, Dharmapala moved to Calcutta and established his activities there. He was interested in getting monks educated in Indian universities for missionary and social work. The monks who followed him to Calcutta, such as Naravila Dhammaratana, were exposed to the Indian Nationalist movement, and many of them located themselves at Vidyalankara. Indian monks such as Rahula Samkrityayana visited and worked at Vidyalankara. Although Vidyodaya also had Indian visitors, these visitors were not politically involved. Groomed in an indigenous anti-imperialism by Dharmapala, the monks at Vidyalankara, in the post-Dharmapalite era, turned to the Marxists who were articulating their own Marxist anti-imperialism.

The king named George the Fifth, in whose dominions the sun, as though unable to over-reach his sway, never sets, may he live long, steeped in glory.

May Your Excellency too, Lanka's noble Ruler, be ever victorious. May all prosperity be yours. With joy do we welcome you on your arrival here.

In prowess like the lion-king, in glory like the sun, may Sir Herbert Stanley, Governor of Ceylon, flourish, free from blemish, full of compassion, advancing the world's weal, as bright as the full-moon in the autumnal sky.

Your Excellency, for want of knowledge the people of Ceylon suffer interminably. Shake (off) their thirst, you of pleasant and joyous speech, rout the darkness of ignorance; kindle the torch of knowledge; thus may your glory, like a banner, fly.

Appointed by the emperor supreme among the lords of the earth, have you come to Lanka, as her ruler, to further her prosperity? May all good be yours; may you, this day exert yourself in the cause of knowledge.

Your Excellency, the sun and the moon illumine only that which is visible to the eye; the light of knowledge, cultivated and increased, makes manifest even things unseen. May Your Excellency live long, endowed with the highest happiness, fostering the growth of knowledge in this land. That for you will be the highest service.[3]

While it is possible to consider this a traditional conception replete with images of *cakkavatti* (universal) kingship, it is also possible to describe it as the epitome of servility. The same journal in its 1928 issue published the governor's address in which he refers to the practice of his presiding over the prize-giving "at this seat of learning" as "an unbroken practice undertaken by the governors of the island,"[4] which further brings out the conservative and pro-colonialist position of Vidyodaya. In another act of conspicuous loyalty, *Vidyodaya* of January 15, 1928 carried an editorial wishing the recovery of the ailing George V, which describes in exaggerated terms, again reminiscent at once of formalized traditional respect and abject servility, the "well-known fact of the compassion of both the British empire and the royal family" and the belief of the writer that "there is no one in this human world who has not enjoyed the fruits of the great majesty's compassion." The Sinhalese have always been supreme in their loyalty to their king, and the editor wishes the king speedy recovery "by the power of the Triple Gem." He points out further that "the good that has come to Buddhism from the British crown is immeasurable" and concludes by urging "all Buddhists to do what acts of merit they can, give merit to the gods and implore them to save the king."

3. *Vidyodaya* 3, no. 9 (1928): 271.
4. Ibid., 233.

These sentiments were reiterated in the State Council (legislature) by the Leader of the House Don Baron Jayatilake, which no doubt was part of the expression of formal courtesy, but it was also expressive of both the conservative and imperialist stand of the ruling elite on the one hand and Jayatilake's own sentiment, closely associated as he was with the monastic establishment.[5] The governor's speech also echoed their civil yet servile sentiments and expressed his admiration of the moral and intellectual achievements of the Vidyodaya college.

The connection between Vidyodaya and the imperial government is further exemplified in the relations between the founder of the college, Hikkaduve Sumangala, and the government. His biographer Yagirala Pannananda mentions an incident where the prelate was greeted by the governor Arthur Hamilton at a railway station. Apparently Sumangala's train had stopped at the station to make way for the governor's and the governor, seeing the former, alighted and walked over, which must be considered an act of the highest courtesy by a British Governor. In 1867 the government headed by Governor Hercules Robinson honored Sumangala with the incumbency and title of Sri Pada (*Sri Pada padaviya*). Thus the government's relations with Hikkaduve were excellent and may have facilitated its relations with the college. In 1876 Hikkaduve hurriedly organized the first prize-giving at Vidyodaya so that he could have Governor Henry Gregory preside over it at least once, before his departure in 1877. Thus Vidyodaya was associated with the government from its very inception, its founder's own relations with the government antedating the founding of the college. It appears that it became a custom for the governor to preside over the prize-giving, and the occasion became a virtual state ceremony, with VIPs in attendance. Some of these were attended by many political leaders including Ponnambalam Arunachalam and Ponnambalam Ramanathan.

It is not that Vidyodaya was lacking in some ambivalence. These pro-empire sentiments may have had something at least to do with protocol and propriety so that the college and its leaders could be in the good books of the government. A confession made by the eminent Vidyodaya monk Kalukondayave Pannasekhara expresses this ambivalence. When at the prize-giving of 1915 he received a prize from Governor Robert Chalmers, he was exhilarated, feeling "as if I went to heaven." But in his autobiography Kalukondayave states: "Now it embarrasses me to think of it, to think that I, wearing a robe, went to the feet of a layman and got a prize. But it is not surprising that I did not think that was below dignity to do so. Even my aging

5. *Hansard,* March 31, 1936, 27.

teachers thought that was *raja gavravaya,* a royal honor. The governor of the island aside, even going to a white man [i.e., government agent] and receiving the act of appointment as a nayaka [chief monk] was then considered something very high. . . . Thus the leader of the white rulers who stole the country, as well as minor [white] officials like the agent were then considered gods. . . . In such a country and such a time, is it surprising to consider it a high achievement to get a prize from the leader of the ruling clique?"[6]

This is about the furthest Vidyodaya seems to have gone in its anti-imperialist critique. Kalukondayave is here articulating the standard critique, but he lacks the venom and bitterness with which the Vidyalankara monks articulated it. Besides and more importantly, there is a healthy realism in his attitude, as if to say it is too bad that there is imperialist domination, but it is a fact that it is there, and one should make the best out of the situation.[7] The paradoxical fact that Dharmapala, the greatest critic of imperialism, was associated with Vidyodaya brings out the centrality in his thought of the economic, although it was the ideological content of his thought that in the end triumphed.

By the mid 1940s, the rightist ruling party, their worries made the more acute by the approaching election, were organizing themselves and their forces against the Marxists, especially the LSSP, whose popularity was growing daily. Among the forces opposed to the Marxists, the most powerful were the country's major newspapers, especially those of the Lake House group. This was in an era when the print media were the dominant and the most persuasive. The Lake House papers were joined by the nationalist newspapers *Sinhala Jatiya* and *Sinhala Bauddhaya,* the latter founded by Dharmapala. That Dharmapala's ideological progeny were supportive of the status quo with its slavish acceptance of imperialism, although ironic, brings out the divide between the pragmatic and the ideological in his work and the fact that the balance could well have tipped against ideological. It did in the 1947 elections, which returned the existing pragmatic leadership to office. But that outcome only exacerbated the divide and made the ideological impulse more virulent. The 1947 election frustrated the traditional nationalist elite, especially the monks, and made their resolve stronger, which

6. Kalukondayave Pannasekhara, *Svyamlikhita Sri Pragnasekhara Caritapadanaya,* 93–94.

7. It is possible to speculate here that, had Vidyodaya, with this realistic view of imperialism, triumphed over Vidyalankara with its bitter and paranoid view, the fate of the country would have been different. It would, then, have been placed on the path of realism, accommodating the necessary evil of imperialism and using it to the country's advantage. Such an attitude also would have bred pluralism and a willingness to accommodate ethnic and other minorities as well as tolerance and the creative accommodation of dissent.

led to their victory ten years later in 1956 and to the implementation of an ideologically based nationalist program. In 1947 however, a substantial section of this elite, the rural petit bourgeoisie, supported the ruling rightist elite, as did the Vidyodaya monks.

In addition to the newspapers, there were other publications—posters, pamphlets, broadsides, and booklets—designed to stall the progress of the Marxists. There was in particular a poster that depicted a burning stupa and proclaimed "Save Buddhism from Marxism." The public speakers, especially the Vidyodaya monks and their students spread over the countryside, painted fearful portraits of Marxism and Marxist societies. For example, it was claimed that if the Samasamajists (Marxists, socialists) come to power, mother and father both will be "comrades." This was an insinuation that incest was lawful under Marxism. The effect of this propaganda was such that an incestuous father charged in court claimed in his defense that he was a Marxist![8] People were told that children are snatched away in socialist societies and brought up in institutions. These charges served to raise elemental fears about religion, family, and basic social relations. Among the cruder attempts to ridicule socialism was an imitation of Orwell's *Animal Farm*. Failing to bring out the genuine and powerful indictment of dictatorship under the pretence of socialism, as Orwell's work did, this work attempted a crude caricature of the LSSP. In this booklet, called *Nari Ugula* (The Jackal Trap), the socialists were derogatorily cast as jackals, a species that is cunning and lowly in Sri Lankan folklore. A further example of crude ridicule of Marxism was the use of the names of international socialist thinkers and activists, such as Marx, Lenin, and Trotsky, to name pet dogs, another lowly animal in the indigenous animal hierarchy.

THE HERITAGE OF THE BHIKKHU
A Charter for Activist Monks

It is in this context that Walpola Rahula wrote *The Heritage of the Bhikkhu* (hereafter, *The Heritage*),[9] a work that has influenced the monkhood more than any other in the recent history of Sri Lankan Theravada Buddhism. Indirectly, it also influenced in critical ways the society as a whole. Two factors

8. U. Saranankara. *Satanaka Satahan* (Colombo: Janata Lekhaka Peramuna, n.d.), 167.
9. The Sinhala original was first published in 1946 under the title *Bhiksuvage Urumaya*. Subsequent editions are: 2d ed., rev. (Kalaniya: Vidyalankara Press, 1948); 3d ed. (Colombo: Godage, 1992); English trans. (New York, Grove Press, 1974).

are worthy of note here. First, although *The Heritage* is associated with the name of Walpola Rahula, rightly so because of his brilliant articulation of its ideas, it is nevertheless a collaborative work. The ideas expressed in it were collectively generated and held, although it was Rahula's precision of language that gave the work its distinctive imprint. Second and conversely, *The Heritage* is not an isolated document; it is rather the most prominent of a cluster of texts that heralded the birth of the new order envisaged in Dharmapala's work. The seed from which this family of texts grew was *The Declaration of the Vidyalankara Pirivena* (hereafter, *The Declaration*), a brief programmatic statement written by Yakkaduve Pragnasara and issued by the Vidyalankara monks in 1946 that defined the vocation of the monk as social service.[10]

The polemic brevity of this document by definition needed elaboration and the more so because of the hostility it provoked in the powerful political and press establishment. So, around *The Declaration* we find the growth of a sort of commentarial literature extending, elucidating, and defending it. As would be clear from the above discussion, this commentary was oral to begin with and continued to be so. But paralleling that, and giving *The Declaration* more teeth and muscle, a number of printed texts came into being. The central work in this cluster of texts was *The Heritage,* but it included, among others, the newspaper *Kalaya,* which was published between March 14, 1946 and December 25, 1947, Rahula's *The History of Buddhism in Ceylon* (hereafter *History*), and the prolific work of Yakkaduve Pragnarama.[11] The *History,* widely considered a work of scholarship, is actually an exemplification of the Dharmapalite paradigm, written to document and celebrate the idyllic society, monkhood, and kingship of that paradigm. *The Heritage* projects that paradigm to the future. Since these texts have as their objective the restoration of Dharmapala's ideal order, alleged to have existed prior to the colonial era, in particular the restoration of the monk to "kingship," they can be called restorative texts.

The Sinhala original of *The Heritage,* entitled *Bhiksuvage Urumaya,* was published in 1946, the updated English translation appearing in 1974. The gap of nearly three decades between the Sinhala original and the English translation bears testimony to the tenacious topicality and the socio-political importance of this slim volume. Lucidly written, *The Heritage* is at once naive and sophisticated, rhetorical and scholarly, and simplistic and brilliant. It is a manifesto ostensibly based on historical and sociological analysis. It is a

10. This is reproduced in *The Heritage,* 131–33.
11. For a sample of these writings, see Yakkaduve Pragnarama, ed., *Pavidi vaga ha sasun maga* (Gangodavila, Nugegoda: Deepani Press for the Vidyalankara Sabha, 1970).

justification of and a charter for monks to involve themselves in social activism (politics robed in social service). It is an attempt to restore to the monk his alleged precolonial status by telling him to rearm himself for a society that has progressed while he has languished. It bears the imprint of the Sinhala Buddhist nationalism of Anagarika Dharmapala. Its other influences—Protestant Christianity, Indian nationalism, and neo-Hinduism,[12] which were also products of Western and Christian influences—are largely mediated through Dharmapala although paradoxically he was opposed to most of them.

Publication of *The Declaration* dramatized and launched what we can now discern as the second aspect of the Dharmapala program, namely the nationalist agenda, and in a more proximate sense precipitated a national controversy concerning the participation of monks in political activity, which in turn encapsulated both the flowering and the destruction of the socialist movement. Yakkaduve Pragnarama, the author of work, credits the document with paving the way for an island-wide Vidyalankara campaign to educate the people on the evils of capitalism, the benefits of socialism, and the importance of gaining total and sovereign independence with no allegiance to the British crown—and also with enabling the monks who had hitherto been confined to their rural monasteries to help people alleviate their *dukkha* (suffering), not only of the other world but this world as well. The *Declaration* is thus the enfranchisement and enablement of the hitherto cloistered monk to break out into the open and perform social service. It is the germ of the idea that grew up to be *The Heritage*. The following sequence of events is narrated by Yakkaduve, regarding the origin and publicization of *The Declaration:*

Early in 1946 the idea was expressed by some prominent political leaders that it is inappropriate for monks to engage in public activities like politics. Before that some of the same politicians had asked the help of the monks

12. In particular the Ramakrishna mission, which modeled itself on the Buddhist Sangha. However, their dedication was social service, an idea derived from Christianity. They were ordained by means of administering to them the five precepts of social service. The five precepts idea is reminiscent of Buddhism (see Udakandavala Saranankara, *Satanaka Satahan* [Janata Lekhaka Peramuna, n.d.], 157). Rahula may have consciously or unconsciously borrowed from this reform movement the idea of social service as the monks' vocation, although he had in mind politics, and although as we know his major inspiration was Dharmapala. Since he could not openly advocate politics, he used the term "social service" as a cover. Social service in Rahula's sense lacked both the morality and commitment of the Vidyodaya monks we have discussed and of the Ramakrishna renouncer. This is amply demonstrated in the kind of monk that this idea bred, namely a monk driven by self-interest and material gain whether employed as a teacher or handling vast sums of foreign aid ostensibly in "social service" projects, such as teaching pre-school children. See chapter 5 below for some examples.

during elections, which the Vidyalankara monks had refused. Thus their idea now, that monks should not participate in political activity, was not an impartial statement but an expression of the fear that monks would indeed participate but not on their behalf. Those concerned were a group of able, young, and educated monks with nationalist and socialist ideas, on the Vidyalankara faculty. The core of this group included Walpola Rahula, Yakkaduve Pragnarama, Kotahene Pannakitti, Kalalalle Anandasagara, and Nattandiya Pannakara. On the evening of February 8, 1946, Yakkaduve and Rahula, who was then secretary of the Vidyalankara Sabha, the governing body of the college *(pirivena),* went to see Dr. Nicholas Attygalle, the president of the Sabha, and in the course of discussions on various matters relating to the college, brought up the question of monks and political activity. Dr. Attygalle expressed the view that it was of the greatest importance to make, at this time, a statement of the position of the college regarding the issue. Yakkaduve expressed the fear that a public statement on the subject might cause problems for the pirivena. Dr. Attygalle responded, "That is all right. We will see about that." Upon return to their quarters the two met informally in Yakkaduve's room with others of the group, which included Kosgoda Dhammavamsa and Kudirippuve Pannasehkara in addition to the three others mentioned above. A discussion ensued as to the idea expressed by the president, Dr. Attygalle, and it was unanimously agreed that a public statement should be made. Writing was assigned to Yakkaduve, who prepared the statement, fully in accordance with *dharma vinaya* and *sasana* practice. The two, Yakkaduve and Rahula, took the statement back to Dr. Attygalle and explained the contents to him in English and in Sinhalese. Attygalle approved it as excellent and asked the monks to get it approved by the Vidyalankara faculty and to release it to the press. On February 13, 1946 the faculty was summoned and the statement read to them, which they approved unanimously. Yakkaduve also explained to the faculty the possible (adverse) consequences of *The Declaration* to the college. The principal, Kirivattuduve Pragnasara, signed it and it was released to the press. It was also printed in the form of a pamphlet and distributed.[13]

While there is no doubt that the above is something like what happened, this is as polemical a statement as *The Declaration* and *The Heritage* themselves were. First, there is a contradiction in the chronology as outlined by Yakkaduve. According to it *The Declaration* was written after Yakkaduve and Rahula saw Dr. Attygalle on February 8. Since *The Declaration* was read to the faculty and issued on the 13th, it should have been written between the 8th and the 13th. In fact, according to the copy of *The Declaration* reproduced in *The*

13. Yakkaduve, *Pavidi vaga ha sasun maga,* 95–99.

Heritage, the principal of the college, Kirivattuduve Pragnasara, signed it on February 2, which suggests that the sequence above is a construction. It rather suggests the possibility that the monks were long convinced of what their political position was going to be and that they were astutely trying to get the support of the powerful figure of Dr. Attygalle, the president of the Sabha, which apparently they succeeded in doing not only here but later as well, as we shall see below. This is a remarkable victory for the monks because of Attygalle's class position and political affiliation with the then powerful leadership that soon crystallized into the UNP. It is also an early hint as to the autonomy of the monks from the socialist ideology and leadership with which they seemed allied, despite their verbose espousal of Marxism and their apparently cordial relations with the Marxist leadership. No doubt there were Marxist sympathizers among these monks, but to them religion, culture, language, and nation (race, ethnic group) were primary. No doubt they were concerned to raise the living standards of the people, but this was largely at the ideological level. They provide no clues, apart from slogans, as to their understanding of how to actually help the people, which is something, whatever their success, that the Vidyodaya monks at least tried. Thus we are back with the two aspects of the Dharmapala agenda, economic development and Sinhala Buddhist nationalism. The Vidyalankara monks would embrace the latter, although this was not clearly discernible at this early stage. In fact, there are hints of concern about people of other religions and ethnic groups, but these are soon forgotten and they become preoccupied with the unity of language, religion and the state.

The statement provoked prompt and intense hostility from the political elite, headed by D. S. Senanayake, Minister of Agriculture and Leader of the House, and his colleagues including J. R. Jayawardene and Sir John Kotelawala. They were forcefully supported by the entire press establishment led by the Lake House group of newspapers, such as the *Dinamina, Silumina* and the English dailies the *Ceylon Daily News* and the *Ceylon Observer.* Paradoxically and perhaps suggestive of the Vidyodaya slant towards the established authority, *Sinhala Bauddhaya,* the weekly founded by Dharmapala and the voice of Sinhala Buddhism, joined the anti-Vidyalankara forces, as did monks like Yagirala Pannananda, the biographer of the Vidyodaya founder Hikkaduve Sumangala.

D. S. Senanayake and his group tried to have *The Declaration* withdrawn. Having failed in that attempt Senanayake tried to get that done through the executive committee of the Sabha. At his request a meeting of the Vidyalankara executive committee and pirivena staff was convened on March 23, 1946. Attygalle warned Yakkaduve beforehand that Senanayake was going to ask the monks to withdraw the *Declaration*. Yakkaduve prepared a statement to the effect that it was not the policy of Vidyalankara to declare publicly anything it later plans to withdraw or to withdraw anything publicly declared.[14] The statement continued: "We hope from this campaign to make Sri Lanka a *dharmadvipa,* to enrich Buddhism, and to make people free of suffering and disease and make them whole; and to make monks a category of people who do not simply exist [doing nothing] but who work selflessly for the good of the religion and its adherents."[15] During the six-week period between the original announcement of *The Declaration* and this meeting the controversy had swelled to national proportions. Some supporters of Vidyalankara withdrew their support and others threatened to do so. Some published their withdrawal of support in the newspapers, to which others responded by announcing support.

The meeting of March 23, in case it failed to persuade the monks to withdraw the *Declaration,* was meant to be a session to brief the members of the executive committee prior to a general meeting scheduled for the next day. It lasted from 7 P.M. to midnight. D. S. Senanayake said: "This movement now afoot, that it is all right for monks to join politics, is a shrewd act of the Communists and Samasamajists [Trotskyites]. They have contrived to get this executive committee and staff involved in it. If we do not defend ourselves against this, Buddhism and this pirivena will be endangered." Here is Senanayake's statement verbatim, as it was taken down by the secretary, Walpola Rahula: "They have started this *vyapare* ("campaign") to destroy our *varige* ("clan"). I will protect that somehow. What saddens me is that because of this *vyapare,* Buddhism and Vidyalankara pirivena will be destroyed." Yakkaduve's reply to Senanayake was also taken down verbatim by Rahula: "Honorable minister, this *varige* thing, the honorable minister will protect wouldn't he? The Mahanayakas will protect Buddhism. We will protect Vidyalankara. That way, this *vyapare* wouldn't hurt anybody, would it?" This was a courageous statement to hurl back at the most powerful man in the country. Rahula assesses its significance as follows: "If not for Yakkaduve's courage and determination, the pirivena could at that moment have succumbed to the power of wealth, and obeyed it. The movement [for nationalist socialism] waged for the benefit of the country would have got extinct."[16]

14. Ibid., 101.
15. Ibid., 102. This expresses the dominance of Dharmapalism in the ideology of these monks, and the exclusivist nature of their definition of "the people" as Sinhala Buddhists. The implicit failure to recognize other people recalls the Mahavamsaic conception of non-Buddhists as non-people.
16. Ibid., 97.

Attygalle, the president, conducted the next day's general meeting adroitly. First, he cleared the scene of the press, which he knew was biased and hostile. Next, he had *The Declaration* read, and he ensured that questions and answers remained short. He then introduced the following motion himself: "While it is desirable that in places of learning like pirivenas, politics is to be taught as a discipline, those who teach or learn it should neither work for a political party by joining it nor advocate the program of a particular party or a political system."[17] Member D. N. Jayatilleke promptly stood up and proposed that the assembly accept the two proposals, one by Yakkaduve (i.e., *The Declaration*) and the other by President Attygalle. This was promptly seconded by member D.C. Jayatilleke. The president then declared the motions accepted by the assembly, declaring it unnecessary to take a vote. Clearly the procedure, including the prompt proposing and seconding of his motion by the Jayatillekes, was managed by the president, and surprisingly so because of his close relations with the political elite of which he was himself a member. This suggests that he had a strong sense of loyalty either to one or more of the monks personally, to Vidyalankara as an institution, or to the principles in *The Declaration*.[18]

The Declaration, in addition to whatever it declared, was also a declaration of war on the elitist, constitutionalist establishment. Until now there was some hope among the elite that the errant monks would in the end befriend them. But with *The Declaration,* a line was drawn in the sand. Behind the thin veil of social service, monks were going to take arms against the elite, and behind the veil of defending Buddhism, the elite was trying to resort to every possible means to stop the monks.

It is necessary before proceeding further to say that the Vidyalankara monks' account of what happened is itself part of the family of texts surrounding *The Declaration.* The account, which may be true in its core, has elements of mythic elaboration. We already referred to the contradictory nature of the date given by these monks for these events. In addition, other accounts, far from making these monks heroes, portray them as a mafia

17. Ibid., 104.

18. A grateful Yakkaduve wrote: "If the proposal about our Declaration were put to the vote that day, it is not possible that no more than three lay members would have voted for it. It is miraculous that our president Dr. Attygalle, having known that clearly, took such great pains to prevent the Vidyalankara Declaration and the Vidyalankara monks from the ignominious ridicule of the Vidyalankara Sabha within the Vidyalankara premises itself. What loyalty! What renunciation of his own party imperatives! This is the more so when one considers the long-term relation Dr. Attygalle had with the Honorable D. S. Senanayake and elite membership like Wijayawardene, and the fact that on the previous night at the executive committee meeting he got to see and hear well what the Honourable D. S. Senanayake said in opposition to our Declaration" (ibid., 105).

within Vidyalankara organized to further their private ends. A distinguished monk of the same college has asserted that the entire drama of The Declaration was a clever manipulation by the core group of monks involved to collect vast sums of money, presumably for political activity, but in any case without any form of accountability. According to this account, Principal Kirivattuduve Pragnasara, under whose hand The Declaration was issued, wanted no part of it but succumbed under duress. It is alleged that these monks hatched an elaborate plan to raise funds by tapping the trade unions controlled by the LSSP. Apparently the plan was to levy one rupee per trade unionist. It was conservatively estimated that Rs. 500,000 would be collected monthly, assuming that, of the 700,000 members, 200,000 would fail to conform to the levy. This would add up to Rs. 6,000,000 per year, which was a colossal sum, equivalent in today's (1999) currency to Rs. 70,000,000—approximately one million U.S. dollars.[19] In the light of these differing views and the internal inconsistencies of the account, it is possible that the exchange between D. S. Senanayake and Yakkaduve supposedly taken down "verbatim" by Walpola Rahula, and which lionizes Yakkaduve, is part of the histrionics of the event's representation.

The next move of the opponents of The Declaration was to enlist the support of the orthodox monastic hierarchy in Kandy and in the provinces and to try to institute a purification (sasana sodhana). The first public meeting for the purpose was held at the Kalaniya Vihara on March 31, 1946. A body known as the Kalani Sasana Sodhana Mandalaya was formed, and, with the support of the orthodox monks and the establishment newspapers, legislation was prepared to empower the Mahanayakas to derobe "political monks" and to fine and/or imprison them.

In response to this the Vidyalankara monks formed the Lanka Eksat Bhiksu Mandalaya (The United Bhikkhu Organisation of Lanka) in May 1946. Its purpose was to broaden and stabilize the Vidyalankara political program, and to engage every monk in the island in a clear political commitment with no references to traditional sectarian (nikaya) and other differences. In addi-

---

19. See Naravila Dhammaratana, Hadipannala Pannaloka (Sandalankava: Sandalanka Co-operative Printers, 1954), 103–106, 139–49. The magnitude of these sums evoke the funds allegedly being handled today by some of the enterprising monks discussed in the next chapter.

The core group of these monks allegedly harbored so much hatred for the UNP and its conservative leadership that they were willing to go to any lengths to try and defeat them at the next elections, hence the need to justify their political activity. Allegedly these monks had no interest in the college or its tradition of learning despite their loud professions to the contrary. Gnanavasa's critique (see below) and his fear of monks getting involved in the revolution (the color red than the color ocher, as he put it) lends some support to these allegations. What is not emphasized in these accounts is the nationalist hegemonist agenda that lay beneath the reputed Marxism, of which they do not seem to have had any understanding anyway.

tion to defending themselves from the impending threat of derobement, fining, and imprisonment, the monks also sought to ensure the passage of the Free Education Act that was facing opposition in the State Council; to make Sri Lanka a socialist, sovereign, free state with no affiliation with the British crown (because Dominion Status then being negotiated was not considered full independence); and to take a stand at the approaching election campaign of 1947. These were popular proposals, and it is clear that the monks were using them in the short run to defuse the legislation that would empower the Mahanayakas to control them, and in the long run, to empower themselves.

The event also brings out a perennial tendency in Buddhism, the attempt by monks to march towards lay behavior and the counterattempt by the laity or by a section of the monkhood itself to stop it. This instance brings out more, the clever combining by monks of a popular program (free education) with laxity in behavior, so that the laxity will either go unnoticed or will be ignored. Yakkaduve became the secretary of the newly formed monk's organization *(mandalaya)* thanks to his acquaintance with networks that could help recruit members from different parts of the country. So far without a voice, they founded a weekly newspaper, known as *Kalaya* (Time). A campaign of writing in this weekly convincingly attacked the Sasanasodhana proposal so that it would be deprived of adequate support when taken up in the State Council.

Yakkaduve and Rahula were the theoreticians of the movement. Because of his international eminence, Rahula's work is generally known; Yakkaduve's, in contrast, is relatively unknown, although in many ways Yakkaduve's contributions both as writer and activist are great. There were other writers as well. Thus, altogether in the movement we have the works of Rahula, of Yakkaduve, and of various writers who converged in the weekly, *Kalaya,* which was in fact founded for the purpose of defensively establishing the ideas of *The Declaration.* There were, in addition, peripheral writings that bolstered these ideas. The process also led to a further declaration, on the verge of independence, *The Vidyalankara Declaration of Independence.* These documents sowed far and wide the seeds of the nationalist and socialist agenda among the elites of the villages; the harvest, ten years later, was a bloodless revolution that brought about in its externalities, though falling far short in spirit, the society that Dharmapala envisaged. As already noted, Rahula's main works are the *The Heritage* and *History.* Yakkaduve's are more complicated and scattered. These works as a whole, along with their adversarial texts, encapsulate the indigenous sociology of politics of the era. While Rahula's writings, although quite clearly polemical, conformed to the accepted format of traditional scholarship, Yakkaduve's work was more scholastic than scholarly. His use of the spoken idiom gave his writings a rusticity and a popular appeal that superseded Rahula's. This was enhanced by the turn of his phrase and by the allegorical style he sometimes adopted. His writings in *Kalaya* and *Vanakata* (1946) were, in his own words, indications of "the path to take."[20]

This was not all. Since the matter was hardly one of altruism on the part of the monks or the elite which opposed them, the monks were attacked on all kinds of grounds, other than *The Declaration*. Indeed, any basis whatever that could be used to attack them. One of these was the allegation made by J. R. Jayawardene (minister of finance, later president), who charged that Vidyalankara monks had secretly espoused the idea that the Buddha was not omniscient and that karma and rebirth are false theories;[21] he also claimed that monks were advised to abandon such heresies by the then principal of the college, Lunupokune Dhammananda. Yakkaduve dismissed the charges as the falsifications of a man who, over a period of thirty years, had not set foot on the pirivena grounds more than a few times but who pretended to have known the late principal well. He added that, as is well known to historians of Buddhism, questions relating to all kinds of doctrines were raised and debated not only at Vidyalankara but at ancient centers such as Nalanda, and Vikramasila, and that such discussions are a common activity at these colleges. He also accused Jayawardene of trying to portray the Vidyalankara monks as a group plotting to destroy Buddhism by suggesting that for this purpose they were seeking the help of Marxism. Yakkaduve's position was that if Marx said later what the Buddha said first, what are the Vidyalankara monks to do?[22]

MONASTIC PUNDITS
The Commissioners' Critique

Early in the election campaign of 1956, candidate S. W. R. D. Bandaranaike, leader of the Sri Lanka Freedom Party (SLFP), publicly accepted a report

---

20. Pragnarama, *Pavidi vaga.,* 169.

21. Ibid., 154.

22. This reflected a general tendency at the time for Sri Lankan Buddhist intellectuals to demonstrate the compatibility between Buddhism and Marxism. This was partly an attempt to counter the established elite's attempt to get some monks and others to portray Marxism as the enemy of Buddhism. A perceptive discussion of the compatibility between Buddhism and Marxism is Martin Wickramasinghe, *Budusamaya ha samaja darsanaya* (Colombo: Gunasena, 1948); rpt. in *Martin Vicramasimha krti ekatuva* (Dehivala: Tisara, 1994), 13:321–462.

published by a Committee of Inquiry set up by the Ceylon Buddhist Congress as the prospective blueprint for a broad spectrum of policy.[23] One of the main recommendations of this report as well as of the report of a commission[24] appointed to recommend procedures to implement these proposals was the establishment of a Buddha Sasana Mandalaya for the care and enrichment of Buddhism. One item in that project was a plan to provide for the education of monks. In keeping with this, the Bandaranaike government conferred university status on the two Buddhist monastic colleges Vidyodaya and Vidyalankara in 1958.

There was, however, from the beginning a built-in dilemma that arose from the policy of replacing English with Sinhala as the medium of instruction,[25] which was implemented by the new government in 1956, ostensibly to help the education and mobility of mostly poor rural children.[26] Previously, since children were educated in the English medium, there was no problem of language when they proceeded to university education, which was in the English medium as well. As the university (only one was in existence then) showed reluctance to take on the task of teaching in Sinhala in view of the absence of Sinhala qualified teachers and Sinhala books,[27] the government was suddenly confronted with the problem of masses of students qualifying for admission to the university whose medium of instruction was incomprehensible to them. The two newly created monastic universities promptly accepted this challenge and offered to admit these Sinhala-medium students. The original intention in creating the pirivena universities, however, was simply the elevation of the two colleges Vidyodaya and Vidyalankara to university status. This meant that they were going to be exclusively or preponderantly monastic universities and that their curriculum was going to be confined to the traditional fields of study and research in which the monks had expertise. The admission of lay students seeking university education to these new universities changed the situation drastically: it meant that the lay/monastic balance in the student population was going to be reversed, with the lay students gaining an overwhelming

23. *Bauddha toraturu pariksaka sabhave vartava* (Balangoda: Dharmavijaya Press, 1956). An abridged English version is published under the title *The Betrayal of Buddhism* (Balangoda: Dharmavijaya Press, 1956).

24. *Bauddha Sasan Komisan vartava,* Sessional Paper 18 of 1959 (Colombo: Government Printer, 1959).

25. English was replaced by both national languages Sinhala and Tamil. This discussion is confined to the replacement of English by Sinhala.

26. Exactly the reverse of this has taken place as a result of this measure.

27. Properly speaking, Sinhala and Tamil. This discussion relates only to Sinhala.

preponderance; consequently, the curriculum needed to be changed to accommodate modern arts and science subjects for which alone the lay students had preparation, thus tipping the curriculum balance also greatly in
favor of the new majority of lay students.

There was also the thorny question of female students. As reflected in the
Buddhist literature, proximity to females had from the earliest times been
viewed with deep anxiety verging on phobia by the monastic orthodoxy.
Thus not only was the acceptance of lay students at loggerheads with the
original vision of a tranquil monastic university, but having let the tide of
secular studentship enter the hallowed precincts of the monastic university,
there was not going to be any going back. The tenor of monastic student life
was going to be overwhelmed by the intrusion of the secular curriculum and
the sheer numbers of lay students and by eventually opening the doors to
female students. As it turned out, all this happened. More importantly, the
conferral of secular university status on these two institutions led to the
extinction of a distinctive indigenous tradition of pirivena scholarship.[28]

In addition to the destruction of an indigenous tradition of learning,
which ironically was the result of an ostensible attempt to strengthen it and
make it flower, the short-term effects of the establishment of the two universities were disastrous. These arose from the administrative ineptitude and
alleged nepotism and cronyism of the monks who presided over the universities at their inception. From accounts of informants, what obtained at that
time was not institutional organization but chaos. As this was becoming
increasingly obvious, the government appointed another commission to in-
quire into the working of the universities and to recommend measures for
their efficient operation. In their report,[29] the three commissioners, upper-

---

28. The founding of Vidyodaya and the Vidyalankara colleges, and subsequently other similar colleges in several local centers, had earlier led to a resurgence of indigenous scholarship. Vidyodaya in
particular produced a large number of erudite monks who produced impressive editorial and commentarial work. Among these were Mahagoda Gnanissara, Ohalpola Devaraksita, Borukgamuve Revata, Yagirala Pannananda, Valivitiye Dhammaratana, Bentara Saranamkara, Kahave Ratanasara, Baddegama Piyaratana, Rayigama Indajoti, Madugalle Siddhartha, Devundara Jinaratana, Kalukondayave
Pannasekhara, Palannoruve Vimaladharma, Valivitiye Sorata, Dehigaspe Pannasara, Kotmale Dhammananda, Suriyagoda Sumangala and Valivitiye Pannasara. In addition were Hikkaduve Sumangala, the
founder of Vidyodaya, Ratmalane Dhammaloka, the founder of Vidyalankara, and Ratmalane Dhar-
marama of Vidyalankara. The colleges also produced lay scholars, including Veragama Punchibandara,
Thomas Karunaratna, Hedrick Jayatilaka Appuhamy and U. P. Ekanayaka. For an account see Sarath
Wijesuriya. "Piriven sampradaya ha bauddha adhyapanye vikasaya," *Sambhasa* 1, no. 1 (May-August
1990): 17–27. A random example of editorial work in this tradition is *Vimanavatthu-Petavatthu* by
Morontuduve Dhammananda of Vidyodaya (Colombo: Sri Bharati Press, 1927).

29. D. C. R. Gunawardene et al., *Report of the Universities Commission,* 1962. Sessional paper 16
of 1963.

class Buddhist public servants, expressed sympathy with of the views of the Sasanarakssaka Bauddha Mandalaya, a Buddhist modernist association and lobby.[30] This organization emphasized the exemplary nature of of monkhood and the need for the preservation of monastic morality, often referred to as *mahanakama,* "the [noble] state of being a monk," or "monkness" as we may gloss it. In their report the commissioners expressed great concern that the imposition of secular, complex, and unfamiliar structures on the ancient colleges would inevitably destroy monkness. They were particularly concerned about the consequences of the receipt of salaries, first by monk-professors at these universities and eventually by large numbers of monk-graduates qualified in marketable secular subjects; about the problems of close physical interaction between monks and their fellow female students; and about the impact of secular qualifications on the rate of derobement and consequent depletion of the Sangha's demography. In their piety, concern for their religion, and most of all their neo-Buddhist conception of an exemplary Sangha, the commissioners were unmistakable in their condemnation of and unsparing in their invective toward the moral state of these salaried monks.

First of all, the commissioners draw attention to the fact that these colleges owed their new status as secular universities to the policy on the medium of instruction and the failure of the existing University of Ceylon to teach in Sinhala. They pointed out that by "waving a magic wand" the monastic pundits were raised to university heights, thereby insinuating that it was the status and prestige of these positions that the monks were lusting after. And on the question of closing the door to female students, the commissioners asked why, in a state-funded institution, half the eligible candidates are ungallantly denied their place merely because of their gender: "Were the learned pundits who were now fairly well assured of the likelihood of their being safely and comfortably installed in the lofty seats of higher learning worried about the future of the young bhikkhus, if they were permitted to drink deep at these two new fountains of learning in the exhilarating company of the fair sex?" They further went on to point out how the monks ingeniously devised a method of channeling their paychecks to their accounts in a way that gave the appearance of the money being paid to a trustee.[31]

The commissioners also characterized the bill presented to Parliament to

---

30. In their report, the commissioners list a copy of the submission made by this body to the Senate on the Pirivena Universities Bill, which expresses their concerns. See Appendix D of the report.

31. Gunawardene et al., *Report of the Universities Commission,* 23–25. The parenthetical references in this section are to this report.

create the pirivena universities as an ill-considered and irresponsible piece of legislation. Since so many experienced and responsible people were involved, the Commissioners found it unbelievable that this legislation went through, and they speculated that this could have happened only due to "some major compelling force" (30–31). This force was none other than the "political bhikkhu," who seems to have "dictated policies, dominated public affairs, and incited actions which people in their normal senses would not have considered even possible. They were most powerful at the time this bill was being drafted and were responsible in large measure for inflaming the racial and religious passions that erupted in such sickening fashion in the early part of 1958." They add: "We are mentioning this as we are unable otherwise to account for the strange behavior of the many persons and authorities who were associated with this bill. The actions of the authorities should, in our opinion, be viewed against the background of the unholy terror that stalked the country in these dark days" (31). These "political monks," as we know, are none other than Rahula, Yakkaduve, and their colleagues at Vidyalankara. Thus the commissioners are squarely and in no unmistakable terms laying the blame not only for the sorry state of these universities but also for the "inflaming of sickening racial passions" at the door of the Vidyalankara monks.

In this the commissioners removed the shroud of "social service" these monks used to cover themselves and exposed them for pawning a valuable and ancient tradition of learning for the gold of professorial salaries, privileges, and status; for pretending to cry about country, language, nation, and religion when their real interest was gaining for themselves positions of power and wealth; and for doing so at the cost of inflaming racial tensions. The commissioners were careful to let the readers know that this evaluation of the monks was not just theirs: "Almost invariably [those citizens who gave evidence] took the view that the establishment of the two universities has brought about a violent and meaningless breaking away from the ancient traditions which had stood the test of time, and that it had almost reduced the Sangha as understood in this limited sense, to the position of laymen." They also maintained that it was "altogether an ill-advised step which, if not promptly retraced, would have disastrous effects on the entire Sangha" (36).

This put the ball in the court of the Vidyalankara monks, and it was Yakkaduve who responded most vigorously. It is important to note here that the true object of the commissioners' critique, though specifically arising from their study of the universities, was the "political monk."[32] The theoretical

32. In the national controversy that raged in 1946 after the Vidyalankara monks declared their intention to participate in politics, these monks were known as "political bhikkus." In the critique

justification for the political monk appeared, as we know, in *The Declaration* and its elaboration, *The Heritage of the Bhikkhu.* Thus the response to the commissioners belongs to the broad category of commentarial texts on *The Heritage.* Yakkaduve's own characterization of his response was that it was an attempt to meet the arguments of the "Commissioner Buddhists" on scriptural *(dharma vinaya)* grounds. That this response should be considered part of the cluster of texts surrounding *The Declaration* and *The Heritage* is clearly seen in the inclusion in Yakkaduve's response on scriptural grounds a chapter where Rahula does the same on historical *(aitihasika)* grounds, which in fact is no more than a summary restatement of arguments in *The History of Buddhism in Ceylon.* This supports my contention that the latter work, widely held in awed respect as a work of scholarship, is a polemical work and is best understood in relation to the rest of the literature that grew around *The Heritage,* its seed, *The Declaration,* and the family of adversarial texts that range from the propaganda of the Lake House group of newspapers and other journals, to oral texts such as the speech of D. S. Senanayake that precipitated *The Heritage* "by way of a public reply," to Henpitagedara Gnanavasa's *What is the Heritage of the Bhikku?* (discussed below) and its unpublished twin by Akuratiye Amaravamsa, and to the report of the commissioners.

"COMMISSIONER BUDDHISTS"
Yakkaduve's Response

The argument of the commissioners was the modernist Buddhist one that paying salaries to monks would render them unworthy of the respect of the laity. The commissioners further recommended that even with no salary, a monk should not be an employee of the state (189), a statement reminiscent of the injunction for monks not to take part in politics. This argument repudiates the whole thrust of *The Declaration* and its progenic literature starting from *The Heritage,* and it represents, as noted above, the recurring tendency for the monkhood to infiltrate the secular world and for a laity concerned with the monks' morality to censor that move. Yakkaduve responded with vigor and tortuous detail and denounced the "Commissioner Buddhists." This critique,[33] since it crucially touched the role of the monk in the new social order, is in fact part of the process of elucidating *The Declaration* and

---

offered in the *Report of the Universities Commission Report,* the commissioners were resurrecting an old debate.

33. Originally published in a limited "desk top" edition of 200 copies, this is abridged and reprinted in *Pavidi vaga ha sasun maga,* 185–344. The parenthetical references in this section are to this work.

its comprehensive reincarnation, *The Heritage.* It is highly polemical, as indeed this entire body of literature is, although underneath the polemics some sociologically valid observations are discernable. Yakkaduve contends that reactionary forces are arrayed against him and identifies seven categories of reactionaries who, by portraying minor offenses of modern monks, especially young student monks, as serious offenses that defeat monkhood, threaten to cause a large-scale derobement by monks thereby made to feel worthless and guilty, leading to a depletion of the monasteries (185–87). His intention therefore is to elucidate, "according to *dharma vinaya,* the Buddha's thought, *sasana* genealogy, the tradition of teachers, and my own conscience" (188), the true nature and ethical status of these offenses and "thereby bring freedom from anxiety to the harsh and rare monastic life that is so valuable to country, nation, and religion" (187). He also frankly admits that his arguments based on *dharma vinaya* are also interspersed with "bombardments of the conspiratorial false views of virtueless opponents" (190). The following are Yakkaduve's contentions.

The commissioners' report is nothing but an attempt to take revenge on the monks for their role in demolishing the old order in 1956, and in particular for providing university education to the children of the poor. Yakkaduve equates this with the elite opposition a decade before to the free education campaign, which he claims was spearheaded and made possible by the efforts of the monks (194).

According to *dharma vinaya,* the fact that a monk is paid a monthly salary neither renders him unsuitable to receive lay respect nor causes the loss of even an atom of his morality. If a monk is free of the four *parajikas* (heinous offenses that "defeat" monkhood) and is adorned with modesty (*lajja bhaya,* "shame and fear"), and if he duly purifies himself of the minor offenses he might have committed, he is fully deserving of lay respect. Receiving a salary is a minor offense (206). It is neither *parajika,* nor *sanghadisesa,* nor *sthula,* nor even *cullaccaya,* but a *pacittiya.*[34] Such an offense is not an injury to morality *(silvipattiya);* it is only an injury to etiquette *(acaravipattiya)* (208). Thus accepting a salary does not take away a monk's right to receive the respect of laymen.

The commissioners and their advisors are labeling as *dussila* (immoral) virtuous monks who are also friends of country, nation, and religion. Such people cause demerit to themselves and prevent benefit to many gods and men, and are extinguishers of Buddhism (210). The Buddha refused Deva-

---

34. These are vinaya offenses (violations of vinaya rules), listed here in descending order of gravity for characteristic rhetorical effect.

datta's request to insist on extreme asceticism because he had omniscient understanding of the variability of human behavior, and he was tolerant of individual approaches to the goal of liberation.

People are impressed not by virtue but by its appearance. Hence the respect accorded to the Vinayavardhana and Tapasa movements.[35] It is hypocritical for the commissioners to consider monks as enjoying "princely pleasures" while they, out of greed for merit, invite monks to their houses for alms-givings as if they were royalty.

Derobing, which the commissioners view with alarm and attribute to monks getting educated and earning degrees, is a natural phenomenon that was rampant during the Buddha's time. Monks leave robes because of irresponsible and harsh lay criticism. Movements like Vinayavardhana and Tapasa and the assassination of Prime Minister Bandaranaike (by a monk) lead to monks derobing. Thus the reason for monks leaving robes is not university degrees but the variable ability to follow monastic vows in the context of human emotions and forces innate to individuals.

The argument that monks use monkhood for mobility cannot be used as a critique because it is fully in accordance with *dharma vinaya* to use sangha resources so long as one is in robes observing the rules (280). A young person very rarely enters the order of his own will. He does it mostly to please parents, teachers, or others. Sometimes monks seek out clever boys and ordain them. Had the boy been a layman, he would have received educational qualifications anyway by means of scholarships and free education. If scholarships to lay students, which come from public funds, are acceptable, why is funding a young monk from the monastery's resources unacceptable? Those who give up robes turn out to be productive citizens. That is better than being in robes and violating monastic rules.

In the minds of the commissioners, monks should do nothing but go into

35. Vinayavardhana is a movement that came into prominence in the 1950s. It was highly critical of established monasticism on the grounds of luxurious living and moral decadence. It advocated and effected, among its adherents, an avoidance of monks, where necessary using laymen instead. This was an anti-ritualist movement. For an account of the movement see Michael Ames, "Ideological and Social Change in Ceylon," *Human Organization* 22, no. 1 (Spring 1963): 45–53; Steven Kemper, "Buddhism without Bhikkhus," in Bardwell Smith, ed., *Religion and Legitimation of Power in Sri Lanka* (Chambersburg, Penn.: Anima Books, 1978).

The Tapasa (ascetic) movement was a similar condemnation of established monasticism for the same reasons. Its adherents, a handful of mostly young men, defied the established order by conferring ordination on themselves and traversed the countryside in measured steps, kindling an enthusiastic public interest. For perceptive accounts of the movement see Nur Yalman, "The Ascetic Buddhist Monks of Ceylon," *Ethnology* 1, no. 3 (1962): 313–28; Michael Carrithers, *The Forest Monks of Sri Lanka* (Delhi: Oxford University Press, 1983), 104–36.

the forest and clear the path for nirvana, without engaging in teaching or the study of any books (289). Yakkaduve here ridicules the critique that monks promise to seek nirvana when they gain admission to the order: "A young boy does not know the meaning of the words he repeats during the ceremony of ordination. But as he grows up, if he is under good guidance, he will probably try to tread the nibbanic path" (290).

The literature shows that *sanghadisesa* violations befell even the *arahants* (saints), so why talk of detailed rules (as the commissioners do) for mere worldly *(prithagjana)* monks? Anyway, monks know how to purify themselves, and the laity does not need to tell them how, nor worry about sangha purity.

Since there is no possibility of reaching nirvana in this birth, the next best alternative is to work for reaching nirvana in a future birth. Asceticism is not the only way to do this. Even if all the vinaya rules are followed, will nirvana be reached? Monkhood is purity of mind (299). In whatever luxury a monks lives, monkhood exists if the mind is pure, and whatever the austerities a monk practices, there is no monkhood if his mind is impure. Monkhood is not exterior appearance (300–301). People today look not for morality *(sila)* but its appearance. Yakkaduve here keeps making a distinction between vinaya rules and "rules of monkhood" *(sramana pratipatti),* thereby making the vinaya mechanical and inorganic. "If a monk lives without violating even some vinaya rules, that is a valuable and noble attempt; but if such fierce impurities of monkhood as desire, miserliness, jealousy, hatred, craftiness, haughtiness, pride, hypocrisy, harassing others, exasperating others, and revengefulness thrive in his mind, what is the use of his observing those vinaya rules?" (302–303).

On the question of monks and salaries, Yakkaduve takes the example of a salaried monk who spends some of his salary on his living expenses and spends the rest on his pupil's education and well-being. He only violates *nisangipatici* (Pali, *nisaggayapacitti*), but in spending the money thus he would be practicing *sramana pratipatti* (the rules of monkhood) and shaking off *sramana dosa, sramanakasata,* and *sramana mala* (the impurities of monkhood); traveling fully the *sasana* path; and getting closer to purity of mind *(cittaparisuddhi).* Further, argues Yakkaduve, accepting a salary is not *parajika,* not a *sanghadisesa,* common among monks and which even affected the arahants who abolished all defilements, not a *thullaccaya,* which is literally a "big [gross] violation," but a violation of the fourth order, an *apatti* that is low in *dosa (atthulla);* a microscopic offense *(khuddaka apatti);* it is a lean offense *(lahukapatti);* and only a violation of etiquette *(acara vipatti).* Monkness is more serious than observing rules (303–304). To label monks, in newspapers and commission reports, as fallen from purity for accepting salaries without thereby examining the rule in the context of the vinaya is a crime and a destruction of the sasana *(sasana vinasa)* (304). The Buddha instituted vinaya rules only after the *prathamabodhi,* the first twenty years of his Enlightenment. Till then the disciples observed monkness to perfection. The Tripitaka shows that disciples in the *pascimabodhi,* the period after the first twenty years of Enlightenment, declined in *mahanakama* (304–305).

Involvement in building works, the "vocation of the books," and meditation are recommended as ways of expelling defilements such as lust *(kama),* anger *(krodha),* the rusting of monkness *(sramanamala),* the staining of monkness *(sramanakasta),* and the polluting of monkhood *(sramanadosa)* (307–308).

The Buddhists of the Sasanaraksaka Bauddha Mandalaya (who supported the commissioners), these "Commissioner Buddhists," and the robed men who were their advisors are uttering nonsense when they say that the use of money makes monks *parajika* (311).

The texts instruct that mind and body of young monks must be engaged in something, according to their tastes. If this is not done, their minds will be filled with natural things such as sexual thoughts *(kama samkalpana).* They will either leave robes or pollute monkness and bring discredit to themselves and the sasana (311–12). Even in ancient times, *granthadhura* ("vocation of the books") was followed by young monks, with the old and weak following the *vidarsanadhura* ("vocation of meditation"). Most of the young monks of today will, when they get old, undoubtedly meditate full time and engage in *vidarsanadhura,* following the culture of monkhood. Till then, if we do not let young monks attenuate the power of impurities and thus engage in monastic practices by devoting their lives to activities useful to our country, nation, and religion, the result will be, as we can all witness, not only a pollution-induced diminution of the Order but its extinction (312).

There are even today monks who do building works *(navakarmanta).* Young monks trained in academic study are not interested in such work. They cannot in any case do such work full time. They cannot be meditating full time either, because of their unruly youth. There are no more *dana, pirit* and *pamsukula* in the country (i.e., these have declined in number) which rules these (i.e., ritual services to the laity) out as a full-time activity. If they do not work in *granthadhura* (as the commissioners want them to) by engaging themselves in teaching as they have always done, and which is what they like to do, and which they do in keeping with monkness, and which constitutes a service to country, nation, and religion—how would they be expected to spend their monastic lives? (313).

The commissioners are trying to artificially create a sangha of aging meditators and servile young monks amenable to the wishes of the elites by means of not allowing them to teach even in a pirivena and even without pay, when it is in keeping with both vinaya and custom, and even when it is a way to make their monkhood successful (313).

To summarize some other points Yakkaduve makes: He (a) defends the teaching of astrology on the grounds that it is needed to determine the times for *uposatha* (confessions) and defends the teaching of medicine as well; (b) argues that, irrespective of whether you call it salaried jobs or service, teaching is what the monks did until the advent of Christian supremacy in the field of education; (c) opposes mixed education in the new pirivena universities, contrarily to its advocacy by the commissioners, arguing that since what is important for women is "unblemished character" (an euphemism for virginity), they should have a separate college. (This is the male position, no longer much in vogue, that women need be educated, if any, only up to a point.)

YAKKADUVE'S RESPONSE
An Appraisal

In this detailed response, Yakkaduve defended traditional monasticism replete with its inequities, property holding, and general involvement in the web of mundane social relations. Indeed he asked for more laxity and established a precedent for other monks to do the same. Rahula and Yakkaduve both claimed that these activities and possessions do not in anyway compromise morality. The commissioners, as did the ordinary people, found this unconvincing. They found the visible asceticism of meditators, which Yakkaduve derides, to be a more convincing index of morality than conventional monasticism.

It is not that the Commissioners wanted all monks to go to the forest and meditate, as Yakkaduve rhetorically asserts. What they were concerned with is inner virtue. It is simply easier to suppress disbelief that a monk is virtuous, when he owns little, meditates, and is a recluse than it is when he owns property, does not meditate, and is involved in political activity. Yakkaduve talks about morality. But the image of the monk he portrays is that of the ordinary representative of established monasticism, who is less convincing as a moral person than a meditator or forest monk.

It is true that a young boy, at admission, does not know the meaning of renunciation and he needs "good guidance" to tread the nibbanic path (290). But little is done in established monasticism to give him that "good guidance." What we hear instead, from informants and from written accounts are quarrels between teacher and pupil, the teacher's miserliness and the resulting alienation of the pupil.[36] Where training is given, it is to obey the teacher unquestioningly and to perform ritual, for the benefit of the laity, which may be moral but may also not be so at all. The whole point, made by young monks over and over again, is that there is no such guidance, one reason for which is the absence in the teacher-monk the qualifications to do so. Besides, senior monks are too busy managing property or doing politics to advice, train, and motivate their pupils in morality. Yakkaduve is again talking about the ideal, forgetting the reality.

When Yakkaduve says "Monks know how to purify themselves," he is referring to the vinaya acts of ritual purification. But the issue involved here is morality, which has nothing to do with ritual. Further, while he invokes vinaya here he dismisses it when it suits him, as we saw above.

In this response, Yakkaduve takes as axiomatic the fact that the possibility of reaching nirvana does not exist, which indicates that his position is the orthodox monastic one. In contrast, there are heterodox Buddhists, both lay and monk (lay meditators and forest monks), who believe that nirvana can be reached here and now. Yakkaduve's position highlights the problem in traditional monasticism and in traditional lay Buddhism: the infinite postponement of the nibbanic goal precludes a serious attempt at moral development and instead encourages a propensity to make merit by hook or crook, which leads to a preoccupation with it and a greed for it, as perceptive monks such as Rahula and Kalukondayave have pointed out. The motivation for merit making is the very mundane one of luxurious future births brimful with sense pleasures and, increasingly now-a-days, for gaining mundane goals here and now by resort to ritualism and cultic activity (like *pirit, bodhi puja,* and vows to the Tooth Relic). Motivated by grossly material goals, these activities, far from having a moral purpose, are utterly bereft of even the tranquility of mind achieved by the ordinary folk in simple acts like offering flowers under the quiet full moon. The corollary of this kind of cultism for furthering grossly mundane goals is the involvement of the practitioners with ethically questionable economic adventures and sometimes violent crime.

When Yakkaduve complains of people looking not at morality but its appearance, his real purpose is to try to debunk the ascetic monks, radically critical laity, and the Vinayavardhana movement. He claims that violations of vinaya are not as serious as harboring within oneself jealousy, hatred,

---

36. See, for example, Bo. Nandissara, *Loku hamuduruvan vetatayi* (Haputale: New Royal, 1991). This work is discussed in chap. 6.

craftiness, haughtiness, pride, hypocrisy, vengefulness, and the tendency to harass and exasperate others. Statements by both lay and young monk informants frequently show clearly that these qualities are not uncommon among monks, which would make them innocent of both vinaya and morality, to use Yakkaduve's own distinction. Monkness no doubt is more serious than rules, but informants assert that it is reassuring if rules are observed.

Yakkaduve says that most of the young monks of today will meditate when they get old. The problem here is that there is no evidence of this. If this is true, we should find old monks of today meditating. Who are "old monks" anyway? In the present context, namely his rebuttal of the commissioners, the contrast is between young and old. Since monks over thirty cannot be considered young, we must consider monks over thirty to be "old" in Yakkaduve's sense. But rarely do these or even older monks meditate. Rather, they are engaged in enterprises, employment, politics, ritualism, and such other mundane activities, including writing chauvinist and racist articles to newspapers and other popular publications. Given the above, it is not a bad idea to "create aging meditators" and "servile young monks," as Yakkaduve alleges the Commissioners are doing.

Yakkaduve's case for monks engaging in building works *(navakarmanta)* is contrived and labored. Such work is part of the routinization of monasticism. This is attested to by the fact that other monks argue the opposite. For example, Hendiyagala, one of the three Vidyodaya monks whose work I discussed at length, far from advocating such work, singles it out as obstructive to even proper social service, not to mention the contemplative life to which Yakkaduve makes these activities integral. Thus for Hendiyagala, navakarmanta, rather than being an aspect of Buddhist monastic life, reveals an "ignorance of Buddhism."[37]

Underneath his rhetoric, Yakkaduve is attempting to defend the monastic status quo and all its worldly accoutrements (and their new extensions like salaries) against the modernist Buddhist critique of Vinayavardhana and other groups who advocate a pure Buddhism reminiscent of Weber's ancient Buddhism. The defensive nature of Yakkaduve's position is expressed in the tiresomeness of his textual details which we have just quoted and into which he reads meanings favorable to him. For example, he splits hairs to show that accepting money is not a vinaya offense that is injurious to morality *(silavipatti)* and argues that it is only an injury to etiquette *(acaravipatti)*. He is sophistically juggling with words when in fact accepting a salary is contrary to the ideals of monkhood, as expressed, for example, in the tenth precept

37. Hendiyagala Silaratana, *Gramasamvardhanaya,* 21–22.

of the basic morality of the monk, the promise not to touch silver and gold. Besides, by saying that vinaya observance may not necessarily reflect inner morality he relegates vinaya to a mere externality, ignoring the fact that various elements of vinaya-based behavior are not discrete items but integral parts of a code whose meaning is inner purity;[38] and that externalities like demeanor are in fact integral to internalities like those reflected in, for example, the *uposatha* confessions. Yakkaduve's is a mechanistic and, especially for an Elder *(thera)*, a strongly contrived view of vinaya, denying its moral purpose and treating it as mere ritual. It is a self-contradictory reversal of his own advocacy of morality as a reality rather than an external appearance.

We can further make the following observations on Yakkaduve's critique. In defending salaries, he refers to a salaried monk as spending half of his salary on the education of his pupil. This is a hypothetical monk and while some may indeed do this, the more prevalent practice is for the monk to keep the salary for himself.[39] Yakkaduve advances, as does Rahula, the argument that in ancient times the study of books (i.e., the ancient equivalent of salaried social service) was done by the vigorous young monks, leaving meditation for the old, and he complacently assumes that the young monks of today, after earning and enjoying salaries, will take to meditation in old age. This is an importation in two-stage form into Buddhist monastic life of the four-stage progress from mundaneity to renunciation in puranic Hinduism. As such it is an implicit admission of the fact that monastic life is largely a form of lay life. The fact that such an admission is consistent with his and his colleagues' advocacy of the role of the monk as social service in fact gives them away. Thus what we see is a camouflaged attempt to make a case for the monks to behave like laymen, a development feared in the folk Buddhist conceptions of the extinction of Buddhism at the end of another 2,500 years, when it will be a common sight to see monks sitting by water with fishing rods in hand and wearing lay clothing except for a piece of yellow thread. It would appear indeed that the definition of the monk's role as "social service" has set in motion this process of secularization. Within the short period of

38. For an excellent discussion of the moral significance of vinaya, see John Holt, *Discipline* (Delhi: Motilal Banarsidas, 1981).

39. This is overwhelmingly brought out by the evidence of informants and reflected in the literature. See Nandissara, *Loku hamuduruvam vetatayi.* Salaried monks, like other monks with incomes, support their kin rather than their pupils. Correspondingly, young monks are supported by their kin. Some do support pupils but this is more the exception than the rule. Monks supporting their kin and kin supporting the young monks indicate a weakening of the act of renunciation, a development aided by many other recent developments, primary among which is the decline in the length and quality of a young monk's pupillary association *(nissaya)* with his teacher.

about fifty years, much less than the 2,500 years of the popular imagination, monks appear to be involved, as in some cases discussed below, in activities that are not in spirit dissimilar to fishing, robed revealingly in only a piece of yellow thread.

Yakkaduve elevates "activities useful to our country, nation, and religion" that young monks are enjoined to do as performers of social service into a quasi-spiritual activity. Basing himself on the scriptures, Yakkaduve argues that such activity, while engaged in maintaining monkness, is potently attenuative of impurities, thus directly linking social service with the path of liberation. This is a variation on the simpler Dharmapalite theory that monks must work for the uplift of the people, following the Buddha's exhortations. It reverses the Rahulite theory that monks must first achieve high spiritual states and then work for the people (though this is inconsistent in Rahula, especially in view of his idea that monks have come to see social service as their role due to social changes). The crucial terms here are what Yakkaduve refers to as "according to monkness." Rahula concurs, although in a convoluted way, when he talks about the need for a moral component in the monk whose role is social service. Like most other things in Sri Lankan Buddhism, the problem here is the difference between theory and practice. For, it is widely held that the new social service monks are devoid of monkness. Further, the ideal universalist morality of the monk is severely compromised in the context of the comprehension by Yakkaduve and his colleagues of "nation" *(jatiya)* as exclusively Sinhala Buddhist. Indeed Yakkaduve's writings, reminiscent of Dharmapala's, are interspersed with racist terms such as the derogatory reference to the Tamils as "illegal immigrants" *(kallatoni)*. If we take Yakkaduve's case for young monks being encouraged to doing things ceaselessly, such as organizing religious building works, so that their minds are kept away from sexual and other defiling thoughts, the problem is that such monks continue doing such work throughout their careers without ever graduating to the contemplative life of Yakkaduve's claims. In fact, what we find in practice is that it is not the young but old monks who do these. Besides, such organizational activity has assumed grotesque and exploitative form as brilliantly described and condemned in no uncertain terms by the early Rahula.[40]

40. *Satyodaya* (Colombo: S. Godage, 1992). First published serially, 1930–34. Examples of garish constructions are found everywhere. This is in fact a favorite pastime of the monks. It was criticized in no uncertain terms by Dharmapala and his hero giants. Often such new constructions are made at the expense of existing tasteful structures—through either their neglect, ensuring their ruin, or their outright demolition. The process was already visible enough in the early twentieth century for perceptive observers to draw public attention to it. See Ananda Coomaraswamy, "An open letter to the Kandyan

Yakkaduve's sophistry is further demonstrated in his equating modern salaried employment in the teaching profession with the ancient *granthadhura* (vocation of the books), while Rahula and Yakkaduve when suitable to them interpret *granthadhura* as "social service." Further Yakkaduve defends the study of astrology by monks as being needed to determine the date of the *uposatha* (confession). This circumvents the true critique of the commissioners, which is the absurdity of teaching astrology as a university subject, and the implied critique of monks practicing astrology, clearly tabooed in the *katikavat* (colloquia) literature as a beastly science. One could with equal reason argue that since monks should learn to mend their torn robes, they should be taught all the technical and managerial knowledge necessary to run a garment factory.

Yakkaduve's opposition to the admission of female students to the new universities is based on the grounds that Vidyodaya and Vidyalankara were men only institutions, and they just happened to be granted university status. In his view there should be a separate university for women because what is important for women is "unblemished character," implying that women's education is a secondary matter and could be of inferior quality. Incidentally, as the commissioners pointed out, it is not true that the two colleges were simply granted university status; rather, two entirely new universities were established. Discriminatory denial of admission to these publicly funded universities on gender or any other basis is not defensible.

Yakkaduve's writings, as do those of his colleagues, refer constantly to "country, nation, and religion," a usage we have traced to Dharmapala. What they have in mind are Sri Lanka as a territorial unit, the Sinhala ethnic group, and Buddhism. The union of the three terms in this usage makes the territory of Sri Lanka one that belongs exclusively to the Sinhala Buddhist ethnic group. As the ethnic conflict has progressed, the religious factor has become attenuated to the extent that Sinhala Christians are included in the group to whom Sri Lanka belongs, even though in given contexts the supremacy of Buddhism is unambiguously asserted. This usage provides us with a clue to the worldview of these monks and their secular counterparts, for whom Sri Lanka is a Sinhala Buddhist political entity. It is striking that no spokesman of this group has ever spoken clearly and specifically about the fate of the

chiefs," *The Ceylon Observer*, 17 February 1905, pp. 5–6. The editor of the *Observer* footnoted his support by describing the "redecoration" of the structures as "irreverent, careless and unsuitable" and as "a source of regret to those who worship there." He adds: "Mr Coomaraswamy thinks it would be well if the Buddhist priests would interest themselves more actively in the protection and proper treatment of the structures with which their lives are so intensely associated."

minorities in that political entity. Alternatively, it has been vaguely suggested by some exponents of this worldview that the minorities would be part of this socio-political entity insofar as they merge their own cultural identity with that of the Sinhala Buddhists. Stated differently, the worldview expressed in the usage "country, nation, and religion" envisages a hegemonic Sinhala culture empowered to place its stamp on other cultures in order to bring about a homogeneous utopia.

Most striking of all, Yakkaduve's defense fails to address the significant issues raised by the commissioners. For this reason it comes through as an uninformed and sloganistic document. Correctly understood, the critique of the commissioners is twofold. First, they point out that the leading monks of the two pirivenas, at the establishment of the pirivena universities, removed the senior classes, their good teachers, and their extensive libraries to the universities, thereby ending the long and healthy tradition of monastic learning which had received international attention and even the admiration of the colonial masters. Second, the formerly pirivena monks, namely Yakkaduve and his colleagues, who took over the administration of the new institutions were devoid of the basic qualifications to set up and run a complex modern educational institution, with the result that they grossly mismanaged their trust, much to the detriment of these fledgling institutions. The second point, the question of qualifications, is a very significant one, and it expresses a social problem of no small measure. It is the troubling phenomenon of monks making public utterances on matters on which they are not qualified to do so, thereby influencing policy in ways that are detrimental to the public interest, a point we shall consider later on.

Finally, the cluster of texts produced by Yakkaduve and his colleagues at Vidyalankara bring out in full fruition the hegemonic Sinhala Buddhist ideology rooted in Dharmapala that lay dormant in the *Vidyalankara Declaration* and its amplification, *The Heritage of the Bhikku*. Whereas the monks at Vidyodaya accepted the pragmatic and economic aspect of Dharmapala's message, the Vidyalankara monks took over its racist and ideological aspect. As noted above, Dharmapala's anti-imperialism, which these monks had imbibed, brought them in contact with the youthful and anti-imperialist Marxist movement of the time.[41] Some of these monks addressed public meetings, in the mid 1940s, from the same platforms as the Marxists to whom they gave electoral support. But as soon as they realized that the Marxists wanted no part of Sinhala Buddhist hegemonism, they abandoned

41. Dharmapala's anti-imperialism refers literally to opposition to imperialism and is not related to the Marxist definition of imperialism as an extension of capitalism.

the latter.[42] Just before the campaign for the 1956 elections, they offered their support to any political party that accepted their "Ten Principles," which was a code word for Sinhala Buddhist hegemony. Candidate Bandaranaike accepted and thereby inaugurated an era of ethnic politics that has led to a near total breakdown of the social order.

THE HERITAGE OF THE BHIKKHU
Orthodox Critique

We shall now proceed to a detailed orthodox critique of Walpola Rahula's *The Heritage of the Bhikkhu* by a well-known scholar monk. This is followed by an anthropological assessment of *The Heritage.*

In 1948, two years after the publication of *The Heritage,* another scholar monk, Henpitagedara Gnanavasa, published a response to Rahula. The title of his book, *Bhiksuvage Urumaya Kumakda?* (What is the Heritage of the Bhikkhu?),[43] summarizes its purpose, namely that the heritage of the bhikkhu is not what Rahula says it is. This work of a hundred pages, about the same length as *The Heritage,* is in agreement with the latter in claiming that, for the past two thousand years, monks have guided the society's progress and that the lost dignity of the Sangha should be restored. Both emphasize the need for education, but in two different senses, *The Heritage* advocating modern secular education and Gnanavasa, the traditional. Consistent with this, and except for the more or less superficial similarities just noted, *Bhiksuvage Urumaya Kumakda?* is the polar opposite of *The Heritage.* Gnanavasa bluntly

---

42. For some perceptive observations on this, see Michael Roberts, *The 1956 Generations: After and Before,* G. C. Mendis Memorial Lecture (Colombo, 1981). I have a different perspective on my friend Michael's idea that it is the doctrinaire stance of the LSSP, their "urbane urbanity" and their "attachment to principle in the face of developing cultural issues in the 1940s and 1950s," that lost them their support base. No doubt this is true. But, I think, rather than leave this at the merely analytical and interpretive level, it is important to mention the obverse, namely, the opportunistic nature of the agenda of the Sri Lanka Freedom Party (SLFP), the crowning error of which was "Sinhala Only." It is under visionless and corrupt leadership that the people's own potential for "urbane urbanity' and "attachment to principle" is undermined. Under able, disciplined, and honest leadership, Singapore, a small city state with practically no conventional resources, was able to achieve an admirable standard of living and opportunities for its people. The most acute crisis in Sri Lanka today is the crisis in leadership, which can do with some urbanity and attachment to principle. Though slightly romanticized, an early modern observer made a reasonably realistic assessment of the potential for urbanity of the people themselves. See Ananda Coomaraswamy, "The Village Community and Modern Progress," *The Ceylon National Review* 2, no. 7: 249–60.

43. Henpitagedara Gnanavasa, *Bhiksuvage Urumaya Kumakda?* (Colombo: Svastika Press, 1948). Parenthetical references in this section are to this text.

claims that what Rahula says is not what the Buddha taught. The work remained unpublished for a year, which means that it was a more prompt response to Rahula than is indicated by its date of publication. The author was persuaded to write the book by his elder brother and teacher, Henpitagedara Gnanasiha, another monk who played a prominent role in the 1956 and post-1956 nationalist politics. In the following pages I give an extended summary of Gnanavasa's book, extended because, unlike *The Heritage,* this work is not available in English. Further, such a summary will help convey with some degree of authenticity the flavor of the argument.

At the foundation of the book are two concepts, *bhavagami* (conducive to rebirth) and *vibhavagami* (conducive to escape from rebirth). Gnanavasa asserts that all action can be categorized under the one or the other of these two. *Bhava* means rebirth or samsaric existence. Thus bhavagami action perpetuates one's existence in samsara, with no release from it. People observe the five precepts and do other virtuous acts to gain merit, not because they seek nirvana, but because they want happy and luxurious rebirths in the form of divine beings or wealthy and powerful human beings. Thus good deeds are done because of a desire to prolong samsara. Any act done with the desire for happy rebirths is an act prolonging samsaric existence. Vibhavagami refers to the opposite action, namely action that is designed to prevent samsaric rebirth. A vibhavagami, a person walking the path of extinguishing rebirth, considers both comfort and suffering as misleading. These opposites as well as success and failure and so forth are viewed by the vibhavagami not as absolutes but as relativities. The vibhavagami path is one that devalues all relativities—comfort and suffering, success and failure, and so forth. The only absolute is liberation, progress towards which is the task of the vibhavagami. It is the essence of the Buddha's doctrine to lead men on the vibhavagami path.

Rahula's main thesis is that the true vocation of the monk is service to others. In Gnanavasa's view, this is to confound Buddhism and the bhikkhu. The welfare of others is indeed the aim of Buddhism. This, Buddhism shares with other religions. But the essence of Buddhism should be sought in what is distinctive to it. This is the vibhavagami path. The aim of the bhikkhu is not the welfare of others but the perfection of himself through self-discipline. Undoubtedly, tasks noninjurious to this primary and unnegotiable commitment can be undertaken as one wishes. The Buddha's injunction to go out and work for the good and benefit of the many refers not to material good and welfare but to the spiritual. There are many socially beneficial teachings in Buddhism and, if these are consciously followed for the benefit of society, that would be a commendable act. But that does not constitute the fulfillment of the truly Buddhist goal. That is only to utilize Buddhist ideas for mundane benefit and to achieve social goals.

It is the essence of the Buddha's doctrine to lead men on the vibhavagami path. The doctrine has no essential link with or interest in the progress of society. Gnanavasa reminds us that the Buddha was criticized by some of his contemporaries as "an ascetic who destroys social progress" *(bhunahu samano gotamo)*. This does not mean that Buddhism has no relevance for mundane society. As a middle path that avoids extremes, it obviously contains numerous teachings that are relevant for the welfare of society. However, if behavior resulting from such teachings contributes to social welfare, that is a by-product that constitutes a benefit to society but not the achievement of the distinctively Buddhist goal.

Buddhism makes a clear distinction between the life of the monk and that of the layman. It provides rules of behavior for the layman. These are the five precepts. Conformity to these enable a life of merit, which will cause rebirth. The precepts do not constitute a path to liberation. The five precepts of the layman are promoters of social harmony. The five additional precepts that, along with these, constitute the basic discipline of the monk have quite a different purpose. These added five precepts—avoidance of sex, money, comfortable beds, entertainments, untimely food—are utterly irrelevant for social harmony. But they control desire and therefore have the utmost relevance for vibhavagami, the path of liberation.

A monk's life illustrates further the vibhavagami path. He is of shaven head. His robes are stitched together ideally from discarded cloth. He depends on others for his sustenance. He considers it a violation of discipline even to earn his living. Such a life is necessary to gain freedom from the idea of the self, but it is utterly inconsistent with service to others. The rules of monastic behavior and the principles that underlie them are incompatible with serving others. Their aim is to set the monk on the vibhavagami path.

Had the purpose of monkhood been service to society, says Gnanavasa, it would have been so designed. As it is, the monk's life is disciplined by numerous rules none of which involves service to others. Therefore, unless the monk who engages in social service is of exceptional moral courage, he would not be able to sustain his monkhood (because of the potential for temptation while dealing with people). If he is not going to sustain his monkhood because of social service, continuing to be a monk is an unnecessary burden.

One could question whether it is not because of the interest in the welfare of others that the Buddha, as bodhisattva, aspired to Buddhahood rather than reaching nirvana as an arahant or a Paccekabuddha.[44] Similarly one could ask

---

44. According to Theravada Buddhism, a person reaches nirvana as a Buddha, a Paccekabuddha or an Arahant. A Paccekabuddha is a silent Buddha, equal to the Buddha in all aspects except that he does

whether it is not for the sake of others that the Buddha instructed his disciples to wander about the countryside for the good and benefit of the many. It is true that both have in view the welfare of others. However the "welfare" meant is not the same as the welfare Rahula advocates. The former is vibhavagami and the latter bhavagami. A disciplined monk teaching the vibhavagami path will not be considered by today's society as performing a service to others.

One could then ask whether service to society is totally inappropriate for the monk. This, says Gnanavasa, is to ask whether it is appropriate or not to consume food. It is, but only certain foods, and at certain times. Similarly, certain services to society are appropriate for the monks and others are not. There should be no objection to employing monks in appropriate types of social service. But with the possible exception of teaching the doctrine, social service is an appendage, not an essential part of a monk's life.

Next, Gnanavasa turns to Rahula's statement that social service should only be done by virtuous, meditative monks (48). But Rahula also says that monks today lack virtue and are a burden to society and that they are too lazy to go into the forest to meditate. It is surprising, says Gnanavasa, if such monks were to suddenly achieve virtue surpassing that of forest monks and then step into social service. On the other hand, asks Gnanavasa, what is the use of meditation, which is an instrument of taming inner defilements, in social service? Is it not like sharpening a razor to go to war?

Gnanavasa argues that service to others in the sense Rahula uses the term is clearly incompatible with the aims of monkhood. He suspects that Rahula is aware of this. This is why he tries to give social service a moral legitimation by insisting that it is only monks more virtuous than even the forest dwelling ascetics who should go into social service. Gnanavasa compares this device to that of the *Mahavamsa* as composed "for the serene joy and emotion of the pious." Rahula's own argument is that the real subject of the *Mahavamsa*, stories about kings, are taboo for monks, and the *Mahavamsa* author is introducing a moral element where none exists purely to cover himself up.

The Buddha permitted the monks to change minor rules, but this was never done. According to the texts, rules were not changed in the first few months after the Buddha's death because there was no agreement as to what the minor rules were. It is Rahula's view that the real reason for leaving the rules unchanged is not this stated one, but the fact that no social and eco-

---

not preach his discovery to others. An arahant is a person who practices the doctrine preached by a Buddha and reaches nirvana, the paradigmatic arahants being the Buddha's disciples. Of these the Buddha alone is a "savior."

nomic changes took place in that short period to warrant changes in rules. Gnanavasa takes Rahula to task for this suggestion. Quoting the texts, he argues that enough changes did take place during the Buddha's own time to warrant changes of minor rules.[45] The texts testify to the monks mingling with laymen and doing such things as riding horses, running, jumping, dancing, and singing, which are clearly changes. Lay society changed as well, as when laymen ridiculed a disciplined monk's measured movements.

For Gnanavasa, the observance of numerous vinaya rules by Theravada monks is proof of the fact that the moral validity of mendicancy and the monastic rules is independent of any social substructure. That is, the moral fortitude and ascetic commitment of some monks have been powerful enough to withstand the forces of "social changes," allegedly resulting in changes of rules. The vibhavagami ideal has triumphed periodically and consistently, as illustrated by the monks Sabhakami, Yasa, Moggaliputta Tissa, Dimbulagala Kasyapa, and Valivita Saranamakara.

The ten points of the Vajjis, proposed by the Vajji monks a century after the Buddha's death, are not accepted even today, twenty-five centuries later. There is no doubt that, though not accepted in theory, some of the ten are accepted in practice, but the relevant fact is that they are not officially accepted, and even in practice not all ten are accepted. This to Gnanavasa is proof of a force that counteracts the socio-economic forces held by Rahula to be invariably productive of change in monastic rules.

Gnanavasa goes on to take up one more of Rahula's arguments in support of changing monastic rules, namely the fact that the Buddha himself changed rules from time to time. This is true, but the Buddha did so when confronted with appropriate circumstances. Besides, the Buddha never changed rules in a manner that would shatter the foundations of mendicancy or that would injure the fundamental rules originally enunciated. The task of the monk is to follow the Buddha's noble example and not to violate the spirit of the freedom he gave to change rules. That is, the monks must change rules only so far as it is necessary to ensure and enhance monastic ideals within a changed social environment, and not for purposes of accommodating and legitimizing lax behavior. Rules should be changed only in such a way that the monk's moral stature is enhanced rather than diminished.

Gnanavasa marshals textual evidence to demonstrate the fact that the vinaya rules were enacted on a pragmatic basis, when circumstances prompted their proclamation. That is, the vinaya texts depict the rules not as static but as a code that grew responsively. When an offense was committed, a rule

45. References here are to the *Samyukta Nikaya* (Gnanavasa, 45–46).

was promulgated prohibiting it in the future. When the monastic order faced changes, rules were changed appropriately, but not abolished. In the postcanonical history of Buddhism, during various periods when monastic morality declined, rather than giving in to "social conditions," appropriate additional rules were promulgated in the form of compendia known as katikavat, as well as other instruments such as the Mihintale slab inscription, the Jetavana slab inscription (in Sanskrit), and the Gal Vihara inscription. In all cases, the purpose was the preservation of the monk's vibhavagami commitment.

Rahula's book, says Gnanavasa, is not an attempt to facilitate the service of monks as guides of men in the vibhavagami path. It is an account of the services rendered by monks towards the mundane progress of society.

It is true that, as Rahula says, from the earliest times, monks worked for the welfare of others. Monks did not hesitate to interfere in the country's political affairs when they perceived trouble. Because of this they changed the course of the country's history more than once. But at all times, they saw to it that these outside activities were not deletions of their inner virtue. It is for this reason that virtuous monks are held in high esteem and pride by the people. Monks acted to enthrone individuals and to save the country from chaos, which are utterly mundane acts. But none of these were allowed to contaminate the ideals of monkhood. Monks have opposed the powers fearlessly and become powerful themselves. Yet, if such a monk violated rules, the Sangha did not hesitate to mete out appropriate punishment. The Jetavana Sanskrit inscription says that not to punish a wrongdoers is itself a crime.

Pursuing Rahula further on the socio-economic argument, Gnanavasa focuses on the former's contention that a specific monastic life with economic interests came into being in Sri Lanka due to socio-economic changes. Rahula's statement is an exaggeration, says Gnanavasa, and the important question is not whether monks controlled property, servants, budgets, and so forth, but whether these violated the foundations of a monastic morality. The answer to this, according to Gnanavasa, is in the Sanskrit inscription of the Jetavana monastery (82–83), which clearly indicates the supremacy of morality. The economic organization was subordinate to the goals of monkhood and was never allowed to compromise the latter (84). Rahula's statement that monks were paid salaries, says Gnanavasa, is a misleading exaggeration, which should be understood against the rule books such as *Sikhavalanda vinisa* and *Sekhiya* and rules which outlaw residence in the monastery for anyone who is "anti-social, anti-Buddhist and conducts a faulty monastic life" (85). While Rahula is keen to show how changing socio-economic conditions transformed monastic life towards worldliness, he omits to mention the inner forces that counteracted and repelled the worldly tendency. The rampart of monastic life did show signs of decay at times, but it was also constantly repaired, and its strength never allowed to vanish (86). Thus it is not the case that monastic rules were increasingly relaxed, but through katikavat and other means new rules were enunciated to meet any relaxation (89). The threat of decay was ever present, but so was the ability of the order for moral rejuvenation. It is clear that what Rahula advocates as "changes" are moral decay for Gnanavasa.

At times Gnanavasa comes to the open about the political rhetoric. The real invitation behind "come to social services," he says is "come to the [socialist] revolution." "Social service," though elucidated in numerous ways, is none other than the revolution. Many contemporary monks have embraced socialism. They value being partners of the revolution more than they do the disciplined morality of the monk.

Expressing the conservative fear of the time, Gnanavasa predicts that "in the future a socialist system of government will pervade the world" (97). The question then is, "Will a role for the monk be left in that world?" In such a system there will be no place for anyone without a job. All employable people will be employed. This is a law in one of the existing socialist states.[46] Such a state will not consider monkhood as a form of gainful employment. The future socialist society will not accept as essential the life style of a bhikkhu organized according to vibhavagami principles. Therefore, the social task of the monk is not politics disguised as "social service" nor social service in the mundane sense, but making a case for himself as the representative of dharma and virtue in the emerging new (socialist) social order. If the monk fails to do so, the messengers of a message that must be conveyed to the future will be extinct. There will be none to carry the dharma to the serene postrevolutionary world in which there is time and leisure for contemplation.

Gnanavasa explains that the "religion" he is talking about is not ritualism but the discipline and morality of the vibhavagami path. Buddhists should give serious thought to a broad program for future religiousness. He is genuinely concerned about Buddhist goals and values, and saving the true path from the threat of destruction posed by socialism.

Here we have a glimpse into the genuine core belief of the best of Bud-

---

46. The allusion is clearly to the Soviet Union. The view that all employable people are employed "by law" in the Soviet Union was part of the elaborate anti-Soviet propaganda of the time perpetuated by the ruling conservative and capitalist elite, its vehemence being testimony to the great anxiety in which they held the left movement, especially the most popular left party, the LSSP.

dhists who see unparalleled nobility in their religious doctrine, but who feel it is fragile and therefore should be protected. This idea is easily taken over by others and, in the name of preserving the religion, used as a justification of aggrandizement. But the question of the fate of the vibhavagami path was a legitimate one in the context of the time.

THE TWO HERITAGES OF THE BHIKKHU
Rahula and Gnanavasa

Let us now assess the two differing conceptions of the purpose of monastic life held by the two prominent scholar monks Rahula and Gnanavasa by critically examining them, relating them to their social and ideological causes, and exploring their ramifications.

The main argument of *The Heritage,* which as already noted is an elaboration of *The Declaration* and therefore the official position of the Vidyalankara College, or the most powerful faction of that college at the time, is that it is fitting for monks to engage in politics. This is supported by (a) giving "politics" a broad definition, (b) arguing that monks have played a political role from the earliest times, and (c) appealing to the law of change. We shall begin by critically elucidating these.

The first thing to note about *The Heritage* is that it is a response to a political and ideological challenge. Its literary devices—exaggeration, understatement, sarcasm, wit, and so forth—make it further obvious that *The Heritage* is more a value-imbued, activist document than the scholarly treatise it is often mistaken to be. Its "facts" are primarily derived from the *Mahavamsa*. This does not make the "facts" untrue, neither does that make them true. What is clear is that these "facts" are necessarily selective, given Rahula's explicit admission that the work is a response to the political and ideological position that monks should not participate in "politics." Besides being polemical the book is also a manifesto, a call to action, which contributes further to its value-imbued status. Nevertheless, *The Heritage* comes through as a perceptive, stimulating, and challenging work.

From the above, it will be clear that *The Heritage* inevitably downplays the aspects of monastic life in ancient Sri Lanka that did not involve relatively highly visible social involvement. The most obvious of these is the preoccupation of the monk with his own liberation. The tension between ascetic absorption with oneself and involvement with the secular society in a mundane, ministerial, or ritualistic capacity has always characterized the history of Buddhist monasticism. Rahula's tautological statement that, in ancient times, monks were held in high esteem because of their social involvement, or that the socially involved *dhammakathika* monks were judged more important for the religion than the ascetic *pamsukulika* monks, understates the strength and esteem of the latter category.

Periodic proclamations of the orthodoxy in the katikavat compendia and inscriptions demonstrate the strength and tenacity of the rules of discipline, whose purpose was the direction of monks towards their own liberation and away from social involvement and working for the benefit of others. Asceticism and orthodoxy were positively evaluated and safeguarded by the broad framework of tradition, which consisted of (a) the traditionalism of monastic socialization; (b) the monk's participation in what Hocart, after Buddhist monks, called "the heredity of master and pupil,"[47] i.e., the sharing of moral substance between teacher and pupil, which also emphasized prolonged association with a teacher, until the pupil's moral strength reached unassailability; (c) monastic ritualism, especially the *upostha* (confessions), and ritualistic and disciplined ministerial relations with the laity; and (d) the threat of excommunication backed by the coercive power of the state. None of these are effectively present today.

Rahula's ideological position includes the approval of monks engaging in activities for the welfare of others as long as these activities did not impede the religious life of the monk (*The Declaration,* quoted in *The Heritage,* xx). The ideal political bhikkhu of *The Heritage* is of pure character, altruistic, upright, and honest. This is a position that all monks must necessarily take because "the religious life" or morality is an indispensable component of the very definition of monkhood. That is, whatever a monk does in practice, he must at least externally adhere to the rules and image of the monk.

Monks receive legitimacy and esteem precisely to the extent that they exemplify such an image. Monks who do not conform to this image may yet have power derived from political or economic functions, and could have clout, sometimes literally, but no esteem, and the clout is strictly related to political and economic resources. When these resources dry up, the monk loses all power.[48] Therefore the position that the vocation of the monk is

47. Hocart, *Kings and Councillors,* 77.

48. An example, replete with physical clout, is Galeboda Gnanissara, who lost power at the assassination of President Premadasa and even more at the election of the United Front government in 1994. Reportedly, the present government has been contemplating demolishing some of the commercial structures that Galeboda has built on public walks near his monastery, pretending them to be structures built for altruistic purposes. That the government has failed to accomplish this objective and is hesitating provides a clue to the tenacity and the reincarnative capabilities of politically agile monks, of which Galeboda is a shining example. Others without these gifts, however, could wither away, although they might be reborn at the election of a government hospitable to them. Behind this phenomenon are the mutually reinforcing machinations and magical beliefs of corrupt and ruthless politicians and other power manipulators.

social service inherently contains the idea that such a monk should be virtuous. But this could be and often is merely an ideal to be invoked in public. Many monks who took to "politics" in the broad sense of social involvement ended up compromising the rules of discipline. Those who took to more specifically political activity have shown no greater moral capacity than lay politicians. Rahula imagines that "the political bhikkhu" will even become a Buddhist tradition, like *granthadhura,* the vocation of the books. This has partially come true. The political bhikkhu has come into being, but not the morality which in Rahula's conception is indispensable to that monk.

Rahula is critical of the Christian missionaries both for their attempted subversion of Buddhism and for their role in trying to portray the monk as a recluse from society. But, like some other critics of the missionaries, he is here influenced by the very missionary activism and ideology he criticizes. That is, the monastic social role he advocates and even some aspects of his conception of Buddhism puts him in the category of "Protestant Buddhist."

The role Rahula claims for the monk of ancient Sri Lanka and envisages for the ideal future monk is closer to that of the Christian minister than of the ideal Buddhist monk. When Rahula says that a monk is not a selfish person who would accept the laity's generosity and will give nothing in return, he is defensively incorporating a new "unselfishness" into the conception of the monk, because "selfishness" is a standard Christian critique of Buddhism. In orthodox Buddhist belief, merit would accrue to a person looking after the needs of the monk, but it is not a thing the monk can or need to give, because merit is an automatic result of the act (though monks have cultivated the ritualism of explicitly granting merit for good deeds done). Thus, strictly speaking as an automatic result of the good deed, but in ritual convention as an act of the monk, merit is exchanged for good deeds and moral instruction (the receipt of which is itself a good deed), but Rahula is really not interested in this. He in fact ignores this mystical dimension of exchange. He is actually saying that the monk must return the laity's gifts by counter-gifts of political activity, which in his definition means social work, teaching the illiterate, giving medicines, health instruction, conflict resolution, technical advice, and so forth, which are mundane benefits, as are granted by Christian ministers to their flocks.[49]

Rahula's "Protestant Buddhist" attributes are further apparent in the state-

---

49. Young monks of today, two generations younger than Rahula, are echoing the idea that they should not accept anything for nothing but should instead give "from the monastery to the village." This is, however, neither spontaneous nor altruistic, because the motivation behind such giving is that of combating Christian evangelical groups.

ment that the early wandering monks preached, not philosophy and meta-physics, but simple moral ideas conducive to the material well-being of the generally poor, illiterate, unclean villagers, who they asked "to engage in just and moral trades, to do hard work, not to cheat customers, and not to be lazy" (*The Heritage*, 5). While these are certainly traceable to Buddhist texts, they sound more like Protestant virtues. These ideas, although present in Buddhism, are not prominent, and they have not had a sustained effect on the social order, as is obvious to any field worker and indeed implicit in the need for their present advocacy. In the idea of the "social worker monk" as a pervasive social force (deriving from Dharmapala), Rahula is implicitly and idyllically attributing to early Buddhist society in India and precolonial Sri Lanka an idealized prosperity and dynamism that has vanished due to the colonialist era deprivation of monks of their social service functions. The idea is inferred not from any reliable evidence but from the behavior of con-temporary Christian clergy. The idea of a social service monk of this type also implies a cultural problem that requires the presence of an activating force for a sleeping population.[50]

The ancient event that heralds to Rahula the importance, to monastic life, of service to others is the first-century B.C.E. "victory" of the *dhammakathika* over the *pamsukulika* monks. This distinction, which has no basis in the canon, is the result of "social changes and change in outlook of the people" (*The Heritage*, 27). Rahula is silent about what actually these changes were. This "victory" represents an inversion of the orthodox position and clearly was made possible by scholarship, "the power of intelligence and knowl-edge" (27). The "victory" consists of the acceptance of the view that study (which implies teaching) alone is adequate for the stability and longevity of the Sasana. The concern here is not the attainment of liberation, but the preservation of the Sasana, which became the reverberating cry of Sri Lankan Buddhism. This view represents the coming into being of a monastic estab-

---

50. This resonates with the lines of the Sinhala national anthem, which implores Mother Lanka to keep awakening her children constantly, giving them new life (*nava jivana demine nitina apa avadi karan mata*), making it quite obvious that the children are lifeless and eternally sleeping. It is no surprise that Dharmapala took as his major task the awakening of these children. As mentioned in chapter 2, images of closed eyes, sleeping, and awakening abound in the exhortations of Dharmapala. Ananda Sama-rakone's lively original lyric read "giving us new life, awaken us again, O mother" (*nava jivana demine navata apa avadi karan mata*). Composed under the British yoke, "navata" meaning "again" made sense, as the state of being asleep was linked to colonial domination. But some time after independence, *navata* ("again") was changed to *nitina* ("forever"), giving us the present image of eternal sleep in the national anthem. The opening of the original, *Namo namo mata*, was changed to the *Sri Lanka mata* of the present version on the quasi-astrological consideration that the original word configurations were inauspicious. In the original version the sleeping children, once awakened, are capable of staying awake.

lishment. The position is that practice is unimportant for the stability of the religion, and that the two spheres, precept and practice, could be embodied in two different types of monks, the scholars and the ascetics. From "unimportant to the stability of the religion" it is a small step to "unimportant altogether." This expresses a mutually fertilizing incentive for nonpracticing monks to be scholars and scholar monks to be nonpracticing. From the recent data we have, it is the scholarly (educated) monks who have an elective affinity for nonpractice. It is not surprising that Rahula is concerned to establish the importance, if not the adequacy, of precept (scholarship) because he is a scholar himself. Though no one advocates the abandonment of practice, this is what in fact happens, with rare exceptions.

The acceptance of scholarship as sufficient religious commitment has other implications. It alters the status of monks as virtuoso travelers of the fast path to liberation and puts them on the slow path of the layman. What is envisaged for them in their vows is the fast or true path. The slow path is one of merit making, which ensures more re-births and which relegates liberation to a distant, ever receding and ritualized goal. The path for the laity is slow because they are considered to lack the strength of will to travel the difficult and true path. Thus, by elevating precept above practice, the monks have, from the point of view of liberation, taken a retrograde step.

The formal acceptance of the validity of precept over practice puts on a conceptual foundation the idea of the monkhood as an establishment and a temporal power, thereby legitimizing aspects of behavior contradictory of monastic rules. It in effect takes away the regimen of the monks and liberates them in a different sense, namely to act in ways they think fit. The true and clear commitment of the monk is the other-worldly goal, and when that is taken away, the monkhood is freed of its basis and monks can engage in any activity. Their access to knowledge widens the range of such activity, and they can be very innovative. Some of these activities may well be moral and not out of keeping with the rules of discipline. But when the floodgates are open, as when knowledge is elevated over practice, there is no inner way to control the activities of monks, whereas such control is the essence of the renouncer's commitment. The controls are then exteriorized and become part of the control system of the broader social order, namely state regulation and public opinion. In particular, during times of radical social change, as in contemporary Sri Lanka, these external controls can become ineffective, and monks can engage in areas of action that are far from orthodox. Periodic reform movements and proclamations (like katikavat), constitute evidence of an order that is constantly tempted to disregard its traditional constraints. Sociologically, although not in terms of liberation, this is not an invariable disaster. Freedom from the strict ascetic rules provides the monks with an opportunity for creative application of ideas in their own self interest, as individuals or the group as a whole, and in the interests of the society.

Rahula argues that in ancient and medieval Sri Lanka a complex system of property was established for the monks to live in comfort because the monks were performing a useful social function. That is, the grant of property was not done for merit. This is doubtful because, although the socially useful work of the monks was acknowledged, and may even have been the primary reason for lavishing the monks with wealth, the element of merit was also present. Another possibility is that while the idea of remuneration for service was the primary reason behind supporting intellectually active monks, merit was the dominant reason behind the support given to many ordinary monks, who catered to the laity's ministerial needs or who just lead a virtuous life (like the forest monks). That mystical sanctions were used to discourage theft of the produce of monastic properties shows the opposite was true as well, namely that giving to the monastery bore mystical fruit, that is, it was meritorious. Rahula's argument ignores this mystical dimension and treats the monkhood merely as a socially and culturally useful professional stratum that was remunerated for its work. In other words, Rahula is making the point that monks were useful and productive members of society and not a burden to it. The implication is that monks who meditate are socially useless. "Usefulness" is here understood in completely mundane terms. Rahula's analysis ignores the value placed on asceticism in ancient times, which was probably as high as it is today. Why does Rahula take this position? Because, although he is "objectively" analyzing the past, his real objectives pertain to the present. He is doing at least two things. First, aware as he is of the criticism that monks are lazy and do nothing, he is asserting that this is not the case, or need not be. Second, he is justifying for the monk a position in contemporary society in which he can play a variety of roles, especially a political role, roles which may well be materially profitable to the monk.

Rahula's emphasis on "changing environmental circumstances and economic conditions" (*The Heritage,* 39) as the engine of change in monastic structures is related to his deemphasis of mystical factors, for example, his theory that monastic endowments were made by kings and chiefs purely because the monks were performing a useful mundane function. Mystical factors, as already pointed out, cannot be ignored in a sociological understanding of monastic wealth and of the procedures of its administration. Apart from mystical factors which involve religious belief, other factors were also at work (with or without the presence of religious belief). The most important of these was the overarching conception of kingship that has been well documented, which calls upon the king to support the religion, the inverse of which is the political use of the practice in terms of legitimizing his authority. Endowment of the monasteries can also be viewed as an integral part of the traditional polity, the essence of which was chronic instability. Raids and plunder were part of this state of affairs, which made both social and psychological demands on the king to endow the religious establishments. It is thus simplistic to think of monastic endowments as remuneration for social service. To do so is to impute to a past society our contemporary notions of remuneration. It is also to justify contemporary monks earning salaries for "social service," as Yakkaduve does in his rejoinder to the commissioners.

Rahula advocates a diversity of mundane activities for the monk. A monk can stay in robes and still practice almost any art or craft, science or profession. Examples from the practice of art and literature are supplied to support his position. He points out that the monks painted or got others to paint the shrines, were sculptors and writers of literary works. While the vinaya texts prohibit monks to paint or cause to paint figures of men, women, and animals, or even guardstones, they are allowed to paint or cause to paint flower and creeper motifs (*The Heritage,* 40, n. 3). Rahula's evidence shows that monks were allowed to cause only religious themes to be painted. (But today, monks paint secular subjects.) He says, quoting Coomaraswamy, that Buddhism became the patron rather than the opponent of the arts. Almost surreptitiously he is forgetting the distinction he himself documents between painting that monks are allowed and not allowed to do. He seems to suggest that monks can paint anything, which resonates with the idea that under the label "social service," monks can do anything.

The practice of writing provides even more apt illustrations. All literary works of ancient Sri Lanka deal with religious themes, which establish their legitimacy as subjects for monks. Once that broad acceptance is secured, monks have smuggled worldly themes of war, murder, sex, and violence into their works as the medieval literature, in particular the Jataka tales and the work of Totagamuve Rahula, illustrates. The same is true in the writing of the *Dipavamsa* and the *Mahavamsa,* the theme of which, stories about kings, is taboo. The *Dipavamsa* gets around this by stating at the end of every chapter that "even such powerful personages were subject to death and decay" (quoted in *The Heritage,* 42–48). The *Mahavamsa,* as observed before, ends its chapters by saying that each was composed "for the serene joy and emotion of the pious." Rahula cites these approvingly as illustrations of how monks circumvented a rule of discipline in their attempt to be useful to society. He is advocating the same for today's monks when he challenges his conservative critics and argues in favor of monks receiving the training and qualifications needed to function in a modern society.

To Rahula the writing of the *Mahavamsa* is a definite sign of the greater participation of monks in national activities. From this time onwards they began to engage in public affairs (*The Heritage,* 48). This is another way of saying approvingly that monks became actively involved in politics, even armed struggle. Rahula provides a list of examples, from early times to the coming of the Dutch, when monks allegedly rose to the occasion whenever the country was in danger, either from external threat or civil war, and played a prominent political role protective of the Sinhalas and Buddhism. The monks considered it "their task" to protect "the country and religion" (89). Indeed he suggests that, had it not been for the "ready and prudent acts of the monks, the nation and the religion would not have endured" (89). The implication of this is the gradual development of the idea that religion is something to be protected rather than integrated into the value system of the society. Atrocities can be and have been committed in the name of protecting and preserving the religion. Popular religiosity in the form of ritualism devoid of and indeed destructive of morality and supportive of immorality can be and are practiced similarly. Thus the paradox of violating the ethical norms of Buddhism in the very act of their ostensible preservation.

Rahula takes to task the British and the chief monks of Asgiriya and Malvatta for the act of appointment that made the recipients "spies" of the British government. He says the statement of the chief monks derives authority from the non-Buddhist governor and not from the Council of Sangha (*The Heritage,* 76–78). Rahula has so far been arguing vehemently and approvingly of the changes that have taken place in the Sangha that have enabled the monks to play a central role in politics and society. That role has been enacted within the context of the close association between the monks and the state. From this perspective, that is, by Rahula's own logic, it is difficult to find fault with the chief monks' relationship with the governor, who is the king's representative. Vidyodaya as we know took this position. It should be recalled that according to the Kandyan Convention kingship was not abolished but transferred to the king of England. Besides, although in fact this lapsed, in the Kandyan Convention the British undertook to safeguard Buddhism and its ministries. Rahula is clearly objecting to white colonial rule and not to the connection between the governor and the chief monks. Besides, in the past de facto non-Buddhist kings, like the Nayakkars, made connections with the religion for political and ceremonial purposes. In fact, it was not the "Sangha Council" but the king who appointed the chief monk, although lower appointments were made by the chief monk or the Sangha Council. Further, an important criterion in appointing a chief monk was loyalty to the king, which in Rahula's language would be equal to "being a spy for the king." Thus Rahula's position is inconsistent, because, if he is arguing for a connection between state and religion as an integral part or an exemplification of the monk's work as social service, it should be applicable to all situations irrespective of whether the king is foreign or native. As colonial rule progressed the native chiefs and the monks were distressed not at the connection between the non-Buddhist government and the Buddhist religion, but its severance.[51]

A further point relevant here is the possibility that the patronage provided by the British government before 1847 laid the foundation for a certain degree of stability and cohesion to the monastic centers Asgiriya and Malvatta. In precolonial times these centers held no common property; it was the British government that made a grant to them as totalities. The *viyadam padiya,* the allowance paid to the chief monks at Asgiriya and Malvatta that Rahula mentions (38), was a British innovation. It is indeed possible to argue that had the monks taken more creative steps to keep up with the new British colonial government and the new society it was ushering in, they would never have lost the preeminence they, according to Rahula, enjoyed for over two millennia. Instead of resenting what Rahula sarcastically calls the "Exalted English Government," the monks should have used the political shrewdness that kept them in the center of society for centuries to infiltrate it. They should have sent their students in numbers to modern schools, including Christian schools. That step would have given them the qualifications to belong to, rather than feel estranged from, the new society that was emerging, which is in fact what Rahula is advocating. It would have kept the ablest monks satisfied in their achievements, rather than frustrated by a system from which they felt alienated. That would have made them happy men and true patriots, rather than the disgruntled chauvinists who have in recent times constituted the main obstacle to the emergence of a peaceful, prosperous, and healthy society, adding insult to injury by expecting the laity to accept them as "guardian deities of the nation" *(jatiye muradevatavo).*

Rahula takes aim at the class of alienated Sinhalese who are western in customs and ways of thought. "They neither understand *bhikkhus* nor do they realize the national services performed or performable by these *bhikkhus.* Brought up according to the teachings of the missionaries, they believe that

---

51. The British government formally ceased its patronage of Buddhism in 1847. See K. M. de Silva, *Social Policy and Missionary Organisations in Ceylon, 1840–1855* (London, 1965).

bhikkhus should keep out of national activities and limit themselves only to receiving alms, chanting *pirit,* performing funeral rites and preaching sermons. They believe that *bhikkhus* should live a life limited to the four walls of their temples" (*The Heritage,* 95).

This critique is intended to meet the argument of D. S. Senanayake and his followers, who maintained that monks should not be involved in politics. It is true that some of those who hold this view are Christians or went to Christian schools. But the overwhelming majority of those who hold this view were trained not by the missionaries, but in the schools of the Buddhist Theosophical Society. They are, in Obeyesekere's usage, "Protestant Buddhists," or "Buddhist modernists," i.e., products of the very nationalist movement Rahula admires and attributes to the work of the monks. Having imbibed "Protestant" virtues and read books on Buddhism in English written by "Protestant Buddhists," they rightly comprehended the heritage of Buddhism as inner discipline, and saw that the monks had neglected this. They took over the Buddhist revival and also encroached into the monastic preserve of meditation, neglected by the monks.[52] These new Buddhists, also paralleling the Protestant analogy, were the business classes. But unlike the Protestants, the Buddhists gave up only one kind of ritualism, namely, pre-Buddhist exorcistic cults (and now as we see, not even these, or only a minority did). They continued to practice Buddhist ritual, in fact with greater intensity, as their business interests flourished. It is these classes that needed monks for pirit chanting, religio-economic and politically competitive merit-making ceremonies, and alms giving commensurate in lavishness with their business successes. It is this Buddhist class, of which the outstanding personality is Dharmapala,[53] rather than the alienated and Christianized Sinhalese that defined the monk as a morally based ritual figure who should not involve himself in politics. Monks were used by this class for the specific activity of merit making, an activity that Rahula generally devalues, although monks have performed such ceremonies for centuries, and with greater elaboration with the coming of Mahayana. Members of this class needed monks only to ensure a rebirth as good if not better than their present one. As Rahula rightly perceives, "political monks" would disrupt their undisturbed political and economic exploitation of the lower strata, insofar as

52. On this, see Richard Gombrich and Gananath Obeysekere, *Buddhism Transformed;* Michael Ames, "Social and Ideological Change"; Steven Kemper, "Buddhism without Bhikkhus"; Kitsiri Malalgoda, *Buddhism in Sinhalese Society,* all cited above.

53. Dharmapala did want monks to be socially involved, which is the basic thesis of this work, but that is quite a different exercise from the politics of the monks to which these classes object.

these monks were allied with leftist forces. This certainly was the major reason behind the campaign against them. Another reason is the view that for merit to be the more bountiful, the monks had to be virtuous, which, in the view of this class, the political monks were not.

There is some ambiguity as to whether Rahula advocated changes in the monkhood that would violate the essentials of monastic discipline. On the one hand, Rahula is emphatic on moral and spiritual values, because he says that monks who take to the social service of "politics" and work for the welfare of others should be on an even higher spiritual plane than the ascetic monks. This position is reiterated elsewhere as well. However, there are other statements that clearly contradict this and suggest a thoroughgoing approval of even doctrinal changes and changes in rules of discipline, as in his approval of the statement of Barua that the rise of various sects is "a sign of health [and] . . . clear proof of the increased vitality and power of expansion and adaptability of Buddhism" (*The Heritage,* 14). Sociologically, this is a perfectly valid position, but the question is whether it is in keeping with the spirit of orthodox Buddhism that Rahula claims to adhere to.

Rahula's thesis that monks must engage in social service is again a position that is sociologically valid but doctrinally indefensible. Besides, as Gnanavasa points out, he bends the meaning of the Buddha's exhortation to the monks to work for the good of the many in a way that violates its meaning and spirit. We are also aware that Rahula's is a manifesto, and a justification for monks to arm themselves with qualifications and be effective and powerful social actors and activists. Rahula makes it clear that in the pursuit of that pragmatic goal all else is irrelevant. In one of the areas he wants monks to be active, the defense of religion and nation, he, like the author of the *Mahavamsa,* approves of even violence. We are then forced to wonder whether Rahula's emphasis on spirituality and morality for social service monks is not a fig leaf to cover the moral indifference that must accompany such an uncompromising goal orientation. Indeed, the emphasis on morality can be understood as a tactical element in that goal orientation, intended to confer legitimacy on it, a soothing cover that veils the rough edges of the proposed "social service."

On balance Rahula the sociologist and activist triumphs over Rahula the defender of orthodox morality and spiritual values. The best evidence of his sociological insight and activist zeal is found in his analysis of the monk's plight in *The Heritage.* It is as if there are four noble truths about the monk's suffering—that it exists, has a cause, a cessation, and that there is a path to that cessation. It is the cause of the monk's plight that attracts Rahula's attention the most. Rahula says:

All social welfare activities hitherto undertaken by the bhikkhus fell into the hands of the missionaries, and their power loomed large. . . . With the missionaries asserting their power under the Christians, the position of the *bhikkhu* began to deteriorate. As the Buddhist monks could not adapt themselves to suit the changed political, economic, and social situation, they were rendered useless to society. Nor did they receive an education to prepare them for these new conditions. They had no plan of action. Their word was no more respected. Laymen had nothing to learn from them. Therefore . . . laymen dissociated themselves from *bhikkhus* and the bond between the laity and the clergy declined. *Bhikkhus* lost their places and positions in society. Functions and privileges which they enjoyed were usurped by, or fell into the hands of the missionaries. (*The Heritage*, 90–91)

Moreover:

Thus the *bhikkhu,* circumscribed with regard to personality and education, was by force of circumstances driven to limit his activities to the recitation of the *Suttas* (*pirit* chanting), preaching a sermon, attendance at funeral rites and alms-givings in memory of the departed, and to an idle, cloistered life in the temple. In spite of this melancholy and abject situation into which the *bhikkhu* was forced, any remnants of Sinhala Buddhist culture in the country, particularly in the rural areas, . . . had been preserved and maintained by the *bhikkhus* themselves. (*The Heritage*, 91–92)

Here Rahula is sociologically at his best. He has perceived the most important reason for the monk's loss of status, which is his failure to adapt to a changing social environment, like a species that failed the test of natural selection. This rendered him useless to society. Why did they fail to adapt? Here again Rahula's insight is remarkable. They failed to adapt because they did not have the education to do so. Because they had no education, they had nothing to tell laymen that was useful for them in the emerging new social order. The laity therefore dissociated themselves from the monks. In fact they did more. They found that their new western education could teach them more Buddhism than the monks could. Armed with this new knowledge, the laity were, as mentioned above, taking over the one last bastion of the monks, meditation, thereby usurping the monk's exclusive fast path to liberation which the monk in the meanwhile had abandoned.

The monk was "circumscribed both with regard to personality and education," forced to limit his activities to the ritual needs of the laity, and made to conform to an "idle, cloistered life." This acutely perceptive analysis reiterates Rahula's idea of the monastic vocation as a dynamic social one. The monk's work is in the world, playing roles as any other prominent member of the society does, and he must be fully alert to his social context and adapt himself to its changes. Not to do so is to face extinction as far as a prominent role in society is concerned.

The analysis also brings out Rahula's conception of the Christian minister as a person well adapted to perform tasks in a changing world and thereby to continue in its esteem—and therefore as a model for the monk who is desirous of being useful to and be recognized by society. It brings out the "Protestant Buddhist" in Rahula insofar as he idealizes, even as he criticizes, the Christian minister as a dynamic actor in society and condemns the rural monk as "idle," a common western, especially Protestant, perception of Sri Lankans (indeed of most people they colonized), a perception which is echoed in the reverse by natives whose image of Europeans is one of hyperactivity. In the same Protestant spirit he devalues ritualism, to which he says monks have been reduced by their failure to qualify themselves for the new social order, although in fact for the society, both the numerically preponderant peasantry and surprisingly the urban elites as well, ritualism constituted most of the religion. It is not altogether clear whether Rahula is totally devaluing or writing off as impracticable the true Buddhist path of meditation towards gaining release from samsara, but one has to assume that he is not. If so, in his view there are only two worthwhile things that a monk can do—liberation of himself, and helping others. The latter in Rahula's view applies to the mundane sphere alone and excludes ritualism. He seems to be saying that monks are not seriously doing anything toward liberating themselves and thus they might as well do something for others.

Despite their "melancholy and abject situation," the monks are still preserving Buddhism and Sinhala culture, particularly in the rural areas. That is, they are still involved in some activity. This is consistent with Rahula's theory of adaptation and survival. The new society touched the rural areas the least. Therefore, in these areas the monk is in his environment, where he knows the political ropes and where he is a seasoned player of the power and status games. The place and functions of the monk were relatively unaffected in the areas where he was the adept and the authority. In the ritual arena, the monk was in control even in hostile territory, the urban areas where the new social order was most manifest. Ritual function is one that cannot be usurped by a nonspecialist group. Hence the monk's continued control of this sphere in the urban environment. That is, the question of adaptability to change is relatively much less important in spheres where the monk is the exclusive specialist. Whereas in the secular area where he has no exclusive rights, he must adapt or perish. That is the price of being in a place where they ought not to be in the first place. If they choose to be there, as they did, then they should take the decision to its conclusion and learn the ways of the new society. This is the force behind the move, in the immediate post-1956 era, to establish a monastic university by conferring university status on either Vidyodaya or Vidyalankara. As it happened, both these were granted university status.

The modernization of the monk by equipping him with modern knowledge and by employing his services "to take up the challenge of the work [of serving society] in consonance with the needs of the modern world and international requirements" is not just a simple happening in Rahula's view, but a manifestation of "the natural process of history that cannot be stopped" (*The Heritage*, 97). Like the coming of the Marxist revolution, it is an inevitability. The symbol of decline in this view is the traditional, monastery bound, "idle" monk. But that monk performs a function in the village in particular and in the city as well. Is Rahula advocating the abolition of that function, which consists of merit making ceremonies, offering of *dana* (food) to the monks, funeral ceremonies, chanting of pirit, ceremonial expositions of the doctrine and so forth? With the devaluation of exorcistic and other folk cults in the twentieth century, these "Buddhist" ceremonies have in fact gained greater popularity and religious importance. Along with the fast path to liberation ideally trodden by monks (but in fact not, except for a very few virtuoso meditators and forest monks), these rituals constitute the sociological phenomenon of Buddhism. Besides, it is not impossible that a temple-bound, ritual-performing, apparently "idle" village monk is also a serious meditator. To argue that such a monk ought to become a social service worker is to advocate throwing away the baby with the bath. And we have already wondered whether Rahula wants neither the baby nor the bath. A rural monk who attends to the ritual needs of the villagers and who is also a serious meditator may appear sedate externally. But actually he may be alert and too busy following the true heritage of the bhikkhu to work for "nation and religion." For such monks, though rare, do exist. An outstanding example is the Venerable Rerukane Candavimala of the Vinayalankararama, Pokunuvita (who died recently, aged one-hundred years).

The enigmatic nature of *The Heritage* becomes apparent when we consider the coexistence in it of a well-argued case for a modern cosmopolitan education with the parochialism of the disastrously successful attempt to establish the hegemony of Sinhala as the one official language of the island.

While saying that "the services rendered by the pirivenas from the last quarter of the nineteenth century have enabled Buddhist monks to develop their knowledge and education," Rahula adds that "this education, however, was not full and complete in relation to modern times" (*The Heritage,* 95). In his discussion of the coming into being of monastic universities, he says "there was no possibility of obtaining financial assistance from the government in order to provide bhikkhus with a system of education in keeping with the demands of modern times." Making his case further, he states that "leading *theras* (senior monks) and lay Buddhist leaders, lacking in vision and wisdom, objected to Buddhist monks studying English and other modern languages and subjects in the area of modern knowledge" (96). These statements reveal disagreements regarding the meaning of Buddhism and the monk among different people, specifically, in the conflict between Rahula and D. S. Senanayake, between two broad categories of people. Both claim to be "Buddhist," basing their claims on different strands of Buddhism. The "establishment" emphasizes orthodoxy and the other-worldly goal. The rebels quote Buddhist texts to "prove" that Buddhism is "service to others," which they claim monks have always done. But what they must do to serve others changes according to social and economic changes. Both have hidden agendas, the one conservative and the other radical. The one emphasizes liberation from samsara, the other liberation from the woes of this world. Despite obstacles, says Rahula, a small group of monks "who had a deep love of learning and a desire to contribute towards advancement of the religion and nation made a valiant effort, in the face of many difficulties and personal hardships, to obtain the modern education which was denied to them. They continue to do so even today" (96). As a result of this effort, "The present generation of bhikkhus study not only the *Tipiṭaka* . . . but also expose themselves to a knowledge and awareness of contemporary problems through the wider media of newspapers, journals and modern books" (96).

The ideal envisaged is that of a complex, rich, cosmopolitan education that emphasizes not only modern western languages and humanistic, scientific, and technological knowledge but also the traditional learning of the country. This is a synthesis superior to both the field of traditional knowledge, which has hitherto been the only one available, and an education, like that of the westernized elite, that is exclusively western. The products of this synthesis would be people of learning, steeped in their tradition but cultivated in the powerful and important knowledge deriving from the European tradition. Such people would be confident, complex, and sophisticated individuals of taste and discrimination capable of defining the true national interest and distinguishing true patriotism from the narrow assertion of ethnic, linguistic, cultural, and religious extremism. They would be fully qualified and confident citizens of the world rather than narrow, anxious parochialists. Unfortunately, the exposure of monks to modern education has so far failed to bring forth this ideal monk.[54]

The above quotations defining Rahula's conception of a proper education for a modern monk (applicable to laity as well) appear at the conclusion of *Bhiksuvage Urumaya,* the original Sinhala version of *The Heritage,* published in 1946. The English version was published in 1974. The intervening years saw the momentous events of the post-1956 assertion of Sinhala Buddhist hegemony and the carrying out of a nationalist agenda. "The movement initiated by *bhikkhus* in 1946 . . . assumed larger proportions in several ways after independence" (*The Heritage,* 99). In a postscript to the English version, Rahula describes the events up to the mid-1970s. The ideological difference between the original version and the postscript is striking. In the original version, nationalist sentiment exists, but only underneath the account of the historically activist role of the monk. The crowning achievement of this version is its analysis of the causes and a cure for the predicament of the modern monk. That prescription is to achieve a blend of the old and the new, a blend in fact achieved by a few exceptional monks like himself, as just noted. The events described in the postscript are of a different character. With the same sense of enthusiasm that he exhibited for a cosmopolitan education and culture, he is, in these later pages, advocating a narrowly Sinhala Buddhist culture. He approvingly describes the achievements of the post-1956 era. The common man gained some self-respect and self-confidence, which was psychologically important. "National and Buddhist culture was given a more prominent place. Sinhala was declared the state language" (104).[55] Public transport and port cargo handling were nationalized. A Paddy Land Act gave security of tenure to the tenant cultivators. A ministry of Cultural Affairs was established. National art was revived. Vidyodaya and Vidyalankara were granted university status. In this discussion Rahula comes through as an advocate of providing higher education through the Sinhala medium. He complains that despite the Sinhala language policy, instruction at the University of Ceylon remained English and rural students did not comprehend their teachers. Thus, he says, "when Vidyodaya and

54. A beginning was made in the late 1980s in the appropriately named Manava Hitavadi Bhiksu Sangamaya (MHBS), The Association of Humanist Bhikkhus, but it ceased to exist. See chapter 7.

55. Presumably Rahula is content with the theory or "precept" of these changes, for in practice they have yielded more loss than benefit. The elevation of Sinhala in particular, leading to the discriminatory treatment of Tamil, has contributed more than any other factor to the turmoil the island has gone through for the last twenty years. Rahula's uncritical view of these developments reveals a narrowness of vision that seems to characterize even the most educated members of the Sri Lankan Theravada monkhood.

Vidyalankara were given university status, the medium of instruction was obviously Sinhala" (112).

Somewhat like his attitude to orthodox monasticism, there is some un-fathomability as to what Rahula's real position is regarding education and what its medium should be. This is in the postscript. In the text, education clearly means modern education, the higher portion of which is to be im-parted in English. He says in the postscript that 'a fairly good knowledge of English, a good working knowledge in fact, was absolutely necessary for reasonably paid employment" (111). And he adds: "In 1945, a free education plan was introduced. Many schools . . . were opened in predominantly rural areas. In most of these schools English was taught as a second language at the elementary level."

If English was "absolutely necessary" to secure reasonably paid employ-ment, the government, one must suppose, was on the right track in intro-ducing English to the "many schools" opened in the "predominantly rural areas" where, unlike in the cities, English was not available to children as a home language. It is then baffling to see why Rahula is hailing the nationalist victories, which cried for Sinhala only, or why he, as a member of the Bud-dhist nationalist groups, promised support to the party that would make Sinhala the only state language, dethrone English as the medium of instruc-tion, and deprive the children of the "predominantly rural areas" the sole opportunity to learn the language (English) which is "absolutely necessary for reasonably paid employment." It is clear that Rahula of the 1946 *The Heritage* is different from the Rahula of the 1974 postscript. The implications of the Sinhala-only education that Rahula espouses contradict his own re-markable espousal of modernism. As mentioned above, these moves also destroyed the traditional education centered on the pirivena, leaving behind a younger generation of monks rooted neither in the indigenous tradition nor that of the westerner.

These are contradictions inherent in a position that tries to advocate uni-versalism and parochialism at one and the same time. They are the contradic-tions arising out of the unresolved conflict between Rahula, the traditional monk however nontraditional he appears to be, and Rahula, the intelligent, thinking, and cosmopolitan individual. Rahula, the brilliant rebel of *Satyo-daya* has steadily moved away from both brilliance and rebellion. It is a mea-sure of the hold the Sinhala-Buddhist hegemonist ideology as a worldview has on individual monks that a man of such gifts could be willingly reduced from freedom to enslavement within that ideology. The ghost of the empty titles of decadent Sri Lankan monasticism he scorned has returned to him in the guise of a Burmese title and claimed him to inmateship in the phantom world of monastic titledom. This unbelievable transformation of a monk of extraordinary talent raises questions as to the ability and legitimacy of even the most informed of monks to intervene in matters of national policy as they insist they should.

If *The Heritage* is polemical, Gnanavasa's *What is the Heritage of the Bhikku?* is no less so despite its appearance as an impeccable exercise in logic.[56] But this does not render these works useless. In the process of articulating their polemical stands, both monks have made contributions to our understanding of socio-political issues. We have already referred to Rahula's perceptive analysis of the condition of the monk as related to his failure to adapt to the rapidly changing society. To do so the monk should gain qualifications by studying important modern languages and modern secular subjects. The sociological impact of this is quite a different matter and has led to ironic and disastrous results.

Gnanavasa's is a more interesting contribution. First, we have in his analysis the affirmation that, while early Buddhist texts may contain many statements that relate to mundane issues, the core of Buddhism consists of an ultramundane quest. This contrasts with the standard sociological view of Buddhism, which assigns equal value to philosophical, magical, behavioral, and other phenomena found in the literature and practice of Buddhism. Among sociologists, the striking exception to this is Max Weber, who encapsulated in his conception of "ancient Buddhism" a single-minded ultramundane quest, which he considered a religion "without a deity, without a cult," and "a religious technology of intellectually schooled mendicant monks."[57] Such a religion could not possibly become a world religion, but since it obviously is one, Weber theorized that the only explanation of this is that later Buddhism, as contrasted with ancient Buddhism, incorporated into itself at the popular level such elements as divine intercession and heavenly existences, transforming the Buddhist societies into gardens of magic. It is this

56. Knowledgeable informants have pointed out that *What is the Heritage of the Bhikkhu?* is the result of an assignment given to the senior Henpitagedara by D. S. Senanayake, which the former handed over to his gifted student and younger brother Gnanavasa. There was in fact a second and longer refutation of *The Heritage* by Akuratiye Amaravamsa of the pro-establishment Vidyodaya, which was enthusiastically accepted for publication by the UNP propagandist Ananda Tissa de Alwis, on the orders of Sir John Kotelawala, Minister of Transport and Communications (and later Prime Minister). The manuscript, an only copy, apparently disappeared mysteriously on its way to the press. One is tempted to speculate, given the headiness of the days, whether this may not have been an act of sabotage organized by interested parties. Information of Akuratiye Amaravamsa, author of the work and present (1999) principal of Vidyodaya. It is no coincidence that a refutation of *The Heritage* should come from Vidyodaya, with its long history of association with the establishment and its pragmatic nationalism.

57. Max Weber, *The Religion of India* (Glencoe: The Free Press, 1958), 204–30.

folk understanding of Buddhism that the commonplace anthropologist and
sociologist has declared to be Buddhism, and at that behavioral level it no
doubt is. This, however, cannot deny the autonomy of what might be called
the core Buddhist system, or Weber's ancient Buddhism, built around the
Four Noble Truths and the Noble Eightfold Path. It is this conception of
Buddhism that Gnanavasa has in mind when he defines the vocation of the
monk as the vibhavagami path.

Were one to ask Rahula what Buddhism is, this is the answer he would
give, as in fact he has done in his internationally known book *What the Buddha
Taught.*[58] The Rahula of *The Heritage* and *The History,* however, is different:
that Rahula agrees with the common anthropologist/sociologist to accept
what Buddhists do as Buddhism. There is no other way he could approvingly
narrate the story of Buddhism in Sri Lanka as one of monastic domination
and king-making, a domination based not on an objective consideration of
evidence but on propping up as real the imaginary monk of Dharmapala on
the basis of selective evidence. Thus Rahula advocates "ancient Buddhism"
as true Buddhism when it suits his purpose of declaring to the world, in a
fashion reminiscent of Dharmapala, that Buddhism is the only truly rational,
intellectually appealing, and modern of all religions; the only truly compassionate and nonviolent of all religions; the noblest of them all. There are no
king-makers and no warmongering soldiers in yellow robes, no spears with
relics in *What the Buddha Taught.* Second, in *The Heritage* and in *The History* it
suits Rahula to be an advocate of a Buddhism that glorifies social intercourse
with lay society, particularly elite society; a way of life close to what Dharmapala called "the hedonism of Kalidasa," for which there are parallels going
back to the Buddha's time; the receipt of salaries and other forms of material
remuneration; ethnic exclusivism and Sinhala Buddhist hegemony; militancy
in politics; and violence, war and the spilling of blood in the name of "preserving the religion." We may observe here that this duality is pervasive in
the Sinhala Buddhist culture and constitutes a bifurcation of Buddhism into
the noble religion to be idealized, boasted about to the world, offered flowers and incense, listened to with rapt devotion, televised and so forth, but
not to be lived by; and a ritualism to be resorted to as the practicing religion.
This consists of the usual food offerings to monks, ceremonial and rituals
like pirit and, increasingly since the 1970s, *Bodhipuja*s. The purpose of this
religion is merit making, but increasingly in recent times (and especially
for socially mobile middle classes and anxious politicians) that purpose has
expanded to involve the successful achievement of specific mundane goals,

58. London: Gordon Frazer, 1959. Available in several languages.

which include the cancellation of demerit acquired in actions like fraud and murder routinely committed in political and economic competition and in the act of governance. In this expanded version, this religion consists of an incorporation into "Buddhist" ritual of the folk religion that propitiates gods, demons, and "goblins," various kinds of magical acts, including black magic for the destruction of enemies, and the magical persuasion of members of parliament to vote for or against motions.[59]

For numerous practitioners of this religion, the intention is the achievement of these goals—merit in general or some more specific mundane goal—unperturbed by any ethical considerations. In fact, some of the ritual activity is designed precisely for the unethical achievement of a goal or, as just mentioned, to cancel the ill-effects of unethical activity in goal achievement. In addition, this religion also constitutes a politicization that includes accommodation of the attempts by monastic pressure groups in the formulation of national policy; ritual acknowledgement of particular hierarchical or other prominent monks while little heed is paid to them and their sayings; and the use of monks in politics. It further includes the exclusivist identification of Buddhism and Buddhists with "country and nation." The anthropological usage "Sinhala Buddhism" needs to be expanded to include all these phenomena.

Let us return to Gnanavasa's Buddhism and his critique of Rahula based on that Buddhism. To him the "social service" that Rahula defines as the vocation of the monk is a code word for "revolution." This is an exaggeration because in Rahula it is actually a code word for "politics." Gnanavasa's reading is perhaps not without some justification, because "politics" at the time meant "revolution" insofar as the alliance contemplated by Rahula and his Vidyalankara colleagues, in contrast to the Vidyodaya monks, was with the revolutionaries (Marxists). It is apparent that Gnanavasa is well-read in Marxist and other contemporary literature, and in fact appears to be a closet Marxist, because he seems to accept the Marxist theory of the class struggle climaxing in revolution and the prediction that after the revolution, all will live happily ever after in peace, happiness, and tranquility. This is a normal thought process for a Sri Lankan intellectual and humanist of the time, which Gnanavasa was. But he has a deep dilemma: while he finds the socialist soci-

---

59. President Premadasa allegedly used Kerala exorcists to apply charmed oil on M.P.'s seats so that they would vote against the motion to impeach him. While we do not know the details of this, the Hansard does record C. V. Gooneratne, M. P., answering the president's ceremonial request to sit down by complaining the he could not do so because there is oil on his seat, and Richard Pathirana, M.P., alleging that some Kerala exorcists were seen performing black magic in the chamber. Hansard, vol. 74, no. 1, 24 September 1991, p. 2, col. 1, and p. 3, col. 2.

ety both inevitable and acceptable in terms of utopian equality, justice, tranquility, and so forth, he is deeply concerned about the brave new world's cavalier attitude to religion.

Gnanavasa rejects Rahula's parochialism, which equates religion with nation and country. Such an equation is irrelevant in the face of the great problem that mankind of the machine age faces, namely, how to make the machine the servant rather than the master of man. This is a thought that connects Gnanavasa to a cosmopolitanism that embraces figures like Gandhi and Charlie Chaplin, which makes him a rare member of an order that typically delimits its vision narrowly and exclusively to the Sinhala Buddhist world. Gnanavasa's proposal that the monks urgently plan strategies so that the sublime word of the Buddha is ensured an important place in the emerging world order constitutes a conviction that Buddhism must be integrated and made meaningful to life in all its ethical resplendence. That is, in the this-worldly sphere of Buddhism, Gnanavasa's interest is not in "country and nation" but in nonviolence, universalism, urbanity, and cosmopolitanism. This is a departure from the bifurcated Buddhism mentioned above, and it expresses Gnanavasa's understanding of Buddhism as a religion to be practiced rather than fetishized. Whereas Rahula's theory is a secularization of Buddhism, Gnanavasa's is a spiritualization of society.

A sample of Kalukondayave Pannasekhara's elegant handwriting. This page dedicates his autobiography to his teachers and the Sangharaja Valivita Saranamkara, founder of the eighteenth-century Buddhist revival.

The library of the Venerable Kalukondayave Pannasekhara at the Sugatabimbaramaya monastery, Navagamuva. The sign says, "Sri Pragnasekhara Library." Beyond the impressive exterior, the library itself is in a poor state of maintenance, and is inhabited more often by bats than human readers.

Continuing Hendiyagala Silaratana's good work, his student Henegedara Siddharta founded a cooperative bank, known as the Cooperative for Employment and Income Generation (*Seva niyuktiya ha adayam utpadanaya sandaha samupakaraya*). Interest rates are often as low as 1 percent while the outside bank rate for comparable loans can be as high as 15 percent. With justifiable pride and a sense of dedication, he mentioned that while other banks close at 5:00, his is open whenever a customer knocks on the door. The chart on the wall proclaims some of the bank's successes.

Walpola Rahula, monk and scholar. He wrote *The Heritage of the Bhikkhu*, a master-crafted manifesto for monastic activism and a powerful work that influenced the recent history of the monkhood as no other did.

The front cover of Rahula's *Bhiksuvage urumaya* (3d edition, 1992), the original Sinhala of *The Heritage.*

Walpola Rahula addressing a meeting of monks convened to condemn the proposals for sharing power with the minorities, known as "the Package." The Mahanayaka Palipane Chandananda of the Asgiriya Chapter presided. (Courtesy of *Upali Newspapers*; photo: Denzil Pathiraja, 1996)

The monastic establishment characterizes the Package as equal to the break-up of the country. In a ceremony held at the Palace of the Tooth Relic in Kandy, a monk leader of the anti-Package movement, Gammaddegama Gnanissara, joins his lay colleagues in lighting three lamps united in a single flame, symbolizing the unity of the "Threefold Sinhala," a synonym for the medieval Sri Lankan polity. The term, incidentally, evokes more the idea of a federalist than a unitary state. (Courtesy of *Upali Newspapers*; photo: Cyril Vimalasurendra, 1996)

At a meeting organized to oppose the Package, Paravahara Pannananda, the chancellor of the Ruhuna University, sets a copy of the document on fire. Burning the books of opponents is a historic feature of the Indic tradition. Recent events show that the practice can be extended to include the opponents themselves. (Courtesy of the *Sunday Times,* Colombo)

At the Mahindaramaya, Borella, monks help unload provisions for the soldiers of the Sinhala army, symbolically supporting the war. (Courtesy of *Upali Newspapers*)

Echoing Anagarika Dharmapala's Internationalist Buddhism, but much diminished religously, Sri Lankan monks have forged links with foreign lands. Here, a delegation of Thai monks led by Phrakru Kittivarporn is being led by the host, Ahangama Ananda, of the Vijayararma Vihara, Frederica Road, Welawatta, Colombo, for participation in a religious ceremony. (Denzil Pathiraja, 1996)

(Top) The Vidyalankara monk Mapalagama Vipulasara, well connected to Japanese benefactors, welcomes the Japanese monk Kyuse Enshino in Colombo, Sri Lanka (K. Rupasinghe, 1996); *(bottom)* the latter in turn felicitates the former in Kyoto, Japan (Alex David, 1996). (Both courtesy of ANCL)

The Christian practice of celebrating birthdays, long accepted by Sinhala Buddhist elites, is becoming increasingly popular among elite and socially mobile monks. Presumably oblivious to the mundaneity of its symbolism, Palipane Chandanada, Mahanayaka of Asgiriya, cuts a cake presented to him on his eighty-fourth birthday by a Singaporean devotee. (Courtesy of ANCL; photo: Gamini Ranasinghe, Dinamina, 27 April 1998)

Galeboda Gnanissara, alias Podihamuduruvo, of Gangaramaya, Colombo, raises a threatening finger to warn an injured yet defiant participant of a demonstration against him. (ANCL, 1996)

Young monks make donations to a JVP supporter at the 1996 *Bak maha viru samaruva,* the annual commemoration of the martyrs of the JVP-led youth rebellion of April 1971. Even considering the fact that the donations are for a "cause," the sight of monks making material donations to a layman is unusual. (Sudath Malaweera, 1996)

Young monks protest the erosion of democratic rights, the presidential system, Emergency Rule, and the "plunder called privatization." The multilinguality of the placards restates the broad significance of these issues, as opposed to narrowly Sinhala Buddhist ones, while Coca Cola advertisements mingle with the placards contrapuntally. (Ajit Seneviratne, 1996)

Young monks in a protest march, c. 1989. (Sriyantha Walpola, 1989)

Monk students of the Pali and Buddhist University demand representation and, in a playful reference to the relative youth of the vice-chancellor, also demand to know where his pacifier is.

Broadminded radical monks, a rare breed, mingle with likeminded Catholic priests at an annual May Day celebration held at St. Michael's Church, Polvatta, Colombo, during which the Catholic priests, wearing the multivocal hammer-and-sickle symbol on their stoles, bless the implements of the workers. Monks in the second-row seats behind the priests, are graciously renouncing their "rightful place." (ANCL, 1991)

Undergraduate monks in between classes at the Colombo University. (Sriyantha Walpola, 1989)

SOCIAL SERVICE:
THE ANATOMY OF A
VOCATION

We have seen in the previous chapters how Dharmapala, with great perception, understood the potential role of the monks in national regeneration.
The choice of the monk as the instrument of regeneration was made not
only for the pragmatic consideration of the presence and preeminence of
monks in the village but also for their symbolic significance as surviving remnants of kingship. Dharmapala felt kinglessness to be a grave loss because he
believed that its paternalistic presence would have ensured the nation's security, prosperity, and unity. He made the forlorn statement that Sri Lanka
could have survived at least as a princely state like Baroda or Travancore "had
not the traitor Ehelapola sold the country to the British."[1] Judging by the
symbolic value of kingship particularly in the orient (Japan and Thailand),
this is a justifiable evaluation.[2] Conceivably, kingship could have averted,
among other problems, the source of the greatest danger that Sri Lanka faces
today, the absence of a national consensus.

   We have in a previous chapter discussed the work of three monks—Kalukondayave, Hinatiyana, and Hendiyagala—who tried to embody this ideal
of the monk and became soldiers and hero-giants of regeneration. There
were numerous lesser known such soldiers, but these three were exemplary.
Their careers show the pervasive influence of Dharmapala, and they seem to
have endeavored to qualify themselves in terms of the stringent criteria that
Dharmapala envisaged and enforced.

   1. Guruge, ed., *Return to Righteousness,* 513–14.
   2. Sir Archibald Lawrie thought similarly. See Ananda Coomaraswamy, *Mediaeval Sinhalese Art,* 2d
ed. (New York: Pantheon, 1956), 15.

Of the major figures influenced by Dharmapala, Rahula is enigmatic. It is
clear that Rahula was not an orthodox Dharmapalite soldier in the sense that
Kalukondayave and others were. To begin with, he did not show Dharmapala
the kind of deference that these other soldiers did, although he was clearly
respectful towards Dharmapala's work. This becomes clear when we reflect
on the following two points: First, unlike Kalukondayave, who appropriated
Dharmapala as his teacher, Rahula does not even make explicit reference to
him in such a way as to acknowledge any influence or inspiration. In *The
Heritage* he only mentions Dharmapala's name once and that in a list of
people who "made life-long sacrifice . . . to rehabilitate the honorable heritage of Buddhism" (94). In one essay in a collection published in 1978, he
pays tribute to Dharmapala for his contribution to the restoration of Buddhism in India, its establishment in England and elsewhere, and for instilling
self-respect and a sense of pride in their culture in the Sinhala people. But
the essay, which reveals no personal influence, is only three pages long and
appears to have been a short commemorative address he delivered at the
centenary of the reformer's birth in 1964.[3] Second, on the first page of the
4×4 inch notebook that was the first diary that Rahula (at that time Dham-
madassi) kept in 1924, at the age of 17, we have a curious piece of evidence.
It is titled *Danagatayutu Karunu* ("Facts one should know"). As we know, this
is the very well-known title of Dharmapala's column in the *Sinhala Bauddhaya,* which was the primary medium through which he captivated the interest of, and inspired, thousands of people, lay and monastic; and the primary medium of recruitment into his army of regeneration. Such an
evocative title notwithstanding, the miscellaneous contents make a drab diary. The entry for March 4, 1927 contains a list of addresses of some monks
and nationalist leaders, which includes the addresses of Dharmapala in England and Switzerland. Without reading too much meaning to this, we can
infer the following: (1) Rahula was actively interested in the nationalist
movement and was inspired by Dharmapala; (2) the fact that foreign addresses, of Dharmapala as well as some others, are recorded suggests actual
or potential correspondence, and forebodes Rahula's travels and renown in
different countries in later years; and (3) the fact that the diary uses the title
of Dharmapala's revered column leaves room for contradictory interpretations: it might signify idealization or its opposite. It is of course possible that
this represents nothing more than the youthful appropriation of a catchy

---

3. Walpola Rahula, *Zen and the Taming of the Bull* (London: Gordon Fraser, 1978). It is noteworthy,
however, that Dharmapala would find greatly unacceptable Rahula's scholarly sojourns in Zen and Mahayana in this book (and elsewhere), which further confirms Rahula's excludability as a true Dharmapalite soldier.

phrase. On balance what we can conclude is that Rahula, while inspired and influenced by Dharmapala, was by no means a soldier or disciple in the sense that Kalukondayave and others were.[4]

Further, while Rahula is indebted to Dharmapala's original insight regarding the prominent role of the monk in precolonial society for his definition of the monk's vocation, his is a definition that differs from Dharmapala's. First the Dharmapalite monk is an inspiring activist, who though accorded a high place in the village, is an ascetic and a humble soldier. In contrast, the monk depicted in Rahula's writings culminating in *The History of Buddhism in Ceylon* (1956) is a powerful kingmaker who is heavily endowed or salaried and lives in comfort. He is rewarded for his scholarship, which must have included the kind of literary study that Dharmapala considered the hedonism of Kalidasa. Second, whereas the Dharmapalite monk is an honored and able leader, the Rahulite is much more: he is supremely powerful. Rahula's ancient monk is much involved in politics and comes through strongly like a projection into ancient and medieval times the "political monk" of the 1940's with his fantasies of power and acceptance in elite society. Third, the Dharmapalite monk is a rural activist involved with the peasantry. While he is involved with the whole range of their problems, his activity is primarily economic. In contrast to this the monk of Rahula's work is an urbanite, as indeed his ancient counterpart was. We know that Kalukondayave, Hinatiyana, and Hendiyagala toiled in the village, but Rahula and his colleagues were ensconced in Colombo. While the latter addressed meetings in rural areas periodically during election campaigns, their major mechanism of addressing the public were the Colombo-based media. Corresponding to the above dichotomies, the Dharmapalite monk was involved with peasants whereas the Rahulite monk with urban, unionized workers. In sum, the Dharmapalites are economic monks whereas the Rahulites are political monks. Fourth, and related to the above, the Dharmapalites, working in the villages on specific problems, had to be specific in what they had to say. In contrast, the Rahulite monks were and are articulators of broad ideas such as those regarding language, religion, and culture, which essentially had to be general and sloganistic. In short the Dharmapalite monk is a technician and the Rahulite monk an ideologue. Fifth, returning to the question of morality, Rahula argued that monks who do "social service" should be so spiritual that they should, before going into social service, have attained some of the high spiritual states of the Buddhist path. This is quite different from the attitude of the Vidyodaya monks who, while assuming that the social service monk remained a monk and observed

4. The information on Rahula's diary is from Gunadasa Liyanage, *Valpola Rahula Hamuduruvo* (Nadimale, Dehiwela: Buddhist Cultural Center, 1994).

basic monastic morality, were unconcerned with spiritual heights. Hendiyagala in particular was explicit in keeping social service separate from spirituality, which is both a more realistic and more convincing position.

This high spiritual standard for the monk is, further, different from that
of Dharmapala. The Dharmapalite ideal of the monk is part of an integrated
conception of society and therefore sounds convincing, whereas Rahula's
spiritually advanced exemplar does not come into being naturally but is a
deus ex machina to help Rahula out of the moral vacuum of his conception
of society. The latter is a labored import and an afterthought designed to
clothe in morality and legitimize Rahula's aggressive and ideological "political monk." Two models of monkhood clearly emerge. First, the monk exemplified by Kalukondayave, Hinatiyana, and Hendiyagala, and second, the
monk defined in Rahula's work and elaborated by his colleagues Yakkaduve
and others. Understood broadly, the Vidyodaya monks exemplify the first
model and Vidyalankara monks the second. We should recall here that these
two models typify the analytically separable two moods, pragmatic and ideological, economic and political of Dharmapala.

Whereas Kalukondayave and his Vidyodaya colleagues worked out the
quite unromantic nitty-gritty of regeneration, Rahula and his Vidyalankara
colleagues went for its colorful, emotional, ideological, and flamboyant aspect. This latter aspect included an anti-imperialist rhetoric for which Dharmapala set the tone and precedent; emphasis on language and culture and on
the identity of the Sinhala race and Buddhism, with their fortunes mutually
intertwined; activism, including strike action in alliance with the Marxists;
oratory that ignited passions of class and dreams of classlessness; confronta-
tional activity replete with dramatic events like Rahula's Robin Hood appearance at a mass rally;[5] arrest and detainment along with the socialist
leader Philip Gunawardena for inciting strike action; violent scenes such as
the one where Rahula and some others were assaulted by establishment
thugs; and the rash *Kälaniya Declaration of Independence* on the eve of the official arrival of Dominion Status negotiated by the ruling conservative elite.[6]

---

5. This meeting was held at the Galle Face Green. See Liyanage, *Rahula,* 128. Similar defiant appearances of the outlawed LSSP leaders, and the drama of their jailbreak, became part of the legend
that both reflected and helped grow the popularity of the Marxist leadership.

6. On January 6, 1947, less than a month before the arrival of independence, the Vidyalankara
monks declared independence from British rule. The reason for this was the theory that the independence that was about to dawn was mere Dominion Status and did not mean full independence. This
was a theory propagated by the Marxists with whom the Vidyalankara monks were in alliance or sympathy. This declaration was also a symbolic attack on the westernized constitutionalist elite, who were
inheriting power from the British. It became a real attack just before the elections of 1956, which
helped dethrone this elite and inaugurate an era of Sinhala Buddhist hegemonist politics. For *The Kälaniya Declaration,* see Rahula, *The Heritage,* 134–36.

Most relevant from our present point of view, the Vidyalankara monks' interpretation of the Dharmapalite agenda gave a particular twist to their conception of the monk's role. This interpretation questioned and endangered the traditional definition of the monk's morality—that is, his *mahanakama,* or "monkness." Hence the prolixity and defensive frenzy with which the Vidyalankara monks discussed mahanakama in contrast to the silence on the subject at Vidyodaya.[7] The dialogue on monkness has continued ever since, indicating that the question of what constitutes this state is far from resolved, while a new morality or its lack has come into being, and a new monkhood based on it.

The broad picture is then clear. As we know, the Dharmapalite agenda was twofold: raising the living standards of the people and restoring to the land as a whole a Sinhala Buddhist cultural and moral stamp presumed to have existed in precolonial times. The Vidyodaya monks took up the former, and became the hero-giants of rural development, inspiring many foot soldiers. In contrast the Vidyalankara monks embraced the latter. The Vidyodaya monks visited and worked in individual village communities and literally got their feet dirty. The Vidyalankara monks proclaimed lofty nationalist slogans, keeping their feet up and dry. The Vidyalankara monks were talkers. The Vidyodaya monks were doers. While these contrasts were thus starkly visible to independent observers, the Vidyalankara monks saw themselves as doing the same "social service" as their Vidyodaya counterparts.[8]

It is not the case that the kind of activity—sloganistic, urban-based, ideological—that the Vidyalankara monks were engaged in was totally devoid of an element of "social service." A good example, and one often cited with pride by their apologists, is their support of the Free Education Bill. There is no doubt that they made a contribution to this.[9] But this pales in comparison to what might be called "antisocial service," which resulted in the swift transformation of what looked like radical activism into a total and pervasive program of Sinhala Buddhist hegemony, and a systematic bulldozing away of

7. See *Pavidi vaga ha sasun maga.* Here, Yakkaduve is taking the standard *dhammakathika* position which was elaborated down the centuries toward more and more worldly gain and "sensuousness," and adapting it to modern conditions. On the increasing worldliness of monastic life as reflected in literature, see Martin Wickramasinghe, *Sinhala Sahityaye.*

8. In defense of his position that the role of the monk is social service, Rahula mentions that some monks are already doing this, clearly having in mind the Vidyodaya monks. This is, however, merely a fig leaf, because the "social service" he had in mind was politics, with an attendant extension of the boundary within which monks can act.

9. V. Nalliah, M.P., and a Tamil, complimented the Vidyalankara monks in Parliament on their contribution to the Free Education Bill (Hansard, 15 May 1947, col. 1664). See also Liyanage, *Rahula,* 117. But as noted above, the role of the monks in the passage of this bill was not completely altruistic. It was part of a package the rest of which was their justification of laxity.

reason and common sense in favor of an outpouring of ideology and exclusivism.[10] They took the worst of Dharmapala and made it the foundation,
ironically, of a *dhammadipa* ("island of righteousness"),[11] ignoring his best:
while Dharmapala envisaged a Sri Lanka with Sinhala Buddhist dominance,
it was envisaged not as an end in itself but as a means of gaining economic
prosperity. In Dharmapala the economic is dominant and ever-present although the ideological is never far behind. In Rahula and his Vidyalankara
colleagues, the economic is completely absent with a corresponding sover-
eignty and dictatorship of ideology.

In the Dharmapalite paradigm, the supremacy of morality is unques-
tioned and paramount. In the Vidyalankara conception of the monk, as already pointed out, the moral stature of the social service monk, although
granted, is unconvincing. What we have in the Vidyalankara version is not
morality as such but an attempt to smuggle it in for purposes of legitimizing
"social service." Further, while Dharmapala's exhortations had a profoundly
emotional content and appeal, they were never devoid of an ascetic dimension, the entire goal of methodical economic activity being not just worldly
prosperity and happiness but a good afterlife and eventual liberation from
samsara. Especially as elaborated by Kalukondayave, such prosperity was a
certitudo salutis auguring well for future rebirths and spiritual evolution. In
Rahula and his colleagues, this ascetic aspect is missing. Instead, what is in
evidence is a reiteration and extension of monastic privileges, including the
modern equivalents of "the hedonism of Kalidasa" or "sensuousness," to use
Dharmapalite terms. Dharmapala knew fully well the dangers of monks giving up normal rural pastoral functions and taking to academic studies, as his
remarks on the pirivena monks illustrate.[12] This is what Kalukondayave, a

---

10. Consider for example Yakkaduve's use of *rata, jatiya, agama,* which appropriates to the Sinhala
Buddhists the entire island of Sri Lanka. This as we know is a usage introduced by Dharmapala. It is interesting and telling that Yakkaduve's exclusivism has two broadly visible stages: First, Sinhala Buddhists to
the exclusion/subjugation of others; and second, monks to the inclusion/subjugation of the laity. The
logical progression of this is for a small coterie of elite monks to exclude others and rule, a theocratic/
oligarchic system but authoritarian as opposed to the village based theocratic/democratic blend of
Dharmapala. In fairness to Dharmapala we must also remind ourselves of the moral, nonsensuous and
abnegating nature of the leadership of that society. In the theocracy of the Vidyalankara ideologues,
laxness is advocated even for monks, as the critique of the "Commissioner Buddhists" make clear.

11. I learn from Professor Charles Hallisey that the term *dhammadipa* occurs in Buddhaghosa.
However, other authorities note its near absence elsewhere in the Pali literature (Professor Steven
Collins in a private conversation). This makes it probable that the recent popularity of the term among
nationalists is related to Dharmapala's use of it. While it is possible that Dharmapala borrowed the
usage from Buddhaghosa, it is equally possible that he invented the term. In either case, the popularity
of the term is probably no older than the twentieth century.

12. Guruge, ed., *Dharmapala Lipi,* 134.

pirivena monk, took care to avoid through his relentless activity. His scholarly work is all in Pali and Sinhala as opposed to Sanskrit, the voluptuous and dangerous language of Kalidasa.[13]

The Dharmapalite call to action constituted a liberation for gifted, dynamic young monks who had left the villages and come to the Vidyodaya and Vidyalankara pirivenas in Colombo. This took these monks on two paths. The first was represented by the true Dharmapalite soldiers, of whom the best exemplar is Kalukondayave. Dedication to the task at hand consumed all of Kalukondayave's time. Thus his liberation from the bonds of the cloister did not represent a freedom of the wild ass. Rather, it represented a higher bondage which was nevertheless intellectually and emotionally satisfying. It meant no mundane enjoyment and no respite from hard work. It did not in any way adversely affect his moral state as an ordained monk. It gave him no freedom from the constraints of the vinaya rules and his monastic vows: within the unshaken foundations of his belief, there was neither the possibility nor the need to ask for or expect any. There was no need therefore to amplify his voice and proclaim to the world, "Look world, my monkness is intact." There was no reason to go out of his way and talk about his monkness or theorize about it in general. The important thing for these monks was not their liberation (from bondage to a laity) but the people's regeneration.

For the Vidyalankara monks who represented the second path of Dharmapalite action, this order was reversed. Most of their literary output in the mid 1940s was an attempt to justify relaxation of vinaya rules and still claim monkness. As the later events demonstrate, it was their liberation from ritual services to the laity rather than the people's regeneration that was important to them. Stated differently, the Vidyalankara idea that the monk's vocation is social service has been revolutionary in that it has provided the monks with an excuse to seek profits and other secular goals and satisfactions in an unprecedented manner. It has opened the flood gates and has given rise to a new monkhood that many thoughtful members of the culture view with alarm.[14]

Thus for the Vidyalankara monks, liberation from rural duties was not a commitment and a dedication anew to a higher duty as it was for the Vidyodaya monks and as it was intended by Dharmapala. For them it was instead the impulse and precedent for exploring evermore the possibilities of expanding the outer limits of morality, so that activities traditionally consid-

13. Kalukondayave was a prolific writer and the author of the longest book in the Sinhala language. His major works are cited elsewhere. See pp. 69–70.

14. The commissioners expressed this concern when they investigated the universities in 1963. See chapter 4.

ered out of bounds could be brought within the bounds of monkness. We
have already referred to the most dramatic example of this: Rahula's labored
attempt to engage in politics by calling it social service. For, while Rahula
and his colleagues theorized about politics being the same as social service,
the outcome was that they were politically active, with nothing honestly to
show as social service. Further, according to the hushed evidence of some
informants, this is the least of the morally questionable things these monks
did. The activities of the "gang of five" of which Rahula was the center has
now become part of the general folklore among a stratum of knowledgeable
monks and laymen. Apart from these activities, a wide range of informants
have also expressed their belief that one well-known Vidyalankara monk was
involved in smuggling precious stones concealed inside statues.[15]

It is not the case that the monks who became soldiers in the Dharmapalite
project of regeneration were total ascetics with no interest whatsoever in
individual expression and recognition. A reader of Kalukondayave's biography gets the clear impression that he enjoyed himself in his various public
activities, but his enjoyment was always subdued and disciplined. Similarly,
while he enjoyed recognition, he was quite put off by ostentatious and
pompous public welcomes which he quietly plotted to flee. The same is true
of his attitude toward titles and honors. He accepted and felt proud of the
academic and hierarchical honors he received, which he equanimously considered just and fair rewards for hard work. In all likelihood he would have
rejected any honor or title he considered undeserving.

SHATTERING OF THE FOUNDATIONS, OPENING OF
THE FLOOD GATES

Although Dharmapala was the first to conceptualize and advocate a socially
activist role for the monk, it was Rahula's restatement of Dharmapala in *The*

---

15. Informants who do not have any reason to make fabrications have described these activities
both in a general way and in the form of actual incidents. See U. Saranankara, *Satanaka Satahan* (Colombo: Janata Lekhaka Peramuna, n.d.), and Naravila Dhammaratana, *Hadipannala Pannaloka* (Sandalankava: Sandalanka Cooperative Printers, 1954).

Traditionally, precious stones were buried in stupas and sometimes in image houses, as a symbol of
the preciousness of the stupa or image. If the claim about smuggling is true, it is telling about the
changes in the monkhood that an educated, prominent monk would come to hold a very different
meaning of precious stones, a meaning, apparently formerly subscribed to only by thieves and treasure
hunters. A recent incident of this type, the damaging of the "pillow" of a reclining statue of King
Vasabha's era by treasure-hunting thieves, was reported in the Sinhala daily *Divayina* (early June 1995).
Similarly, *Ravaya* of 9 August 1998 carried a long article on the theft of the golden Buddha statue at the
Piyangala vihara in Bibile.

Heritage that reverberated in the country and that led to the association of his name with the idea that the monk's vocation was social service. In the mid 1940s, the rural development movement led by the Dharmapalite soldiers came to a sudden halt. This coincides with the activities at Vidyalankara that we are concerned with, of which the 1946 publication of *The Heritage* was the herald and landmark. While the Vidyalankara activities did not cause the end of rural development in any simplistic way, the contemporaneity of the two events cannot be a mere coincidence. What then was the connection? The following answer can be suggested.

As already mentioned, the rural development movement of the Vidyodaya monks was a quiet affair, whereas the propagation of the ideology of *The Heritage* was a consciously organized campaign that constituted major propaganda. The ideology, further, was proclaimed within a highly charged political context, namely the eve of the first national election under the Soulbury Constitution (1947) and one in which a number of charismatic young Marxist leaders were bidding for power. This added to the visibility, audibility, and receptivity of the message of *The Heritage*. When the original articulation of this message was made in the decades before the 1930s by Dharmapala, there were only a handful of monks ready to hear it. Hence Dharmapala's frustration and criticism of the monks. As the Vidyodaya-led rural development movement got under way, the number of such monks slowly grew. By the time *The Heritage* made its vociferous entry in the mid 1940s, a much larger number of monks had received advanced education either at one of the Colombo pirivenas or at those in the provincial towns. For these monks, the message of *The Heritage* was music to their ears: these gifted, ambitious, and educated monks, having tasted the delights of urban life and having experienced a widening of their horizons, had developed a distaste for the traditional ritual duties that *The Heritage* stigmatized as chanting pirit, accepting alms, and participating in funerals (91, 95). That is, by the mid 1940s, thanks to the production of graduates at the Colombo pirivenas Vidyodaya and Vidyalankara and at their branches established in many provincial towns by their respective alumni, there was a flowering of monastic education into which was blended a taste for an urban lifestyle, giving rise to a monastic middle class.[16] This class was greatly attracted to the message that a monk's vocation was not traditional ritualism but social service. And it became the carrier of the idea. Besides, since some of these monks had by then accepted socialist ideas and had the desire to take part in politics

---

16. The formation of this class was made possible, after its foundation was laid by the rise of the new pirivena education, by the revivalist agenda that came into being after 1956. Monks were already on their way to forging this class when they were met halfway by this agenda.

in opposition to the ruling elites, the message that politics was social service was greatly welcome. (Hence the bitter opposition of this elite to "political monks"). In their eagerness to hear this message, these monks quite forgot that the rural development work of the Vidyodaya monks was also "social service," in fact more so than theirs, which was plainly politics. Further, with its association of potential power, politics was more exciting than the humdrum rural economics that may have appeared to these monks as only once removed from rural ritualism. In this context, it is no surprise that the rural development movement built painstakingly and with evangelical fervor by the hero-giants of Dharmapala had little chance of survival. Many gifted and ambitious young monks, who would have taken to rural development, were enticed by the more flashy "social service" as propagandized by the Vidyalankara monks. Politics, primarily in the form of nationalist ideology, drowned the sprouting rice fields of economics and common sense that was the message of rural development.

From our discussion above, it should be clear that Rahula's restatement of the vocation of the monk constituted a change from Dharmapala's original formulation. Almost invisible at first glance, that change was subtle but profound. It signified a change of focus of the monk's activity from society to himself. In the Dharmapalite conception, the monk was the best available resource for the task of national regeneration. He was the agent of doing good to others, to the society as a whole. In contrast, despite much swearing on the part of *The Heritage* that the monk's work was for the benefit of others, the stigmatization of the rural ritual role of the monk, which constituted the testimony and essence of the bond of reciprocity between him and the poverty-stricken villagers who supported him, gave these monks away. It bared the desire of these monks to do things that are facilitative of acceptance by modern nonrural lay elites as explicitly advocated, in another giveaway, by *The Heritage*. Thus "politics" in the activities of these monks, rather than meaning "social service," which is altruistic and universalist, remained true to its narrowest and least ethical meaning of seeking benefit for themselves either directly or indirectly through courting the acceptance of a modernizing lay middle class, and by means of pressure group activity. The latter was possible through the custody they claimed of religion, language, culture, and nation, which amounted to fanning the flames of Sinhala Buddhist nationalism. This is *The Heritage*'s second and proud message, which reveals to us its true intentions. For if Rahula's intention is "the good of the many and the benefit of the many,"[17] as the Buddha exhorted the monks to work for, it

17. As we know, this itself is a misappropriation of the Buddha's words to suit the project of the monks since by this exhortation the Buddha meant the spread of the dhamma and not "social service,"

is inconceivable, not to mention illogical, that "the many" meant only a chosen ethno-religious group. Further, in constituting a pressure group to advance Sinhala Buddhist interests, as the postscript to the English edition of *The Heritage* makes clear, these monks knew that their own personal interests would also be automatically advanced.

The severing of the bond between the monk and the villager in the denunciation of ritual service thus contained the seeds of the evolution of a new monk whose altruism was nebulous and self-proclaimed rather than specific and objective. This is a monk who claims that his morality resides not in the objective conformity to rules but within himself. If truly understood, this could be a development with a profoundly positive social consequence, but it was not. This new monk typically entered the university and earned a degree in a secular field of study, which may be a natural or social science subject or the study of literature. "The hedonism of Kalidasa" would certainly be a part of the latter. The first generation of these monks were the first graduates of the newly created Vidyodaya and Vidyalankara universities. Every year their ranks swell as a new class of graduate monks enter the group. These are salaried monks, typically teachers, who by virtue of their full time employment and assignment in a secular professional capacity have no time for ritual services to the laity, even if they wish to do these. In the early stages of their evolution as recruits to this particular monastic vocation, they can be first spotted in the cocoon of the university, freely associating with other students, both male and female, and enjoying the privileges and immunities of studentship, including strike action and "ragging."[18] These monks feel they should be academically qualified, salaried, and in other ways allowed to do "as laymen do," as elaborated below.

The sociological validity of *The Heritage*'s central thesis (that monks languished while the lay society advanced; that they have nothing to say to the laity; and that therefore they lost status among the elite laity) brings out the real reason behind the argument that the vocation of the monk is social service. On Rahula's own admission, the motivation for this definition is to gain

---

which in Rahula's definition ranges from politics to teaching about cleanliness. Our concern here however is with the contrast between the universalism of the Buddha and the parochialism of these monks.

18. "Ragging" is the rite of initiation of freshmen into university studentship. A custom borrowed from British universities, it was once a benign and enjoyable part of university life. It has now taken monstrous, potentially criminal, and clearly pathological form in Sri Lankan universities, exhibiting class hatred and sexual perversions. As conducted now ragging can cause severe physical and emotional injury. In 1997 two freshmen died in ragging incidents, which led to new legislation requiring heavy punishment for ragging offenders, which is unlikely to dampen the zeal or creativity of ragging enthusiasts. While physical injury is visible and potentially treatable, there is little concern about emotional injury. Monks rag only their own kind, although there is nothing to prevent them witnessing the ragging of lay students.

lay, especially elite, acceptance (91). This became apparent not only to Rahula but to the monastic middle class that came into being after the establishment of the pirivenas. The education of this other-worldly middle class was traditional: both in content and pedagogic style it belonged to a past society. With the establishment of the colonial system the elite status that the monk literati enjoyed in that society passed on to the English-educated modern intelligentsia, which constituted the middle and upper classes. When Rahula talks about "laymen" having nothing to learn from monks, what he has in mind is not the laity as a whole but this particular section, namely the elite. It is this class, not "laymen" as a totality, that "dissociated themselves" (91) from the monks, and it is the bond between monks and that class, and not the laity as a whole, that "declined." In the precolonial system, since the monks were an intellectual elite, the "laymen" of Rahula's usage here, i.e., the upper classes, did have something to learn from them.[19] Thus what Rahula is defending here is not the interests of the monkhood as a whole but its upper stratum from whom the lay upper stratum traditionally had something to learn.

Like Rahula, this upper stratum of monks could well have been without any belief in ordinary ritualism, and without any time for such activity. It is that class of monks, and not the rural monks, who would be miserable having to do only rituals for the laity. The large majority of the monks were quite happy with the ritualism that constituted the basis of the bond they had with the people; "social service," such as teaching literacy, was marginal. When Rahula talks about "energetic and enterprising monks" who "would not like to sit idle, satiated with the sanctity afforded him within the temple precincts, devoting his life only to receive alms, chant pirit, perform funeral rites, and deliver the usual sermons" (97), he is speaking not of the ordinary monk, who would have no such problems, but of an elite, like Rahula and his Vidyalankara colleagues—an elite not only because they were educated but also because they were "energetic and enterprising." Such monks, says Rahula, would instead like to "liberate their country, nation and religion" (97). This is a noble thought indeed if only Rahula and colleagues understood what that mission truly meant and made sure, as Dharmapala wanted them to, that the monks had the moral and professional qualifications to do this service.

19. In the Sinhala original of *The Heritage,* there is no mention of "something to learn." It says "*bhiksuvagen gihiyanta prayojanayak nati viya*" ("monks became useless to the laity"). Since Rahula approved the translation it is justifiable for us to think that what Rahula meant was "useful knowledge." The two usages suggest the equation of "useful" monk's work with secular knowledge.

In his postscript to *The Heritage* Rahula narrates with satisfaction the progress of the nationalist agenda and expresses optimism for a new role of the monk that would reunite the monkhood (i.e., its upper stratum) with the lay elite from which it was estranged at the advent of colonialism. On Rahula's own criterion, for this to happen, the monks must have something in the secular field, for example in social or political matters, international affairs, the sciences or the aesthetic fields, that they can say to the laity. Rahula considers the change in the medium of instruction a great victory and a justice. That, according to Rahula, opened the door to higher education for students from rural areas and young monks (112). In fact what has happened is ironical and has made Rahula's dream of uniting the monastic middle class with its secular counterparts recede further: while the monk (and the rural youth) no doubt received some education, the change to Sinhala as the medium of instruction closed the only door they had to English and further increased the advantages of upper class children who had access to English over those who knew no English. The reality as opposed to the fantasy is that the Sinhala language carries very little modern knowledge when compared to the nearly unlimited sources of knowledge available to the users of English. Thus, these monks, educated in Sinhala, still have nothing to say to the lay elite, and the only use of these monks for these elites is still the ritual one. Contrary to Rahula's expectations, "Sinhala Only" has functioned to perpetuate the gap between the monk and the lay elite rather than to bridge it. Belated realizations of the importance of English issue from unlikely quarters. An article in *Divayina,* the nationalist Sinhala daily, states: "While talking about university education, it is necessary to mention the medium of instruction. Today the majority of jobs go to those who know English. But in the arts faculties, which produce the majority of graduates, the medium is Sinhala. The majority of graduates has only a weak knowledge (if any) of English. The fault is entirely in the education system, which excludes English. If the medium is English, that will help the employment problem, as it will other problems. This should not be the excuse for any anxiety about the national language."[20] This is a sober and realistic position about the medium of instruction.

Thus, the Sinhala Only policy, especially in its extension as the medium of instruction, despite Rahula's hopes and dreams, has far from ensured what he thought it would, namely the rise of a monkhood that can be taken seriously by an educated laity. In this respect the monkhood appears in less favorable light when objectively compared to institutions like the Christian

20. *Divayina,* 26 April 1966.

priesthood, which has access to English and other international languages.[21] What the Sinhala Only policy has ensured rather is as follows. First, it has ensured that the young monk (along with his secular counterpart, the rural youth) is left behind in the race for employment, as the writer just quoted says, thereby depriving the nation of the potential contribution of exceptional talent that on statistical probability must be present in this large group. Second, politicians consider monks to be useful to them as "stage props," as some young monks put it, and therefore try to use them in their race for power. But they cannot give the monks anything substantial in return. However, the nationalist agenda obliges the politician to give the monks something. Therefore, this agenda has ensured a ceremonial recognition to be accorded the monkhood, giving it a false prominence in the state-owned and private nationalist media and elsewhere. This takes the hilarious and hypocritical form of seasoned politicians going to the Mahanayakas of Asgiriya and Malvatta and unconvincingly asking for "advice."

It is a measure of the delusion of the monkhood, proof that a modern education still evades the monks and they still have nothing to say to the laity, that the monks are unable to see through this facade. It is revealing of the monkhood's narrowness of vision that they have not even grasped the argument about their condition that Rahula has expounded so perceptively and lucidly, namely that to gain elite acceptance they must gain a basic knowledge of contemporary trends in national and international affairs and of the generally known advances in the natural and social sciences and the arts. Far from such a contemporary awareness, even the most intellectual of these monks, including Rahula, seem to lack, for example, the simple knowledge that the modern state is a certain specific kind of historical and legal entity, that Sri Lanka is a modern state that consists of people belonging to different ethnic and religious groups, and that the premodern polity was, neither in Sri Lanka nor elsewhere in the world, a "unitary state." Hence they constantly and glibly talk about "country, nation, and religion," meaning by that only the Sinhala Buddhists, which makes the demand for a separate

---

21. In the medieval world, when local European languages were undeveloped, Christian priests broadened their perspectives by the study of Latin and Greek. Similarly, Buddhist monks learnt Pali and Sanskrit, and by that means had something to say to the laity. With the establishment of the pirivena universities, traditional pirivena education has declined dramatically and monks have lost their knowledge of these languages and become monolingual, which prevents their gaining a comprehensive knowledge of even the one language they know. Their perspectives have narrowed into chauvinism or false socialism, and they have nothing to say to the laity even considering the latter's own monolingualism, leaving the monks where they were, namely as ritual specialists. See Dayan Jayatilleke, *Sri Lanka: The Travails of a Democracy* (Kandy: International Center for Ethnic Studies, 1995), 148.

state more logical and reasonable than the separatist ideologues have ever made it out to be. The reason for this distorted view of contemporary Sri Lanka that monks hold is their lack of the kind of education that Rahula envisaged for them despite himself, which would have updated their thinking from medieval to contemporary times. It is one of the stark and unbelievable facts of contemporary Sri Lankan Theravada that there is not one single monk who can truly be described as an urbane intellectual who has imbibed contemporary knowledge and has developed a contemporary outlook and sensibility. Paradoxically, after a period of youthful sojourn in that mental state, Rahula himself returned to being a typically narrow-minded Buddhist monk.[22] Thus, while there are monks with modern academic qualifications such as university degrees, including Ph.D.s from local and foreign universities, they still have nothing to say to the sophisticated laity, which thus cannot be blamed for looking at them as nothing but recipients of alms, chanters of bana and pirit, and performers of funeral rites. This statement obviously has the qualification that those in the category of educationally qualified monks who have teaching jobs, do have something to say, but that is limited to the classroom. There are a handful of monks who teach in the universities, and in their specialized areas they may have something to say to their audiences. But this is also a limited and classroom audience, and it is well recognized in any case that the general level of university teaching in Sri Lanka is low due largely to the monolingualism of the teaching staff. There are a few distinguished scholars in the universities, but they are very much the exception and they are not monks. Furthermore, the educational qualifications of these monks have had no effect on the foundations of a monastic culture long emancipated from the openness of mind and spirit of free inquiry that is often considered the hallmark of the Buddha's doctrine. It is obvious that the monkhood represents a "routinization of charisma" in Weber's sense and has long been interested in land and other forms of booty, monopoly over education, perpetuation of caste and other forms of inequality, and pressure group activity for the maintenance of its privileges by appeal to one or another variation of the chorus "country, nation, and religion." It is apparent that there is something in the socialization of the monk in this system that acts as an effective deterrent against the intrusion of the freedom of mind,

---

22. A newspaper cartoonist corroborates. Referring to Rahula's transformation he says: *"Olu palu unat attayi kivve ekala, Pasukala nisaru de desuve ape pavatayi"* (Although they broke his head he told the truth. Of late he utters nonsense because of our sins). *Divayina,* 26 July 1991. "Broken head" refers to an incident in 1947, in which Rahula and some others were assaulted by thugs, widely believed to be candidate (later Finance Minister, President) J. R. Jayawardene's, in election-related violence.

civility, and urbanity that Buddhist scholars and apologists claim for Buddhism's pristine form.

Besides ensuring that the monks continue to have nothing to say to the lay elites, the nationalist agenda with its Sinhala Only policy has ensured that the monks along with the rural youth, who are also denied access to English, are left behind in the race for employment and open mobility. It has ensured a decline in all fields of academic and artistic activity, with the university degrees now meaning little more than a knowledge of notes from lectures delivered by a faculty whose knowledge itself is sketchy, making a mockery of the literacy levels that are proclaimed as the country's achievement. It has ensured the preparation of the ground for the subversion of democratic institutions, adventure capitalism, terror, anomie, and the violent call for a separate state.

In *The Heritage* Rahula visualized a middle class monk who is learned in modern western languages and in modern secular subjects. "Social service," the work such monks would do, Rahula speculated, would gain acceptance as a new monastic vocation or *dhura,* comparable to the two classical ones, grantha dhura (the vocation of books) and vidarsana dhura (the vocation of meditation). This monk indeed has come into being, except for the difference that, in contrast to the ideal modern monk of Rahula's paradigm, this monk is not necessarily or commonly altruistic. Rather, what has happened is, as an inevitable outcome of the stigmatization of the rural-based ritual service that constituted the basis of the reciprocity and bond between monk and layman, we have a monk who has been set free and given a modern secular education, however poor its quality, with no questions asked.

That monk, instead of being the center of a village community as Dharmapala wanted him to be, is the center of himself. He is typically a university graduate who is either salaried or has a comfortable income either from traditional or new sources. The latter can be local enterprise or in a few cases foreign funds. Liberated from ritual duties to a specific community, such a monk imagines his community to be geographically the entire country and demographically the Sinhala Buddhists. Service to such a nebulous community is unspecific and sloganistic. This faceless and ephemeral community contrasts with the known village community to which the traditional monk is bound with bonds of neighborhood, kinship, and ritual duty. This nebulous community is reached through the mass media or through political or quasi-political meetings on subject matter that is ideological and chauvinist, with no meaningful reference to or impact on economic/pragmatic thinking or activity.

In appearance and demeanor this new monk is markedly different from the traditional monk. For example, he wears well-groomed short hair (mockingly referred to as the "samanera cut") and possesses mannerisms different from those of the traditional monk. He may reside in a monastery without necessarily being an organic part of the social life of that monastery, and he may occasionally be found residing in a house of his own attended to by servants. In a few cases his belongings may range from expensive luxury cars to investments. His lifestyle may be a variation on the traditional regarding consumption patterns but may sometimes verge on "the hedonism of Kalidasa." He was conceived in the imagination of Dharmapala in his hour of need for soldiers and hero giants—and delivered by Rahula. But he has grown into a caricature of what Dharmapala defined him to be, an epitome of hard work, wisdom, and above all morality. Dharmapala's conception liberated him from traditional rural bonds, but instead of entering into a new set of bonds with the village, as Dharmapala envisaged, this monk has fled the village community, morally, physically, or both. Dharmapala wanted this monk to set himself free from his traditional anchor but stabilize himself on a new one. Instead, this monk has become anchorless. He has, in the process of his new socialization, been sent to a pirivena and then the university rather than grow up under the traditional tutelage *(nissaya)*[23] of a teacher-monk until a basic behavioral if not a moral code was woven into the fabric of his life. *The Heritage* has allowed this monk to convert the freedom from rural bonds to a freedom of the wild ass labeled "social service." This new social service dhura has freed and secularized the monk in ways unprecedented since the infancy of Buddhism, when, in the soteriological turmoil of the Buddha's time, groups of wayward monks tried unsuccessfully to practice a hedonistic life while remaining in robes.[24]

I shall now focus on how the liberation from ritual service (provided by *The Heritage*) has enabled monks to abandon their traditional bond with the rural community and to embark on any activity and seek success in the areas of power, wealth, and influence. It is necessary before this to discuss briefly a treatise written by a monk that further extends the boundaries of morality or "monkness" heralded by *The Heritage*.

EXTENSION OF THE MONASTIC BOUNDARY

The book we are concerned with is *Vartamana Bhiksu Parapura* (The Contemporary Generation of Monks; hereafter, *VBP*) by the monk Horatapala Palita,

23. Nissaya refers to the customary requirement of a young monk to stay with his teacher for a period adequate for him internalize the ways of a full-fledged monk.

24. Whether this is historical or fictional is difficult to determine. Either way, the descriptions of this in the Buddhist texts has only one purpose, its denunciation.

published in 1970.[25] A slim volume of 56 pages, it is strongly influenced by
The Heritage and related works, especially those of Yakkaduve, as we shall
see below. It accepts the monk's vocation as "social service" but takes the
position further by the candid admission that social service means politics.
It is of particular interest to us because it claims that its views are not just
those of one individual but representative of the views common to young
monks of his generation. Since the author is a graduate, we can legitimately
understand this to mean not just "young" but "young and educated." In this
sense the work represents a trickle down of the ideas of *The Heritage* into the
more educated and therefore influential section of the monkhood.

The book is, first, a critique of different segments of society, both lay and
monastic. Traditional monks are criticized for their greed for meaningless
titles, for their property interests, and for maltreating their pupils. Monk di-
rectors of pirivenas are criticized for corrupt practices to swindle state funds.
The hierarchical chief monks are criticized for polluting the honor of their positions by signing statements *(nivedana)* on various issues written by someone
else, usually politicians. The laity are taken to task for their criticism of monks,
which the author considers ignorant.[26] Both monks and laymen are criticized
for certain rituals that Palita considers to be hypocrisies. Second, the book
makes a case for a council *(sangayana)* to revise the vinaya rules so that they
reflect realistic standards of behavior applicable to modern conditions. That
is, vinaya rules are to be revised to conform to existing behavior rather than
the other way around. In this sense, it is a frank admission of the fact that the
rules are not followed at present. The basis for this suggestion is the position
taken in the texts that grew around *The Heritage,* especially those of Yakkaduve
(see chap. 4), that monkness depends on the four basic vows a monk under-
takes at ordination.[27] It is the violation of these that constitutes defeat *(parajika)*
of the monkhood. Vinaya violations are thus considered remediable and non-
fatal to monkness. This in turn is based on the Rahulite theory, expounded
in *The Heritage,* that these rules are a product of time and place and thus have
no universal and timeless validity. That is, these rules are cultural and enjoy
no autonomy. Since morality in relation to the realization of ultimate truth

---

25. Horatapala Palita, *Vartamana Bhiksu Parapura* (Gangodavila: Ranjani Printing Works, 1970). In
an unpublished paper I have discussed another work on the same theme, Jayasiri Manoratne, *Sangha
samajaya prabhavaya ha Pariganaka Yugaye Bhiksuva* (Origin of the Sangha Society and the Monk of the
Computer Age [Colombo: Godage, 1992]).

26. Laymen criticize senior monks for violating vinaya rules and young student monks for their
unorthodox behavior including eating at night, which *VBP* considers necessary for poor, hard working
students whose meals are meager and lacking in nutrition. *VBP*'s answer for criticizing senior monks
echoes Yakkaduve's.

27. These are vows to refrain from killing, stealing, sexual offenses, and falsely claiming supernatural powers.

has by definition to be universal in validity, and therefore, autonomous, this amounts to a denial of a moral base and meaning to vinaya.[28] The question of time and place regarding vinaya is a pillar of the Vidyalankara position. The *VBP* position on this and several other matters, such as the defense of salaries, is a rehash of that of the Vidyalankara monks.

VBP's next point consists of a critique of existing inequalities, suggestions for an economic program (and this includes a program of distribution of monastic lands, which are extensive, among the lay needy), and the establishment of a common fund from existing monastic resources to support student monks. Next, *VBP* suggests the idea of a Sangha Court and attributes its prevention so far to the bickering between chief monks.[29] It takes an economic view of the problem of alcohol and other toxic substances such as ganja (marijuana), and it says that people take to trafficking in them because of unemployment. Temperance has led to the production of illicit brews, and therefore true temperance should constitute the rehabilitation of the individual.

What is most surprising to come from a Buddhist monk here is the suggestion to evaluate distilling arrack, the farming of livestock, and fisheries in economic rather than in religio-cultural terms. *VBP* argues that the vast sums of money that were being paid to India to buy eggs could be saved by producing them locally. The consumption of eggs further will contribute to a healthier work force. Arrack should be produced because it makes economic sense: the country derived significant income in the past few years from the production of arrack. (This brings the Dharmapalite reformation full circle in the sense that Dharmapala's entire effort was to empower monks to get rid of immoralities that produce degeneration, of which alcohol was the prime culprit.) The state-owned Sugar Corporation, says *VBP*, is kept solvent due to the profits made by distilling arrack. The growth of animal husbandry will help alleviate the problem of unemployment. It is foolish to use religious and cultural criteria to make decisions about fisheries.[30] The prosperity of Japan, an eminently Buddhist country in *VBP*'s view, is dependent on fisheries.

28. I have already alluded to writings that take a different view. See John Holt, *Discipline* (cited in chap. 4, n. 38).

29. The idea of a Sangha court is also a suggestion made by the Buddha Sasana Commission. *Buddha sasana komisan sabha vartava*, Sessional Paper 18 (Colombo: The Government Press, 1959), chap. 6, 187–207. For a critique of these proposals, see Havanpola Ratanasara, *Buddha sasana komisan sabha varta samalocanaya* (Colombo: Gunasena, 1961).

30. Sometime after the publication of *VBP*, some monks obstructed a state plan to implement a village-based freshwater fish farming program. But, according to newspaper reports, the same monks performed a religious ceremony on board a fishing trawler and chanted pirit to ensure the success of a state-sponsored trawler fishing venture. Monks also perform Bodhipuja and other ceremonies to bless the army.

The proposals for a new monkhood are based broadly on the idea that the monkhood should be "like a flowing river" (54), constantly adapting to its environment. The *VBP* proposes an empirical study to determine what the frequently violated vinaya rules are, with a view to abolishing them. While this in principle sounds dangerous, it appears that *VBP* does have some concern about monkness: "Monkness is public. [A monk] must live in an open world. The honor and hopes of a whole cluster of people that includes teachers, parents, and supporters is dependent on the life of one monk. To protect these is to protect the heritage of monkness" (53). While this is reassuring, it is clear from the above that *VBP* has gone further than any other in advocating the revision of rules in the direction of laxity. Further, it is curious that the control envisaged in the above definition of monkness is external (namely, honor and hopes of a cluster of supporters), whereas the standard Vidyalankara defense of nonconformity to rules (as indeed *VBP*'s in other contexts of the work) is that it is internal and not visible to critics, who therefore should not worry about it.

VBP explicitly says that "the entire monk society, monk life, should be subjected to a change" *(parivartanaya)* (55). The first ingredient of this is economic independence from the laity: "Monks should not be self-deceiving hypocrites and must find their own livelihood. To expect to live on the charity, the support of others, even in the name of religion, is an injury to self-respect, an insult to being human" (55). This is a radical idea that challenges the reciprocity between monk and layman for which the noneconomic and nonproductive attribute of the monk is pivotal; and the idea of "self-respect" is a far cry from the doctrine of no-self. The effect of this would be an independent monk who pursues his own interests and performs ritual functions, if any at all, exclusively on a voluntary and selective basis as opposed to the obligatory nature of ritual performance in traditional practice. The *VBP* is explicit on this: "The monk must stop advising the laity *(anusasana)* and preaching *(bana)* and let every person arrive at his own decision and understanding. Religion, good behavior *(sucaritaya),* and ethicality *(pinpav)* are inherent to individuals and cannot be imparted by another. Doing prayers, rites, blessings for others like deity priests *(devala kapuvan)* do, should be given up" (55).

It would not be difficult to recognize that these are the ritual services *The Heritage* (after Dharmapala) characterizes to be the lot of the uneducated rural monks. Thus *VBP* represents the realization of what is advocated in *The Heritage,* a new dhura (vocation), as Rahula put it. To state this differently, this is a reaffirmation—let us keep in mind the author's statement that these ideas are not his own but of his generation—and an announcement of the arrival of that new vocation, that, as we shall see in the next section, we might call *nagaravasa* or *titthavasa*. The central question is that of monk-ness—the extent to which monkness can be saved from injury or total defeat under these new circumstances, despite promises and optimism by the Vidyalankara monks and this new generation. As we already saw, the source of constraint that the preservation of monkness requires is claimed, contradictorily, to be external at one breath and internal at the next. A pervasive lay critique of the monkhood, which is often expressed informally but also in correspondence columns of newspapers, shows that the public is skeptical of the morality of these monks. The public moreover is insistent on the ritual services that these monks, from Rahula and his Vidyalankara colleagues to the young monks of the *VBP,* would rather not do. Thus, from the point of view of the Rahulite theory of a modern "social service" monk, we are back at the fundamental and tragic monastic condition: the monk is still most sought after by the laity for ritual services, and he still has nothing to say to the laity, a state far from that which *The Heritage* in its postscript in particular confidently anticipates.

VBP then could be described as a mirror of the contemporary state of the monastic "middle class" monks, toward which the monkhood in general seems to be moving. *VBP* advocates not the practice but the preservation of Buddhism. That is, the generation of young monks represented by this work are in full conformity with a long tradition of Buddhist monastic history, going back to the second century B.C.E. victory of the dhammakathika monks over the pamsukulika. The idea of preservation originated in the conceptions of nobility *(ariya)* of the doctrine and its supreme rarity *(paramadul-labha)* and was enhanced by local threats to the physical safety of the monks vividly imaged in the Buddhist literature as danger from thieves, fire, water, harlots, and hostile kings, and also by foreign threats imaged in the burning, pillage, and vandalization of monasteries and edifices.

According to *VBP,* earlier innovators such as the Rural Development monks and their followers all have misinterpreted the exhortation of the Buddha to work for the good and benefit of the many, interpreting this to be worldly benefit, whereas it truly refers to the other worldly. In this *VBP* is in agreement with the traditionalist Gnanavasa, the advocate of vibhavagami as the monk's true path. Since *VBP* advocates a revision of the vinaya rules and is in other ways unorthodox, this amounts to an admission that they are not on that path and are therefore, not true monks. Their monkness thus derives from their self-appointed role of preserving the doctrine and from a certain morality claimed by them to be inherent in them, their actions and style of life notwithstanding. The former (preserving the doctrine), a valid function in the ancient and medieval eras, is now particularly questionable because of the redundancy of human preserving agents in a world rife with efficient, reliable, expeditious, and safe technologies of preserving and multiplicating.

When compared to that of the Vidyalankara monks, the Sinhala Buddhist nationalism of the *VBP* is a milder form that at least allows room to think with some degree of rationality about economic matters. The Vidyalankara monks were, as we know, totally noneconomic. In this context, the *VBP*'s opposition to Poya (full moon day) holidays is also relevant, because such holidays are economically disruptive. Elements of ideology, however, are present and cannot be underestimated.

If monks are going to earn salaries, they can be like laymen in other ways, as these monks seem to want to be. Short haired rather than shaven headed, groomed, socializing, seeing films and plays and TV shows, listening to music, enraptured by cricket, using cosmetics, eating in restaurants, the gap between monk and layman has narrowed. There is also, to add to this, the denial of the ancient reciprocity and relation with a particular lay community, i.e., the monks finding it undignified to accept the laity's generosity. With this, it is possible to envisage a new kind of professional monk, independent of the laity, and, as observed before, having relations with a laity voluntarily and selectively. For the majority of these monks, this can be only an approximation to be carried out with subtlety, providing ritual services gleefully only to some, typically middle class clients and doing it as a chore to others, typically the poor, illiterate villagers. Although these monks are unwilling to accept lay generosity, the laity would not want to have it any other way, which brings us back to the uncomplimentary way (from the monk's point of view) the laity looks at the monk's social utility, as chanters of bana and pirit and performers of merit generating rituals.

MONKS AS ACTIVISTS
Social Service in Action

I shall now return to the question of how the liberation of the monk has led to an opening of the floodgates for them to do more or less as they please. "Monks" here refer typically to those with a modern education, often a university degree, but the idea of the monk's vocation as "social service" has, as we observed before, trickled down to the less educated monks who live in village or small town monasteries as well. This does not mean there are no traditional monks, the kind described in *The Heritage* as illiterate, lazy, and ritualistic. On the contrary, the large majority of the monks still belong to this category, in the sense that the kind of modern monk who embodies the new dhura envisaged in *Heritage,* which we have labeled nagaravasa or titthavasa, and illustrated in the cases we are about to discuss, are few. But except for a few of the older generation of rural monks, the large majority which we just called traditional have imbibed to a greater or lesser extent the trickled down ideas of *The Heritage* as to their vocation. This is particularly so in view of the acceptance by the media of this definition of monkhood, which thereby is repeatedly broadcast. Monks are the preeminent consumers of the media in the villages, and they are likely to come across the idea frequently. The two extremes of monks—traditional and modern or new— are relatively small categories, with the group in between constituting the overwhelming majority of the monkhood. This majority has either accepted or is favorably disposed towards the idea of "social service" as the monk's vocation. Yet they are entangled in the web of local social relations in such a way that they cannot shake off their traditional ritualistic bond and reciprocity within that web. Supported by social and political changes, the new monk's role is now institutionalized, contributing to the birth of a new monk whom his progenitor Dharmapala would find unrecognizable. The number of monks who are fully "modern" in this sense is still small, but there is a much larger number whose basic orientation is "modern." Those in full bloom have launched themselves in various kinds of enterprising activity, thus constituting an astounding displacement of goals. They further constitute the rise of a secondary and realistic individualism in the monkhood as contrasted with the primary and ritualistic individualism represented in relinquishing family ties and dramatized in the ritual of ordination.

This new monkhood can be illustrated by some specific cases. All bring out the indispensable precondition, the liberation of the particular monks from traditional monkhood. Some of the activities of these monks even resemble "social service," but, while there are some monks who are genuinely interested in social service, serious questions arise about others and their activities. Moreover, the "social service" of these monks does not compare favorably with that of the Christian ministers and priests from whom the idea was borrowed. For example, in Sri Lanka misuse or embezzlement of funds is rare or nonexistent among the Christian clergy involved in well-funded "social service" activities.[31] Since liberation from bonds to a particular laity or gramavasa (village dwelling) constitutes the major objective

---

31. There are several organizations that help the poor run by the Christian clergy in Sri Lanka, for example Satyodaya, located in Kandy, headed by Fr. Paul Caspersz. Another is a similar organization run by Fr. Tissa Balasuriya, a radical priest excommunicated by the church for writing a controversial book, *Mary and Human Liberation* (Colombo: Centre for Society and Religion, 1990).

criterion that defines these monks, we shall call their vocation nagaravasa
(city dwelling). In doing so we are merely placing a label on the new dhura
Rahula asserted "social service" would come to be.

Dramatically successful enterprising monks share several characteristics.
They typically come not from the *Raja Maha Viharas* or "Royal Temples" that
own extensive properties and that are typically located in the interior of
the island but from the urban monasteries located in the western seaboard,
particularly Colombo, the only large city and the capital of Sri Lanka; or if
they actually come from a rural monastery they have nevertheless successfully gained a foothold in an urban one. Thus they parallel the nonlanded
entrepreneurial class of the secular social order. They are educated monks,
graduates of Vidyodaya or Vidyalankara from the time they were privately
owned colleges, or from the more recent era (after 1958) when they were
converted into state-owned modern universities with broader secular curricula. They are typically innovative, gifted monks who use their educational
accomplishments and creative gifts to establish connections with foreign
countries, in particular with the rich Buddhist countries of East Asia. It is
telling that no connections of this type exist with Burma, a fellow Theravada
land with which Sri Lanka had historical monastic ties that were intense in
the last two centuries, but which is not an entrepreneur's paradise. These
monks also typically have important connections with the western world,
including Australia. It is as if they have converted their formidable gifts and
educational qualifications into equivalent capital reserves. Although they
exhibit the spirit of innovation, they are typically the pupils of, or in some
other way closely connected with, a prominent monk, who would, in the
case of the most dramatically successful of these monks, give them their
initial boost. There is a pattern of internationalizing themselves, a pattern
ultimately rooted in Dharmapala's foreign mission. It is almost exclusively
through the foreign connection that these monks have raised vast sums of
money for their projects. Dharmapala himself was an accomplished fund-
raiser,[32] but there is never any doubt that these were disbursed responsibly
and in keeping with the purposes for which the fundraising was done, which

---

32. Naravila Dhammaratana, who worked as a Dharmapalite missionary in India, recounts an incident where Dharmapala instantly assumed a deeply meditative posture before welcoming some East
Asian pilgrims who promptly made donations. At their departure Dharmapala awoke from the assumed
blissful transic disposition and asked the disciples present, "How did I do?" This shows how well Dharmapala knew what all spiritual fundraisers or "divine entrepreneurs" know—the appeal of serenity of
appearance to pious and vulnerable donors. See Naravila Dhammaratana, *Hadipannala Pannaloka,* 120–
21. In fairness to Dharmapala, there is no evidence that the funds he raised were expended on any
other than the intended projects, like the revival of Buddhism in India.

is not altogether the case with these monks. Various international associations, some with substantial economic resources, have sprung up, as in the case of Kananke Dhammadinna and the ICAAP discussed below. The popular network is the Asian region, both East and Southeast.

An interesting example is the World Buddhist Congress, of which there is an all-Sri Lanka branch. In 1991 a new branch was founded (strictly speaking, rendering the existing branch no longer all-Sri Lanka), and a delegation participated in the sessions of the World Young Men's Buddhist Congress held in South Korea. This was led by Kotavila Pemaloka, director of the Piriven Vihara, Vidyavardhana Pirivena, Dehivala, who was elected vice-president of the Congress. On 28 May 1991, the same monk held a ceremony at the Vidyavardhana Piriven Vihara for officially accepting a large bronze Buddha statue from Thailand donated by two Thai donors, Mr. Kanok and Mrs. Valee Devahastin.[33] The ceremony was attended by V.I.Ps who included the Thai Ambassador Apinan Pavanath and his wife. The Pirivena, said Kotavila, was founded by his teachers in 1936 with a humble beginning. Valamityave Kusaladhamma, Principal, Vidyalankara Pirivena, emphasized the close relations between the two pirivenas (his and Kotavila's), mentioning past students who have grown up to serve the Buddha Sasana and the people, including Kirinde Dhammananda, the Chief Sanghanayaka of Malaysia and Singapore, and incumbent of the Buddhist Vihara, Kuala Lumpur.

This event and the delegation to Korea illustrate one kind of enterprise that essentially is a method of using foreign connections to improve the image and esteem of a monk and his monastery, with political and economic possibilities always lurking in the background. Some further examples: A Thai Buddhist delegation led by the Venerable Phrakrusanghakicca Visud presented Thai candles, traditionally offered before *Vassa* (rain retreat), to prime minister D. B. Wijetunga at Temple Trees, his official residence.[34] Umale Jinaratana, president, Sri Lanka-Thailand-Japan Friendship Association, gave a gilded Buddha statue and a *navagunavala* (string of prayer beads) to all those who came to observe *sil* or to worship during Vesak at his vihara, the Sudarsanaramaya at Umale.[35] In February 1991, Hadigalle Pannatissa, incumbent of the Agrasravaka Vihara, Maligakanda, and of the Sanchi Vihara, and Chief Sanghanayaka, India, welcomed at the Agrasravaka Vihara a delegation of Japanese led by the Ven. Moyitoku Horiye, incumbent, Shokani Temple, Japan, and the nun Tokusho Okomura. In the picture depicting

33. *Sunday Times,* 9 June 1991.
34. *Ceylon Daily News,* 8 July 1991.
35. *Divayina,* 29 May 1991.

Chapter Five

the ceremony are Banagala Upatissa, Chief Sanghanayaka of Japan, Kiniyavala Palita, and Matara Ratanapala.[36] In his speech Hadigalle praised the rise of Japan after its defeat in World War II. Banagala, Director of the Japan-Sri Lanka Buddhist Center (in addition to being Chief Sanghanayaka of Japan), also spoke. Without mentioning former President J. R. Jayawardene's name, he alluded to the former's San Francisco speech supporting Japan at the end of the World War II (where Jayawardene quoted the Dhammapada verse "Hatred is not ceased by hatred").[37] During Vesak 1990, the Mahanayaka Osako Kimura of the Jigenj temple of the Singosu sect and eleven others were to arrive in Sri Lanka to join celebrations and discuss the projected Industrial University to be built in the Uva province at the cost of 400 million rupees ($8,000,000). Leadership for this was provided by Galeboda Gnanissara. Umale Jinaratana went to Japan for preliminary discussions on 13 November 1990. The Japanese delegation was to participate in Vesak celebrations at the Umale Purana Viharaya, in which the First Lady Hema Premadasa was to participate.[38]

Not all our "new" or nagaravasa monks are involved in this kind of "social service." As contrasted with those monks who have successfully tapped large-scale financial resources, there are others whose enterprise or talents have been channeled in other directions, as the cases below illustrate. But let us start with examples of the former.

Banagala Upatissa is the director of the Yoshida Free Nursery Institute at the Abeysekararama monastery, at Sapugaskanda, near Kelaniya. Preschool education is the area best represented in the projects of these enterprising monks. Several monks have been successful in recruiting Japanese philanthropists or organizations (usually individuals rather than organizations) as contributors of what appear to be substantial funds. Banagala is a pupil of Hadigalle Pannatissa, a Vidyodaya monk and Dharmapalite missionary in India who is the incumbent of the Agrasravaka Maha Vihara in Colombo and the Sanchi Vihara, India. He is also the chief Sanghanayaka of India, a system of chiefships which is a part of this new monkhood.[39]

36. *Divayina,* 14 Feb. 1991.
37. *Divayina,* 14 Feb. 1991.
38. *Divayina,* 15 Nov. 1990.
39. With the gradual consolidation of Sri Lankan Buddhist monasteries in different parts of the world, we have an interesting Janus-faced development. On the one hand, monks have adapted to the cultures of the host environments in numerous ways, for example, making Sundays rather than full moon days the ritual days and gaining licenses as marriage registrars. On the other, these monks have had an abiding interest in gaining status at home by seeking titles, typically, nayaka or chiefships of the relevant countries. This reflects the dramatic rise in the numbers of the expatriate Sri Lankan Buddhist communities, which brings the foreign context closer to the indigenous, by the gradual introduction

According to Hadigalle, the series of events that led his pupil Banagala to the successful establishment of the institute are as follows.[40] In 1976 Takiko Yoshida, a Japanese millionairess, was on a pilgrimage to visit the Buddhist sites in India. Madam Yoshida, referred to by Hadigalle and others as "Mother Yoshida," was born to a distinguished Buddhist family on the island of Kyushu. She studied Japanese culture and literature at the Jotogakukan College in Tokyo and became a poet and painter. She married Dr. Kishi Yoshida and became the director of Yoshida, a well-known private hospital in Japan, presumably one source of her wealth. During her visit to India, she was impressed by the tranquility, expository skills, and demeanor of Banagala. She learned of Sri Lankan Theravada from Banagala and visited Sri Lanka in 1977, a visit Hadigalle describes as "a blessing to our country." "The pure Buddhism of Sri Lanka, the virtuous Buddhist people, the values of Sri Lankan women, the pleasant behavior of the sons and daughters and the natural beauty of Sri Lanka captured the heart of Mother Yoshida," writes Hadigalle. With this favorable impression she resolved to provide funds "for the upliftment of Buddhism and the people of this country." Banagala drew the philanthropist's attention to the close relationship between the monastery and the school in Sri Lankan Buddhist culture, and he indicated to her his desire to open a nursery school "in the shade of the Bodhi tree of the Abeyesekararama Vihara in Sapugaskanda." "Considering the sons and daughters of Sri Lanka her own," Madam Yoshida offered to fund the project, which was opened on 26 June 1979, the first of such schools to be established with Japanese support. Others were to follow, "due to the successful forward march of the Yoshida Free Nursery Institute." Speaking the language of an entrepreneur, Hadigalle describes the institute as providing job opportunities for young Sri Lankan women through the course in Nursery Educa-

---

of more and more indigenous religious phenomena. This development is also a function of the class nature of beliefs. For example, when the Washington Buddhist Vihara was established in the 1950s, its major supporters were the western educated elite civil servants, some of whom were Tamil Hindus or Christians, and ritual was at a minimum, with the propagation of the dharma among the Americans as the major goal. But today the supporters are a much larger community of Buddhists of a mixed class composition, who are keen to duplicate in their new domicile the ritual life of the old country, constraining the monks to focus more on them than on the American seekers of the dharma. As in the case of the titles at home, these foreign chiefships carry no administrative or other authority and have no meaning to anyone but their givers and recipients. This system is a parody and phantomized version of the disciplined and dedicated worldwide missionary project that Dharmapala envisaged and worked tirelessly to achieve, and a feeble echo of the Asokan *Dharmavijaya,* world-conquest by dharma. These comments do not devalue the work of the few dedicated monks involved in missionary work. See also chap. 7 below.

40. *Divayina,* 24 May 1991.

tion started by the Yoshida Foundation. Besides, the young women who successfully complete the course, which is "assisted by specialists," and who "show excellent results" will get the opportunity of "getting a theoretical and practical training in Japanese educational institutions." "Madam Yoshida continued her support and appreciation of Theravada by building a Theravada Buddhist Vihare in Japan. This was opened on 24 May 1984 by the then Sri Lankan President J. R. Jayawardene. Further she started a program of training Theravada monks in Japanese language and culture, all expenses paid, and thereby opening the way for propagating Theravada in Japan." The Yoshida hospital also provides free medical attention to Sri Lankan Buddhist monks. In addition Madam Yoshida has supported the Lady Ridgeway Children's Hospital in Colombo and provided emergency relief to Sri Lanka.

A witness to the horrors of World War II, Madam Yoshida is committed to peaceful relations between nations and considers seeing a child educated at Sapugaskanda complete his or her higher education and accept a responsible position in Sri Lanka to be the crowning moment in her life. On 22 May 1991 she was honored with the national honor "Sri Lanka Ranjana" by President Premadasa. A mix of tradition and modernity, fact and fiction.

In 1991 the Naritasan monastery of Japan donated 1.4 million rupees out of the 5.8 million rupees it pledged toward an art center in memory of the renowned actress Rukmani Devi, the *Rukmani Devi Kala Niketanaya* to be constructed in Negombo at the cost of 8.3 million rupees.[41] Banagala was present at the ceremony at which the Venerable Hishiki Shoei, incumbent of Naritasen, presented the donation to President Premadasa. He mentioned that the remaining sum would be donated in a few weeks. What is of interest here is the patronage shown towards President Premadasa in two ways. The niketanaya was constructed by the Tower Hall Theatre Foundation, one of the president's favorite projects. Second, at the same ceremony, the Venerable Hishiki Shoei donated 1.4 million rupees, "in response to a request made by Ven. Banagala Upatissa" to the Sevana Fund, an even greater pet project of the president. These donations in fact are the springs of the president's gratitude to Japan (symbolized in the national honor awarded to madam Yoshida) and to Banagala, the apparent incubator of the golden eggs.

Bandagiriye Somavamsa, a student of the scholar-monk Baddegama Vimalavamsa, studied at Sri Lanka Vidyalaya, headed by Vimalavamsa. To continue his education he joined the Shiro Ume university in Japan. As in the other cases, the mini-mythology of these monks, perhaps initiated by themselves, is important. "When he came back [from Japan] and opted to crusade

41. *Ceylon Daily News,* 20 June 1991.

for a properly imparted preschool child education, he had many detractors. They opined that he should go in for setting homes for the destitute. But he had different views."[42] Bandagiriye's response was that the monastery had been a home for the destitute from ancient times [which is not true] and that it is important to eradicate the causes of destitution. Initial training of a child to develop his innate intelligence was a way of doing that. With this conviction he, with the assistance of child experts such as Professor Kubota Hiroshi, founded in 1985 the National Children's Educational Foundation, declared an approved charity by the government in 1986. "I could have led a very happy life of a bhikkhu in Japan," the monk is quoted as saying, "but I wanted to serve the future generations in my country. That was why I studied child education." So we have the pattern of bodhisattva-like sacrifice and "renunciation" on the one hand and the sense of "social service," reminiscent of *The Heritage,* along with the underlying or undisclosed premise of the dynamism from within and the availability of Japanese support.

With Japanese assistance Bandagiriye made a study of Sri Lankan preschool education. According to the article quoted above, this study took Bandagiriye "to almost all Montessori or preschool child education centers over several years." (This is a doubtful, because, on the writer's own evidence, there are an estimated 30,000 such schools in the island with 200,000–300,000 children and 2,829 teachers.) The report's conclusion is that Sri Lankan preschool education had no unified aim, lacked structure, did not make use of the available resources, and lacked trained teachers. The government has accepted the report, according to the article, and is using its findings as a basis for legislation for standardizing and controlling the schools. It was natural for Bandagiriye to successfully crusade for the establishment of a foundation with adequate resources to rectify the problems of preschool education his research uncovered. It is clear from the article that the research uncovered conditions that would appeal to philanthropy— small and poor classroom space, and lack of scientific teaching. His idea that it is better to have no preschool education than have it unscientifically lends urgency to the need for a foundation to address the issue.

The National Children's Educational Foundation, founded in 1985, is located at the Mulleriyava New Town on a four and a half acre lot donated by the government. This donation suggests the direct or indirect involvement of the government or some individuals in the government. In this location, the Foundation houses "the central preschool education system and consists of classrooms, teacher training programs, swimming pools, and all other

42. Eric Dewanarayana: "Crusader for pre-school education," *The Island,* 11 Nov. 1990.

facilities to make learning the most interesting episode in a growing child's life." The Foundation is jointly managed by Sri Lankan and Japanese educationists. The Foundation's programs include assistance to other schools, training of teachers, and granting scholarships for teachers to be trained in Japan. Ten kindergarten schools have already received support (in 1990). Setting up a Technical College is being planned. Units are being opened "in almost every district" to implement the Foundation's programs widely. Bandagiriye's broad aim is to develop "a national scheme of education with international assistance." A fitting conclusion to this account of Bandagiriye is his election to the presidency of the Rotary Club of Kolonnava, hailed in the newspapers as a milestone in the history of Theravada.

The source of foreign capital for enterprising monks is not always a foreign individual or organization. Sometimes expatriate Sri Lankan Buddhists make donations as well. An opportunity arose for Parakaduvue Saranamkara, incumbent of Asokarama, Kalutara North, when a young businessman working in England, presumably originally from Kalutara, visited the monk and offered to help "develop" *(diyunu karanta)* the vihara. Such "development" is the common ambition of rural monks. The monk's reaction, revealing the sentiment of *The Heritage,* was that the vihara can wait, and it was more urgent to help the poor fishermen who are in need of food and housing. The monk took Sedrick Manuven, the potential donor, round the huts of the fishermen. Manuven invited the monk to visit London, where he arranged other expatriates to meet him and learn about his plans. They not only made contributions but gave the monk a BMW. In a reminiscence of the Buddhist habit of mind to reduce things to their elements and of contemplating impermanence, the monk told the news reporter that the elegant and milky white BMW was, underneath its glitter, "a heap of metal," subject to decay, and that it should be sold forthwith for its market price of 8 million rupees so that he could use the money to build something presumably more permanent—houses for the 153 shanty dwelling fisher families.[43] In addition, the monk plans to build these houses by the beach in Kalutara North, in the residential neighborhood of the local rich, as a modest one man's contribution to diluting the class system.

This monk differs from those in preschool education in several ways. They have a steady source of financial support. His is support towards one specific project. Their resources are vast and appear inscrutable. His is limited and clear. Their copious resources enable them to endear them to the government, which has given them concessions. This monk needs the land on

43. *Divayina*, 20 March 1991.

which to build houses and, at the time of reporting (1991), he was still waiting for the government to act.

Kakanke Dhammadinna directs another nursery school established (in 1977) and run with the support of Japanese funds, the Shinnyo-en Nursery School at Pamankada, near Colombo. Housed in a spacious and beautifully designed building by a well-known architect, the school employs about twenty young female teachers, with as many classes each consisting of about twenty children (400 in all). Kananke's luxurious, air-conditioned office occupies a central and strategic point in the design of the building, providing the office with an excellent view of the classrooms, inclusive of the teachers. An exuberant young monk whose preferred language is English, Kananke expresses revolutionary ideas concerning the monk's status and role in society. He is the recipient of a doctoral degree in English literature from an Indian university, and he plans to work for another doctoral degree in England or the U.S.A. Kananke is co-founder, along with "The Venerable Dr. Juin" of Japan, of the International Cultural and Peace Promotional Association (ICPPA). According to newspaper reports, presumably supplied by Kananke,[44] "the Venerable Dr Juin" is a writer and head of several religious bodies in Japan, and a student of Indian Philosophy, who studied at Rissho (Buddhist) University and founded in 1971 the sect Myohozan of the ICPPA. This is "the only private cultural organization in Japan devoted to the arts, education, and cultural activities."[45] On 31 May 1991 Dr. Juin arrived in Sri Lanka leading a delegation of forty members, to participate in the foundation-laying ceremony of the headquarters of the ICPPA, which has branches in the U.S., U.K., Japan, and India. According to the *Daily News* report, the parent institution is located in Sri Lanka, and it suggests that Kananke, the co-founder, is a major player in the association. According to the *Divayina* report Kananke was to be given a distinctive honor, the fifth person to receive it and the first non-Japanese, by the ICPPA, which suggests some inbreeding. Besides, the *Divayina* report describes Kananke as the Chief Sanghanayaka of Japan, whereas the *Daily News* report gives the honor to Banagala. Thus these accounts reveal certain baffling contradictions. The ICPPA honor for Kananke was to be ceremonially presented by Prime Minister (later President) D. B. Wijetunga.

According to the *Divayina* report, Kananke studied English at the Gaya College of the Magadha University in India, where he was the first to read for an M. A. and excel in English literature, a feat to which his spoken English at

44. *Ceylon Daily News,* 31 May 1991.
45. *Divayina,* 31 May 1991.

any rate provides little credible testimony. This was achieved in 1976, while he was concurrently engaged in missionary work at the sacred grounds of Buddha Gaya. Next, he entered the best Pali Buddhist university in India, Nalanda, for postgraduate work. Here he gained a gold medal, the first time a Sri Lankan was awarded this honor by Nalanda. Subsequently he joined the Benares Hindu University, where he did his doctoral work.

The picture these accounts portray is far from clear regarding Kananke, his qualifications, affiliations, and status, and the personalities involved in these activities. What is clear is that he runs the Shinnyo-en Nursery School and apparently controls a considerably large sum of money. The accounts suggest some competition between Kananke and Banagala, as in the reference to both as the Chief Sanghanayaka of Japan.[46] Both seem funded by Japanese individuals or institutions and both seem eager to receive the then (1991) government's acceptance and recognition, which appeared to be forthcoming. Kananke's personal history, especially his academic record, which emphasizes many "firsts," seems quite baffling and contradictory.

In the first week of March 1992, Kananke was remanded without bail on charges of embezzlement of funds. On March 30, the court was to consider allowing bail.[47] In August 1992, Kananke appealed to the court for the restoration of his rights to enter the premises of the school on the grounds that he is a trustee of the Shinnyoen Lanka Free Nursery School, and he claimed rights to the property on which the school is situated. The property was owned by Swarna Abhayanayake and D. L. Srikanthi Rodrigo, who donated it as an irrevocable and absolute Sanghika gift to the monk Hadigalle Pannatissa, who in turn gave the land on a ninety-nine-year lease to his pupil Kananke to establish an international Buddhist center.[48] From news reports and other second-hand sources,[49] the allegation appears to be that Kananke levied thousands of rupees in admission fees on students when in fact the Japanese donors had already met all admission expenses, and that he defrauded the Customs Service for Rs. 507,213 because this amount has been obtained from Japan to pay custom duties on bathroom fixtures imported for the school when in fact Customs had agreed to exempt the items from duties.

Silogama Vimala is a pupil of the prominent scholar-monk Baddegama

46. Since Kananke and Banagala are pupils of the same teacher Hadigalle, this might indicate some "sibling rivalry."

47. *Divayina,* 17 March 1993.

48. A Sanghika gift is a gift ritually offered to the Sangha as a whole. This is considered infinitely more merit generating than gifts to individual monks. In reality a Sanghika gift becomes the private property of a specific monastery if not an individual.

49. *Ceylon Daily News,* 11 Aug. 1992; *Divayina,* 17 March 1992.

Vimalavamsa, and his work illustrates a more complex enterprise. A university graduate, he is the executive director and incumbent of the Mahinda Social Welfare Buddhist Center and chairman of the Sri Lanka NESEL Foundation.[50] The projects of this Center and Foundation are listed as (1) Sri Wimalawansa Children's Educational Institute; (2) Sponsorship Program—Low Income Group; (3) Program for distribution of free clothes; (4) Mihindu Pre-School; (5) Library; (6) Self-employment Project; (7) Diploma Course in Child Development; (8) Japanese Language course; and (8) English Language Course.[51] A unique project not mentioned in this list perhaps throws some light on the more subtle aspects of these enterprises, including their high-level political links. This is the erection and ceremonial opening of a stupa known as the Mavpiya Mahasaya (Mother-Father stupa) on 25 May 1991 by President Premadasa. The ceremony was given wide publicity by the state-controlled television and newspapers in addition to full page "advertising supplements" in the major newspapers. The page in the *Daily News* of 25 May 1991 was paid for by Messers. Premadasa Group, Jewelry and Gem Merchants, and the one in *Divayina* of the same day by nine businesses, most of them car or car parts dealers all located in Colombo. The stupa is part of a complex of buildings already completed, for which contributions in the form of various items such as the *dolosmahe pahana* (lamp of the twelve months), the pinnacle of the stupa, the relic chamber in front of the stupa, the portal to the stupa, the land on which the pavilion of urns is built, and the electric lamp inside the stupa were donated by individuals associated with various businesses, several of them members of the Mahinda Social Welfare Buddhist Association. The name of one of these businesses, "Kadavata-Mikado," suggests a Japanese connection. According to a felicitatory newspaper article by the monk Mapalagama Somissara,[52] the bell-shaped stupa is 75 feet high from its base *(valimaluva)* and 85 from the ground. The interior of the stupa has two floors. The upper floor houses the pavilion for Buddha relics. The lower floor is divided into two areas of 8,400 square feet each. One of these is a preaching hall and the other the "internment site of the parental felicitation receptacles"[53]—in simpler language, urns *(manjusa),* 13 centimeters high, weighing one gram, made of a "special metal," and gold plated. These are available for those with filial piety to deposit parental relics and are to be enshrined in the allocated space. No men-

50. I have not been able to decipher what "NESEL" stands for.
51. Advertising Supplement, *Ceylon Daily News,* 25 May 1991.
52. *Divayina,* 25 May 1991.
53. Advertising Supplement, *Ceylon Daily News,* 25 May 1991.

tion is made in the advertisements or news stories as to whether these are freely available or are to be paid for, but the Sinhala advertisement contains a photograph of the urn with the inscription, "Deposit a parental felicitation receptacle on behalf of your parents in the pavilion adjoining the Mavpiya Maha Saya, erected at the Mahinda Social Service Buddhist Center, Ranmutagala, Kadavata," which suggests a price tag. Above the picture are two verses[54] wishing the two parents the attainment of nirvana and the admonition: "Ever make offerings, and pay respects to your parents who nurtured you with incomparable parental love."[55] The cost of the stupa is fourteen million rupees, and the funds were donated by the Japanese monk Ryushu Kawasaki. To quote Silogama:

> The work of the shrine room of this center had been complete and the most venerable Ryusho Kawasaki was invited to the center for the opening ceremony of the shrine room, and on this day after the ceremony, he asked me what I intend doing next. I told him about my desire to construct a pagoda to commemorate parents. The most Venerable Kawasaki assured me that he will look after its expenditure. That is how the construction work in regard to the pagoda was started.[56]

Silogama's thoughts on the stupa expressed on the day of the ceremonial unveiling are of interest in our understanding of the sociological meanings of this project.[57] He related the idea of honoring parents to the Buddha, and considers it a Bodhisattva quality to do so. The Buddha in a previous birth rescued his mother by swimming in the sea for days with her aloft. At the end of this heroic act the mother wished him Buddhahood for being so devout towards her. In a more direct reference to the project at hand, Silogama recalls how the Buddha, after the cremation of his stepmother, carried the ashes, wrapped in a piece of cloth, in his begging bowl and enshrined them in a stupa built in her memory. The ashes, the bowl, and the stupa here become an archetypal parallel of the parental remains, the urn, and the present stupa, conferring on the project unassailable authority and legitimacy.

---

54. *samma sambudu sarana labeva / nimmavak nati guna sihihveva / Dhamma dasa akusal duru veva / amma mage nivan dakiva / / soya nivan maga dora haradeva / dayabarin sausata sanasava / kiya dipu bana sihiyata eva / piyananata mage nivan labeva.*

   May there be the Buddha's refuge / May I remember (her) endless virtue / May (her) ten demerits disappear / May my mother reach Nirvana // May the door to the path of Nirvana open / May all beings be loved and content / May I recall the *bana* (he) taught (me) / May my father reach Nirvana.

55. *Asama sama daru pemin oba hadu vadu obe demavpiyanta samara puja pavatva garu buhuman karanna.*

56. Advertising Supplement, *Ceylon Daily News,* 25 May 1991.

57. *Ceylon Daily News,* 2 May 1991.

Next, Silogama reminds us that "mother is living Buddha in our homes" and next to her is the father, and he recalls how it was his father who asked him whether he would like to get ordained as a monk. When he replied "yes," it was his mother "who shed tears of joy and happiness." He credits his parents as the two most important people who enabled his "national, social, and religious contributions as a Buddhist monk." He also attributes the speedy progress of the work first on the Center and then on the stupa to his "fervent belief, that some divine power is behind me, protecting, guiding, directing, and helping me in my endeavor," and he believes that divine power to be his father, "reborn as a deity of correct belief" *(samyak drstika deviyeku).* He pays tribute to three other fathers, "the most venerable Ryusho Kawasaki," whose role is perhaps even more important than that of the divine power, his "teacher father" *(guru piyanan vahanse)* Baddegama Vimalavamsa, advisor to the stupa committee, and President Premadasa who ceremonially declared open the stupa. He then proceeds to the "extraordinary Japanese custom" of commemorating dead parents on Mother's Day and Father's Day and sug- gests that the government declare March 1 Parents' Day, which, had it been accepted, would have added one more to the long list of Sri Lankan public holidays. The letter written by the benefactor Ryusho Kawasaki hails the project as "one of the greatest creations in the recent history of Sri Lanka."[58] What is more important from our point of view is the sense of gratitude once again expressed towards Sri Lanka for the speech made in San Francisco by the former president, J. R. Jayawardene, urging support for Japan in the darkest hour of its history. "When we look at the post-war development in Japan we always remember the former president of Sri Lanka. We Japanese can never forget the historic speech made by your president in San Fran- cisco, saying that 'hatred cannot be conquered by hatred.'" For President Premadasa, the idea of honoring parents is not new, because he had already named the home villages of his mother and father Mavgama (mother village) and Piyagama (father village) respectively. Thus there is empathy between the ideas of Silogama and the President.

There are several underlying meanings that are striking, and they center on the powerful political and economic threads that connect the key person- alities and their ideas. There is no doubt that filial piety and associated senti- ment are not only existent but felt to be important by these personalities. But that does not explain all or even most of the factors just discussed. Thus it is clear that the donor has both a personal and nationally dictated interest in playing the crucial role he did. References to President Jayawardene's

58. Supplement, *Ceylon Daily News,* 25 May 1991.

speech have been mentioned over and over again by important Japanese political and cultural figures. For President Premadasa the occasion afforded
an opportunity to relive and replay a sentiment that was personally and politically meaningful to him. Indeed, the ceremony looked much like one of his
own, and the state media coverage made it more so. Further, it echoed the
propensity for building various meaningless and monstrous structures so
characteristic of his Gam Udava celebrations.[59] Next, the contributions to
the Center and this project by various businesses cannot be isolated but must
be understood as meaningfully related to the totality consisting of the planning, financing, construction, ceremonial opening, and public legitimation
of the stupa. Thus we can think of the project as having a nucleus of sentiment surrounded by powerful political and economic forces in which the
key players make common cause.

The benefactor Ryusho Kawasaki refers to Buddhism as "the golden
thread that binds the hearts of the Japanese and the Sri Lankans" and hopes
that "the friendship between Sri Lanka and Japan will be strengthened and
be firmly bound by this pagoda."[60] Silogama emphasized, as we just noted
above, the Buddhist significance of honoring parents, that it is Bodhisattva-
like to do so. And an important aspect of the Bodhisattva is doing good to
others. At one level Sri Lanka and Japan are doing good to each other and
being grateful to each other for good actions. Here we have full equality. At
another level, equality is inherently impossible, because Japan is the giver
and Sri Lanka the recipient. This is the undeniable inequality arising from
relationship to wealth, accentuated by other disparities including the state
of industrial development and technology. The stupa project provides two
emblems of this: the "felicitation receptacle" or urn is a distinctively Japanese object, and the idea of urns containing ancestral relics subjected to
mass entombment is a characteristically Far Eastern one and is consonant
with the strong patrilineality and developed ancestral cults of these cultures.
It would seem a strange idea to most ordinary Sinhala Buddhists.

---

59. Gam Udawa means "village awakening." This is one more of the numerous manifestations of
the idea of "rural development," and it illustrates the extremes to which misunderstanding of this commendable idea can be taken. Premadasa held lavish celebrations each year when in a selected village a
specific number of houses—the number was determined by his birthday, for example 65 houses for
his sixty-fifth birthday—were given to the allottees. These "houses" were constructed in a great hurry
to meet the celebration deadlines, which places their longevity at great peril. In addition, replicas of
ancient stupas and other religious sites and of public buildings like the Colombo municipal building
were built at the site, at a colossal waste of public funds. It was widely believed that these construction
activities also involved extensive corruption in the procuring process. These constructions seem to have
been conceived within the president's illusions of grandeur that equated him with the royal builders of
the past. See Josine van der Horst, *Who is He, What is He Doing?*

60. Supplement, *Ceylon Daily News.*

The so-called attempt to introduce Mahayana and the nursery schools discussed above,[61] along with the stupa project, would represent, to some Sri Lankans, a form of imperialism, as the following illustrates. The writer is Ratna B. Ekanayaka, director of the Child Welfare Institute, and the piece is entitled, in a reference to the birth story of the Buddha as the perfectly generous Vessantara, "*The Vessantara Jatakaya* imported from Japan":[62]

> It is a surprising avalanche of money. At least in excess of two lakhs (200,000 rupees). Over forty Japanese guests. The anniversary of a children's home. In the vanguard is our Jewel, the Sangha. In between, the nuns of Japan. It is high festivity. Gifts to all the participating children to fill their hands. Though it was a children's festival, gifts to all adults to fill their hands as well. If all festivals are full of gifts like this one, there is no need for advertising.
>
> Thirty rupee (i.e., expensive) rice and curry packets alone for 1,500. The home's children just like Japanese dolls. They are covered in Japanese clothing. Their music and dancing, everything according to Japanese styles. How enchanting!
>
> Comfortable vehicles every day for the children to be brought to the Children's Home. They can go in a comfortable vehicle right from their doorstep. They return to their doorsteps in the same vehicles. Sri Kanta (the Goddess of Prosperity) has descended on that Children's Home in person. But she has come from Japan. . . .
>
> How nice if this is true of all Children's Homes in our country. Many Children's Homes go begging to feed its hungry children. But milk is overflowing for this Children's Home.
>
> We have no displeasure with people coming from Japan to make milk flow for our children. Our pleasure is dampened only when we wonder what the obverse of this money contains.

The writer goes on to express concern about children's minds being stamped with Japanese culture. Will this not create a future population that will mentally live in Japan? Will not Mahayana then get institutionalized here? Some members of the Sangha Jewel (monks), born in Theravada, are trying to fly over to Mahayana. These are the monks who are driving children over toward the Mahayana sharks. Some Theravada monks are trying to go over to Mahayana. These are the monks who bring Sri Lankan children to the brink of Mahayana. Younger monks who have fallen to the lure of Mahayana will

61. Palpola Vipassi, another monk in the Nursery School enterprise, well-funded by the Japanese, was accused, in the early 1990s of trying to establish Mahayana. The monastic hierarchy reacted swiftly to influence the government to nip the alleged attempt in the bud.

62. *Lankadipa*, 31 March 1991.

usurp the [Theravada] hierarchy [of Sri Lanka] while they are complacently stooging the politicians. They will also recruit, from the Children's Homes, pupils who will carry Mahayana forward.

This is an example of Sinhala paranoia about the vulnerability of their culture.[63] However, it does contain a kernel of truth. The critique is valid not for its cultural protectionism which, as in the past, would prove to be a failure. Its validity rather is related to the magnitude of foreign capital that is flowing in, and the possibility that much of it may be directed to activities for which no public accountability exists. In no sphere of Sri Lankan life is public accountability a priority. Yet that does not erase the reasons for concern about this particular flow of foreign capital, which some monks have manipulated with great skill.

It is relevant to note the value that the Japanese apparently continue to bestow on J. R. Jayawardene's support of Japan at the conclusion of World War II. On 1 May 1991, Jayawardene gave a talk at the Metropolitan Hotel, Tokyo on "Buddhism in Sri Lanka and Japan."[64] He mentioned how, on his way to the peace conference in San Francisco in 1951, he stopped in Japan, desirous of meeting Buddhist leaders. He met the well-known Japanese Mahayana scholar D. T. Suzuki who, when requested to explain the differences between Mahayana and Theravada, asked, why emphasize the differences, why not the similarities? Here, the president made two diplomatic acts that are also made by enterprising monks. First, he subtly reminded his hosts of the San Francisco conference, for which the Japanese remain grateful to the president and to Sri Lanka, and second, he emphasized the common bonds, rather than the differences between Sri Lanka and Japan.

Galeboda Gnanissara, popularly know as Podihamuduruvo, is one of the best known Colombo monks in social service. Among the talented, energetic, and resourceful monks that we are concerned with, Galeboda stands out as teeming with energy, ideas, and organizational skills. He took charge of the monastery, the Gangarmaya, located beside the beautiful and stinking Beira Lake, while he was young, probably in his twenties, apparently because of the illness of his teacher. In 1974, when I first met him casually long before I started fieldwork on the present project, he was overseeing the first of his many building projects, a sacred ordination space in the water *(udakuk-*

---

63. Instances of this paranoia are extensive and varied. Its agents are, for example, the CIA, America in general, India, the Tamils, the Muslims, the Christians, the World Bank, and now Mahayana! This is a national-level expression of the local and domestic paranoia expressed in the suspicion of magical and other harm that can emanate any moment from kinsmen, neighbors, fellow workers, and even friends.

64. *Ceylon Daily News,* 3 May 1991.

khepa sima) in the lake opposite the monastery. Looking even younger than his relatively tender age and with a powerful and persuasive demeanor, he eagerly explained to me the project at hand. At my answer to his question about my professional identity, he responded that he had traveled all over America on a Greyhound bus. Later I heard of his many feats, which I could not verify but which are unlikely to be anything but the truth. An early one revealing his skills and potential was the building of an Alms Hall at Malvatta, the center of the Siyam hierarchy in Kandy, which he persuaded a well-known Sri Lankan Parsi businessman to finance. Tapping piety across religious boundaries is a skill at which he was later to show consummate ability. According to the story I heard, the unusual dynamism and success of the young outsider apparently alarmed the sedate hierarchy at Malvatta, which thanked him and politely intimated to him that his services were valued but no more needed.

The apparent attempt at the conquest of Kandy thus aborted, young Galaboda retreated to Colombo. As if to tell the world that, while he may have retreated, he was not incapable of bringing Kandy within his compass, he built an ornamental parapet around the Beira Lake that is a replication of the one around the Kandy Lake, and which symbolically declares Kandy's status as a celestial city. Further, he inaugurated the Navam Perahara that copies and vies with the Kandy Perahara as a glorious nightly spectacle. So he brought Kandy to Colombo.

While the major entrepreneur monks we have described above derive their capital from overseas, Galeboda is successful in both local fundraising and foreign aid. He has incessantly knocked on the doors of local businesses and has been, to all appearances, well rewarded. Similarly he has received funds from many foreign sources, one of which is a USAID grant of 24 million rupees, massive by Sri Lanka standards, made in 1992.[65] The aggressive persuasion he has exhibited in fundraising has also successfully brought him close to politicians. In fact, he no longer seeks politicians—they seek him. In any given evening many members of the upper echelons of Colombo society may be seen visiting him for his blessings. These include politicians, businessmen, professionals, uniformed officers, and high bureaucrats, all of whom receive a *pirit nul* (charmed thread), which is tied around the wrist. His blessings and pirit nul are considered highly efficacious by the clients who are nervous competitors in politics or in the "open economy." This in

---

65. *The Island,* 24 June 1992. According to USAID, only a portion this grant was made. The remaining portion was to be paid upon specific approval conditions. Galeboda refused compliance, thus blocking USAID's path to completing the grant.

particular is a remarkable fact, considering the normal processes of religiosity in which clients rush to ascetic monks, not worldly ones, to profiteer from the power and charisma of the ascetic exemplar. One source of Galeboda's power seems to be that of the reliquary that he holds up so that the client's forehead touches it in worship, which presumably conveys to the client a charge of magical power. The other source of his popularity is apparently the perception of him as a repository of a certain amoral power efficacious for worldly success. There is a mythology around him, sometimes enhanced by a ceremonially enacted Sai Baba style regal demeanor, that credits him with magical success in dealing with brute power. Thus he is supposed to have once slapped a police officer of some rank. He is said to have approached an unruly elephant fearlessly and calmed the elephant, although in another version (or another occasion) the elephant was less cooperative and he had a near miss. He is also once said to have made a police officer, under threat, release some illegal loggers, allegedly his men who the officer had the temerity to arrest. Again in Matara he confronted and vanquished the thug of the local market, and apparently subjected to arson some dwellings of the poor that were in the way of his social service there. (The victims went to court, and Galeboda was found guilty and asked to pay compensation; the matter was also taken up in Parliament.)[66] The shift from the ascetic exemplar to a figure of amoral mystical power like Galeboda is an urban middle class version of the ritual tapping of the forces of black magic in the folk religion, and, especially when located in a monk respected by the middle and upper classes, it raises disturbing questions about the society in which

---

66. Mangala Samaraweera, Minister and member of the Cabinet, stated in Parliament that once Galeboda drove in a Mercedes to the Market at Nupe, Matara, displayed a gun and damaged a building (apparently in an effort to scare away the tenants so that he could gain mercantile occupancy). He described Galeboda as a monk "who says he is the head of the Gangarama at Hunupitiya which is a half religious and half business establishment." Samaraweera also stated that he could not believe that such a monk can act in kindness and compassion towards the people. He asserted that it is well known that the monk tied (protective) pirit thread on the wrists of the ruling military and political leaders in the age when six hundred true sons of the Buddha (monks) were killed in cold blood and burnt by the roadside. The minister tabled two police reports recording Galeboda's setting fire to the houses of two poor women. On 1995.08.01, the plaintiff of one of these incidents of arson, P. L. Maryhamy, came to a settlement when Galeboda Gnanissara paid her a settlement fee of Rs. 10,000. The minister further stated that in 1988 Galeboda illegally occupied the old Dutch market at Nupe, Matara, which is an archeological site and state property, and he did so by using the thuggery and influence of the then government. The opposition of the local people to these activities is muted because of threats. Galeboda has also acquired land around the Beira Lake, by the use of political thuggery, and is using the land for commercial purposes. Hansard, 22 September 1995, cols. 507–12. *Yuktiya* of 5 November 1995 reported this with the headline "*Gangaramaye Podihamudurvo mara karma dekakata rupiyal 20,000 vandi gevati*" (Podihamuduruvo of Gangaramaya pays Rs. 20,000 for two acts of thuggery).

these middle and upper class personalities occupy politically central and influential positions.

Galeboda's obvious proximity to high places was one nonmystical source of his influence over the taxpaying rich, whose tax brackets he reputedly had the power to lower. His rise in the post-1977 era was meteoric even by his dynamic standards, and one reason for this was his ready access to the then president, J. R. Jayawardene. At the signing of the Accord with India in 1987, Galeboda crossed over to the nationalist protest against it and lost his favor with the president. However, with the accession of R. Premadasa as the next president, Galeboda was in charge again. Premadasa, whose workaholism, restlessness, and brute power resembled Galeboda's own, befriended and supported him until the former's assassination in 1993. It is in this context of proximity to power that we can understand how Galeboda's copious mail, soliciting support and spreading his propaganda, used government envelopes with the logo "On Government Service" and was stamped with the seal of the Government Agent, Colombo, free of postage. With the assassination of Premadasa in 1993 and the electoral defeat of Premadasa's party in 1994, Galeboda lost proximity to high places, but it appears that he has the adaptability to regain it, due in particular to the pervasive belief among Sri Lankans of all strata in magical power, and the psychological needs of political, business and bureaucratic competitors.[67]

Galeboda has rationalized or modernized the traditional dealings that a clientele has with a monastery, giving the changes a distinctively upper class touch. He apparently keeps copious details of the life histories of his clients, such as birthdays and death anniversaries of kinsmen, on which people usually make donations. Galeboda's office sends out reminders to the clients about the upcoming date. The clients need not go through the elaborate process of inviting monks to an almsgiving, bringing them ceremonially and transporting them back, and cooking an elaborate meal. Instead, they can simply send a check and only need to be present at the refectory on the

67. On the same day that minister Mangala Samaraweera made his statement about Galeboda in parliament, another M.P., Mervyn Silva, made a defense of the monk, saying that the minister's speech, he thought, was written for him by Victor Ivan (editor of *Ravaya,* the Sinhala weekly), and the minister spoke on the instructions of (Christian) missionaries to bring discredit to the people of Ruhuna (*Hansard,* 22 September 1995, cols. 555–56). Bengamuve Nalaka also wrote in defense of Galeboda without mentioning him by name. Attacking the minister in a threatening tone (again without mentioning him by name) Bengamuve stated that "character assassination" of the type the minister had done "will not be tolerated." The minister's critique of Galeboda belonged in the category of "serious sin" *(barapatala papa karma).* See *Divayina,* 16 June 1996. Bengamuve and his colleagues kept their word: it is on this minister that they proclaimed the *patta nikujjana kamma,* the act of "turning over the bowl" (see note 81 below).

appointed day at lunch time. The food is prepared at the monastery's kitchen and the clients need only to formally and ritually serve it. Of the ritual services he performs to the city, the Navam Perahara is the most conspicuous, but there is the perhaps more important "pirit truck," an elaborately decorated truck that parades the streets, chanting pirit and sprinkling the purifying and magically powerful pirit water, thereby conveying to the city dwellers and the world his generosity and thoughtfulness.

The center of Galeboda's social service is a school of vocational training, the Jinaratana Vocational Training Institute, which teaches a range of subjects from appliance repair to secretarial skills. Students, some of whom come from long distances, are enrolled in a complex system of attendance which I and my research assistant found incomprehensible independently of each other. Railway tickets and food are provided either free or at discount prices, the former suggestive of Government complicity. In 1991, the Seylan Bank, "in its pursuit of helping the youth of this country secure employment," joined hands with the Institute by making a donation.[68] The sum of 24 million rupees awarded by USAID is reportedly to establish a similar institute in the south in the areas where violence was concentrated during the 1980s revolt of the Jatika Vimukti Peramuna (JVP).[69] Emphasis is on preventing the youth from returning to violence, and the project hopes to train the youth for employment indigenous to the area so that costs are minimized and exodus to the already overcrowded cities discouraged, both of which if true are commendable. During training all trainees are allegedly paid an incentive allowance.

The overall impression is a man of enormous will and energy, capable of great feats of public relations and fundraising, restless and dominant, but all this energy seems utterly misdirected, and for all the effort of teaching technical subjects to wayward youth, allegedly saving them from terrorism and ultra-left politics, the results seem meager, a fate that this project shares with Sarvodaya.[70] Galeboda's effort deserves appreciation if the results are as demonstrable as the hectic activity, the unbelievable energy and drive, the organizational frenzy, and the colossal sum of money wasted annually in producing the garish and meaningless spectacle of the Navam Perahara.

Baddegama Samita, incumbent of Dutugamunu Vihara, Baddegama, ac-

68. *Island,* 27 June 1991.

69. *Island,* 6 June 1992.

70. Sarvodaya is a well-funded NGO headed by A. T. Ariyaratne, who has received numerous international awards for his work. For accounts see Richard Gombrich and Gananath Obeyesekere, *Buddhism Transformed,* 243–52; Detlef Kantowsky, *Sarvodaya: The Other Development* (Delhi: Vikas, 1980).

tive in politics, is a member of the LSSP and was elected member of the Southern Province provincial council in 1992. An interview published in the *Lankadipa* of 26 November 1992 gives us a glimpse of his views. The interview, entitled "It is useless to deliver sermons to the hungry" *(Badaginne sitina janatavata bana desa palak naha)*, reflects his Marxist position. He starts by quoting the scriptures, that once the Buddha insisted that a poor and hungry man be given food before he preached to the man. This, says Baddegama, should not be treated as yet another Buddhist story. This is a serious statement, a warning and good advice. Problems of unemployment and poverty lead not only to starvation but also to unhappiness and family problems. The people are in a state of oppression *(asahanaya)*. Before delivering sermons, we must dispel the conditions that oppress the people. What happens today is the opposite: while people are dying of hunger, the leaders and the media are preaching nonstop. When monks point this out to the politicians, they (the monks) are told that it is improper for them to meddle in politics. Echoing Rahula's idea that a monk's vocation is social service, a monk, Baddegama maintains, renounces the world for the liberation of all people.

All people have basic needs, says Baddegama, and the earth has enough to supply these needs. But in Sri Lanka and elsewhere, these resources are enjoyed only by a powerful minority. To deny food to a child, an old person, or an expectant mother is a crime even worse than an *anantarya karma,* a cardinal sin. And feeding the people is not a difficult task like solving the ethnic problem or creating something new. As such, freedom from hunger is the society's responsibility.

In the West, continues Baddegama, religion is a personal matter. In our society it is inextricably bound with daily life. Politicians, having understood this, use religion to achieve and hold on to power. Even religious leaders use religion for private gain. (This echoes the idea often expressed by educated monks that politicians use monks as stage props to dramatize their own importance and that establishment monastic leaders go along with this, because they benefit by doing so, although this amounts to betraying their rank and file.)

Economic systems based on profiteering were condemned not only by the Buddha, but also by Christ, says Baddegama. This is a critique of the "open economy" and the United National Party (UNP) government, and it echoes the proto-socialist Proudhonist idea that "property is theft," which equates business enterprise with profiteering, a common view among a wide spectrum of Sri Lankans who are broadly speaking opponents of the UNP government and its basis in the market economy. The reference to Christ reflects the new radical monk's pluralistic acceptance of the other religions as part of Sri Lankan religious life.[71] Christian clergy have also condemned the open economy, adding another dimension to the new harmony if not alliance between Buddhism and Christianity, a harmony enabled by, among other factors, the ethnic crisis, which has placed ethnicity above religion.

Profiteering is not confined to the laity. In Baddegama's view, religious leaders are involved in it too. The reference here, apparently broad, is in fact to the landowning hierarchy and some of the modern monks who have ventured into money making in diverse ways. These sentiments parallel those expressed by younger monks who condemn empty titles and super-elitism in the monkhood and advocate distributive justice in the monastery.

In a refreshing view to come from a monk, Baddegama says the war in the north cannot be solved by bodhipujas, *peraharas* (processions), and preaching. This view has clear Marxist resonances, pointing to the real problem as opposed to the superstructures and considering religious ritualism the opium of the people. The statement is also a critique of the traditional monks' support for the government's attempt to deal with the youth uprising by ritual means. Broadly, it is a condemnation of traditional priestly ritualism in the service of a ruling class that oppresses the people, a Marxist critique of religious hierarchies propping up despotic regimes. Baddegama is, however, keenly aware that in the present day setup in Sri Lanka, monastic supporters of politicians often end up being disappointed. Such monks, according to Baddegama, are like those who look after other people's cows—they get only the cow dung. This is a challenge, a ridicule, and taunt at the hierarchy and a reminder that they will only be left with "cow dung."

Baddegama believes that there are real problems in the areas of crime, corruption, and extortion. People are ripped off every day by rapacious political and economic powers, big and small. The remedy for this according to some political and religious leaders is putting up Buddha statues and stupas at every street corner and preaching from the stage. Baddegama mentions Christian leadership as well, but his real targets are the Buddhist monastic hierarchy and other monks who stooge for the government, and the political leadership who are partners in ritualism—bodhipujas, pirit ceremonies, opening ceremonies of religious buildings, and ceremonial deference publicly paid to hierarchical monks for political gain, with no genuine

---

71. Some monks, especially of the Vidyodaya and Marxist traditions, had always been tolerant of other religions and cultures. With the momentum achieved in the nationalist movement culminating in the electoral victory of the nationalist forces in 1956, these became a dwindling minority. Hendiyagala talks admiringly of the Hindu culture he observed first hand in the northern city of Jaffna and recommends that Buddhists celebrate the religious holidays and festivities of other religions of the country. This is striking because it is at variance with the view, now axiomatic among monks and deriving from Dharmapala via Vidyalankara, that Sri Lanka is a Sinhala Buddhist country.

respect towards them. Specifically, the reference is to the endless propensity the former president Premadasa had for building replicas of religious monuments in his Gam Udava sites, and for hopping from temple to church to mosque in a shallow ecumenism.

Baddegama's critique is not without political motive. He is a politician elected to office and will naturally make public criticism of his political opponents. Yet his arguments remain valid.

Bengamuve Nalaka is not in active politics nor is he a major speaker on the political stage. But he is a frequent contributor to the popular press. His views are critical of politics and illustrative of the new monkhood that refuses to remain in the cloister. The following views on education are an index to his political thinking. His main critique is the absence of a "national face" in education, and his contempt for the existing system is expressed in the title of one of his newspaper articles, "The exorcistic dance of education, to the foreign beat" *(Anunge padayata natana adhyapana tovilaya).*[72]

Bengamuve sees in the educational policies today the reason for the country's ills. Higher education in Sri Lanka is based on western models. The graduates of the universities analyze society within western conceptual frameworks, with rare exceptions.[73] This system has not been able to produce the kind of leader suited to the country. The ancient system of education that built the nation has been discarded. We need today a new one based on that ancient system. The entire focus of higher education is development, because of the grip those who control higher education have on power.

Politicians are only interested in achieving and staying in power. They have no interest in building the country or improving the living standards of the people. Universities are controlled by the politicians and therefore cannot be expected to work for the benefit of the people. The Colombo University and the University Grants Commission are both located in the upper-class residential subdivision of Colombo 7, and this environment has swallowed these institutions. They are permeated by the Colombo 7 mentality.[74]

---

72. *Divayina,* 31 Dec. 1992.

73. The writer gives as an example F. R. Jayasuriya, the university lecturer in Economics who fasted against the agreement between Prime Minister S. W. R. D. Bandaranaike and the Federalist Tamil leader S. J. V. Chelvanayagam. This agreement, if consummated and carried out, would have spared the island the present crisis which has taken a hundred thousand lives and displaced a million people.

74. How wrong Bengamuve is cannot be overstated, which includes even his geography when he locates the university in Colombo 7. Bengamuve is flogging a dead horse. What he says about the university is dated by nearly forty years. After the changes introduced by the nationalist policies inaugurated in 1956, the university has steadily lost, since about the late 1960s, its elite status. It is now about 99 percent populated by students from rural, nonaffluent families. The children of the kind of families

About 1985, in response to a solicitation of opinion on how to reform the pattern of higher education, Bengamuve proposed that all entering students be given a six month course on the tanks and on agriculture in the North, Northeast and North Central provinces.[75] The presiding officer, Stanley Kalpage, told him it was a good suggestion, but asked whether Colombo 7 parents would send their children to a thing like that. Underlying Bengamuve's case is a theme that recurs in the thought of many Sri Lankan nationalists, the romantic idea of returning to ancient glory through the magic of the tank and its agriculture, an idea derived from the Dharmapalite theory of Sri Lankan society. This utterly unrealistic theory is also an expression of resentment towards what is perceived as westernization, and its symbol, Colombo 7.

Bengamuve argues that the history of the universities shows that they have done nothing to raise "indigenousness" *(desiyatvaya)* and "nationalness" *(jatikativaya)*. With the conversion of Vidyodaya and Vidyalankara to universities, national and indigenous thinking *(desiya, jatika cintanaya)* was at first invigorated, but soon the new universities were westernized, and even their names were changed. In his view, the powerful influence of the sons of western-enslaved minds prevents the implementation of anything that is suitable to the country. This university bashing ignores the fact that whatever cultural activity has come into being in recent times is the work of the university, in particular Peradeniya. In fact, it is the nationalist anti-intellectualism that took away academic freedom and truly patriotic and meaningful research from the universities.

Western modes are applied in a variety of ways, says Bengamuve. The education system is changed even when a new minister of the same government takes over the department of education. These changes are made not to suit the country but the needs of the multinational companies.

The task of the university teacher, continues Bengamuve, is not to satisfy politicians but to build the society by giving the nation a good understanding of its problems. University teachers should not be vendors of knowledge.

Bengamuve talks about are sent abroad. This stance illustrates the important sociological fact that the underlying anti-western sentiment whose roots go back to Dharmapala remains unappeased despite nationalist policies. The ultra-nationalist Jatika Cintanaya movement, of which Bengamuve seems to be a member or sympathizer, is another expression of this. (See note 76 below.)

75. "Tank" refers to the reservoirs that the nationalists make much of as illustrative of the glory of the ancient Sinhala civilization. They are considered unique to Sri Lanka when in fact they are part of the cultural ecology of the south and east Indian region and in all likelihood originated there. The six months' course recommended here by Bengamuve has more to do with nationalist pride and symbolic assertion of Sinhala dominance in the areas bordering the "traditional homelands" of the Tamils than agriculture. It is hard to imagine what a six months' course on the tanks and agriculture in the North, Northeast and North Central provinces for every university student would accomplish.

Here Bengamuve seems to come to his main point, to which the above is a prelude, namely the suspension from the university faculty of the leader of the Jatika Cintanaya movement, Nalin de Silva. The university has given reasons for this suspension, says Bengamuve, but the real reasons are "well known to intelligent people," i.e., his Jatika Cintanaya ideas.[76] Alluding to the suspension, Bengamuve continues: "on such occasions as this, just protests are interpreted by politicians as rebellions against the government, and they get the police to suppress them." (Bengamuve does not mention that the faculty supported Professor de Silva, despite their disagreement with his views.) When universities are in this sorry state, they cannot do anything to the nation's benefit. Bengamuve uses local clichés and says that these "educational factories" only produce a class that fulfills the needs of politicians. To understand this and act is the supreme responsibility of university teachers and students who have the national interest at heart. Bengamuve darkly hints that terrorism will return to take vengeance on the suspension of Nalin de Silva. The thoughts expressed here are angry and have an eerie resemblance to Pol Potist ideas.

In an article in *Divayina* of 18 November 1990, Bengamuve condemns the havoc played by the advent of the western powers, which led to the snatching away by the missionaries of the national system of education centered in the monastery. The western system of education produces graduates with servile attitudes. Leadership suitable to the country is not produced by this system. In ancient Sri Lanka the monk was above the politician, but close to the people. The monk was devoid of greed for personal gain. That monastic leadership was able to prevent injurious political activity. Now the picture has changed. Politicians only give mock attention to the monks, so that they achieve their goals. Thus, Bengamuve's main complaint is that monks are not given the recognition they deserve, and the reason for that is the laity's western education. The implication of this position is that the society should remain where it was in precolonial times. Rahula in *The Heritage* argued that monks must change with society. Bengamuve is saying the opposite, that the society must turn back its clock and return to where the monks are, namely, the medieval era. But through different means Bengamuve and Rahula are seeking the same thing, recognition for themselves.[77]

According to Bengamuve, Tamil, Muslim, and western forces united with

76. Jatika Cintanaya, or "national thought," is an isolationist movement that advocates indigenousness in lifestyle and thought. It is led by Gunadasa Amarasekera, a dentist and novelist, and Nalin de Silva, a mathematician.

77. In *Divayina* of 11 May 1991, Bengamuve again criticizes the politicians for going to the four *agatis* ("hellward") by will, jealousy, fear, and ignorance, claiming that since this is a Buddhist country, its politics should be measured by Buddhist standards.

organizations of other religions (an euphemism for Christianity) to harass
the innocent little Sinhala nation.[78] He is convinced that there is a conspiracy
to kill the Sinhala nation by resort to two methods. First is the continued
use of the English language in government. According to him English is unnecessary to gain access to modern knowledge, and those who say so are
wrong. They are the same people who say that the Sinhala Only act of Prime
Minister S. W. R. D. Bandaranaike was an injustice to the Tamils.

In Bengamuve's view, the second subtle strategy to kill the Sinhala nation
is the government policy of not teaching Sinhala history. It was a Muslim
minister of education who, according to Bengamuve, stopped teaching Sinhala history in the schools. Because of this Sinhala people under forty have
no love for the nation. That is why this age group is attracted to political
parties without love of country and nation. Even if the children of the nation
die in the thousands, such people feel no pain. The politicians have successfully put the Sinhala nation to sleep. Such people will raise their hands to
even dividing the country. This strategy of putting people to sleep is so successful that even monks have begun to think in terms of political party affiliation. To them their political leader is more important than their Teacher
(the Buddha). Thus the monks who in the past advised the king has now
become a tool of the politicians. The guardian deities of the nation have
become guards of politicians. The politicians have joined hands with the class
of the "certified educated" and are using the deceitful political system called
democracy to put the nation to sleep.

These views hardly need comment. They not only express Sinhala Buddhist extremism but also surprising ignorance. Of all the Sinhala Buddhist
extremist monks, Bengamuve is arguably the most xenophobic. He expresses the beleaguered mentality of the xenophobe with extraordinary resentment. His statement that people who have no love of nation do not feel
pain when thousands of children are killed is both ironic and hypocritical,
because the prime reason why thousands of children are killed is the kind of
extremism he exudes; and because he and other extremist and militant
monks bless the war and send the "children of the nation" to their deaths
under the false shield of magical rites and warmongering songs.

Madoluvave Sobhita is the incumbent of the Naga Vihara, Kotte, and a
popular preacher. He is one of the best known critics of the "open economy."
Madoluvave's picture appeared on the cover of the S. J. Tambiah's *Buddhism
Betrayed?*—which for that reason became the focus of a stormy controversy
leading to the banning of the book in 1996. This bears testimony to the

---

78. Bengamuve Nalaka, "Jatiya nidikarava rata vanasana despalakayo," *Divayina,* 31 July 1996.

political stature of this charismatic monk, who in 1987 was in the forefront of the protest against the Peace Accord that brought the Indian army to the north and northeast of Sri Lanka. Madoluvave is a graduate of Vidyodaya, where he read history. He has qualifications in oriental learning as well and is a faculty member of a pirivena near Colombo. He was a leading member of the Mavbima Surakime Vyaparaya (MSV), the Movement to Protect the Motherland, which arose in response to the Accord and the occupation by the Indian army. He is a critic not only of the market economy ("open economy") policies of the government but also of the traditional monastic hierarchy. He attributes the moral decline of the present era to the excesses of the market economy, and he advocates a return to the "socialist" policies of the previous government.

Madoluvave is well aware of the basic moral problem of Sri Lankan society, the gap between the ritual expression given to moral principles and their abandonment in behavior. There is no country in the world where there is so much bana preaching, says Madoluvave, but there is no attempt to relate it to life.[79] This is reciting your prescription instead of swallowing the medicine. "Today there are many people who recite the *Karaniya metta sutra* before going to sleep. But *Karaniya metta* means 'practice kindness.' There is no use in going to sleep after chanting the *Karaniya metta sutra*. What the sutra contains is a job of work for the wakeful. It is not a sleeping matter. What it teaches are virtues."[80]

Madoluvave refers here to two of the best known Buddhist sermons (sutras), the *Mangala* and the *Karaniya metta*. The choice of the *Mangala sutra* is particularly appropriate, because in that sutra the Buddha is also making the distinction between ritualism and ethical behavior. The sutra is a simple statement that says auspiciousness *(mangala)* is brought about not by ritual or worship but by ethical conduct and strength of character, a position that is in keeping with the Buddhist statement that it is by action and not by birth that one becomes a brahmin. Madoluvave is ridiculing the practice so common among the laity today of getting monks to chant the sutra a hundred thousand times, in the hope of magically capturing its auspiciousness. Similarly, he is ridiculing the idea of people reciting the *Karaniya metta sutra* and going to sleep, which amounts to using the sounds of the sutra, like an amulet of words, for their personal protection, which has little to do with kind-

79. There is some irony here because Madoluvave is in agreement with Tambiah's *Buddhism Betrayed?* But his picture on the cover of this book led to a protest by Sinhala Buddhist extremists who thought they were supporting Madoluvave.

80. *Lankadipa,* 30 June 1991.

ness to others. In this sarcasm and "getting down to basics," Madoluvave reminds us of the Rahula of *Satyodaya,* who also subjects ritualism to candid and scornful criticism.

Citing the custom of "turning over the bowl,"[81] Madoluvave says even kings were not spared of this sanction by the ancient monks. "But today's fate is such that when five monks turn over the bowl, fifteen turn it up." Madoluvave continues: "Today we live in an intelligent society. People used to say 'Yes, Venerable Sir,' to anything the monk said. Now we must argue out issues, logically. Monks today should be able to address an educated audience. They should be well read, learned and knowledgeable about the dhamma. They should lead methodical lives. Young monks should work hard to qualify themselves."[82]

Madoluvave directly relates the social problem of prostitution to tourism, the five star hotels, and the "hotel culture," which are metonymic of the open economy. He brings in here the proposal to build a tourist hotel in Kandalama, near the Dambulla temple, which brought about a national controversy (discussed below). He mentions that the reason for the protest over Kandalama is the fear that what happened to the coastal towns like Negambo and Hikkaduva will happen to Kandalama, presumably the rise of prostitution, both male and female. It is for this same reason that the Catholic priests and fishermen of the area objected to the Kiranavala hotel complex. "Is it not clear from this that sexual misbehavior is on its way to becoming an aspect of our culture?" questions Madoluvave, relating sexual misconduct directly to tourism, a part of the open economy, as if none existed before, especially considering the rampancy of homosexual abuse of the young in the monasteries.[83] "Values and morality have been turned to ashes in the face of the money of the wealth hunting veddahs *[dhana vaddo].*"

Madoluvave's association of the open economy with moral decline is typical of the critique of the government and its economic policies. The specific form of Madoluvave's critique is ingenious, because it identifies the open economy as the violator of the five precepts, the basis of lay morality: the first precept is violated when murders are committed to gain wealth; the

---

81. That is, refusal to accept alms, which is the strongest sanction that monks can make against a lay donor in general, but in fact against the political authority.

82. *Lankadipa,* 30 June 1991.

83. The homosexuality of the monasteries is generally taken for granted, with no notice of it being taken by either the monks or the laity. During field work I came across two painful letters addressed by a young monk to a high official in the Ministry of Buddhist Affairs, asking the official to rescue him from homosexual abuse. This official himself was later accused of sexually abusing his underaged live-in female servant.

second is violated when public money is stolen through corruption; the third when children are prostituted, and so on.

Continuing his discussion of the fate of the precepts, Madoluvave says there was never an age as the present when lying was so common. Radio and television have destroyed the people's capacity to believe. To hear any news of Sri Lanka one has to tune into a foreign broadcast, like the BBC. Next, he refers to a monk who had written to a newspaper a letter highly critical of Bhikkhu Walpola Rahula, but it turned out that that was an impersonation: the person who supposedly wrote the letter never did so. Next, focusing on the violation of the fifth precept, Madoluvave says, incorrectly, that Sri Lankans were known as a nation that despised alcohol. Governor Gregory admitted that establishing taverns during his government brought destruction to this Buddhist country. The heroes of the independence movement emerged from the temperance movement. He decries the relaxation of rules about the production, sale, transport, and consumption of alcohol, objecting particularly to persuasive and appealing liquor advertisements in the media and on posters. This links intoxicants to Madoluvave's favorite villain, the open economy.[84] What is the state of liquor consumption? queries Madoluvave. In 1985, 7,500,000 bottles of liquor were consumed. This is in addition to the village brews like *sini karinnan, ala hodi, hin kendiriya* and *balu kendiriya*.[85] People drink disgusting things like vine spirit, surgical spirit, urea, and substances used in dressing wounds. There is now an arrack substitute called *naki ukkum*, "the milk of the old farts." Then he refers to 50,000 young cocaine addicts. Profiteering in cocaine is identified with the open economy. Punishments are meted out not to the wholesale importers (who presumably are part of the open economy), but those who are caught with a pinch.

Summing up, he says, we live in an age where the *panca sila,* the morality of the five precepts, the basis of lay morality, is cruelly destroyed. The culprit: the open economy. Thus, there is an underlying critique, that of the government. While the validity of the moral critique is beyond doubt, it is equally clear that Madoluvave's is a partisan political critique of the government. An important part of Madoluvave's popular appeal is his moral critique. This appeal in fact *reflects* the moral decline, and is even a part of it. It feeds the fetishization of Buddhism, first by allowing a wrongdoer for the

---

84. Madoluvave refers elsewhere to the prolific production of illicit brews. If this is so even under liberal laws, temperance would boost manifold this dynamic cottage industry.

85. All these are funny folk names for illicit brews, much like "moonshine." These literally mean "sugar biscuit," "potato curry," "mild moan," and "dog moan," respectively.

moment to imagine that he is innocent, and to think of moral wrong either as an abstraction or as something that others do and he does not, and second by magically absolving himself through participating in and absorbing the sound of morality rendered by a charismatic figure.

In this, Madoluvave lends the fetishization of Buddhism the authority of his charismatic personality and thereby, unwittingly and ironically, becomes part of the moral problem. He becomes exactly the politician he criticizes, namely a preacher who does not do anything more effective than preaching. He fails to make the moral and intellectual breakthrough to ensure his passage from preacher to effective activist, for which we have excellent precedent in his Vidyodaya forbears Kalukondayave, Hinatiyana, and Hendiyagala. This is a pity because Madoluvave is a monk of formidable talent, sincerity, and persuasive manner.

Muruttettuve Anada is the President of the Private Hospital Nurses Union and the Public Services United Nurses Union, which covers the entire nursing profession. Like a Ndembu curer who becomes one by falling sick,[86] it is while recovering from illness in hospital that the psychological foundations were laid for Muruttettuve's future trade unionism. He noticed first hand some of the problems nurses faced and realized that the only true solution was unionization. Since then he has led the union and achieved successes. Recently he advocated the appointment of a task force to monitor the activities of private hospitals.[87] "Now a days, private hospitals," he wrote, "are opened like grocery stores." There is no proper regulation of buildings, sites, staffing, cleanliness, or facilities. Some of these hospitals function without resident medical officers, without proper operating rooms, and even proper facilities to sterilize syringes. Thus Muruttettuve is as concerned with patients as with the welfare of the members of the Nurses Union.

Muruttettuve was at the center of a protest in 1988 that ended in tragedy. The government had banned a May Day Parade under Emergency Regulations, but Muruttettuve allowed a meeting to be held at his monastery precincts. The police attacked the meeting, sacrilegiously killing a young student in the temple grounds.

Unupolagama Vajirasiri was educated in the USSR and is now the director of the Sri Vajira Children's Home at Kotte, a home for children orphaned by the war and terrorism. He was impressed by the way the children were cared for in the USSR and resolved to help needy children in Sri Lanka. During

86. Victor Turner, *The Drums of Affliction* (Oxford: Clarendon Press, 1968).
87. *Observer*, 10 January 1993.

the 1983 ethnic violence, he started the home with 101 destitute children, ranging from a few months to 18 years old. From the chaotic start of having to feed, clothe, and house 101 children suddenly, the home has now evolved into an orderly establishment. There are four laymen to work in the kitchen and three in a classroom within the monastery premises. The home has its own baking and carpentry shop. A visiting nurse tends to the sick children. At the start Unupolagama had no support and sold the 96-perch (0.6 acre) block of land that he inherited from his family to pay the bills. The monk, aware of his responsibility, personally supervises the meals, the laundry, the personal cleanliness of the children, and other routine matters relating to the children. The home is deliberately modeled to resemble a real home rather than an institution whose too stern discipline could emotionally damage the children. The first day of the home, when he arrived from Moravara with the 101 children at night, he rose at 3:30 A.M. and cooked the large breakfast necessary. "I live in a children's world, I talk to them a lot. We sing *kavi* (verses) together in the evening. . . . I even play with them sometimes," says the monk, who then asks rhetorically, "Would this thing have worked out if I sat pompously in my *avasa* (monastery) with a *padikkama* (spittoon) chewing betel? . . . I try to spend as much time as possible with the children."[88]

Unupolagama's lay family name "Dissanayake" is given to those children whose parents are unknown, a dozen of them. Although originally Sinhala only, the children are now an ethnic and religious mix, and the school captain is a Tamil boy. The monk is involved full time with the home and has no time for the normal functions expected of a monk. The monastery has actually become a children's home. According to the newspaper report cited here, the monk demolished the image house to make room for the residents. The monk is quoted as saying, "We have enough viharas in this country. I don't have enough space for the children," a statement that elevates social service over religious duties. The only disconcerting aspect is the general contradiction that while the children are taught the Dhammapada—we are told that the monk teaches the verse "Hatred is not ceased by hatred"—there seems to be an undercurrent of Sinhala Buddhism in the venture. The monk wants to inculcate love *(maitri)* in the children "in a country where the virtues of nonviolence are often quoted but seldom followed." Nevertheless, some children want to join the army "to be of service to the country." But some also want to renounce the world. "Taking care of children is a huge

---

88. *The Times,* 5 May 1991. The reference to the spittoon is a conscious evocation of *The Heritage*'s critique of monks as idle.

responsibility. It can't be taken lightly. There has to be total commitment and a lot of love. We have to be just like their parents." This is a commitment more akin to Christian activities than the more traditionally Buddhist ones. Taking care of children indeed is a very unusual phenomenon for a Buddhist monk. It amounts to return to household-like life, as the monk's statements make obvious.

Kiranthidiye Pannasekhara's work is devoted to environmentalism. One of his projects attracted international attention, including a documentary aired by public television in the U.S., and his work is featured in a book on the environment.[89] This was an attempt to stop "slash and burn" cultivation by landless peasants in the Sinharaja forest, virgin jungle in south central Sri Lanka. The villagers burnt the mountain slopes for one season of cultivation and, abandoning it, moved over to a nearby area to do the same. It both destroyed the jungle and contributed to erosion. The monk understood that the only way to stop this was to remedy its cause, namely, the landlessness of the villagers. Using his status as a monk to invade the well-fortified offices of senior bureaucrats, he succeeded in getting the government to alienate land for cultivation of permanent crops and for building a homestead for each of the landless families. In addition he started a reforestation program for the burnt up areas, which included the distribution of scientific information. He involved school children in the program, so that an environmental awareness is instilled in their impressionable youth. Paralleling Unupola-gama of the orphanage project, this monk also relegates religious duties to a secondary place. A bodhi tree was planted, but only after the practical program of planting secular trees on the eroding mountain slopes was completed. A traditional monk would have given the sacred tree precedence. Further, he also remarks that religious duties, which are important, can wait until the mundane problems are attended to, echoing the priority given by the Dharmapalite hero-giants to economic problems.

Elle Gunavamsa combines militancy and music. To be more precise, he is a songwriter. He was widely held to be a strong supporter of the then existing Premadasa government, having first supported and later became disillusioned with the Jayawardena government. In this, and in a certain militancy of personality, he resembles Galeboda discussed above. His words and tone, though not the volume, are as militant as those of Galeboda. The *Observer* of September 1991 reported that his song "The Greatest Wealth" won the first prize at the Commonwealth Song Competition of 1991 held in En-

89. Lloyd Timberlake, *Only One Earth* (New York: Sterling, 1987), chap. 3, pp. 41–60.

gland. Alexandra Jones, the Deputy Director of the Commonwealth, was quoted as saying that 33 entries from 17 countries competed for the prize.

An interesting proposal made by Elle Gunavamsa, and also echoed by several other new monks, is that monks be made the legal authorities for registering marriages. His argument, expressed at a meeting to open a Japanese-funded nursery school in Oruwela,[90] is that the Sinhala Buddhists are keen to receive the blessings of the Sangha at every occasion from birth to death but forget the monk during the second most important life event, the marriage ceremony. This is an incorrect statement; monks do not participate in all lay rites of passage. Clearly, this is an attempt to imitate Christian clergy and to socially and symbolically make the monastery a place where people get married, and thereby make a monk's life more secular and more "social." This idea of the monk as a fit person to officiate at marriages is now becoming accepted by some educated Buddhists. During fieldwork in 1997 I encountered two instances where monks officiated in marriage, one in a five star hotel. The newspapers carried a photograph of a monk ritually pouring water on the joined hands of a Singapore couple in a ceremony held in Sri Lanka. Having monks participate in the marriage ceremony is a logical extension of *The Heritage*'s "social service" but perhaps hardly one anticipated by its author or his predecessor Dharmapala.

The idea of marriage licenses to be issued by monks is one example of the influence of monks based in the West, who experience cultural pressure from the society in which they live to model the monastery after the church. Some monks living in the West have been authorized marriage registrars for some time, just as they have also been licensed drivers of motor vehicles, and it is possible that, although the conditions were ripe in Sri Lanka for monks to make this demand, the immediate inspiration for the idea came from their western contacts. This innovation is quite radical because, as noted elsewhere, in traditional Sinhala Buddhist thought, monk and marriage were mutually repellent, and there is tension in the conception of the monk between auspiciousness and its opposite. While according to "true" Buddhism, the monk is auspicious (as is made quite explicit in the *Mangala sutra*), in actual cultural practice the overwhelming force of the broader South Asian idea of the inauspiciousness of the world renouncer has had an effect on the popular conception of the monk. It is entirely in keeping with the Dharmapalite conception of the monk that he is auspicious (although Dharmapala does not seem to have entertained these popular categories). Thus it is no surprise that monks are eager to overcome this negative image

90. *Lankadipa*, 11 Jan. 1993.

as much as the Buddhist modernist laity are keen to "invent tradition" and have monks officiate at their marriages.[91] Young rural couples who, with education, imbibe the nationalism and "Protestant Buddhism" of the city middle classes sometimes ask monks to attend and bless their marriages.

What this demand forebodes, like many other recent changes, is the slow and imperceptible secularization of the Sangha, a desire to be more "social," which indeed is an important psychological meaning of "social service" to the monks—they are often more interested in "social" than "service." The participation in the marriage ceremony is particularly interesting for its negation of the traditional mutual repellence between monk and marriage. It is also an attempt to redefine monkhood as "pro-life" in the sense of pro-mundane as opposed to the traditional image of him as a life-negating re-nouncer, an ill omen to associate in any auspicious (i.e., "pro-life") endeavor, or to encounter as the first thing in the morning, the beginning of a day of raw mundaneity.

Elle Gunavamsa's songs are in keeping with his general posture. They are militant and warlike. In fact, according to some reports, his are among the songs played by the army to boost soldier morale in battle. A well-known cassette of songs is titled *Bala Senagata Samara gi* (Memory Songs for the Soldiers). These songs are given in the appendix to this chapter.

First of all, we should know that these songs were published by the Sri Lanka Broadcasting Corporation, i.e., by the state, which provides a particularly clear perspective of the extent to which monks can, if they see eye to eye with the state, get things done. This also illustrates, I think, how monks can use state resources, as when Galeboda gets the state to pay the postage for his solicitary mail. It is said that Elle Gunavamsa was greatly favored by the Premadasa government. Similarly, the less political and the more economic monks, best illustrated but not exclusively by the nursery school directorate, are clearly in a symbiotic relation with the government.

Even in translation, which waters down the effect of these songs, the sentiments expressed are strongly exclusivist and xenophobic. The militancy Elle Gunavamsa exudes in conversation is powerfully condensed in them. The landscape is familiar: religion, country, and race; the sword that should not be sheathed unless it is smeared with blood; the recurring evocation of Dutugamunu, his brave mother, and his superhuman ten soldiers; and an appropriately middle class concern with the purity of women, whose sole task is the production of brave sons. A proper evaluation of the xenophobic power of the songs should constitute a close analysis of the imagery and

91. For an excellent discussion of this, see Richard Gombrich and Gananath Obeyesekere, *Buddhism Transformed*, 255–73.

music, which is outside the scope of the present task. However, it is possible to make the general statement that the songs are set to stirring martial music, with a predominance of wind instruments and percussion which recalls the traditional war drums *(gaman hevisi)*. The statements that connect the dominant theme of violence with images of religion and worship—that fighting accrues enough merit to reach Nirvana, that the country, religion and race are the speaker's Triple Gems—are startling, but perhaps not any more than bodhipujas held almost daily to bless the armed forces or the Mahavamsaic conception that nonbelievers can be killed with impunity. The images of commitment, mortal combat, females joining battle, and so forth are curiously more applicable to the enemy envisaged in the songs than they are to the Sinhala army, with its reputation for corruption at the top and defection at the bottom.

For our present purposes, it is adequate to draw attention to a critique of the songs that appeared in *Ravaya* of 10 February 1991, written by the pseudonymic columnist *"Podi hamuduravo,"* which means "junior monk." It is a column that exclusively deals with monks, and the writer is purportedly a monk.

The critique opens with a reminder about monkhood: an ordained monk commits an unforgivable crime that defeats *(parajika)* his monkhood and results in expulsion from the order if he commits an act involving sex, theft, killing, or spiritual claims. The songs, argues the critic, are instigations to kill and therefore constitute a defeat of monkhood for the songwriter Elle Gunavamsa. He makes special mention of Elle Gunavamsa telling the soldier that he will reach nirvana for fighting the enemy and that the drawn sword not to be resheathed unless it is smeared with blood. Can a person wear the Buddhist robe and say things like this? asks the writer. Further, he points to the fact that the songs are sung by some of the most popular singers of the country, who thus profiteer by using hatred. The title of the column parodies that of the cassette, *"Bala senagata samara gi"* (Memory Songs for the Soldiers) by calling itself *"Bala senagata marana gi"* (Killing Songs for the Soldiers). The writer scornfully refers to the silence of the Sangha hierarchy on this while they made a big fuss about "the Mahayana terror," considering it a more fierce terror than the JVP.[92]

Rambukana Siddharta is a songwriter whose work is mild when compared to the incendiary songs of Elle Gunavamsa. Rambukana does not fix on any one subject. His themes are many and varied. He has written songs that

92. The references here are to (a) the Sangha's overreaction to the alleged attempt by Palpola Vipassi to establish Mahayana in Sri Lanka, and (b) the late-1980s terror led by the rebellious Sinhala Youth Organization, the Janata Vimukti Peramuna (JVP).

evoke religious feeling, monkhood, monk-lay relations, and peace. In some
of his songs, Rambukana is critical of society. But he is never strident. There
is something gentle about the way he approaches his subjects, even when he
is critical, an exercise in which he successfully uses folksy humor:

> Though we talk bana endlessly
> Though we hear bana endlessly
> In our behavior we are—
> Yet in the jungle, in the jungle

The Sinhala I gloss as "endlessly" is *nirantare* and jungle, *vanantare*, which
alliterate resonantly. In the next lines he says:

> Wonder whether there is something
> In us [the Sinhalas]
> That makes Bodhisattva virtues
> Not stick.

Underlying this delightful understatement is a perception of the moral crisis
in contemporary Buddhism, already stated in the previous lines. Again,
mildly satirizing the excessively formal and once-a-year generosity shown
by merit-greedy Buddhists during Vesak, Rambukana writes:

> The good deeds of all
> Are at Vesak time
> I wonder, to be seen by whom.
>
> Nourishing one's vanity
> And reaching Nirvana
> I wonder how the two
> Walk the same path.

Rambukana's target here are Buddhist profiteers who put up garish pandals
and free food stalls and inflict food on already stuffed crowds that throng to
see them at Vesak, especially in the cities. While they expect merit from
these, these activities are self-flattering exhibitions of vanity and advertisements. Hence Rambukana's playful dilemma of "wondering" how morality
and pride can walk together. Thus, in different images, sounds, and allitera-
tions, he continues the critique that the Sinhala Buddhist morality is a show
with no substance. In this Rambukana is sophisticated both sociologically
and aesthetically. He is doing social service in his own way, by drawing atten-

tion to the foible of ritualism that appears in the guise of morality. After the blood and thunder of Elle Gunavamsa, the following words belong to a different tune indeed:

> Mothers, fathers
> alms-give
> a drop of your love
> to extinguish the volcano
> of hatred.
> Let peace be king.

Public discussion of changes in the Sangha have concerned the moral state of being a monk, or "monkness" *(mahanakama, bhiksutvaya)* to which we have already referred. "Moral" here is used in the very broad sense, so that a monk would be considered moral if he follows the basic rules of demeanor and decorum. Rambukana's songs reaffirm this image.[93] Rambukana sings hauntingly about a little monk walking decorously away from the village, beyond a field where children of his age are playing. The same positive evaluation of monkhood is conveyed in images of mild but nevertheless unmistakable disapproval of a young monk, derobed, walking towards the village as a layman. In this Rambukana brings out the most serious question about modern monkhood, namely, how to be modern and a monk.

The sixth precept requires that monks do not listen to songs or musical instruments, and not witness dance and comic shows, much less be actively engaged in the production of any of these. While the observance of the precepts has been imperfect in general, one of the precepts that actually has been rather consistently observed in Sri Lankan monasticism is the one about monks engaging in music and dance. Thus a credible justification is necessary if a monk were to participate in the production of popular music. During the early decades of the twentieth century songs were written by monks, but to all appearances, the initiative came from a composer who already had a composition that simply needed a lyric.[94] This kept monks in the background or totally unknown, the song being associated with the singer alone.

---

93. So does Jayasena Jayakody's novel *Piccamala* (Colombo: Dayavansa Jayakody, 1985).

94. It is interesting to note that in keeping with the inter-ethnic communication and harmony of the times, some of these Buddhist and Sinhala nationalist songs, written by Buddhist monks, were sung by talented Muslim singers. This is one among many indications that keep turning up that illustrates the inclusivist current in the history of Sri Lanka. This demonstrates that, had the natural growth of the relations between peoples not disrupted by ideologues, people would get on with their lives, with little consciousness of ethnicity.

Further, these early songs were either exclusively religious or religio-nationalistic counterparts of the more concrete restorations of the ruined cities, for example *Danno Budunge,* now a quasi-national anthem, written by the playwright John de Silva. In contrast to these anonymous or background-dwelling early songwriters, Rambukana is a highly publicized and popular creator of songs. The fact that there has not been a murmur, either from the monks or the laity, that Rambukana's songwriting may be possibly contra-veneous of the seventh precept is partly at least testimony to the acceptance of the ideology of *The Heritage,* that social service is the monk's role. When Rambukana talks about music (in a poetic prose of his own) it is this that he emphasizes:

> We should consider it a good fortune that mature creative intellect has been thoughtful enough to consider . . . music as not confined to mere aes-thetic enjoyment but utilized for the progress of society.
>
> In determining the answer to the question "of what use is music?" human-ists have been more progressive than some artists. The march, along with the people, of those artistes who have grasped the truth of this, is undoubtedly cause for auspicious fruitfulness.[95]

Referring to the popular musician Kapuge in the same essay, Rambukana writes: "Kapuge, an artiste with a clear political vision . . . and brimful tal-ent is not one to be forgotten in the attempt to bring about an age of human-ism." Then he goes over an entire list of musicians and credits them with talent and striving towards a humanistic society. Thus, Rambukana repre-sents, like the young monks of the Manava Hitavadi Bhiksu Sangamaya (MHBS),[96] a stage of advancement beyond *The Heritage*—a stage at which

95. *Silumina,* 12 January 1992.

96. The Lawasia Human Rights Standing Committee report of 7 June 1985 mentions the MHBS as a group that is taking initiative to reestablish communication and trust between different communi-ties in Sri Lanka. The report notes that "the leaders of this new organization wish to awaken their brethren to the fact that, consequent upon excessive Sinhala-Buddhist fervor, many injustices and injur-ies have been inflicted upon innocent people." A letter written by Mandavala Pannavasa, a young monk and leading figure in the MHBS, was published in the weekly journal published in Jaffna, *Saturday Review* 4, no. 3 (6 April 1985). I wish to thank Elizabeth Nissan for helping me secure copies of both the Lawasia report and Mandavala's letter to the *Saturday Review.*

At one stage in the present research I was of the opinion that the MHBS was the beginning of a reformation in the Sangha, a genuine breakthrough in the Sangha's evolution into a society of sophisti-cated, dynamic, moral, cosmopolitan men. This optimism gradually vanished, although my faith in the pioneers of the movement is still intact. Far from forging ahead, this group had great difficulty in surviving due to some of them being targeted by killers of one group or another during the repressive and violent 1980s. Some of them fled the country, and some left robes, and I can only hope none were murdered. The fact that this movement made no impression on the Sangha is a commentary on its entrenched conservatism, its moral state as well as the society as a whole.

they talk more about "humanism" than "social service." But they are different ways of saying the same thing: that the monk's role is not ritualism but social activism, which will dispel any lingering doubt about the compatibility of song writing and the sixth precept.

The ten basic monastic precepts do not include a specific prohibition of painting. But rules outside these precepts strictly limit the freedom a monk has to paint. These rules prohibit monks from painting all but religious figures and decorative patterns. During the eighteenth century, when the monkhood had "declined," monks did paint. For example, the finest examples of late medieval paintings, those at the Degaldoruva temple, are the work of a monk, Devarangampola Silvattana. In recent times, we have two relevant examples: First, Manjusri, one of the finest painters of contemporary times and a founding member of the '43 Group. While some of Manjusri's works are on religious themes, most are not. They are the work of an accomplished artist with a contemporary sensibility. Second, Mapalagama Vipulasara, a colleague of Rahula, from Vidyalankara who gained publicity as a sculptor. In terms of theme, in contrast to Manjusri, Vipulasara's work is religious, but in terms of aesthetic accomplishment it is mediocre and cannot claim any proximity to Manjusri's exquisite work. While Manjusri had no strong involvement with any ideology, Vipulasara is a Vidyalankara monk of the 1940s who is most likely to have come strongly under the influence of *The Heritage*.

Katuvana Piyananda is a young monk whose work as an artist is explicitly justified, like Rambukana's songs, in humanistic and "social service" terms. According to a review,[97] Katuvana's themes are varied. But a substantial proportion deals with social themes, especially the rebellion of the youth, not by romanticizing it but by an attempt to depict its pathos—for example, a gun barrel as the teat of a bottle from which an infant sucks its first drink of milk, a mother suckling a bullet as if it were a child, and the Buddhist apocalypse as a shower of bullets. These startling juxtapositions, though aesthetically unremarkable, are an attempt to portray the futility and pathos of war and terror. We might recall here that a large number of young monks were killed by death squads, who even had coined, in a cruel manner, religious sounding names for specific tortures.[98] In these works Katuvana is, like Rambukana, a young monk whose ideas are closer to the humanists of the MHBS,

---

97. *Divayina*, 18 August 1991; Brochure for "Passage of Emotions," the ninth exhibition of paintings by Katuvana Piyananda, The Lionel Wendt Art Center (Colombo), 1994.

98. *Vinivida* 15 (July 1988): 2 refers to a torture known as "dharma cakraya danava." The death squads were mobilized in the 1980s by the police and the intelligence units of the army to suppress the JVP rebels, among whom were young monks.

at any rate consciously, than to the "social service" idea of *The Heritage*. Katuvana has another justification for painting, which also echoes *The Heritage*'s
idea that the monk, although devoted to social service, should be of perfected virtue. This is his view that painting is a form of meditation.

Katuvana's awareness that his engagement in painting could be open to
the criticism of being inappropriate for a monk is seen in his rather defensive
statement that painting does not fall into the category of "tabooed art" *(garhita vidya)*, unlike music, comic shows, and dancing. Historically, all these
were gradually incorporated into the monk's sphere of experience, but always with the justification that they had been given a religious coloring and
content. Modern monks, like Katuvana, produce secular work, and *The Heritage*, with its explicit theme of "changing with the times," is the text in relation to which they justify and legitimize their work. Accordingly, it is not
surprising that Walpola Rahula, the author of *The Heritage*, says of Katuvana's
work, that "painting to create pleasant emotions within a person is very
much in accordance both with the heritage and the role of a monk."[99]

THE KANDALAMA PROTEST
A Social Drama

Inamaluve Sumangala, one of the most dynamic and colorful of the political
monks of recent times and a child par excellence of *The Heritage*, orches-
trated in 1992 a religio-political event of exceptional anthropological interest. Its sequence can be well understood within the typological framework
of the "social drama" proposed by Victor Turner.

The idea of social drama, implicit in Turner's earliest work, *Schism and
Continuity in an African Society*,[100] is more explicitly articulated in different
degrees of detail and refinement in much of his later work.[101] In a minimum
Turnerian definition, a social drama is "an objectively isolable sequence of
social interactions of a conflictive, competitive, or agonistic type" that "may
provide materials for many stories, depending upon the social-structural,
political, psychological, philosophical, and, sometimes, theological per-

99. Brochure for "Passage of Emotions."

100. Victor Turner, *Schism and Continuity in an African Society* (Manchester: Manchester University
Press, 1957).

101. See *The Drums of Affliction; Dramas, Fields and Metaphors* (Ithaca: Cornell University Press,
1974); *From Ritual to Theatre* (New York: Performing Arts Journal Publications, 1982); *The Anthropology
of Performance* (New York: Performing Arts Journal Publications, 1986).

spectives of the narrators."[102] Our analysis is concerned with one such "objectively isolable sequence," the rupture of relations between Inamaluve and his hierarchical superiors, but this is intertwined with others, the most important of which is that between the same monk and the secular powers, which I contend is a later phase of the "social drama."

In Turner's definition, the social drama is "processually structured" in identifiable phases of public action. First, there is a breach in the regular norm-governed social relations "made publicly visible by the infraction of a rule ordinarily held to be binding, and which is itself a symbol of the maintenance of some major relationship between persons, statuses or subgroups held to be a key link in the integrality of the widest community recognized to be a cultural envelope of solidary sentiments." This breach or rupture in relations leads to an irrational and contagious crisis, which is the drama's second phase. As Turner puts it, "when antagonisms become overt, ancient rancours, rivalries and unresolved vendettas are revived." The irrationality includes "temperamental dislikes, unconscious desires and aggressions, re-animated infantile anxieties, as well as the conscious envies and jealousies which break loose when a major normative knot is cut." Most public crises of this sort have liminal characteristics, not the sacred liminality hedged by taboos, but a "menacing stance in the forum or agora itself" and "challeng-[ing] the representatives of order to grapple with it." In the third phase, we have "the application of redressive or remedial procedures," ranging from informal mediation to performance of public ritual or recourse to legal machinery. In this most reflexive of the phases, "the community acting through its representatives, bends, or even throws itself back upon itself, to measure what some of its members have done, and how they have conducted themselves with reference to its own standards." The fourth and final phase "consists either of the reintegration of the disturbed social group, or of the recognition and legitimation of irreparable schism between the contending parties."[103]

The Kandalama sequence of events, though by no means perfectly within this typological framework, are eminently comprehensible in its terms. These events both fall short of and exceed this framework. There are at least two major social-dramatic movements here, one arising from the rupture of relations between Inamaluve and his religious hierarchical superiors, and the other, at a later stage, between him and the overarching secular powers. But the issue is much more complex than this. I contend that the subtext of the

102. Turner, *Anthropology of Performance,* 33.
103. Ibid., 34–35.

second rupture is part of the complex and elaborate process of legitimation of irreparable schism of the first rupture as defined in the final phase of Turner's typology. The first rupture went almost unnoticed as a public event. It was in fact not a truly public event: it was a private matter between Inamaluve and his group and the Asgiriya hierarchy, with the state in the background as the arbiter. It is the second rupture that attracted public attention and mobilized the kinds of passions and aggressions, and reasons and irrationalities envisaged in the conflict phase of Turner's "processual structure." Besides, in the public eye, there was little or no relation between the first and second ruptures; indeed the first rupture, as just noted, was little known. But a closer look shows the inextricable intertwinings of the two, making them a single social drama of national dimensions. Let us now turn to the sequence of events.

In a news report emblazoned with the heading "Buddhist monks to set themselves on fire," a national newspaper, the *Island* of 27 June 1992 claimed that this action of the monks was part of a mass protest campaign that was being organized against the construction of the Kandalama hotel complex. No one set himself on fire. But the alarm about the possibility represented the climax of a series of events related to the proposed building of a hotel complex, mainly for tourists, at Kandalama, on the shore of a tank (i.e., a reservoir) that has come to bear that name, located 15 kilometers to the west of the thirteenth century cave temple and monastery at Dambulla in central Sri Lanka.

Inamaluve Sumangala, the principal opponent of the hotel project and therefore the central actor in the conflict, emphasized two points.[104] First, Dambulla is a primordial and autonomous center of Sri Lankan Buddhism, on a par with Sri Pada and Anuradhapura.[105] Second, Dambulla is associated with struggles of liberation against foreign invaders, and it has acted as a catalyst in launching movements to repel them. Inamaluve gives examples: the monk Tissa of Dambulla gave refuge to the fleeing King Valagamba when he was attacked by South Indian invaders, fed him the *pindapata* (begged) food and reunited him with his dissenting ministers. Armies were organized and a struggle launched to regain the country from Dravida rule. Centuries later, the rebellion of 1848, known as the Matale Revolt, was launched at

---

104. This account is based on an interviews with Inamaluve (1991), other informants, and newspaper reports. For a naive panegyric which blindly amplifies Inamaluve's position, see Lakshman Piyasena, *Vave banda hotalaya* (Ratmalana: Sarvodaya, 1994).

105. The imprint on this mountain peak, Sri Pada, is believed to be the Buddha's footprint. Anuradhapura is the first great Buddhist sacred city in Sri Lanka and a premier pilgrimage center.

Dambulla in an attempt to free the nation from the British. Thus, points out Inamaluve, whenever the country, nation, and culture were threatened, the Dambulla Raja Maha Viharaya (The Great Royal Monastery of Dambulla) assumed leadership to work for the country's unity and the continuity of "the Sinhala state." It is important to note here the multivocality of some of the terms used. For example, in the characterization of Valagamba's struggle as an attempt to liberate the country from *Dravida*—rather than South Indian—rule and the reference to the *unity* of the country we have clear evocations of the present Dravida attempt to divide the country and the Sinhala attempt to keep it together.[106] The statement that the Matale Revolt "gave life to national unity" again evokes the present threat to "national unity."

Inamaluve's next point is the relation of Dambulla to Asgiriya. In theory all Sri Lankan monasteries, except for those of the sects that came into being in the nineteenth century, i.e., the Amarapura and Ramanna nikayas, belong to the Siyam Nikaya which consisted, until recently, of the two "chapters" Asgiriya and Malvatta. In effect, monasteries have enjoyed local autonomy even during periods when a political centralization of sorts and related royal power enabled a certain degree of centralization of the Sangha. The Asgiriya and Malvatta monasteries have enjoyed the right, which the British government upheld if not established, to make appointments to the major Buddhist centers, one of which is Dambulla.

Inamaluve's explanation of this relation is as follows: when the British quelled the 1848 rebellion, they took into custody the Dambulla monks, plundered the monastery, destroyed the treasures, and burnt the libraries.[107] Monks went into hiding. Some were caught and tried by a military court, but were acquitted. But the British wanted to take no chances, and the agent of the British government in Kandy summoned the Asgiriya monks and asked them to explain why the Dambulla monks acted in this treasonous and disloyal manner. The reply of the Asgiriya monks was that the Dambulla monks knew no Pali and did not know how to preach in Pali and that is why they acted against the British government. The insinuation is that the Dambulla monks were rustic and uneducated, which made them unruly. Turner, the British government agent, then ordered Asgiriya to take the

106. The Sinhala for "unity" is *ekiya bhavaya,* which is the same emotionally charged term used by Sinhala Buddhist extremists as a rallying cry against devolution. It is incorrect when used, as Inamaluve does here, to refer to ancient Sri Lanka, for no such unity existed, the political system being "galactic," i.e., non-centralized.

107. These are standard tropes to describe foreign invaders of Sri Lanka, and are best exemplified in the *Mahavamsa.* They represent stylized statements and cannot be taken literally. Inamaluve's description here is mythical and is part of the elaborate texture of his broad project.

Dambulla monks under them *temporarily* (presumably to civilize them, through Pali, so that they would behave with due deference to the British government).

This explains why, since 1848, Asgiriya appointed a chief monk to Dambulla. Under the British rule, this chiefship, known as the Dambulla *padaviya*,[108] was securely established within Asgiriya. Why? "The rebels [against the British] are here [in Dambulla] and the loyalists [to the British] are there [in Asgiriya]." Inamaluve's comment evokes Rahula's theory that the British adopted a policy of creating a monastic hierarchy of imperialist stooges who would spy on the rebels in the areas of their jurisdiction. "The power of the loyalists grew limitless, the rebels became refugeless." Gradually, the person given the padaviya assumed the title *viharadhipati* (incumbent), which was wrong; because the appointment was a padaviya (title) and not incumbency. In the meantime the Dambulla monastery grew and diversified into four monasteries by means of pupillary succession.

By 1980, continues Inamaluve, the Dambulla monks had become tired of the hegemony of Asgiriya and held a series of discussions aimed at liberating themselves and asserting their autonomy. The manner in which they asked Asgiriya for their freedom is instructive again for its resonance with *The Heritage*. "The British government does not exist anymore. Do not continue practices ordained by the British government." The words again recall *The Heritage*'s allegation that the British used the hierarchy to spy on their fellow sect members. Inamaluve kept using the term "freedom struggle," which implies a parallel between the island's domination by the British and Dambulla's domination by Asgiriya. In 1980 they drew up a "giant petition," signed by the people and leaders of the area—Members of Parliament (M.P.s), Assistant Government Agents (AGAs), monks, presidents of the Sasanaraksaka Sabhas (Religion Protection Societies) and so on—asking the Mahanayaka of Asgiriya to rectify the error. The Mahanayaka accepted the position of the petitioners but told the delegation sent that he must consult his colleagues before making a decision. The rest of the story, both about how the Dambulla monks consummated their liberation and about their anti-hotel protest, brings out how dynamic, educated monks are spurning both the traditional trappings of ceremony that bring them only ceremonial recognition as "tools of politicians" or "stage props" and the traditional ritualism of the monk, and are thereby bringing themselves into effective con-

---

108. A major incumbency is known as a *padaviya,* literally "position" or "fiefship." The padaviya-holder controls the incomes from the land, which, as in the case of Dambulla, could be substantial. The padavi system represents the adaptation of the monastic order to the "feudal" secular system of medieval Sri Lanka.

tact with social and political forces that are real and meaningful in a modern socio-political order.

The Mahanayaka's reply never came. In 1980, after much waiting, the Dambulla monks took the defiant step of establishing a chapter of their own. The Secretary, from the founding up to the present, is Inamaluve. The most senior monk of the now four-fold Dambulla monastery is the president, and the two next senior monks are the vice presidents. Even in this allocation of offices we see the able hand of Inamaluve at work, which combines tradition with modernity, the ascribed status of seniority with the achieved status of qualification, which he himself represents, being a university graduate. Further, the same impulse to be modern, and to become meaningful and acceptable to an educated modern laity, is evident in their decision not to use the traditional titles Maha Nayaka and Anu Nayaka, using rather the more democratic and modern "President" and "Vice President." In this the Dambulla monks are sending a message to all other "chapters" that retain the traditional titles, and ironically so, because Dambulla monks are the "rustics" as opposed to the supposedly sophisticated dwellers at Asgiriya and Malvatta. In their choice of modern terminology, they are mocking the traditionalists, especially their erstwhile overlords, the Asgiriya hierarchy.

Inamaluve is as able a strategist as he is a dramatic narrator. He spices up the narrative, heightening its drama by counterpoising the protagonists, in keeping the Shavian principle, no conflict, no drama. Already, as we noticed above, he has defined the protagonists in David and Goliath terms: the lone rebel vs. the establishment, with evocations of colony versus imperial ruler. He next refers to the Asgiriya's tactic of trying to sow dissension, which he referred to as Kautilyan, among the united four monasteries of Asgiriya, which consisted at the time, of about sixty monks. "We [Dambulla monks] . . . educated ourselves on the importance of autonomous rule. After we established the Sangha Sabhava (Sangha Committee, Council), we met fully and frequently." The last sentence evokes a fundamental value in Buddhism, the rule that monks must meet fully and frequently, which is the palliative against dissension—the greatest danger to Buddhism. To cause dissension is a heinous crime. Thus, when Inamaluve accuses Asgiriya of sowing dissension, he is accusing them of a serious moral failing. At the same time, he associates them with Kautilya and Hindu statecraft, as opposed to the Buddhist. He is associating them, by extension, with Hinduism, the dark force that has been depicted by monastic writers as the historical foe of Buddhism. He is drawing a contrast between the Buddhist theory of rule by concord and the Hindu theory of rule by dissension and associating the already imperialist Asgiriya with the latter. In this cluster of meanings, there lurks somewhere a further one, that of the separatist war, which is launched by "terrorists" who are Hindus and who in their attacks have ravaged Buddhist sites and killed Buddhist monks, as in the case of the massacre of the novices at Arantalava, and who are threatening the "unity" of the island.

As a part of building concord through full and frequent meetings, Inamaluve succeeds not only in uniting the four Dambulla monasteries but also in bringing under the umbrella of the Sangha Sabhava about thirty-nine other monasteries in the vicinity which he vividly and hegemonistically calls "branch monasteries" *(sakharama),* thereby raising the membership of the Sabhava to ninety-three. Inamaluve understood the value of developing the idea of common interest as a means of maintaining solidarity among the monasteries that constituted the Sangha Sabhava. In this strengthening of the local group, Inamaluve perfected his rebel position in relation to Asgiriya. He had in view an idea that only a far-sighted person could entertain, namely, the legitimization of the Dambulla autonomy in vinaya terms, which is to establish their own ordination. The vinaya rules allow monks in provincial areas to ordain novices by the simple means of a congregation of five ordained monks. Thus the crowning sequence in the establishment of Dambulla autonomy was to hold an ordination of their own. It is this consummation towards which Inamaluve worked fervently, but it was by no means his primary motive. Autonomous ordination, rather, is the legitimization of the rebel group as a provincial power, held de facto by Inamaluve. Ideally by this act Dambulla becomes a separate yet legitimate expression of the universal Sangha, but more importantly, it becomes a reconstituted socio-political reality that the modern political and economic order has to reckon with. It is this clout that was made visible, tested, and revalidated in the challenge to the hotel complex, the second sequence of the social drama.

In 1985, in the first ceremony held by the rebel group, five novices, one a pupil of Inamaluve's and four from the other monasteries, were ordained. Reiterating his rectitude, Inamaluve described this as an act in keeping with "the rules enunciated by the Buddha" *(Buddha niyamaya),* implying the unassailability of the act and defiance the rules of all others. Once again criticizing in one stroke the traditional hierarchy and embracing the modernity advocated by *The Heritage* and, at the same time, claiming moral superiority deriving from Buddhist universalism, Inamaluve and his colleagues claimed to have rejected the "narrow divisions" *(patu bheda)* of caste, region, and chapter and to have made ordination at Dambulla open to all. Asgiriya, like the rest of the Siyam Nikaya, is caste exclusive,[109] and the openness of the

---

109. Although ancient Buddhism was an anti-caste movement, it gradually accommodated caste as it did other social institutions. The Siyam sect of Thai origin, established in the eighteenth century, is restricted to the Goigama, the uppermost in the Sinhala caste system.

new group was described as a "need of the times." The ceremony received "a great deal of media attention," according to Inamaluve, which was probably not spontaneous but helped by his energy and skills. Up to 1990, that is, in a period of four years, thirty-seven monks were ordained. This included those who came from afar, from Hingurakgoda, Nikavaratiya, Kurunagala, Trincomalee, and Amapara, bearing testimony to the open-door policy of the group. In a further innovation, customary gifts given by candidates to the ordination teachers were abolished. This fitted the pattern we have seen, repeated over and over again, of making a radical statement, namely a condemnation of the traditional hierarchy for accepting gifts. As Inamaluve put it, even ordination has got caught in "the wave of commercialism" *(vanija ralla)*, senior monks receiving substantial gifts and later selling them to vendors.[110] In this Inamaluve can once more claim to be on the side of the original "pure" Buddhism in which morality is what matters and gifts have no place. Like much of what preceded, this act proved extremely popular with young monks and their families and supporters who cannot afford lavish gifts. It also appeals to the educated classes, who emphasize morality rather than ritual or the social organization of the religion. Not only do these monks refuse gifts but they do so truly with a vengeance: they arrange accommodation and food for ordination candidates and their families, friends, and supporters. The costs are shared by the Dambulla monks and their lay supporters.

The deemphasis of the economic dovetails the emphasis placed on the moral. Inamaluve pointed out that they were not concerned as to what caste the novice belonged to but looked into whether the novice had knowledge of the required texts. Preoccupation with caste and other traditional considerations are obstacles that make it difficult for the Sangha to make a successful transition to the twenty-first century, says Inamaluve. He points out that their former overlords did not agree with what they were doing (i.e., giving up caste exclusivity). But educated monks with a modern outlook gave their approval. Thus the battle is not just one of emancipation from Asgiriya, but one between tradition and modernity, stagnation and changing with the times. The desirability of change and modernity is sharpened by the identification of modernity and change with an ethical dimension of which tradition-bound stagnation is considered bereft.

The conservative forces persisted even after the successful completion of several ordinations. They still had one card left in their hands, namely, their

---

110. I discuss below a different, fiction-based critique which incidentally conveys some of the flavor of the traditional system of ordination with its heightened inequalities between the hierarchy and the ordinands, and its elaborate system of gifts. See chap. 6.

formal relationship with the state, which gave them the authority to register monks, who are issued certificates to the effect that they have been ordained. All monks, at their ordination, are required by law to be registered with the Ministry of Buddhism. Thus, while the Dambulla monks duly informed (in duplicate, Inamaluve added) the Commissioner of Buddhist Affairs about their ordinations, the Commissioner failed to register them. When they wrote letters of inquiry, the Commissioner wrote "slippery replies." Inamaluve here astutely returns to the broader and spiritually more important and morally and ethically powerful issues. From his higher moral ground he could plainly tell the commissioner, as he did, that "the morality of the ordained needs no certificate, but there is a legal requirement, which, if not met, there is some lingering doubt, and monks may be unfairly treated for that."

Inamaluve soon found out the reasons for the Commissioner's inaction and slippery answers. The Mahanayaka of Asgiriya had exerted pressure, through the highest levels, on the Commissioner to prevent registration. At this Inamaluve made an appeal to the Supreme Court, stating that the Commissioner had failed to act according to the law and asking the court to issue a writ of mandamus requiring the commissioner to comply, and to recognize the new group as a new chapter of the Siyam Nikaya under the name *Rangiri Dambulu Sangha Sabhava* (The Sangha Assembly of the Golden Rock of Dambulla).[111] Inamaluve's action is again consistent. In these details about registration, his last battle for autonomy, he portrayed the traditional hierarchy as a partner with politicians in the perpetuation of morally reprehensible acts. This is an allegation frequently made against the hierarchy, which is often stigmatized by younger monks as "stage props" for politicians. In contrast, Inamaluve portrays himself as the moral force, going through the proper channels, the judiciary. Within six months the court issued an order requiring the Commissioner to accept the establishment of a new chapter and to register the monks in question as duly ordained by the new chapter. Inamaluve also maintains that the term "sect" should refer only to doctrinal differences—which do not exist in Sri Lankan Buddhism. Therefore, the so-called sects should actually all be chapters, with minor behavioral or external differences, usually of sartorial style.

111. I am unaware of the antiquity of the usage "Rangiri" (Golden Rock) to preface "Dambulu vihara" (Dambulla temple). While the usage may go back to the time of the construction of the temple, the honorific/romantic "Rangiri" is never used in ordinary parlance. Inamaluve's propagandistic use of the term is now appropriated by the nationalist media, which confers on it a new reality and validity. Thus the plain old solid Dambulla rock of popular usage has become a "Golden Rock."

HOTEL PROTEST OR RITE OF PASSAGE?
Extension and Celebration of Dambulla Autonomy

The Dambulla monks, as already indicated, are charting a new course for themselves. For example, we noticed how they have brushed aside old customs relating to the ceremony of ordination and treat lay and monastic visitors to the ceremony not as subordinates to be patronized but as guests. They, along with their lay supporters, have "become activist," in Inamaluve's words, in an attempt at self-help. The monks regularly visited the villages "to participate at an activist level in the problems of lay supporters." This kind of activity would certainly be satisfying in itself. But that is not enough to satisfy the status yearnings of able, articulate, educated monks who seek acceptance and status as central actors in a new social arena. They want to be freed from the shackles of tradition, and they are determined not to be outpaced by a changing society. And they would lose no time in using opportunities that arose to cast themselves as central actors in socially and politically charged situations. Besides, understood within the framework of the "social drama," their self-determined secession from Asgiriya remained unconceded by Asgiriya despite it being an accomplished fact. Thus it was paramount that they seek legitimacy for their new status through appeal to the only alternative they had, the moral authority of the total social order.

An opportunity for this arose when the government allocated land on a fifty year lease to a private company, Aitken Spence, to construct a hotel complex in Kandalama. It was a tailor-made opportunity for Inamaluve to dramatize and consecrate the newly won autonomy of the Dambulla chapter, and to claim legitimacy for it. The event also gave Inamaluve the opportunity to cast himself in his favorite role as the underdog taking on the powers, David taking on the Goliath of big business and no less a power than the government. Inamaluve could not only cast himself as an enemy of rapacious business and corrupt politics, but also, simultaneously, as a pious lover of threatened animals and a protector of the trees and the streams and the environment in general. Further, he could cast himself as the defender of the poor against the rich; of the idyllic village against the encroachment of the city; of indigenous culture against its invasion by decadent capitalist ventures and tourism equated with neocolonialism; of humanism against the heartless pursuit of profit; and of interfaith activism against narrow religious partisanship. The opportunity for all this was there, and Inamaluve seized it.

As in the case of the breach with Asgiriya, Inamaluve has constructed his own story, a story that is now believed to be fact by many. Many of the journalistic defenses are based on the "facts" of this story. According to him, the Kandalama reservoir was built by King Bhatiya.[112] In 1946, the Department of Agriculture rebuilt and enlarged it to build a colony. The land belonged to the Dambulla Vihare. Agriculture Minister D. S. Senanayake appealed to the chief monk to give the land to the project. He agreed "because it was for the benefit of the poor." Inamaluve is here implying that to make cause with the poor is a Dambulla tradition. When the tank was rebuilt, the high-water mark rose. The new water mark swallowed an ancient village, and, in keeping with the legislation, the inhabitants were evicted and resettled on land on the lower side of the tank, which Inamaluve claims is infertile land. It is on the site of the original village, from which the poor were evicted, that the Government proposed to build a hotel "for foreigners." In Inamaluve's view, this is illegal, because the project violates the legislation that gave the monastery's land for the benefit of the poor. Inamaluve agrees that tourism is acceptable and hotels are needed, but they should be built in appropriate places. Already fifty acres of protected forest have been destroyed, he claims. The tank has been filled in on the hotel side, to protect the future hotel. Thus he claims the tank, along with the environment, have been destroyed. Besides, tourism will bring immoral activity, as it has been alleged in the case in the coastal towns. The problem says Inamaluve, is that there is no national policy on tourism; and the Dambulla chapter is expressing its opposition to the harm the hotel project would do to the "agro-economy" *(krsi arthikaya),* culture, and the environment.

Agro-economy, culture, environment—no better themes are imaginable in contemporary Sri Lanka to gain high profile attention, and in the Turnerian terms employed here, for Inamaluve to launch the second phase of his social drama. "Agro-economy" not only evokes the traditional attachment the people are supposed to have for their way of life; it is also full of associations of a much more potent idea, that of the idyllic village community centering on the tank, the temple, and the field. These three form part of the present day nationalist and middle class view of the ancient idyllic village community. Now considered indigenous, this romantic idea of the village community is borrowed from western conceptions of the village community and the idealized life of the peasantry, whose own view of their life was one of drudgery mercifully punctuated by some communal ribaldry and religio-theatrical alleviations. The idea first entered the Sinhala-speaking middle

112. There were two kings named Bhatiya, Bhatiya I (38–66 c.e.), also called Bhatikabhaya, and Bhatiya II (203–27) also called Bhatiya Tissa. Inamaluve's narrative does not say which one of these he is referring to. This is immaterial, however, because Inamaluve is inventing a myth, in which he claims antiquity for the tank.

classes through Dharmapala. The writings of Ananda Coomaraswamy contributed to the idea of a noble peasantry living in idyllic harmony in its natural and social environment. The major recent writer who idealized the village and coupled with it the stupa, the tank, and the paddy field to construct
a distinctive Sinhala culture was Martin Wickramasinghe. Sinhala poets of
the "Colombo Period" like Mimana Prematilaka, Sagara Palansuriya, and
P. B. Alvis Perera directly borrowed from English romanticizers of the countryside, adding another dimension to the idea of the idyllic village.

The idea also received a boost from an unlikely source, the anthropologists and Buddhist scholars, through two concepts. The first is the concept
of the "Buddhist State" proposed by S. J. Tambiah, Heinz Bechert, and
Trevor Ling, who understood the Buddhist state as a symbiotic relation between the king, Sangha, and the people; and second, Edmund Leach's use of
the term "hydraulic society" to refer to the ancient Sri Lankan irrigation-
based civilization. Leach's work, however, was hardly a romanticization because he "deconstructed" the formidable tank by pointing out that the large
reservoirs were not the work of some one single hero-king but systems that
evolved over time—a point that cut down to size some of the tank building
hero kings.[113] Leach's term "hydraulic society" gained wider currency in Sri
Lanka through the work of the historian R. A. L. H. Gunawardhana.[114] This
term has now trickled down into the nationalist-romantic-idyllic vocabulary
as *vari samskritiya* (hydrolic culture), restoring the idea of the romantic hero-
centered tank that Leach so imaginatively demolished. Inamaluve's term *krsi
arthikaya* belongs to the same family of romantic-propagandist terms as *vari
samskritiya* in contemporary ideological jargon and is probably inspired by it.
That is to say the idea behind the term *vari samskritiya* and even the term itself
is of western origin, just like numerous other items of "national" culture.

The idea of the Buddhist State trickled down to the Jatika Cintanaya
ideology through the work of Gunadasa Amarasekera.[115] One or another
version of this idea is now nearly epidemic in the newspapers and other
media. In this we see a fascinating migration of ideas from intellectuals to
demagogues via an intervening range of interpreters, and the resulting unin-
tended, unconscious, and unwitting complicity of intellectuals in the manu-
facture of socio-politically potent ideas of which they would want no part.
In another contortion, the stupa-ricefield-tank trinity has been used in re-

---

113. Edmund Leach, "Hydraulic Society in Ceylon," *Past and Present* 15 (1959):2–25.
114. R. A. L. H. Gunawardhana, "Irrigation and Hydraulic Society in Early Mediaeval Ceylon,"
Past and Present 53 (1971): 3–27.
115. On Jatika Cintanaya, see note 76 above.

cent times as a model for inventing other trinities, like the school, the police, and the monastery of President Premadasa.

By the use of the term "agro-economy" *(krsi arthikaya),* Inamaluve tapped into this vast socio-emotional reserve in contemporary Sri Lankan ideology. Inamaluve's use of it is again evidence of his mastery of the political use of words. The term is full of associations of the romanticized past in which agriculture was central and allegedly ensured total prosperity. It also evokes the tank, which was the basis of agriculture, particularly rice cultivation. "Culture" evokes the entire gamut of ideas and feelings associated with a glorified past, the ravages of foreign domination, and the importance of nationalist revival. In addition, the term taps into the popular idea of identifying and reconstructing ruined structures, each of which would be a monument to past glory. Dambulla is a primary religious and cultural site, and Inamaluve stated that the hotel project also threatened ancient archeological sites, which he claimed are abundant in the vicinity of the project. In addition, he also claimed that there is a hidden treasure, which introduced an element of mystery. Finally, the environment. In addition to nationalist and socialist sentiment that seeks to protect the environment from foreign capitalist ventures, the environment is a modern concern, fashionable within social and intellectual elites. Thus Inamaluve assembled together a set of themes that are of contemporary interest as subjects worthy in themselves and as issues of intense politico-emotional potential.

What action did Inamaluve take? He wrote to the President, asking him, as a Buddhist, to abolish the project. He organized a petition with a thousand signatures from "Protect Buddhism" Societies, saying that what the people need are roads, electricity, irrigation, and a way to market their produce, very Dharmapalite ideas, and not a hotel. Twenty-two peasant associations were mobilized to write to the President, but to no avail, except for an acknowledgment, and a visit by some cabinet ministers, both of which were, according to Inamaluve, perfunctory.

Inamaluve was of the opinion that the land is crown land. For that reason, in his view, which he put out as the view of the local people, Aitken Spence is a squatter, and the government was in the position of giving protection to a company that was perpetrating an illegal act. That is the kind of democracy Sri Lanka has, lamented Inamaluve. Thus the critique of a hotel project was transformed into a political critique of the existing regime. Meanwhile, Inamaluve visited the U.S., where he gave an interview to the Los Angeles based *Sri Lanka Express.* He enlisted the help of the incumbent of the monastery in Los Angeles, Valpola Piyananda, to contact U.S. environmental groups and through them to address a petition to President Clinton. Clearly,

Inamaluve correctly understood the petition as a propaganda weapon to advance causes that are not necessarily those the petitions make explicit.

Undaunted by the government's indifference, Inamaluve moved on to the next stage of dramatically making visible his protest, which until then was confined to petitions and small-scale expressions of disagreement. He organized a Satyagraha—a large-scale, nonviolent protest—that brought the matter into the arena of active politics. On 12 June 1991 three thousand monks and 50,000 lay people (by Inamaluve's estimate) gathered on the gently sloping rock at the entrance to the Dambulla temple and performed the Satyagraha. Inamaluve by now had assembled a coalition of representatives of all the major Sri Lankan religions—Buddhists, Hindus, Christians, and Muslims—which gave the protest a strong multi-religious tinge. Inamaluve's penchant for depicting his struggle as one of an underdog taking on the powers is reasserted in his description of the government trying to prevent the Satyagraha. Many people were turned away by the use of force, he says. Despite this the Satyagraha attracted media attention and was, in Inamaluve's estimate, a great success. "The government was burnt," he said, and the proof of this is in the reaction: the government organized a poster campaign to discredit Inamaluve and the protest. This campaign proclaimed that the sacred ground of the Dambulla temple was desecrated by "hoisting a cross on the rock," a reference to the cross the Catholic participants carried and displayed during the protest. The posters identified the guilty parties as Inamaluve, who was derided as a pseudo-monk (*hora sangeya*, "thief monk"),[116] and as A. T. Ariyratne, a major supporter of Inamaluve and leader of the *Sarvodaya* movement, who was called a "profiteering boutique keeper" *(mudalai)*.

According to Inamaluve the poster campaign was intended to break the coalition and divide the religious groups, but the tactic backfired. It contributed, he states, more to generating goodwill among the different religious adherents. The government persuaded certain monks, who were its allies, to issue public statements denouncing the protests. But in Inamaluve's view impartial and intelligent observers rejected them. Delighting in what he imagines as the upshot of the enemy's tactical folly, Inamaluve believes that, if not for the posters, the coalition would have ended, and the unity among religious leaders (not religions, he adds) would have collapsed. As a result, on 2 January 1992, the day the President addressed the nation from the palace of the last king, a giant protest, known as the "satyagraha meditation,"

116. This is colloquial Sinhala for the Pali term *theyya samvasika*, which questions the legitimacy of a monk's ordination.

a semantic combination that presumably reflected the event's multi-religious composition, was staged in the coastal town of Ja-ela. The well-known preacher and popular monk, Madoluvave Sobhita, was a participant. Among the participating Catholic priests were Oswald Firth and Oscar Abeyratne. Unlike the sit-in on the Dambulla Rock, the protest proceeded unmolested by the government, which only took away the protestors' loudspeaker permit half an hour before the meditation. The permit was restored when Inamaluve reasoned with the police and pointed out their democratic right to criticize the government.

This was no longer a protest against the establishment of a tourist hotel beside a scenic man-made lake in the vicinity of a monastery, which is an ancient Buddhist site. It never was. In fact what we see is a brilliant and resourceful monk, trying to gain legitimacy for his newly established subsect by attracting the attention of elite members of the society. He was trying to break away from tradition while at the same time combining the usable parts of tradition with modern resources such as the media and anti-colonial, anti-imperialist, and anti-capitalist ideological sentiment, and adding to that a splash of moral rectitude. Here Inamaluve acted in a manner that is representative of a whole generation of middle aged and younger monks with secular qualifications, most of whom are emerging from the traditional role of rural ritualist, though not as visibly as he is.

Theirs is the role and definition of monkhood advocated in *The Heritage.* This role has now been absorbed, four decades after its original advocacy by Walpola Rahula, as a legitimate part of the culture of monasticism. Many educated monks now openly state that monkhood is a vocation of active benefit to society, with the other-worldly or nibbanic content relegated beyond even the secondary place ritualistically assigned to it in traditional monasticism.[117] Being actively beneficial to the world is, of course, full of possibilities for political ramifications, as the protest over the hotel complex amply demonstrates. For example, by the time the protest reached the stage of the sit-in at the Dambulla Rock, it was already highly politicized and rife with opposition, not to the hotel but to the government—broadly the UNP government with its policies, enunciated in 1977, of the "open economy" and free-rein capitalism, and more specifically the government of President Premadasa, both for continuing those policies and for its repressive acts. A master of nuance, Inamaluve made a distinction between the unity of reli-

---

117. For a recent explication, see *Bhiksuvakage vagakima bauddha darsanaya samajayata kiyadimayi* ("The responsibility of the monk is to explain the Buddhist philosophy to society"), *Ravaya,* 18 May 1997. This title notwithstanding, the author's aim is to interpret Buddhist morality as a social philosophy.

gious leaders rather than a unity of religions, the latter being a direct and sarcastic reference to Premadasa's "all religions are true" theory and his penchant for hopping from temple to church to mosque in front of TV cameras. Inamaluve's reference to the nonviolence of his protest is as much a characterization of his work as a condemnation of the ruthlessness, repression, and authoritarianism that were the hallmark of the Premadasa regime. It is no accident that the second large-scale protest, the meditation at Ja-ela, coincided with Premadasa's address to the nation on 2 January 1992. Inamaluve reaffirmed his work as a refusal to keep silent when a national service needed to be performed, echoing *The Heritage*'s (and Dharmapala's) prescription, and the alleged historic role of the monk. While the whole affair was a problem for the government, it was an opportunity for the opposition, and some opposition politicians, like Dinesh Gunawardena, joined the protest, taking its politicization further.

In terms of the vocabulary of the "social drama," the protest over the hotel project constitutes the fourth stage, the stage of resolution, when the rupture between Asgiriya and Inamaluve, having been deadlocked at the level of the two parties and the government, is now played out in the court of public opinion. For this Inamaluve needed an issue on which to rally a convincing range of groups and interests that would validate his position in relation to Asgiriya in the process of his validating his position on the issue. Here his position as himself vs. the hegemony of Asgiriya was transformed into himself vs. the government, which restated his view of the traditional Dambulla position as rebel vs. the powers.

KANDALAMA
Interpretation and Assessment

Kandalama attracted national attention and engendered enthusiastic public discussion, but none of it, including the discussion in *Ravaya*, which normally makes a sophisticated comment, went beyond reiteration of the slogans that are part of the ideology of the opposition that coalesced around Inamaluve. The single exception to this was a perceptive evaluation of the issues by Jayadeva Uyangoda and Nirmal Ranjit Devasiri, entitled *"Kandalame desapalanaya saha pragdhanaya"* (The politics and capital of Kandalama).[118]

One of Uyangoda and Devasiri's main points is that the movement inde-

---

118. This article was published in both Sinhala and English. Since the English version was not available to me, I have translated the Sinhala into my own English. The Sinhala original appears in *Pravada* 2 (July–August 1992): 7–9.

pendently launched by the monks was swallowed up by the opposition to
the Premadasa-Thondaman alliance and by the electoral platform of several
opposition parties and extremist forces.[119] In their view, this co-option put
an end to the autonomy and potential of the early phase of the movement.
However, a close examination of the protest and its wider sociological context reveals that the conferment of autonomy and potential on the early
phase of the movement is unwarranted.

From two analytical perspectives, the apparent public spiritedness and
love of the environment expressed in the protest are not autonomous. First,
in a sociology of knowledge or Marxist perspective, these are superstructures. Second, from an anthropological point of view, they are part of the
processual structure of a "social drama." Uyangoda and Devasiri repeatedly
recognize the conditioned and nonautonomous nature of these sentiments
later in the paper but they miss the most important reason why they should
do so, namely the relationship of the protest (that expressed the putative
public spiritedness and love of the environment) to the successful rebellion
of the Dambulla monks against the Asgiriya hegemony. Having broken away
from Asgiriya, it was imperative that these monks justify their act in the
public eye and gain legitimacy for it by proclaiming to the world that, unlike
the moribund Asgiriya hierarchy, they are individuals with a contemporary
outlook and sensibility and with the capacity to meaningfully respond to
contemporary issues, a pattern of behavior they learnt from *The Heritage*.
Among the issues that especially appeal to the elites whose acceptance they
seek are the romantic notion of the village community beside the tank, opposition to the post-1977 policies of the open economy, and opposition to
the (then) existing political and bureaucratic leadership as the visible and
obnoxious embodiment of these policies. Public legitimation was necessary
because of Inamaluve's deadlocked position with Asgiriya and the need to
bring to a resolution the social drama that began with his first challenge to
the Asgiriya overlordship. For that he needed another social drama, (or we
can call it, as we have done so far, another phase within the first one). The
protest provided him with that second phase.

Thus, the socialist and environmentalist ideas of the Dambulla monks
were not spontaneous overflowings of compassion for man and beast, nor
for the woods or the streams, but badges of modernity and contemporary

119. S. Thondaman, the powerful trade union leader, lent parliamentary support to the UNP governments both of Presidents Premadasa and Jayawardene. At the 1994 defeat of the UNP, he changed
colors and aligned himself with the new victors, the United Left Front, and has since been a cabinet
member of that government.

awareness. These badges demand that modern secular elites give the monks the recognition that has eluded them since colonialism relegated them to the periphery of society, while providing the laity with adaptive mechanisms to eventually monopolize the society's center. The ultimate inspiration for this, as we have seen, is *The Heritage,* and, we may add, in the case of Inamaluve, the nationalist environment of Vidyalankara in which he was reared. Thus, partisanship for nationalist politics, which went hand in hand with *The Heritage*'s prescriptions for recapturing for monks the center of society, was another source of the socialist and environmentalist ideas of the Dambulla monks. While it appears that the protest missed the opportunity, as Uyangoda and Devasiri observe, to take off into a genuine socialist and environmentalist movement, I contend that the potential for that was no more than a mere appearance, and that opportunity never truly existed. Such an opportunity can exist only in the context of "an enlightened civil society, strengthened by democracy," which Uyangoda and Devasiri rightly define as the effective deterrent to "the invasive nature of capital" (9).

My next disagreement with Uyangoda and Devasiri is in relation to how they apply to this case their theoretical idea that in precapitalist society it is the landed stratum that is hurt by the flow of urban capital to the village. Dambulla is taken by the two authors as a candidate for sustaining economic damage caused by immigrant capital. Thus they see an economic motivation in Inamaluve's environmentalist and cultural protest. According to Inamaluve, the monastery first ceded the land, not to intruding private capital, but to state capital, during the enlargement of the tank in about 1950, which definitely was a loss. The present intrusion of capital in the form of the hotel complex is certainly private, but the land does not belong to the "landed stratum" in this case, i.e., the Dambulla monks, but to the state. The intrusion does not cause any losses to the Dambulla monks. In fact, it might make some gains to them, both in indirect revenues and in Dambulla's enhancement as a cultural center, with the help of the infrastructural gains and tourist traffic the project would bring to the area.[120]

---

120. When the Central Cultural Fund instituted a fee for foreign tourists visiting the Dambulla temple, Inamaluve protested, characterizing it as a shameless sale of religion. Soon after, however, he negotiated for a share of this shameless sale. Subsequently, he did even better. He instituted a charge of his own, over and above that of the Cultural Fund from which he was receiving a share, of Rs. 100 per foreign tourist. This was in 1996, and he has since raised the fee to Rs. 200. Thus, far from incurring a loss, Inamaluve is gaining handsomely from the increased tourist traffic which the Kandalama hotel generates.

The practice of charging foreign tourists in this manner is being increasingly practiced by profiteering monks who emerge from nowhere and claim ownership of historic sites. Among examples, besides, Dambulla, is the famous statue of Avukana. A monk who is essentially a squatter now claims

I argue, however, that the direct interest of the Dambulla monks in the protest is political rather than economic, and is part and parcel of their recent independence from Asgiriya. By definition, that independence means the empowerment of the Dambulla monks to assume religio-political hegemony locally, primarily over the local system of monasteries that Inamaluve explicitly verbally appropriates in his usage *sakharama,* "branch monasteries," and secondarily over the laity of the region, especially given the modernity of the Dambulla monks and their professed elevation of morality over ritual, which appeals to the socially crucial lay elites. This is already apparent in the organization of the Dambulla chapter and the network of interconnections of the Sasanaraksaka Sabhas (Protect Buddhism Societies) of the region. The protest against the hotel project indeed can be seen as, among others, the first substantial test of Dambulla's local hegemonic potency, which was based on this local organizational network. That network withstood the test, because it was through this network that the core of the protest and the work that went into it, including the thousands of signatures collected for the petitions, was accomplished. Thus, in their suggestion that the Dambulla monks possibly have an economic reason for their protest, Uyangoda and Devasiri appear to be trapped in their theoretical framework.

The protest, for the Dambulla monks, was a win-win situation irrespective of whether it "succeeded" or not, because the success of the protest, though desirable, was not their only or even the primary goal. Stated differently, the protest was a rite of passage, more accurately its liminal period,[121] that ordained the Dambulla chapter to full and autonomous cultural and political adulthood. It was replete with its own versions of the features that Turner lists, such as induced, seduced, or nudged in partisanship, contagion, irrationality, resurrection of ancient rancors, rivalries and unresolved vendettas, threat of physical violence, and the invocation of different

---

ownership of the site and charges Rs. 50 per foreign tourist. While monastic property is "private," the indigenous conceptions of ownership of such property never extended to the paintings, images, and edifices that housed them, which were all religious objects, freely accessible to all. It is not imaginable that foreign visitors, like the fifth-century Chinese pilgrim Fa Hien, were asked to pay to see the sites at the then capital Anuradhapura. It is understandable that a fee may be levied for the upkeep of these sites, but if such is to be levied, it should be levied on all visitors, and by the Department of Archeology, the Central Cultural Fund, or some other public institution, rather than allowing private individuals to profiteer from national treasures. See *Yuktiya,* 16 June 1996; *Ravaya,* 14 January 1996.

121. I use Arnold van Gennep's classic definition of the rite of passage as consisting of separation, limen, and reintegration. In a feat of unparalleled sociological imagination, Turner elaborated limen in astonishing ways, encompassing a vast range of phenomena from puberty rites to pilgrimage. Indeed, all of Turner's now fabled work is based on the idea of limen, and no other great corpus in anthropology constitutes such a variegated elaboration of a single idea.

deities. In the protest the monks tested their local networks, and the networks, it appears, responded smoothly to their commands, held national media attention for a period of two years, and helped them emerge as an autonomous local politico-cultural force which both national and local power-seekers can ignore only at their peril. This is demonstrated by the swiftness with which opposition parties embraced the protest and the anxiety with which the government condemned it. Uyangoda and Devasiri are right in their Marxist argument that since the advance of capital is irreversible, protests against it by precapitalist power groups are aimed at various other objectives they desire. This is eminently applicable to the Kandalama protest because, while the Dambulla monks did not succeed in stopping the hotel project, they by no means fought in vain, because their battle itself was their victory.

The rupture between Asgiriya and Dambulla is now an accomplished fact. It is nevertheless not a fact that the Asgiriya hierarchy finds easy to concede. In this sense the social drama has not yet run its full course. Its last phase, namely the recognition and legitimation of irreparable breach, has not yet taken place completely. Thus, even as late as September 1996, five years after the climactic events, in letters written to public figures, the Mahanayaka of Asgiriya clung on to the fiction that the Dambulla incumbency is held by Udugama Buddharkkhita, the appointee of the Executive Committee (Karaka Sabhava) of the Asgiriya chapter.[122] But this refusal to accept the breach with Dambulla is a psychological or self-representational fact of the Asgiriya hierarchy, or a vestigial survival in its psyche, and not a social fact. Such a psychological or representational fact enjoys no objective reality. In contrast to the Asgiriya hierarchy, the society at large has accepted the irremediability and legitimacy of the breach. Here in the society at large the processual structure of the social drama has completed its course. We are thus able to refine Turner's framework by making a distinction between the *social* or *objective* acceptance of the breach and its legitimation, and its *psychological* or *self-representational* rejection, and by positing the possible coexistence of these two in the last phase of the social drama, until final resolution.

The most important point made by Uyangoda and Devasiri undermines their position that there was, in fact, originally a genuine protest, with potential as a permanent vigil against the insidious encroachment of capital. I

122. Letters written to Janaka Bandara Tennekoon, the District M. P. for Matale and to Kumbukkandanvala Nandavimala, a prominent Buddhist monk of the area, dated 20 February 1996 and 14 August 1996. *Yuktiya,* 22 September 1996.

have argued that this was not the case. Uyangoda and Devasiri seem to imply as much when they posit an enlightened civil society strengthened with democracy as the indispensable precondition for a genuine community-based safeguard against the excesses of capitalist intrusion. That civil society is nonexistent in Sri Lanka, as a structural feature; but its ideology is borne by various individuals and groups. A mere summation of such individuals and groups, as long as they are discrete entities, cannot become that civil society. In that state they cannot permeate the social order.

But a beginning can be made, and monks are ideally suited to launch the campaign for a civil society. Monks constantly complain of lay indifference and of being used by politicians as stage props. It is within their power to change that, and one way to do that is by taking the lead in building a civil society. They are ideally suited for this by virtue of their traditional status as "worthy of support and respect," by their alleged historic role as "guardian deities of the nation," and by their profession of a message of universal compassion. It is one of the ironies in the history of society and religion that this has not been forthcoming, despite apparently favorable conditions.

That the protest, despite apparent potential, failed to even raise the hopes for finding in it an opportunity for a movement toward building a civil society is based in the contradictions of the ideology of its leadership, the ultimate source and the most coherent statement of which is *The Heritage*. The call to monks to study modern secular subjects and modern languages and take up the cause of social service in a modernizing society, left to itself, has the potential to open the way to a civil society. But that potential is nullified in the overarching monastic conception of a highly centralized and unitary political order in which Buddhism and Sinhala are elevated to hegemonic status, with an evocative and looming silence on the fate of the minorities built into that order. Despite the apparent concern for the ordinary man and the environment, the protest failed to extricate itself from the mire of ethnic prejudice. Its underlying majority-centeredness was made explicit in Inamaluve's choice of words, already mentioned, and in the support given by the Jatika Cintanaya leader Nalin de Silva. The hotel project was seen, especially by the latter, as another example of Tamil power because it came under the jurisdiction of the only Tamil cabinet member, the Minister of Tourism, S. Thondaman, and some critics paired the minister with separatist leader V. Prabhakaran. For the same reason, despite appearances, the protest did not provide a meaningful opportunity for genuine interreligious understanding. Inamaluve's distinction between religious leaders and religions is instructive. He was careful to insist that the dialogue was between religious leaders and not between the religions. When there was an attempt by the

Buddhist and Christian clergy to talk to the separatist Tamil rebels, the Buddhist monks and the Christian priests made separate trips.

The breakaway from Asgiriya is understood by Inamaluve and his supporters as an act of commendable heroism. Besides, it is an act fully confirmative of the letter and spirit of the Buddhist vinaya, as Inamaluve does not fail to point out. The strength of Buddhist organization in fact was based on its non-hierarchical, non-centralized nature, which allowed flexibility and encouraged creative local innovation. The absence of centralization facilitated conformity to the greatest value in Buddhist organization, the conduct of business through consensus made possible by full and frequent meetings of all monks. Such meetings would be logically and logistically possible only if the Sangha were decentralized into local groups, as in fact they historically were and are today, for, despite the elaborate sounding and multi-titled hierarchies and the so-called sects, the Sangha, at least in Sri Lanka, conforms to its pristine, non-centralized, "republican" form derived, according to authorities, from the premonarchical Indian republics, which were actually known as Sanghas.[123] It is this principle that Inamaluve evoked in justifying his break with Asgiriya, a principle that he rightly traces to the Buddha himself. Thus, knowledgeable monks are not strangers to the validity of decentralization not just in the Sangha but in any social organization. Besides, it is claimed by these monks themselves that the Sangha is a model of organization for lay society. It is therefore incomprehensible to say the least for the monks not to allow that same principle, which has worked so well for Buddhism ensuring its luxurious variety and longevity, to be applied to the secular social order. Whereas breaking away from Asgiriya was a positive and meaningful act, political decentralization to these monks is equal to breaking up the country. With this ideology, it is not surprising that the monks have not been able to come up with any viable and democratic solution to the ethnic problem, and thereby failed to live up to the universalist ethical standards of Buddhism. Were they to come up with that solution, they would gain the status and esteem in society which they claim they once had, and which is now denied to them. Had Inamaluve and the new monkhood he represents been able to resolve the contradictions of *The Heritage* and cross the barrier that keeps them away from a genuinely Buddhist society and state of mind, they would find in Dambulla's liberation from the religious hierarchy in Asgiriya a rationale and rallying point for liberating the habitats of the minority from the centralizing mania of their hegemonic colleagues and their secular counterparts.

123. Trevor Ling, *The Buddha;* U. N. Ghoshal, *A History of Indian Public Life,* vol. 2: *The Maurya and pre-Maurya Period* (London: Oxford University Press, 1966), chap. 10, 185–97.

APPENDIX
The Songs of Elle Gunavamsa[124]

1. My brave, brilliant soldier son
   Leaving [home] to defend the motherland
   That act of merit is enough
   To reach Nirvana in a future birth.

   When you march to battle
   Like the son of Vihara Maha Devi
   May the gods of the four directions protect you
   My son, defender of the land.

   Know that the mother and motherland
   Are nobler than kingly pleasure
   I turned my blood to milk to make you grow
   Not for myself but for the country.

2. Men, men, harken
   This is the sound of the war song, the sound of war
   The noble sound of us soldiers, that destroys enemies.

   They will rather die, they will not return unvictorious
   Hundreds, thousands of others line up for the battlefield

   In peace for the future, proud of heritage
   Love of motherland, let us march for the battlefield.

3. Tears go down eyes, fires go up in the heart
   I know my love, my love, those are for me.

   The day will return when the war fire is out
   Tear at the eye's edge dry
   and [we are] wrapped in one flag.

   If I die in battle don't be alone in the patri-house
   Give bravery to [our] son, O Vihara Maha Devi.

---

124. My translations.

4. Not an inch of another's land on this big earth we want
   Not an inch of this mother earth we'll give, but die
   This earth mother which gave us birth, this earth mother which
      gave us birth.

   We'll shed the last drop of blood
   To defend the land which gave us birth
   We will, like lions, conjure
   Before our enemy our skill [in war].
   Where is a country without a nation
   A nation without a country, where?

5. O heroes, battlefield bound
   Brothers, weapon in hand,
   Teraput abas, Suranimilas,[125]
   Reborn in my motherland.

   My land my nation waits
   With lit eyes, minds, thoughts
   Till [you] win back my country
   Like Dutugamunu's men.

6. Lion cubs, we lion cubs, brave cubs of the three Sinhalas
   Cubs defending the nation's heritage, lion cubs that defend
   the motherland.

   To fight, not to loose, we are cubs capable, in history's span
   Vanquishing enemies all march forward, able and brave soldier
      cubs.

   To be together under a single flag, let us march to the front hand in
      hand
   All one mother's, all one land's, let's march singing the song of war.

7. It is not to be king that I bear weapons. I defend my land as Gamu-
   nu's son.

---

125. Teraput aba (Theraputtabhaya) and Suranimila are soldiers of Dutugamunu.

Country, religion, race are my triple gems. Children, I make a to-
    morrow in your name.
For us *helas* [Sinhalas], to be born and die, where's another except
    this earth.

8. O youth, awake, awake, awake, unite in nation's name
    By the power of motherland's heritage, with love of race, with one
        mind, forward march.
    Grandsons of Vihara Maha Devi, reborn lieutenants of Gamunu
    We are the able and brave for ever by the power of this Lanka land.
    A new son has arisen in the distant land, this is not our end but the
        beginning.
    United in the shade of one flag. Unite this is our golden land.

9. It's not that I didn't feel your feelings, you who goes sleepless, at
        the palmyra's boundary, gun in hand.
    It's not that I didn't feel. It's not that I didn't feel.
    The nation's, the country's eye lamps aren't closed. It is at you that
        they winklessly look, of you they relentlessly think.

    A hundred, a thousand of those who aspire
    To join you, there are in the motherland
    A hundred, a thousand these are in the motherland.

10. The sword is pulled from the scaffold, it is
    Not put back unless smeared with blood,
    This is the way of the Sinhala of old
    Who vanquished the foe.
    Son, you must know that is how it was.

    Our able, brave hands, our able, brave minds.
    Are offered, to the motherland, with devotion for the race.

    Wishing the birth of brave sons
    Who comfort the nation
    Our brave mothers safeguard noble custom.
    Daughter, you must know that was how it was.

Ever remember the heroism
That valiant, shining *hela* sons showed
In the bygone *hela.*

Defend the radiance of the motherland's heritage
That the sons of Sinhala ever defended
Offering their lives.

11. O prince of mine defending the land
In the province of the *jambu* leaves
In the palmyra's shade
When are you going to meet me?

Tears pour down eyes, sighs arise in the heart
I fall down in front of the Buddha and the gods
In your name.

Nandimitra,[126] Suranimila rise in the memory
O prince of mine, are you the same as they?

Win my country and return, my lord,
For me to kiss those hands of mine

12. May our Sinhala country have the refuge
The refuge, the refuge
Of the great Sangha.

Let's fearlessly travel the path
That our Tera put aba trod

The Sangha is ever ready
At the front
If the race is threatened

So long as the Sangha robe lasts
So long as the Sangha robe, the Sangha robe lasts

126. One more of Dutugamunu's soldiers.

Our country and race, our country and race
Will shine, O son.

13. If you die in the battlefield my lord
I will come too, bearing arms, I am not lonely

You my lord, do not come [home] without victory
Searching for me here again.

I will come to the battlefield
Searching for you.

Nights are sleepless. Your image
You in the battlefield, you in the forefront
Appears without a break.

I will come to the battlefield
In search of you.

THE CRITIQUE OF THE
MONKHOOD

Niccam aniccam samana vadanti
Ghatassa bhinne kalaham karonti
Danena silena anusasayanti
Haritakim ekaphalam na denti

Everything is impermanent says the monk
But yells at me when the pot is broke
Be moral says the monk, and give
But doesn't give me even a bitter olive.

Pali folk verse, c. eighteenth century, presumably composed by a lay servant of a monastery. (The translation singularizes the plural of the original.)

Cultural critiques of the monkhood spring from an intelligent laity as well as a section of the monkhood, typically young monks. While the critiques by young monks overlap in content with those of the laity, they merit separate discussion because conspicuous articulation of monks' critiques entitles them to autonomous subcultural status. The critiques of the young monks, while not bereft of an ethico-moral content, are too rooted in interests arising from their subaltern state to constitute a genuine inner critique with meaningful reformative consequences. A specific and extreme form of the critique of the monkhood is that of the reform movement Vinayavardhana that came into being in the 1940s.[1] There is finally what might be called a liberal humanist critique articulated by cosmopolitan lay intellectuals. It is important to bear in mind the overlap in content, especially between the first two but not confined to them.

---

1. On this movement, see Michael Ames, "Social and Ideological Change in Ceylon"; Steven Kemper, "Buddhism without Bhikkhus," cited in chap. 4, n. 35.

There is nothing in Buddhism that is more worthy of deference than the three jewels, the Buddha, the Dhamma, and the Sangha, the "trinity" of Buddhism. The extreme respect shown to the Sangha by the laity is derived from this ideology. Every overt encounter between a monk and a layman is characterized by the latter's expression of deference to the former. This is taken to extremes at the formal level, as in the customs of spreading a freshly laundered white cloth on the seat on which a monk is invited to sit and of laymen washing the feet of monks as they ceremonially enter a house to accept alms. However, in the next breath, the laity can be extremely critical of the Sangha. This critique is expressed in the saying that the Buddhists worship the robe and not the wearer. Sociologically, this is not so trivial as it sounds. It encapsulates and expresses the entire problem of the Sangha of today in particular, but it is probably true of other ages as well, for it points to the gap between the ideal and reality. That is, the morality of the Sangha is an ideal to be talked about, but not practiced. At a still broader level it signifies the entire problem of Buddhism: the Dhamma is to be worshipped, preserved, provided for, televised, bragged about, exported, but not practiced. There is another implication: the lay greed for merit. The laity wants merit, by hook or crook. Merit is the greater if the monk is virtuous. Often lay devotees rush to provide the needs of "ascetic" monks because of this. However, for purposes of merit making, any traditionally ordained monk will suffice; having access to a virtuous monk is just a bonus in the merit making investment. The only requirement is that the monk is properly ordained, his inner state being immaterial. It thus follows that, however useful the monk is for satisfying the lay greed for merit, or perhaps *because* the monk does that, the laity's true interest in the monk is narrowly defined. Hence the space within which the monk is accorded respect is delimited. Outside that space, the monk can be the butt of ridicule, or at least an irrelevance. Overt respect is accorded to the monk at all times, but covert critique is never far away.

The critique of the monks is not an exclusively modern phenomenon. An entire folklore satirizes monks' failings and foibles. This satiric lore can be partly explained as the expression of a peasantry's rebellion against an elite, commonly featured in the ethnographic literature. In this folklore, monks are mocked in a good-humored way on subjects such as their indulgences and their relative inexperience of the mundane world.[2] This is a folk critique

---

2. For example, in the story where a layman offers a monk a drink, the following ensues: Layman: Will you have some tea? Monk: No, thank you. — Layman: Will you have some coffee? Monk: No. — Layman: Will you have some orange juice? Monk: No. — Layman: Will you have some scotch and soda? Monk: Not the soda.

that is stylized and lacking in specificity. Our concern here is not this but rather a more focused and rational critique that arises from perceptions of the monks' failure to live up to the expectations of moral rectitude and their transgressions of the boundary within which the laity expects them to live.

"TOOLS OF POLITICIANS AND STAGE PROPS"
The Laity's Critique

One of the most frequent criticisms made about the monks is their support of politicians, especially those in power. This is often expressed in accusations that monks are "the tools of politicians" *(desapalana atakolu)* who act as "stage props" *(vedika sarasili)* for them. This constitutes an inevitable development of the critique, going back to the controversy of the mid 1940s, about monks dabbling in politics. This criticism is leveled at the older generation of the monks in general and the hierarchical chief monks in particular; it is part of the general critique articulated by both the laity and the young monks. The behavior that is criticized includes appearing on the stage with politicians, blessing politicians, and participating in activities sponsored by a political party (usually the ruling one) or the state. For example, for the monks to support the ethnic war, in the eyes of these critics, is not only something inherently unacceptable but also an act of stooging for the government. For example, Timbiriyagama Bandara makes a particularly biting criticism of the monks who support the war:

> The place is an army bunker in Jaffna. A miracle indeed. Amidst weapons of war and soldiers is a monk inquisitively peering into a Tiger bunker with the aid of binoculars. He is our chief monk, the Venerable Rambukvalle Vipassi. Why did he go there? Was it to extinguish the flames of hatred like the Buddha did with the waters of compassion when he appeared at the battle between the Sakyas and the Koliyas? Was it to save, by performing a miracle, the helpless Sinhala and Tamil poor from being reduced to ashes by the bullet and the cannon ball? No. No. In the venerable monk's own words, to see the battlefield with his own eyes, to bless the army so that the war would be fought well. This is indeed a miracle. . . .
>
> The attitude of some of the monks to the war in the north is an expression of both their alienation from the social dialogue of this country and the resulting Sangha decadence.
>
> The primary reason for the revolt of the youth of both the north and south is the economic crisis. That the armed struggle in the north has been forced in the direction of a mistaken extreme due to Indian support is a different question. But to bless the effort to launch the extermination of the

Tamils . . . is unbecoming of a Buddhist monk. In this Buddhist country, where the life of the fallen opponent was spared, war was never so callous as to kill and burn not just the opponent but his wife and children, kinsmen and fellow villagers. And when the idea of a political solution is suggested to replace this slaughter, the chief monks who oppose it are more numerous than the bearers of arms.

According to the Venerable Elle Gunavamsa, who writes war songs, the shortest cut to Nirvana is to go north and kill people.[3]

Virasekara Liyanage, Joint Secretary of the Temperance Society, has also criticized the monks for their role in politics.[4] The following is a summary, but it is close to the vocabulary and spirit of the original:

> The defense that the Sangha declines because society declines is not acceptable. If society is in decline, the first responsibility is the Sangha's, because they did not do their job as guardian deities of the nation. Monks have lost esteem by their willing subordination to politicians: the Sangha should involve themselves in politics but not in partisan politics. Greed for profit causes this decline in the Sangha. All but a handful of monks are maximizing profit, from the state or from wealthy people. They are trying to gain land and other forms of wealth, luxury goods, and titles and honors. The hierarchical chiefs do nothing to stop monks from fulfilling narrow ambitions of politicians. They must provide opportunities for young monks who have correctly understood the role and responsibility of the monk. The hierarchical chiefs did not even bother to ask how many young monks were killed in the recent [late 1980s] terror. Young monks are so disheartened about this that in the last analysis non-Buddhist organizations gain. Monks are seeking privileges not only here but overseas. Many of these have signed the contract of establishing Japanese Buddhism here. The Sangha must understand that it is natural for capitalist governments to try to use the religion of the majority to gain their private ends.
>
> Nobody is threatening or wielding physical force on the Sangha. Influence on the Sangha is wielded through the bribe of privileges. If the Sangha refused to accept these privileges and sided with the people, it would not be possible to bring pressure on the autonomy and the nobility of the Sangha. Even in the case of physical threat to the Sangha members, it is they themselves who must be held responsible. If the majority of the Sangha are bought over by privileges, the monks who try to go against that and protect the people are under attack.

3. Timbiriyagama Bandara, "Sangha samajaye khedavacakaya" (The tragedy of the Sangha society), *Ravaya,* 9 February 1992.

4. Virasekara Liyanage, "Desapalanayata avadanna agamat pavadila," *Divayina,* 2 June 1991.

Virasekara Liyanage, though critical of the Sangha, is a traditionalist in his acceptance of the propagandistic conception of the Sangha as "guardian deities of the nation." He takes this literally and, as logically appropriate, places the blame on the Sangha for not doing their job properly. He claims, as many do and with some justification, that the decline of the Sangha is the result of their willing subordination to politicians. Regarding politics, the writer's position is that the monk should not be partisan, in contrast to what political monks desire. He points out that the Sangha's acceptance of large sums of foreign money, for which they are not accountable, has enabled them to free themselves from traditional bonds. The writer focuses attention on the luxury of the monks, reminding us of the "sensuousness" into which Dharmapala feared they would precipitate themselves. The irresponsibility of the hierarchical and other elderly monks in not showing concern for young monks who were abused by the police is mentioned, expressing also the middle-class Buddhist fear that these young monks are sitting ducks for conversion by evangelical groups, mistakenly referred to as the Catholic Church, much to the church's consternation. The majority of these hierarchical or other prominent monks are willing to tow the government line in exchange for profit and privilege, which causes physical threat to those monks who refuse to do so. The physical force exerted on the Sangha refers to the threats of J. R. Jayawardene and R. Premadasa, who tried to "bring monks in line" and threatened or attacked those who resisted.

That the Sangha chiefs become stooges or lackeys of politicians is a common critique, and we should ask why? One answer to this is the public adulation hierarchical monks express towards political leaders. A good illustration is a Sunday newspaper article by Talalle Dhammananda, which is no less than a panegyric.[5] In this Talalle praises President Premadasa for establishing

---

5. Talalle Dhammananda, "Ratata dayata sasunata kapavena ape janapati" (Our President dedicated to Country, Nation and Religion), *Silumina,* 23 June 1991.

The "stooging for politicians" syndrome is illustrated in the *Dinamina* of 15 September 1991, where the chief monks Rambukvalle Vipassi, Palipane Chandananda, Baddegama Vimalavamsa, Talalle Dhammananda, Madihe Pannasiha, Kamburupitiye Vanaratana, and Pottevela Pannavasa, along with about twenty-five other prominent monks, wrote letters supporting the then President Premadasa, a man widely considered to be a ruthless dictator. Their tone can be gauged from some of the titles of their contributions: *Kapavima vismaya janakayi* (His commitment is astonishing); *Editara nayakatvayak* (Brave leadership); *Samaya uda kala* (He brought peace); *Prasasta sevayak* (A distinguished service); *Akul helima varadiyi* (It's wrong to oppose him); and *Bhedayen torava sahaya demu* (Let's unite and support him). The *Dinamina* is a state-controlled newspaper. It is this kind of statement, which the chief monks issue willingly but uncritically or do so under pressure, that brings them the epithets "yes men," "stooges," and "stage props" for politicians. A further illustration of "stooging politicians" is in the *Dinamina* of 24 Sept. 1991, which published a page of letters from monks praising Premadasa. These are: Muruttetuvwe Ananda, *Honda karana udaviyata udav karanna biya viya yutu na* (We shouldn't be afraid to support

a Ministry of Buddha Sasana and for governing democratically. It is an auspicious sign, says the monk, that the president arrives at decisions such as the one to turn disadvantage into advantage by recognizing all religions, nationalities and political parties. He follows democracy to the letter and consults the Sangha, his ministers, and representatives of the people in these decisions. The president is committed to protecting the religion and to the fivefold improvements: eradication of poverty, protecting the future generation, protecting and enriching the future monk generation, bringing about unity between all nationalities and all religions, and bringing about unity among all political parties. Nearly calling the president "king," Talalle writes that "there is no king who built so many stupas as the president," and he makes a list of these: the Dutugamunu maha saya at the Gam Udawa site at Ambilipitiya in 1985, the D. S. Senanayake maha saya at Hingurakgoda in 1986, the Kataragama Vihara Maha Devi saya in 1987, the Kavantissa maha saya at Anamaduva in 1988, the Sri Mahabodhi maha saya at Mahiyangana in 1989, the Deveni Patis maha saya at Pallekake in 1990, and the Anagarika Dharmapala maha saya at Kamburupitiya in 1991. People, writes Talalle, must contemplate on what a fine example the president is setting to the future generations, by building these great stupas. (All these stupas are fake and, like Premadasa's lavish Gam Udava celebrations, a colossal waste of public funds.)

The article is full of superlatives that metaphorically confer on the president the glory of an ancient great paternalistic king. In view of Premadasa's assassination by a suicide bomber, it is ironic that, in his discussion of the president's practice of democracy, Talalle quotes the Pali saying *Dhammo bhave rakkhati dhammacari* (the Dhamma protects the person who acts according to the Dhamma).

Monks are also criticized for their involvement in rituals that are considered not in keeping with Buddhism. In the article discussed above, Timbiriyagama Bandara quotes an eighteenth-century predecessor, Munkotuve Rala, the author of the *Sangarajavata,* the poetic work on the reformer Valivita Saranankara:

> Not keeping to the dhamma
> Corrupting the laity

---

people who do good); Galaboda Gnanissara, *Janata duka sapa soyabalamin bauddha prabodhayata kriya kala* (He brought about a Buddhist renaissance while helping the people); Vattegama Jinaratana, *Uve maha sangaruvana beragatte premadasa janapatitumayi* (It is President Premadasa who saved the great Sangha jewel of the Uva province); Elle Gunavamsa, *Jatiyata tarjanayak ena hamavitama sangaruvana peramune* (Every time the nation is threatened the Sangha jewel is in the forefront); and Girambe Ananda, *Mata itihasaye sangaruvana araksakala ekama nayakaya janapatiyi* (The only president in recent history who protected the Sangha jewel).

Not learning the renowned doctrine
Practicing astrology and medicine

By these, winning the minds of men
Accumulating wealth
Supporting wife, children
This is the only morality they keep.[6]

Bandara goes on to say: "What we have today are not just exorcisers, but vendors of exorcism. Today there are numerous shrines of the major deities, and subsidiary shrines with signs proclaiming the days and times they [the 'exorcist monks'] can be met. It is like meeting a medical specialist. These shrines are inside [Buddhist] monasteries, or by their side. Thanks to the stupid business community of Colombo and elsewhere, the exorciser monks *(kattadi bhiksun)* and deity priests *(kapu mahatturu)* have been able to make this into a giant business. The latest deity to be led into the Buddhist temple is Sai Baba.[7] In Buddhist temples it has become a fashion to make images of Sai Baba, and wash the ugly dirt of a misbehaving magician." The writer takes to task the prominent monk Talalle Dhammananda for associating himself with the celebration of Sai Baba's birthday. Talalle's name was printed in the invitations as the special speaker at the celebrations held at a Mt. Lavinia monastery. The writer continues, "In this *dhammadipa,* there are false monks *(sranama pratirupa)* who are stupid enough to consider a fraud like Sai Baba to be a religious leader and his magic to be miracles."

"TRI-NIKAYIST ROBE-WEARERS"
The Vinayavardhana Movement's Critique

Striking among the critiques of the monkhood is that of the Vinayavardhana, a movement that came into being in the 1940s that advocated a strict return to vinaya, the code of monastic discipline. Essentially a critique of laxness,

---

6. *daham lesa no hasira — kuladusanaya kara kara*

bana no igena pavara — nakat vedakam purudu kara kara

eyin lova sit gena — vastuva upadavagena

ambu daruvan rakina — pamanamayi un rakina sil guna

These verses refer to the monks in a period of "decline," the eighteenth century, but most of it is commonly, though jokingly, mentioned in today's critique, as the rest of what this writer has to say shows.

7. Sai Baba is one of the most adored "god-men" of contemporary India. One expression of his "divinity" is the production of objects such as jewelry and wristwatches from thin air. For accounts, see Lawrence Babb, *Redemptive Encounters* (Delhi: Oxford University Press, 1987) and Lise McKean, *Divine Enterprise,* 21–23.

it is only an extreme form of the common critique, and it emerges as a
powerful denial of the claim by the Vidyalankara monks that monks should
change according to time and place. Its strident tone exceeds the tone that
characterized the spoken and written words of Dharmapala, although it is
clear that the roots of the movement are in the work of the reformer. It
parallels the development of a contemporaneous movement to go into forest
hermitages such as Salgala and Kudumbigala for the determined pursuit of
liberation.[8] As does Henpitagedera Gnanavasa's work, *What is the Heritage of
the Bhikku?*, the Vinayavardhana movement challenges the conception of the
monastic vocation as advocated by the Vidyalankara monks. The present account is based on Tambugala Ananda's *Dharmavinayalokaya* (The Light of the
Doctrine and Discipline), a work by a monk of the Vinayavardhana movement.[9] The introduction to the work, written by A. Sumanaratne, Secretary
of the United Vinayavardhana Federation *(Sri Lanka Vinayavardhana Ekabaddha
Sangamaya)*, sets the tone for the critique by emphasizing that, of the fourfold
division of the discipleship, although the monks are preeminent, the first
disciples were laymen,[10] and he goes on to point out the contribution to the
Sasana made by the lay disciples, including the "expulsion of the non-
virtuous *(dussila)*, heretical *(Vajji)* monks" and the facilitation of the Councils
(sangayana). The lay disciples, the writer claims, have never done anything
to cause the decline of the Sasana. The decline was brought about by monks
who divided themselves into three sects (nikaya), involved themselves in
politics, and sought wealth, fame, comfort and indulgence: "This great *vajjian* obstacle should be removed, like a piece of dirt in the eye, a thorn in
the foot, a poisonous snake in a house, an epidemic that has embraced a
country."[11]

The main thrust in the body of the text is the same as in the Preface, that
the mainstream monks, referred to here derogatorily as "monks of the three
nikayas" or "vajjis," have no monkness because of their acceptance of luxury
and sensuous living. Monkness, according to Tambugala, is simply not something that can be practiced by living in palatial houses (i.e., monasteries) in
towns and cities, and by becoming owners of property and money.[12]

8. For the best account of these see Michael Carrithers, *The Forest Monks of Sri Lanka.*

9. Tambugala Ananda, *Dharmavinayalokaya* (The Light of the Doctrine and Discipline) (Maradana:
Oriental Press. 1958). Parenthetical page references in this section are to this work.

10. This reference is to Tapassu and Bhallukka, the first, according to tradition, to take refuge in
the Buddha and the Dhamma, the Sangha being nonexistent.

11. A. Sumanaratne, introduction to Tambugala Ananda, *Dharmavinayalokaya,* vi.

12. This contrasts with the Vidyalankara view, best expressed by Yakkaduve, that monks can live
in luxury without violating morality.

Further, writes Tambugala, these monks venerate books that should be despised (17). The example is the *Mahavamsa,* which is most interesting, because of the prominence it enjoys in traditional Sinhala Buddhism, not to mention its central place in the recent colonial-aided representation of the ancient glory of Sri Lanka. The author not only challenges but also ridicules the *Mahavamsa.* The point of departure of the critique is the Buddha's visits to the island as recounted in the *Mahavamsa.* The author of the *Mahavamsa,* normally mentioned with some degree of respect if not awe, is referred as a "robed man by the name Mahanama," and the work is derided as based on "merit books" that are partial fabrications written by panegyrists who pandered to kings and prime ministers to earn favors from them (16). The Buddha did not use even a single flame to tame the demon Alavaka and the fierce murderer Angulimala, but the *Mahavamsa* stories depict him as miraculously producing fires and as conquering the Yakkha inhabitants by cheating. Such books belong to the category of despicable *(garhita)* sutras (16). The mainstream monks who treat these books as venerable sutras are not Theravadins.

"Looked at from the point of view of dharma vinaya," Tambugala writes, "the robe-wearers of the tri-nikayas who live the hypocritical lives discussed above, who live with obstacles to liberation, and who live in pomposity and pride bearing titles like nayaka, anunayaka, and mahanayaka according to nikayas, and like pandita, rajakiya pandita, and aggamaha pandita" (91) do not belong to the Theravada genealogy and have no ordination in it.[13] In another echo of Dharmapala, Tambugala also criticizes the monks for establishing pirivenas, which he considers similar to land ownership. Pirivenas are a luxury and indicate secularization. Monks get oriental degrees and become pirivena administrators (103).

The Vinayavardhana are particularly critical of those who argue for lax behavior because the Buddha allowed the revision of minor rules. The preeminent exponents of this theory that rules can be broken are the Vidyalankara monks, especially Rahula and Yakkaduve, who claimed that the need of monkness is simply not to break the four parajika (defeative) rules. Here this position is explicitly attacked.

Tambugala quotes the *Jinna sutra,* where the Buddha asks the elderly Kasyapa to stay near him because observing the *pamsukulikangas* and the *pindapatikangas* is difficult for an aging man. Kasyapa said that he likes those and got the Buddha's permission to practice those *dhutangas* (111). This is an answer to Rahula, who tries to prove the opposite case. In his attempt to glorify village dwelling and therefore laxness, Rahula gives examples of

---

13. This is Dharmapala's critique almost verbatim.

aging monks opting for these practices because, according to him, these were easier.[14] Here the clear implication is that observing dhutangas was the more difficult. In sum, the Vinayavardhana is here attacking the Rahulite/ Vidyalankara idea that able monks take to *gramavasa* (politics) and that it is only the aged, the less talented, and the feeble who take to meditation, the path to liberation.

YOUNG MONKS' CRITIQUE (1)

"Is it possible that such illiterate monks exist?"

The critique of the Sangha by young monks is epitomized in a critique of Madihe Pannasiha, one of the best-known monks of Sri Lanka today. The nature of the ridicule to which he is sometimes subjected by young monks is a measure of the breakdown of the old order in general and of the traditional relations between senior and junior monks, and it serves to underline the generational crisis in the monkhood. It is an indication of the rise of an unprecedented monastic individualism. Young monks are not his only critics. He is also criticized by the laity, especially the educated young.

Carefully identifying himself only as a "pirivena student monk" but identifiably a young monk, this writer reviews some economic proposals that Madihe had recently proposed.[15] The opening itself is indicative of the absence in the writer of any desire to veil his derision. "When we look at the proposals made to the government by the venerable Mahanayaka," says the writer, "what we feel is embarrassment and a sadness that non-Buddhist clerics will think 'Is it possible that such illiterate monks exist?'" He ridicules the proposals one by one. Madihe had suggested lowering the price of some consumer items and raising the price of others. The writer's response to this is that if the price of eight items is to be lowered, the price of the remaining 990 items can justly be raised. This is a proposal, says the writer, that will

14. Rahula, *The Heritage,* 30; *The History,* 160. Rahula grants that the distinction between the vocation of the books and the vocation of meditation is noncanonical, and the view that the Commentaries express that the vocation of the books is superior is "not in keeping with the original idea . . . that a person of realization even though he has only a little learning is superior to one who has great learning but no realization" (*The History,* 159). It is revealing of the Theravada hegemonism and intolerance of dissent that Rahula, referring the first-century B.C.E. "victory" of the book-vocation monks *(dhammakathika)* over the meditation-vocation monks *(pamsukulika)* says: "Ultimately it was decided that learning was the basis of the Sasana, and not practice. The pamsukulikas were silenced, and the dhammakthikas were victorious" (*The History,* 158).

15. See *Silumina* of 28 October 1990, *Maha na himi sanduni, me yojana ka sandahada?* (For whom are these proposals O your lordship the Mahanayaka?)

eliminate even the meager dana (alms) that young monks at present get. Referring to Madihe's proposal that air-conditioned buses be made available to those who can afford to use them, the writer retorts that the rich do not travel by bus not because they are crowded or because the buses are not air conditioned, but because the private car is an expression of their life style. That difference, says the writer, is found among the monks as well. Monks like him (the writer) travel herded in buses and the chief monks travel by luxury car, either gifted by the government or obtained in other (unethical) ways. The class differences found in the lay society, says the writer, are also present in the society of monks.

"The venerable Mahanayaka has made proposals like this before, and brought ridicule to the Sangha," continues the writer. He cites Madihe's proposal to end terrorism by clearing the entire jungle stretching north from Vavuniya and settling people there. "It was the venerable chief monk's idea that, when this is done, terrorism will cease." Further, says the writer, the Mahanayaka has said that settling people in the newly cleared areas should be proportional to ethnic composition. When do we begin bulldozing the jungles in the south, because there is terrorism there too? asks the writer, and are buildings to be leveled too, or all streets closed because sometimes there are urban guerrillas? "We would like to say that by making these proposals, the Mahanayaka is bringing disgrace to the sasana. . . . It is said that the Mahanayaka is also opposed to family planning, apparently because, with the decline in births, the Sinhala nation will get smaller. We do not wish to discuss this subject, because if we do, we will be compelled to say things unworthy of the robe we are wearing. This is indirectly asking the Sinhalese to produce more babies so that they could continue to be the majority. Does this not increase the family burden and cause further decline in the standard of living? The Mahanayaka puts on his shoulder problems that are not his, and causes laughter in the adherents of other religions, and that is an embarrassment to us."

YOUNG MONKS' CRITIQUE (2)
Ko. Ananda's Parable of Ideal Monkhood

Ko. Ananda, a monk who graduated from Vidyalankara in the late 1960s, published in 1978 a novel entitled *He Siddhartha nam veyi* (His name is Siddhartha).[16] This is a literary work that merits acclaim, but our interest is in

---

16. Ko. Ananda, *He Siddhartha nam veyi* (Colombo: Gunasena, 1978).

its reflection of the contemporary public discussion about the Sangha. The overall sociological significance of the work is as a document that represents the nature and role of the modern monk. The work depicts two monastic worlds, the world of the minimally literate traditional monk involved with the ritualism of his village flock, and that of the modern monk, a generation younger, whose outlook on society and existence is far broader. Though he receives some pirivena education and is adequately trained to perform traditional ministerial functions, the modern monk is a university graduate who has read modern secular subjects, thus combining virtue and traditional knowledge with training in modern secular knowledge. The younger monk, who is the hero of the novel, is an ideal representation of the modern monk envisaged in *The Heritage,* and his mission is not traditional religious work but "social service."

From the beginning the novel shows indications of an idealized content and characters—an ideal chief monk, pupil, and supporters. The chief monk is broadly the traditional monk of *The Heritage,* rustic, uneducated, and ritual bound; but he shows interest in the mundane welfare of the villagers, as if in anticipation of the flowering of this disposition in his pupil, a gifted and extremely honest youth motivated to excel in his work. In keeping with the allegoric nature of the novel, the young novice is named Siddhartha, which is the Buddha's lay name, and which the chief monk elucidates by using the ornate and conventional definitional formula *siddha vu artha atte yamek da he Siddhartha nam veyi* (he who is of realized benevolence, that person in Siddhartha). At his *pabbajja* (lower ordination), the chief monk chants a Pali verse: "making the Sasana shine, and society shine, being obedient to your teachers, learn well the doctrine and practices of the monk" (4). "Making society shine" is an unorthodox admonition, but it brings out the key message of the work: "the role of the monk is not ritual but social service."

The chief monk's own ideal status is exemplified in another way, namely, as a father to the pupil, a metaphor for the teacher-pupil relation common to the Indian tradition in general. He makes only the correct decisions, which contrast with the wrong ones routinely made by teacher monks in the real world of Buddhist Sri Lanka today by denying their pupils the two indispensable ingredients of nurture—support and discipline. Support consists of seeing to all the pupil's needs, including a good education and emotional and financial support at all times. The monks today are generally accused of dispatching their pupils to a pirivena the day after their lower ordination and of failing to support them. This is magnified in the case of young monks who go to the university and need greater financial support. Since food, clothing, shelter, and medication are ideally provided by the laity, though in reality this is far from assured, a monk must substantially support his pupil's education, first at a pirivena and later at the university. This, the chief monk of our text provides unfailingly and with the ideally prescribed paternal care and affection, despite great hardship. He enlists the support of a generous school teacher, who is impressed by the young monk's talent and social awareness. First the young monk is sent to a distant pirivena and later to the university, both costly by village standards. Though he endures some deprivation, the ideal of the teacher's loving paternal support is maintained throughout. For example, when the young monk makes his first visit to Colombo while still a young boy, the teacher notices him gazing at a toy train in a shop window and promptly buys it for him; and later, when, as an idealistic youth working on flood relief, he is taken ill with malaria, the agitated teacher arranges with care and concern the necessary medical attention, going to the extent of screaming at him as a father would for neglecting to take his medicine as prescribed.

What the chief monk refuses to do is as significant as what he does, which takes us to the second ingredient of nurture, discipline. When the supportive village schoolteacher suggests that the young novice should be sent to a pirivena as he has already spent two years in the monastery, the chief monk refuses. The novice should be given more knowledge, says the chief monk, about rituals and texts *(vat pilivet, bana daham)* before he is sent out. The novelist's emphasis here is on the importance of the traditional ideal, known as *nissaya,* that a young monk should spend an adequate length of time with the teacher, until he acquires the solid knowledge, background, experience, and strength necessary to launch himself successfully on the path of virtue and disciplinary accomplishment. All too often, young monks are "admitted [to the Order] today and dispatched to a pirivena tomorrow," as informants often put it, which is a commonly held reason for what is perceived as the contemporary decline of the Sangha.

During this period the young novice not only learns the basic texts known as *bana daham pot* but often also a wider circle of texts as well as the skills and knowledge needed to minister to the laity, such as ritually accepting offerings and preaching. The rituals of the Sangha, such as the observances of vassa and uposatha, and the daily *vata pirit* are also learnt by the novice during this period. In addition, he does all the daily chores, mundane and sacred, of the monastery, not the least of which is to treat the teacher with respect and kindness and see to his needs. Thus, by vetoing the school teacher's suggestion to send the young monk away and by refusing to cut short his personal supervision and his primary role in the socialization of his pupil, the chief monk is dispensing his teacher-father's role with conscience and responsibility. The imparting of ritual and textual knowledge is inextricably bound with discipline or the molding of the raw novice into a full-fledged monk, referred to as the "making" of pupils, meaning "molding" or "socialization." The teacher takes charge of the physical, intellectual, and moral welfare of the pupil, a total responsibility reminiscent of that ideally shouldered by the teacher's "House" *(ghriha, gharana)* in India,[17] and by the medieval European residential university.

The hero of the novel, the young monk, to begin with, has the innate qualities of good nature, intelligence, and a love of the monastic life. He recalls the fascination with which, as a little boy, he first saw a procession of yellow-robed monks, including a very young novice walking in measured steps across the fields (4). Often monk-informants speak of an aesthetic attraction to the monk's way of life as the reason for their entering the monkhood. As a young boy, the prospective monk is obedient to his elders and after his pabbajja he transfers his obedience fully to his teacher. In the monastery he quickly learns his chores and uncomplainingly takes to the rigorous routine that constitutes the making of a monk. He studies with seriousness and determination and when he is sent to the pirivena he adjusts easily to the new life, makes new friends, and becomes an avid reader, taking seriously the sign put up in the library, "Reading maketh a full man." He becomes an exemplary student who endears himself to his supervisors at the pirivena. The same pattern of obedience, discipline, hard work, and intelligent application is repeated at the university level, which as before is crowned with success. As he goes through the pirivena and the university, minor conflicts with the teacher are suggested, but these only enhance contrapuntally the idealized father-son relation rather than detract from it.

This pattern of idealized relations is repeated with the supporting cast of villagers, friends, and fellow monks. The influence of *The Heritage* is obvious in the climax of the story, when the young monk, now a graduate, chooses to work as a teacher in an impoverished village in Bibile, one of the harsh geographical and climatological regions of the island, in preference to a comfortable job in his former pirivena located in the relatively more prosperous and salubrious town of Horana. Here the monk is moved by the poverty that surrounds him, about which we learn from his letter to a fellow university student, whom he persuades to renounce his salaried job and return to the village to devote all his energies to social service, enlisting in it the support of the local youth.

17. This tradition is still continued in some areas such as music and dancing. See Ravi Shankar, *My Music, My Life* (New Dehli: Vikas, 1969).

Thus, selfless service to others is the abiding interest and dedication of the monk. While the reader is given every indication that the young monk is trained in the traditional ministry of the rural monk—for example, we are repeatedly told of his learning vata pirit and bana daham, the standard fare needed to minister to the laity—we hear nothing whatsoever about practicing any of it, except when the monk was still an *antevasika* (residential pupil) of his teacher, prior to his departure for studies. This enhances the theme of social service because what comes through here is that, during his early novitiate, the young monk is an appendage, a mere shadow of his teacher, devoid of a personality of his own. While the teacher is depicted as a good monk, he comes through unambiguously as the illiterate, rustic, ritual bound, somnolent, rural monk stigmatized in *The Heritage*. When the young monk departs the monastery for studies, he also leaves his traditional tutelage and is symbolically reborn as a new and autonomous person who is no longer the shadow of the traditional monk, but who now can embody the new calling of social service. Since traditional monkhood can constitute virtue, and does in this case, the episode encapsulates another of *The Heritage*'s qualifications for monkhood devoted to social service, namely, the need for such a monk to be perfect in virtue, as a precondition to going out on the mission of social service.

In its radical critique of the monkhood, the novel goes beyond *The Heritage*. This critique is implicit in *The Heritage*, but it becomes clearly manifest and vocal only in the work of younger writers. In the novel under consideration, there are two noteworthy occasions in which the author seizes the opportunity to mock and ridicule the tradition-bound Sangha. The first is the *upasampada* (higher ordination) of the young monk. Although he shows little interest in the ritual itself, he is concerned with its inner meaning, which reminds us again of *The Heritage*'s requirement that the monk who goes into social service must, to begin with, be spiritually exemplary. Spirituality is the caterpillar that is going to be the butterfly of social service. The cover of the book expresses this idea in quite different images, a serene figure of a monk in the gesture of expounding the dhamma *(dhammacakka mudra)*, representing spiritual achievement, and a raised fist in the background connoting activism.

The narrative concerning the monk's upasampada opens with a dream. The young monk, in the thick of his studies for his pirivena final examination and in a state of resulting anxiety, receives a letter from his teacher summoning him for his upasampada. The young monk is ambivalent. He does not want to displease his teacher, and he also knows the teacher too well to even try to bargain with him. But he has his examinations, and as a modern monk trained in modern secular knowledge who has assimilated the skepticism and radical activism characteristic of the university, and also as the budding embodiment of the ideal monk of *The Heritage,* he is opposed to traditional ritualism, which ordination is.

To him ordination is not a priority. He is in a dilemma and cannot sleep. When he does snatch some sleep in the wee hours of the morning, he dreams "a great many diverse dreams, like the sixteen dreams of King Kosala" (99). Unlike the king, however, he does not remember any but one, and that, faintly. Five hundred cartloads of goods are unloaded and are stacked up like a mountain in the center of the city. Suddenly, a large number of persons wearing "yellow robe-like garments" make a great commotion. Large crowds of people noisily witness the scene. Gradually, the crowd in yellow becomes quarrelsome. They scramble to grab the various items of goods from the heap. Thousands of crows fly about and caw in a surreal sky, and attack each other. The heap is now garbage that belongs to the crows, and they attack the crowd in yellow, pecking on their heads. The yellow garbed crowd run amok and fall into the lake nearby. They stretch their hands out to be rescued from drowning. The onlookers make a deafening applause.

The meaning of the dream is straightforward. It is a condemnation of the traditional practice of the hierarchy of senior monks, especially of the Siyam Nikaya of Malvatta and Asgiriya, of receiving gifts from candidates who must go to these centers for ordination. The center of the city represents the ordination center, and the one appropriate to our text is Malvatta, located beside Kandy lake. In the dream, the lake doubles as a *Naraka* hell, in which the greedy are reborn, a meaning suggested by the figures driven into the lake, crying for help with hands outstretched to be rescued. The heap of goods is also a heap of garbage, the true owners of which are the scavenging crows. The greedy monks are thus associationally identified with scavengers. Further, crows evoke the traditional sanction against stealing, that those who do will be reborn as dogs and crows. The monks who accept goods for themselves are appropriating common Sangha property for themselves. The crows attack the heads of the individuals in yellow. This is the characteristic mode of attack of the crow, but more than that, in rural Sinhala thought, to be subject to such an attack by so unendearing an enemy is not a compliment. Pecking on the head evokes another idea, the light-hearted view of the villager that the hairless head is the part of the anatomy best suited to receive a gentle knock *(tokka)* of disapproval. The dark and fierce crows are also a subconscious multiplication of the *yama rajjuruvo,* the Sinhala folk variation of the Yama, the Sanskritic king of the netherworld. They send the greedy yellow-clad individuals fleeing to hell, represented by the lake. Thus,

the young monk's innermost self, as revealed in the dream as a whole, perceives monastic traditionalism, especially the greed for material goods, with
disgust, fear, and unequivocal scorn.

This dream is followed by a wakeful critique of the preoccupation of
monks with material goods, especially foodstuffs in the ordination ceremony. The chief monk is anxiously sending out lay supporters to buy foodstuffs: sackfuls of rice; a bundle of good dried fish; and quantities of potatoes,
dal (lentil), onion, red onion, chili, dried sprats, pumpkin, beans, and cab-
bage; five bunches of plantains to be artificially ripened. A village youth, a
friend of the young monk, jokingly asks him, "shall we open a grocery store?"
(101). And a donor states, "We need a truck to carry these" (101).

The form of the ritual itself, which is textually based, is blasphemously
questioned, a striking contrast to the awed respect that traditional monks
show to the texts.[18] The text describes how some female village devotees
ask the junior monk questions that are difficult to answer, largely because of
the intellectual gap between them and the intricacies of the doctrine. The
questions asked at upasampada are simple when compared to the questions
of illiterate village women, which leads the hero to ponder:

> The questions of the *upasakammas* (village female devotees) are complex, but
> one could easily get by with a simple yes or no to the questions asked [of the
> novice] at upasampada.
>
> The junior monk thought that in a way it is not too bad. People will start
> speculating if these questions are asked in Sinhala [i.e., they are asked in Pali,
> which people do not understand]. Do you have any skin diseases? Boils?
> Sores? Asthma? Epilepsy? If these are asked in Sinhala not only the candidate,
> but also his parents, kin, and friends, all these people, will want to hide in
> shame. Not even a doctor will ask all these questions [in a single consulta-
> tion]. On the other hand, don't people get sick? (102)

The reference here is to the canonical *Mahavagga* account of how to ordain
monks. Since the *Mahavagga* is not only canonical but is also considered one
of the earliest and most authentic of the Buddhist texts, the mere fact of
poking fun at it is remarkable, and it constitutes a commentary on the extent
of detraditionalization among this stratum of the Sangha. It is not likely that
the character to whom the novelist attributes these derisive words is un-

18. For example, Henpitagedara Gnanasiha and Henpitagedara Gnanavasa, who "are compelled to
refer to with respectful fear" to what their analytical acumen tells them is a scriptural contradiction: *me
parasparavirodhi bava . . . gavravasamprayukta bhayakin yuktava . . . sandahan kala yutuva ata.* Henpitagedara
Gnanasiha and Henpitagedara Gnanavasa, *Khandaka Vinaya* (Colombo: Ratna Publishers, 1966), 246.

aware of their meaning and significance. It is rather a deliberate attempt to exhibit radical skepticism as something that a modern monk can legitimately and appropriately hold, especially when he is armed with the moral worth of serving society. Thus:

> The other question, the junior monk thought, is one up on this. Are you human? Are you male? Supposing someone who belongs to neither of these categories is a novice, what harm if he is given upasampada?
>
> What will they do if you become a *napumsaka* (hermaphrodite) after you are admitted to the order? One could say the people who do these things (i.e., ritualize ordination) are napumsakas.

The hero is next made to question the relevance of the labored interrogation:

> Aren't there questions to ask that are more appropriately for today? Does your teacher give you any support? Do you treat your teacher well? Do you have money for your education? Do you have robes to wear? Do you live in a great royal monastery, a great monastery, or just a monastery? If you live in just a monastery, you probably have problems getting food. If you live in a great royal monastery, is it not the case that you have endless resources of gold, silver, precious stones, estates, fiefdoms, and so forth? Is it a very nice thing to enjoy them yourself? Isn't it better that you distribute some of that among the poor? Or even after the ordination, isn't it a good idea to loose some fat, along those lines? Does you teacher disapprove of things like that? Do you? Even if both of you do not approve of it, isn't somebody going to forcibly appropriate it one fine day?
>
> If they are serious, these are the questions they should ask, the junior monk thought. But how can they ask them? If they do, they will be the first to get caught, he thought.

These questions continue the critique of the status quo. Monks mistreating their pupils and destroying their careers is allegedly very common. Although not in terms of economic support at the novitiate stage, pupils can also mistreat teachers. Some of the other questions above constitute a condemnation of the vast disparities of wealth that is a feature of traditional Sri Lankan monasticism, and represent an instance where the spirit of *The Heritage* is taken over and radically elaborated by a younger author. Some equitability in the distribution of monastic property hinted here is a theme that has been developed by many young monks. The critique in the following is explicit:

Then, the junior monk remembered things he overheard, one by one, at a previous upasampada ceremony.

"This question about are you human . . . it is the hierarchy, not the candidate who should answer that," said those monks. "Had they (the hierarchy) been human, would they scream at the poor monk, and his supporters, who came for yesterday's upasampada from so far away?"

"The best of all this is [taking novices around] for seeing (dakkavanta). It is a real dakkavima (drive). This can easily be done within the poya-ge (the ordination hall). After doing that mad thing, I returned home ordained—and sick. Imagine going sleepless for days, walking about in damp weather and kneeling in ninety-nine places. I went to the doctor at Warakapola on the way home."

The scene here is one in which the ordination candidate, brought to the central monastery at Asgiriya or Malvatta, is taken round, in the evening prior to ordination, to all the individual monasteries of the complex to "see" the hierarchical elders. In the precolonial society, "seeing" had feudal connotations, when a subordinate had to "see" the lord periodically, taking a gift, which was called dakum. The gift was the eye with which one "saw" the lord, which makes the gift more important than the person, but since the gift-giver has to be necessarily present to give the gift (i.e., "see"), the act of seeing was also a reaffirmation of the subordinate's fealties to the lord. What the candidates are made to do is the same "seeing." They carry a gift (dakum) and go round to each monastery to "see" the hierarchy of the monks. Each visit involves the candidate falling on his knees and worshipping at the elder's feet, after presenting the gift. Hence the reference to the candidate getting sick (a bad knee from too much kneeling). In the case described the newly ordained monk had to see the doctor on the way back to his monastery, and, the text tells us, later that the monk was too sore even to attend the reception given in his honor. The author is punning on dakima (seeing) and dakkima (driving, usually cattle), suggesting that the hapless candidate is led like a cow or a mule.

The pages that follow continue the critique. There is a reference to an ordination candidate who assaulted his teacher for not awarding him the title "the Naga of the court" at an upasampada ceremony.[19] Lavish upasampada ceremonies are compared to village weddings that end in bankruptcy for all parties concerned (105). Next, we are given a picture of traditional monasticism with its landlordism, litigation, teacher-pupil conflicts, struggles for

19. "Naga of the Court" (vahala naga) is a recognition awarded to the best candidate at ordination. See H. L. Seneviratne, "L'ordination bouddhiste à Ceylan," Social Compass 20, no. 2 (1973): 257–66.

incumbency, all gossiped about by monks assembled at the young monks' monastery on the night before his ordination. They chatter, drink tea, and smoke. At one level, there is in this scene the kind of rustic and chaotic merriment that is characteristic of a village festival. There is clowning and an air of comic caricature. But the underlying comment is inescapable. It is one that mocks the traditional rural, illiterate, ritual bound monk, the black sheep of *The Heritage*.

In a light-hearted understatement, one of the monks says, referring to lavish ordinations, that the Buddha would have said "Monks, that kind of ordination, I do not approve."[20] Considering the awe in which the Buddha is invariably held, this attitude is startling. The Buddha certainly is not mocked, but the Pali literary style is, which introduces an unfamiliar levity to the content, which parallels the parody of the textual questions discussed above.

So far we discussed one of the spaces in which the novelist's critique is expressed, namely the description of the upasampada. The next space for the criticism is the university on the occasion of the young monk's first week as a freshman. Undergraduate monks, like lay undergraduates, enjoy a great deal of freedom to flout tradition and convention and have taken to "ragging." Their rag, however, is colored by their monastic culture.

We are told that the rag consists, among other things, of mock ordinations (111), and the hero of the novel is asked by his seniors to deliver his maiden sermon *(magul bana)*. He is given a topic from the *Dhammapada*, but the syllables are mockingly and skillfully jumbled, eliciting roars of laughter from the onlookers. The young monk tries to recite the verse correctly but is shouted down and asked to chant it malsyllabically. The young monk says that is not how it is in the *Dhammapada*, to which a senior responds, in an obvious jibe at the status quo, "it is our regret too, that no body follows the Dhammapada." The young monk is then asked to quote from memory the textual elucidation of the Four Noble Truths. As he starts reciting the passage correctly, the seniors interrupt and ask him to repeat after them a jumbled version, which provokes laughter: "Monks, the Four Noble Truths are three. What two are they . . ." and so on (112). Like the gossiping and clowning of monks the night before the hero's upasampada, this has no direct bearing on our theme of the parallel between the novel and *The Heritage*, but the attitude of irreverence is of a magnitude that is unprecedented.

The next episode of the rag returns to the critique. Addressing the freshman, the seniors tell him:

---

20. This is the stereotyped wording that, in the vinaya literature, characterizes the Buddha's style of answering a question raised during an exigency. The Pali style of doing this is parodied here.

"We are going to mention the names of some well-known monks. All you need to do is tell whether you know them. *Saddharma bhayanaka paca vacana kirti kama mitthyacari Gorakana Ambulananda* [Dhamma terrorizing, sexually misbehaving, bunkum spouting Gorakane Ambulananda]. Do you know him or don't you?" (112)

The fictional name Gorakane Ambulananda is untranslatable but something of its flavor can be conveyed by saying that the first name refers to a very sour fruit and the second to the sour taste itself. The statement is a double critique. First, it is a scornful depiction of the widespread love of traditional monks for high sounding titles, even though these completely lack any substance. This is a temptation to which even scholar monks well known in the West have sometimes succumbed. Second, it depicts the traditional high-status monk as a dharma violating, lying, fornicating monster, adjectives widely believed to be accurately descriptive of some monks.[21]

YOUNG MONKS' CRITIQUE (3)
"To my teacher, with contempt and sympathy"

Another work of fiction critical of the Sangha is Bo. Nandissara's *Loku hamu-duruvan vetatayi* (To the Chief Monk). Like the author of *He Siddharta nam veyi* just discussed, Nandissara is a young monk and a university graduate exposed to modern secular knowledge. The work is a portrait of the typical chief monk (teacher-monk) or incumbent of the monastery on whom rests the responsibility of socializing the next generation of monks in morality, religious knowledge, and exemplary conduct. Like the work just discussed, *Loku hamuduruvan vetatyi* is a sardonic literary work that is reminiscent of the work of the renowned fifteenth-century monk-poet and critic of Hindu

---

21. "Sexual misbehavior" is one of the four major Vinaya offenses that "defeats" a monk and makes a "no-monk" *(assamano)* of the monk. Yet literary evidence is clear for its occurrence throughout history. It is also reflected in folklore, where it is often depicted with folksy good humor. Its treatment in "ancient Buddhism" and the "Protestant Buddhism" of today, however, is much more serious. Cases are reported periodically in the newspapers. A recent dramatic one is that of Ratmalane Siddharta of the Vadihitikanda monastery, who is alleged to have lured four sisters, aged 17, 15, 13, and 11, into the monastery and to have kept them in a secret chamber for a month, sexually abusing them, especially the two younger girls. It is reported that they were threatened at gunpoint and shown pornographic films as a guide to what was expected of them. The monk, incumbent of an ancient temple, is considered to command formidable magical powers, and leading politicians, including past presidents J. R. Jayawardene and R. Premadasa, are reported to have sought his expertise either to benefit themselves or to ruin opponents. With such power and connections in high places, it was reported that the monk had been evading arrest. See *Ravaya*, 12, 16, and 19 October and 13 and 16 November 1997.

ritualism, Vidagama Maitreya, and of the folksy simplicity of the thirteenth-century monk Dharmasena, the author of the *Saddharmaratnavaliya*.[22] The form Nandissara adopts itself is revealing: though fictional, it is perfectly obvious that the work is based on real experience. Nandissara explicitly states that his novel is "an attempt to write an investigative composition *(gavesanatmaka nibandhayak)* on the basis of the experience of living a monastic life," and that it is "a handbook that must be read with equanimity by all chief monks and heads of monasteries *(viharadhipati nahimivarun).*" This is part of Nandissara's literary and communicative tactic. He knows that he has something justifiably critical to say about monasticism, but he does not want to write a straightforward critique. So he takes refuge in the art of fictionalizing, but then he wants it to be perfectly well understood that what he is talking about is not fiction but reality. This kind of subterfuge is resorted to in general under repressive conditions when a writer has reason to be afraid of the personal consequences of his critique. A parallel instance in Sri Lanka contemporaneous with the work of Nandissara is the critique of the regime of President Premadasa which, unable to manifest itself directly, was channeled into oblique expressive forms like oral literature (gossip and "yarns") and the theater.[23] Nandissara takes the further precaution of justifying his critique with an appeal to high moral values and a sense of moral responsibility, lest he be misunderstood or made the target of organized attack by those for whom he critique is addressed. This in its own way affirms the validity of his critique.

The focus of Nandissara's critique is what he considers the typical chief monk or incumbent of a rural monastery. This monk is the widespread and rural refraction of the monks at the centers of the respective hierarchies, the best known of which are the two chapters of the Siyam sect, Asgiriya and Malvatta.

As a work of fiction, there is no story to talk about. Nothing really happens, except that a young boy, perhaps no older than ten, starts life in the monastery at the beginning of the story and the chief monk of the monastery

22. Bo. Nandissara, *Loku Hamuduruvan vetatayi* (Haputale: New Royal Press, 1991). All references in this paragraph are to the Preface ("From the Author"), 7. The work of Vidagama Maitreya referred to here is *Budugna Alamkaraya*, available in different editions, as is the *Saddharmaratnavaliya*. An authoritative edition of the latter is by G. D. Wiyayawardhana and M. B. Ariyapala (Colombo: Sri Lanka Pracina Bhasopakara Samitiya, 1985). For selections of this work recently translated into English, see Ranjini Obeyesekere, *Jewels of the Doctrine* (Albany: State University of New York Press, 1991).

23. That even the theater was not safe is clearly demonstrated in the case of the murder of the journalist, actor, and dramatist Richard Zoysa (see R. Weerakoon, *The Extra-Judicial Execution of Richard de Zoysa* [Colombo: The Star Press, n.d.]). But more veiled and artful theater, exemplified by Ediriweera Sarachchandra's *Mahasara,* got away safely.

dies at its end. In between, for about 65 pages of the seventy-page book, there is a lengthy critique of the chief monk *(loku hamuduruvo),* who becomes a metaphor for the institution of the chief monk. We infer that the narrator, the young boy now grown older, has derobed himself in disillusionment. As he puts it, "Pervading the Sangha society is selfishness, greed, and hypocrisy. One more thing, arrogance. How despicable is it to pretend to observe ten million moralities, mislead, the laity and enjoy the four requisites they provide. . . . But I have freed myself from that prison. . . . I live in a world of freedom within a garland of principles that I have fashioned for myself."[24]

The work invites comparison with *He Siddharta nam veyi,* just discussed. While the two are quite different from each other in style, story interest, and even overt theme, they are the same in their critique. In *He Siddharta nam veyi,* the overt theme, as we know, is the ideal system with the ideal new monk and the ideal father-figure (the chief monk). But this is only contrastive: the real theme is the corrupt system portrayed in the dream sequence, the ordination ceremony, and the ragging incident, and enlivened in the person of the "Dhamma terrorizing, sexually misbehaving, bunkum spouting Gorakane Ambulananda."

Nandissara portrays the typical chief monk as a miser and a greedy grabber of material wealth. He is both an investor and a hoarder. His hoarded wealth is stacked up and locked away, and the bunch of keys to the various safes and cupboards becomes a metaphor for his greed. It is securely tucked between his waist and his "wearing robe" *(andanaya).* It never leaves this sanctuary, not even when he goes to bed and not even when he is weakened and bedridden in old age. He has no interest whatsoever in doing anything about his ignorance and reads no books. Not only does he fail in his duty to socialize his pupils in morality, knowledge, and conduct, he positively maltreats them. He does not trust them. He sows dissension among them, as he does among the laity who support him, so that he can the better use them to his own advantage. He directs his pupils in such a way that he ensures a flow of material goods to himself. He does not part with anything of even the most negligible value and turns away as "sinners" the starving victims of displacement who come to him for food and shelter. He goes on fundraising sprees and keeps erecting useless structures in the monastic grounds.[25] He is very much the opposite of the ideal monk the Buddha compares to a bird, free and unburdened with material wealth, light and able to soar to spiritual

---

24. Bo. Nandissara, *Loku hamuduruvan vetatayi,* 61–62.

25. This is the favorite monastic pastime of "developing the place" *(sthane diyunu kirima),* which is given "dharma vinaya" support by Yakkaduve, *Pavidi vaga,* 307.

heights. Instead, he becomes *bahubhandika,* "multi-itemed," the Buddha's
scornful characterization of acquisitive monks. He bribes his way to titles
such as *vicitra bhanaka, sahityacarya, rajakiya pandita,* although he knows no
doctrine, discipline, or art/science (*dharma, vinaya, silpa sastra*). Finally, the
chief monk, like Gorakane Ambulananda of the undergraduate monks' ragging incident, is "sexually misbehaving."

The work is a humanistic critique of the cultural practice of ordaining
very young boys and depriving them of the simple pleasures of their childhood and the love of parents, siblings, and friends. This is the obverse of the
attraction that young boys reportedly have to the monkhood. Gone is the
warmth of home. The chief monk is cold and cruel. In the story, when his
parents go away tearfully after admitting him to the monastery, the young
boy is in tears with no word of consolation from the chief monk, now ideally
his caretaker and actor *in loco parentis.* When the boy longingly looks in the
direction of the access road to the monastery, the chief monk chastises him
cruelly, saying, "Are you gazing at the road to suck your mother's milk? Pick
up your book and learn it by heart." But the book he has to study, the *Bana
daham pota,*[26] is torn, unattractive, and ancient, and the boy is reminded of
his school books which are filled with pictures. At home he eats from a
beautiful plate. He has to now eat from a black begging bowl the shape and
depth of which he cannot negotiate. At home he wore colorful shorts. Here
he has to wear a robe, stitched all over, without a shape, weighing several
kilos, that constrains the body and turns walking into a task.

NATIONALIST ENTRAPMENT AND SUBALTERNIST PITFALLS
Reflections on the Young Monks' Critiques

Nandissara's work holds up two types of monks as ideals of monkhood. First
is the ascetic monk who, though "village dwelling," is minimally involved
with the laity. The second is the monk born of *The Heritage.* The author
makes explicit mention of Yakkaduve, the Vidyalankara theorist of new
monkhood and colleague of Rahula, and quotes him approvingly. In his admiration of the first type Nandissara is solidly based, but when it comes to
the second, his position is problematic and reveals the fundamental weakness
of the young monk's critique as a universalistic moral critique. In his admira-

26. One of the standard texts monks learn from memory as part of their socialization in established monasticism.

tion of Yakkaduve, Nandissara seems oblivious to the narrow politicization of the monk as a defender of Sinhala Buddhist interests as distinguished from the universalist humanism that is the basis of the Buddhist concern for the human condition.

In sum, Nandissara's work is less an original critique than a well-crafted restatement of the young monks' general critique of the traditional system of chief monks with its involvement with property, empty titles, abuse of pupils, exploitation of the laity, and general moral decrepitude. This is important from an anthropological perspective, because the critique of the monk is not a superimposition from some alien source but an autonomous critique arising from the society, indeed from the monkhood itself. Interestingly enough, it is also in essence the critique of the monkhood made by Dharmapala and Rahula. In Rahula's *The Heritage,* the intention of the critique is *empowerment* of the monk, which is *political,* whereas in Dharmapala's and Nandissara's it is the *enablement* of the monk to render service to society, which is *economic,* a distinction I made previously in relation to the Vidyalankara and Vidyodaya monks.

The young monk's critique of the monkhood is broadly divided into these two streams, empowerment and enablement. Valid in theory, this distinction is not easily operative in practice. Undoubtedly some monks soundly based in moral vigor, like Nandissara, can stay with enablement and prevent themselves from crossing over to empowerment. But most take the easy step to empowerment, not as a positive political power, which the monkhood is inherently incapable of, but more as negative and often socially injurious pressure group activity that is coupled with their turning into modern era reincarnations of the very chief monk that was their original object of denunciation. These are the modern monks (illustrated in some of the case studies in chapter 5) who are different from the traditional chief monks only superficially and externally.

The young monks struggle to gain an education, and, once they do, they are promptly placed at crossroads:[27] they must, like Nandissara, either take the noble path of altruism and become the embodiment of selfless social service, i.e., the best of the ideals of Dharmapala and *The Heritage,* or they must become modernized versions of the chief monk as just defined.

It is clear that most of the young monks, if they get a chance, will tread the path of empowerment rather than that of enablement. This makes their critique of the chief monk of the old system simply a subalternist (or some-

27. Many of them will return to lay life, but that is not relevant for the purposes of this argument. Our concern is with those who continue to remain in robes.

times even tactical) assumption of moral high ground. The moral site from which they speak is not intrinsic but dependent on their subaltern condition, and it is therefore a fragile site. It is easily vulnerable to success, which will enthrone the now subaltern young monk in a position of economic security or sometimes even considerable wealth, which will transfer him to a different site. From that new site he can now practice what he preached against. We have empirical cases of such subaltern monks now ensconced in high positions and correspondingly altered states of consciousness. In this we simply have a new version of the reproduction of monastic culture in which the young monk is socialized into eventually becoming a typical chief monk. Social change in the monkhood thus has only assumed new garb, without going through the fundamental moral transformation it needs.

Far more disturbing is the nature of the young educated monk's critique in the context of a modernizing nation-state and of the cosmopolitan knowledge and attitudes the young monks exposed to modern secular education are supposed to acquire, as anticipated in Rahula and indeed foreshadowed in incipient form in the Dharmapalite conception of the monk. Except for the tiny minority of members of the Manava Hitavadi Bhiksu Sangamaya (MHBS), mentioned in chapter 5, which is now extinct, and a handful of individual monks who are rarely organized or articulate and therefore socially ineffective, the young monks have not succeeded in coming up with the visionary and humanistic critique that alone will raise the monkhood from its depths of parochial, sectional, and purely personal interest and elevate it to the position of esteem in society that it so direly desires, and enable its members to become the true guardian deities of the nation. The indigenous critique of the monks, and of the nationalist elite as well discussed at the beginning of this chapter, remains imprisoned within its premodern, proto-nationalist and bounded conceptions, unemancipated from the framework of the narrow Sinhala Buddhist definition of identity that equates Buddhism with Sinhala ethnicity, and unable to see the light and breathe the fresh air of universalist Buddhist-humanist perceptions that will truly liberate them and the land they claim to have a special dispensation to guard.

HUMANIST CRITIQUE
Anthropological Assessment

Such a universalist-humanist critique has emerged not from the monks but from the laity. In this we encounter once more the monastic condition the alleviation of which was the main intention of *The Heritage,* namely, the fact that the laity has advanced while the Sangha languished has left the monks in the state of having "nothing to say to the laity," as Rahula put it. The laity overtook the monks in practically every sphere, including, as mentioned above, the monks' own preserve of meditation, for today there are more serious meditators among laymen and laywomen than in the Sangha. So it is no surprise that in the area of reformation, which is indispensable to the Sangha if it is to lead rather than follow the lay social order, the laity has set the pace by its constructive critique, suggesting ways by which the Sangha can reform itself, though this has so far fallen on deaf ears, which is itself a commentary on the Sangha's backwardness and intellectual and moral incapacitation all over again.

The universalist-humanistic critique has come from two streams of lay intellectuals: first, the intellectuals of the All Ceylon Buddhist Congress (ACBC), which is the premier lay Buddhist organization, and second, the generality of Buddhist intellectuals. It is outside the scope of this work to enter into a discussion of the first of these critiques, that of the All Ceylon Buddhist Congress, except to say that it is interventionist, and that it presumes to pigeonhole the monk into an idealized, essentialized, and ascetic framework of conduct reminiscent of Max Weber's "ancient Buddhism," denying the monks the self-determination to which they are entitled in defining a social role for themselves.[28] I shall focus on the second, that of the generality of the modern secular educated intellectuals. Journalists figure prominently here, most likely because of the access they have to the media.

Such a critique is articulated by D. Amarasiri Weeraratne, independent scholar and participant in the public debate on issues of Buddhism and society for the last several decades. In an article written to the major Sunday English language newspaper *The Observer* on the Sangha's opposition to the proposals to devolve power to the minorities in the regions they predominate,[29] Weeraratne makes two points critical of the Sangha. The first is that the Sangha has mistakenly denied the existence of an ethnic problem and has

28. The ACBC's conception of the Buddhist monk is partly rooted in Dharmapala, but without Dharmapala's sense of social mission. The denial of this social mission is related to the political conservatism of the leadership of the ACBC in the 1940s, when such definition by the Vidyalankara monks became a political threat to their class and its party, the conservative United National Party (UNP). The ACBC vehemently opposed "political bhikkhus," i.e., the Vidyalankara monks who were an immediate and substantial threat to the UNP leadership in the general elections of 1947. This fascinating and important area remains almost completely uninvestigated by social scientists, except for a brilliant paper by W. A. Wiswa Warnapala, "Sangha and Politics in Sri Lanka: Nature of the Continuing Controversy," *Indian Journal of Politics* 12, nos. 1–2 (April-August 1978): 66–76.

29. *The Observer*, 17 March 1996. This article, as it deserves, is quoted in full in the Appendix to this chapter.

equated the devolution proposals with dividing the country. That is, the Sangha equates Sri Lanka with Sinhala-Buddhist interests. The second is that the Sangha does not have the expertise to pass judgment on an issue of this nature. To quote Weeraratne, the monks "are not experts in political science and their knowledge of international political problems and constitutions is poor." Weeraratne points out that the rise of the separatist terrorist group, the Liberation Tigers of Tamil Eelam (LTTE), was facilitated by the failure of the Sinhala government to settle the question by peaceful means, and that attempts in that direction were opposed and stopped by the Sangha. The Bandaranaike-Chelvanayagam Pact drawn up for this purpose was derailed by Sangha opposition led by Baddegama Vimalavamsa, and the Dudley-Chelvanayagam Pact was similarly derailed by opposition led by Madihe Pannasiha.[30] The All Party Conference convened to resolve the ethnic problem was also "scuttled by hardliners in the Maha Sangha who spearheaded the Sinhala-only chauvinists."

Weeraratne's critique also points out that the government should be run not by monks but elected representatives of the people. "There is no room in the constitution," he says, "to give into pressure tactics of reactionary monks." In a clear reference to Rahula and his colleagues, Weeraratne derides the politicization of the Sangha as "a heritage of apostasies coming down from the Anuradhapura period [that] . . . should be disallowed." He urges a proper reorganization of the Sangha as found in other Theravada countries like Burma and Thailand so that the monks are debarred from "resort[ing] to the present corruptions and apostasies such as politics, business ventures, renting out temple rooms to laymen including LTTE agents,[31] running garages, printing presses, tuition classes, karate classes [and] parking [garages]."

An anonymous columnist of the weekly newspaper *Yuktiya* provides us with a further example of the kind of ethical critique that has evaded the young monks and the nationalists.[32] The well-known monks Walpola Rahula and Madihe Pannasiha had accepted the high religious title Agga Maha Pandita from the military rulers of Burma, who offer it to non-Burmese monks in an attempt to make up for their persecution of the dissenting pro-

30. According to Weeraratne, this triumphant claim for Madihe Pannasiha is made in *Dam Raki Naka* (The Sect that Protected the Dhamma), the caste-based history of the Amarapura Dharmarakshita sect.

31. This refers to the Ramalingam Dharmalingam, reportedly one of the masterminds behind the LTTE bombing of the Central Bank that killed over a hundred people and injured over a thousand. Dharmalingam was renting a room in a monastery. Receiving rent is a violation of monastic ethics.

32. The column "Ilakkaya" in *Yuktiya*, 7 July 1996.

democracy monks of Burma. Radical politician and member of parliament Vasudeva Nanayakkara had publicly denounced Rahula and Madihe Pannasiha for accepting the title. It is a measure of both the moral and the intellectual state of the Sangha that the deputy chief monk of the Amarapura Saddham-mavamsa sect, Talalle Dhammaloka, had taken great offense at Vasudeva Na-nayakkara and asked him to apologize to the Sangha for his temerity. The *Yuktiya* columnist points out that the Sangha leaders, in their greed for titles, had failed to see the ethical problems in accepting a high honor from a military clique that had cancelled an election and imprisoned the democratically elected leader. In this process, these rulers have, according to this columnist, killed thousands of dissenting monks and imprisoned hundreds. He points out that Rahula and Madihe Pannasiha, by accepting the title, are shoring up this bloodstained regime, and that Laotian, Thai, and Cambodian monks approached by the clique have refused it. While the columnist's dismay is understandable, shoring up bloodstained regimes has not been unknown in the history of the Sinhala Sangha, which historically has seen nothing wrong with it. This is indeed the central sociological question: why is the Sangha, the carriers of a message of peace and nonviolence, so attracted to murder and murderers? This in essence is the question that Tambiah raised, and this in essence is the questions these lay Buddhist intellectuals are raising.

Another *Yuktiya* columnist, Edwin Kotalavala wrote an open letter to the Sangha reminding them of their historical misdeeds, including their support of the Sinhala Buddhist king Dutthagamani against Elara, the righteous Tamil king.[33] He points out how the Sangha factions Mahavihara and Abhayagiri of the Anuradhapura era (3d century B.C.E. to 10th century C.E.) took turns in instigating the kings favorable to each to destroy the monasteries and books of the opposite faction. The monks' interpretation of the now notorious *Mahavamsa*-based incident that the thousands killed by Dutthaga-mani amount to only one and a half, because only that many were Buddhists, says Kotalavala, is not the Buddhism he knows and neither it is the Buddhism the monks themselves preach. He gives several examples from the history of Sri Lanka to show the harm done to the nation by the interference in political affairs by monks. He cites two recent events: the monks' opposition to two economically sound proposals, legalizing the tapping of the coconut palm for toddy ("palm wine"), and fish farming in inland waters, resulting in the abandonment of both. He urges them not to do the same at this last chance to peacefully settle the ethnic question:

33. Edwin Kotalawala,"Bauddha Bhiksuva ada koyibatada?" (Whither Today's Buddhist Monk?) *Yuktiya*, 11 February 1996.

It is widely acknowledged that the primary problem the nation has faced after independence is the ethnic question. We must similarly acknowledge that every government since then only complicated this question in their pursuit of [immediate] political gains, and never cared to seek a solution. The present government, whatever its faults, has put forward a respectable solution to this national question. Today a considerable section of your institution [the Sangha] have arisen to prevent the passage of these proposals. The inevitable result of that would be to drag on for years to come this destructive war that has now lasted one and a half decades. . . . You must accept however reluctantly that, on the threshold of the twenty-first century, we cannot go back two thousand years to bring about again the era of Dutthagamani. . . . To talk about a singular *(ekiya)* Sri Lanka or a pure *(amisra)* Sinhala ethnicity in the global village of the twenty-first century is an illusion.

Questions regarding the moral crises in the Sangha have also been raised perceptively by the journalist Lucien Rajakaurnanayake.[34] Commenting on the ironic fact that the LTTE bombs used in the attack on the Central Bank were buried in the compound of a monastery in the Colombo suburb of Narahenpita, and that the incumbent had for ten years had given a room on rent to Ramalingam Dharmalingam, the LTTE supporter who reportedly buried the bombs, Rajakarunanayake writes: "It is time for the Buddhists in civil society to admit the truth that the lives of a large section of the Sangha, revered by the laity and considered their guides and philosophers in life, and in many instances the most strident voices of Sinhala chauvinism, are examples of a clergy in decline. Such situations have been faced by other religions too, which have led to major reforms. It is becoming necessary to question the position and status of the Sangha in the current political, social, and economic system, and their behavior amidst rapidly changing mores and moral values."

Rajakarunanayake confronts starkly the paradox of monks claiming to be "guardian deities" and demanding to be advisors to the government when they do not have even basic knowledge, not to mention expertise, in the areas like devolution of power and economic development in which they are supposed to advise. This is how Rajakarunanayake puts it. He is referring to the lorry that was carrying the bombs buried in the monastery compound: "One English editorial attributed the Kotahena lorry, laden with explosives, to the simple-mindedness of the monks of the temple in permitting its parking there. What strikes me as more important is that today's simple-minded

34. Lucien Rajakarunanayake, "Trade and Politics amidst the Yellow Robes." *Sunday Leader,* 18 or 25 February 1996. The Sinhala version appeared in *Yuktiya,* 25 February 1996.

or naive monk may be tomorrow's Nayaka Thera, Mahanayaka, and who knows, if the trends continue, even the future Sanghanayaka (Sangha chief). Are these the sections that will advise the future governments on matters of policy on Buddhism? And, can they be expected to be solely interested in Buddhism in their advice?" Rajakarunanayake continues: "The trends of today call for a major reassessment of the role of the Sangha in our society. For far too long the Sangha has been politicized, under cover of the argument that they have been the traditional advisors to the kings of the past. The respect that the yellow robe has gained among our people has been abused far too often in the most blatant manner."

Rajakarunanayake refers to the business activities of monks and raises questions as to why it is necessary to raise money by renting monastery land for parking vehicles, letting rooms, and maintaining paying lodges or boarding houses when the needs of the monks are taken care of by the laity's donations. It is time, says Rajakarunanayake, for the Buddhist laity to raise questions about "the trends in the Sangha, their involvement in business, the obvious opulence which many of the leading monks seek." He points out that temple premises are used to conduct karate classes, and preaching halls have been converted to tuition halls, "not necessarily for the advancement of education but because of the income it gives the temple or the incumbents"; and that Sangha members visit politicians "not for any genuine needs of the Buddhist laity, but for special favors for family or business friends and other interests." Running through Rajakarunanayake's critique is the interesting fact that he urges the *laity* to take the initiative in Sangha reform. Consciously or otherwise, Rajakarunanayake is invoking a historic feature of Theravada, that its reforms have come not through inner questioning and rebellion within the order nor derived from its intellect or its "conscience," as has been the case, for example, in Christianity, but by imposition from the outside, which means the laity, typically the king. These have taken the typical form of "purifications" that were centered on factional Sangha politics rather than on any question of moral or ethical significance. The intrusion of the king is partly explicable in terms of the absence in the Sangha of overarching social structures. But the question is more complex, and it relates socio-psychologically to mechanisms of internalization of ethics and morality. I argue below that this is possibly a function of the doctrine of samsaric reincarnation, as opposed to a theory of eternal damnation.

One more element in the moral critique of these writers is their exposure of the monks for their beliefs in magic and cultism, a point that is reminiscent of the scorn that the fifteenth-century Buddhist monk-poet Vidagama Maitreya poured on the believers in Hindu ritualism. The monks provided these critics with good ammunition by conducting the weekly rituals of the Sai Baba devotees in a Buddhist monastery, located on the Bauddhaloka Mavata, "the Light of Buddhism Road." The ritual is initiated by the incumbent himself in front of an altar on which a Sai Baba portrait co-exists peacefully with the Buddha images.[35] A *Yuktiya* editorial uses the fact of a Buddhist monastery holding Sai Baba rituals to bring out the hypocrisy of the elite monks. It points out the fact that the "the chief monks of the three sects, and educated monks and dharma experts like Walpola Rahula and Bellanvila Vimalaratana who are the guardian deities of the nation," make no protest when high officials of a government constitutionally bound to protect Buddhism become worshippers of a magician and holder of false beliefs *(mithya drsti).*[36]

Another element in the moral critique of these writers is their assessment of the reaction to the publication of S. J. Tambiah's *Buddhism Betrayed?* This book caused hysteria in Sinhala Buddhist extremists, both lay and monastic, leading to its eventual banning by the government. Among the best Sinhala-language defenders of the book were the journalists of *Ravaya* and *Yuktiya.* The *Yuktiya* editorial just mentioned discussed the angry and vociferous reaction of the monks when "the professor named S. J. Tambiah wrote the *Buddhism Betrayed* book," and contrasted it with the silence of the monks when high officials of a government committed to protecting Buddhism take to Sai Baba worship. *Ravaya* went to the extent of explaining Tambiah's much misunderstood and misrepresented concerns, and it serialized in Sinhala translation a chapter of the book. The newspaper claimed that it was doing so "to enable the readers decide for themselves whether Tambiah is an enemy of Buddhism or a better Buddhist than those who claim to be defenders of Buddhism."[37] The main stand taken by these writers in their ethical critique concerns the gap between theory and practice, and especially the contradiction of monks preaching nonviolence in one breath and militantly advocating war in the next. In addition, the writers charge the monks with being cultists and magicians who bless the army, which these writers consider to be primitive and non-Buddhist.[38] In essence this is what Tambiah is saying too, and it

35. After the initiation of the ritual, the monk stepped out of the area. Thus the monk did not participate in the community singing and other parts of the ritual, illustrating the incompatibility of the monk with the ritual, although his initial act is participation enough.

36. "Sai Baba vandanava saha Buddhagama surakima," Editorial, *Yuktiya,* 21 July 1996.

37. For a discussion of *Buddhism Betrayed?* in relation to its reception in Sri Lanka, see H. L. Seneviratne, "Tambiah Betrayed," *Lanka Guardian* 20, no. 1 (1997): 13–15.

38. See Ajit Hettiarchchi, "Baudahama saha Yuddhaya," *Yuktiya,* 19 November 1995. This article quotes Walpola Rahula's eloquent exposition, in *What the Buddha Taught,* of Buddhism's nonviolence and condemnation of war and bloodshed, implicitly contrasting this with Rahula's other face, his advocacy of the ethnic war and opposition to the peaceful solution of devolution.

is no surprise that they are keen to let readers decide for themselves what Tambiah's message is.

SINGING A CRITIQUE
Nanda Malini and Sunil Ariyaratne

I prefaced the discussion on the work of Bo. Nandissara above with the statement that creative works like novels and plays are vehicles of critique under certain socio-political conditions. The critique of the monkhood made by scholar and songwriter Sunil Ariyaratne and sung by the gifted and well-known singer Nanda Malini is such a critique and must be considered part of the intellectualist humanist critique of the Sangha. This critique is, however, not exclusively pointed towards the Sangha but embedded in a broader critique of the society, and it is relevant to briefly refer to the broader critique and its context.

The broader critique is part of the opposition of what we might call the moral coalition to the policies of J. R. Jayawardene, who was elected to power in 1977 on a platform of economic liberalization or "open economy." Since the election was an overwhelming victory for J. R. Jayawardene and the opposition was decimated, neither this coalition nor the official opposition were able to "stand up" to the regime. But there was one force that was willing to take on the regime, the JVP (Janata Vimukti Peramuna), the revolutionary movement of the youth. There was thus widespread but secret sympathy in this moral coalition toward the JVP and indeed toward the Tamil youth movement in the North. The songs of Nanda and Sunil, the best known of which were first publicized in the very popular concert entitled *Pavana* (Breeze), constitute one of the most poignant and anguished expressions of this sympathy. With the barring of Nanda's songs from the state-owned radio and television, they were published in the form of a cassette under the same title.[39]

Nanda and Sunil question the monks about their sectarianism, which is based on caste and is without any doctrinal justification. "Is that what you find in the doctrine *(bana)* of our Buddha?" they ask the imaginary monk addressed in the song. They criticize the monks for tying protective pirit threads on "the enemies of the people"; for hoarding money and being miserly; for ordaining kinsmen so that they continue to keep in the family prop-

---

39. They were barred, along with other musicians like W. D. Amaradeva, as punishment for signing a protest against the government's decision to replace the elections due in 1982 with a referendum.

erty that belongs to the monastery; for "laundering the dirty acts of people in high places"; for making money on the poor on ritual and festive occasions; and for seeking titles and other empty recognitions.[40]

It is easy to see that none of this is new: this is the standard critique of the monk. But what is of interest is the fact that Nanda is the best-known Sinhala singer and her songs are very popular, which means that the standard critique of the monk is brought home to the listener, who is part of a massive audience, with renewed and amplified effect. Equally potent is the folksy and economical style of Sunil's lyric, which recalls the folk critique mentioned at the beginning of this chapter. The combination of these two, the sonority of Nanda's voice and the balladic simplicity of Sunil's lyric, is very effective, and it constitutes a complex and unusual integration of the folk and the humanist-intellectualist frameworks of critique.

A QUESTIONNAIRE FOR THE SANGHA
The Challenge of a Young Journalist

Among the journalist intellectuals the most perceptive and courageous commentator on the Sangha's moral crisis is Uvindu Kurukulasuriya, a young *Ravaya* journalist. In several pieces written for his journal,[41] Kurukulasuriya exposes the class foundations of Sinhala Buddhism and takes on the Goliath of the Sinhala Buddhist fundamentalist establishment, which identifies the humanist-universalist critique of Sinhala Buddhism with Eelamist separatism

---

40. This sample from *Pavana* illustrates Sunil's treatment of these themes: *Upasaka amma ipaduna hina kule-mahana karantayi yanne age kolu / uta nikayak venkara taba tibe-apa muni bane ekada hamuduruvane? / pirit nul bandimin jana haturanta-yaturu karali andanaya yata gasagena / apavat venta pera saha le gnativaru-mahana karana ekadayi muni bane ane / kunu hodanta maha tanvala ape rate-pansala tamunna-hage honda vellava / tikat vikunala perahara karanakota-karanduve individa datun vahansela.*

The devotee, born of low caste / Is having her kid ordained / There's a low caste sect for him / Is this what our Buddha said, O honorable monk? // Tying pirit thread on the people's foes / Bunches of keys tucked under your wearing robe / Ordaining kin (so property goes to them) / Is this what the Buddha preached? Oh dear! // Your monasteries are laundries sublime / To launder the dirt of the high of this land / When you sell tickets for the perahara / Won't the relics flee the reliquary?

41. Uvindu Kurukulasuriya, "Sangha samajayata prasna patryak" (A questionnaire for the Sangha Society), *Ravaya,* 29 October 1995; "Anomadassi maha na himiyangen vartamana sangha samajayata" (From the Venerable Anomadassi to the contemporary Sangha Society), *Ravaya,* 5 November 1995; "Gini tabimen sanketavat kale sanghaya vahanselage virodhayada?" (Did arson symbolize the Sangha opposition?) *Ravaya,* 17 December 1995. The contradiction between the value placed on devolution in Buddhism and the monk's vehement opposition to it in lay society has been commented on several of these writers. See also Swaminathan Vimal, "Yuddhaya, balaya vimadhyagata kirima ha bauddha drstiya" (War, devolution of power, and the Buddhist perspective), *Yuktiya,* 23 June 1993. Vimal points out the fact that opposition to devolution is an ideology of the elite monks.

and western-funded NGO activity allegedly designed to destroy Buddhism and the Sinhala ethnic group.

Basic to Kurukulasuriya's argument is the distinction he makes between Buddhism as a universalist ethical system and what he terms "Sinhala Buddhism." This sounds quite familiar, but there are some subtle but significant differences. As a religion Kurukulasuriya's "Buddhism" is without ritual, magic, tradition, culture, processions, ceremonies, faith, devotion, concepts, theories, and even "Buddhism" as a self-consciously grasped thought system. It is merely an ethical and compassionate existence.[42] This, however, is not passive or negative. It refers to the inner ethical development of the individual and positive ethical action guided by a universalist social concern that rejects all parochial categories like caste, creed, ethnicity, cultural or linguistic identity, and locality.

"Sinhala Buddhism" in its manifestation as an elite ideology is mired in all of the above parochialisms. The main function of the Sangha is the reduction of true Buddhism to the parochial elite ideology of Sinhala Buddhism. This is an acutely perceptive observation and exposes the fact that Sinhala Buddhist extremism, with its notions of bounded community, nationalism borrowed from the West, and racist notions of ethnic purity, is a superstructure of the urban-based middle classes; and that, in contrast to this, the generality of the people represents the nonexclusivist and assimilative tradition of open, unbounded community so picturesquely illustrated in the ethnic mix and cultural evolution of Sri Lanka.

Kurukulasuriya's article "Sangha samajayata prasna patryak" (A questionnaire to the Sangha) provides us with an excellent window on his critique. The "questionnaire" deserves to be quoted in full:

1. Would it not be a violation of the Buddha's most basic ethical teaching regarding peace, nonviolence, and societal coexistence to say [as the monks do] that "war must be dealt with by war"?

42. This is remarkably close to, and perhaps derived from, the thought of Martin Wickramasinghe, whose book *Bavataranaya* (Dehivala: Tisara, 1973), a humanist interpretation of the Buddha, was denounced by the monks. One such was a two-volume denunciation by the Vidyalankara monk Yakkaduve, *Bavatarana maga ha Buddhcaritaya* (vol. 1, Nugegoda: Deepani, 1976; vol. 2, Colombo: The Department of Cultural Affairs, 1982). In addition Yakkaduve published a "handbook" on the subject, *Bavatarana maga ha Buddhcaritaya atpota: bavatarana pariksanaya* (Nugegoda: Deepani, 1978), and launched a newspaper and public speaking campaign to propagate his critique island wide (see Preface to the 1982 work cited above, p. ix). A public rally of protest was held on 15 March 1975 (*Bavataranaya*, 5th ed., 1992, iii). See also Martin Wickramasinghe, *Sinhala Sakaskada* (Maharagama: Saman Publishers, 1962), 82–87. The study of Buddhism as a thought system is the precursor of its objectification, its acquisition as part of the paraphernalia of nationalist resurgence, its fetishization, and ultimately its use as an instrument of oppression.

2. The monk Bellanvila Vimalaratana in his translation of John Walters' *Mind Unshaken* says that Buddhists never went to war because of religion. The same Bellanvila Vimalaratana emphatically says this [ethnic] war must continue. What does the Sangha say about this [double talk]?

3. What do you venerable monks who oppose federalism have to say about the Buddha's preference for the federal system of the Licchavis [the Vajjian republics] and the political democracy articulated thereby?

4. Has not the Sangha, which was originally institutionalized in unitary form, now accepted a federal framework due to divisions of caste and sub-caste and other cultural criteria?

5. You accept the principle of devolving judicial power to the various provincial judicial chief monks within a given sect and among different sects. On what basis then do you oppose the same devolution of judicial power in the lay social order, in its regional bodies, as proposed [in the devolution package]?

6. You venerable monks cite the *Mahavamsa* as your authority to say that, during the time of the kings, political problems were solved according to the advice of the Sangha Jewel, and therefore modern political problems must also be solved according to your advice. [Let me then ask you this.] Of the 54 kings mentioned in the *Mahavamsa*, 22 were killed by their successors. Eleven lost the throne because of defeat in war. Thirteen were killed in war. Six were assassinated. Did this fate befall these kings because they accepted the advice of the Sangha Jewel? Or, was their fate a consequence of the meritorious deed of protecting and nourishing Buddhism?

7. According to chapter 42 of the *Mahavamsa*, war plunged the country into economic disaster during the reign of king Dathopa Tissa. [In that national emergency] the king [having had no choice] appropriated [for the country's need] the treasures in relic chambers; melted golden images for the gold; acquired valuable goods that had been offered [to temples]; plucked even the golden pinnacle of [the renowned] Thuparama stupa; and the golden umbrella that sheltered the [great] Ruvanvali stupa. He was a king who much patronized the religion. If, basing itself on the framework of your own logic [of continuing the ethnic war for which it needs resources], the government launches a policy of appropriating for itself the property of the Sangha, would you approve of it?

8. You venerable monks talk with such sadness about landlessness. Would you distribute the vast properties you own among the landless?

9. How do you reconcile war with the following verse that is broadcasted [over radio and television] in the dawn everyday [by you]: *mata yatha niyam putttam, ayusa eka puttha manurakkhe, evampi sabba bhutesu, mana sambhavaye aparimanam...* ?

10. The *Rajja sutta* of the Samyukta Nikaya says, is it possible to rule righteously, without killing and causing to kill; without winning and causing to

win; without suffering sorrow and causing sorrow. What do you venerable monks have to say on this?

11. You venerable monks proclaim that every inch of this island belongs to the Sinhalas. Are you aware of the following statement of Anagarika Dharmapala, the widely acclaimed pioneer of the Buddhist renaissance: "Prior to the advent of the Sinhalese from India the island was inhabited by a non-Aryan tribe allied to the Dravidian race, who were called Yakkhus. The new race came from Bengal as invaders and conquerors."

12. What do you have to say about this statement of Dharmapala's, made in 1908?

13. Is it not the case that, according to this, Dharmapala accepted the concept of Tamil homelands which you venerable monks reject?

14. The Buddha never took sides in a war. How have you venerable monks blatantly taken a side?

15. [In 1994] the Venerable Madoluvave Sobhita said, "Racketeers who charge commissions on weapons, who became millionaires and billionaires that way, want war, the people don't" (*Lankadipa*, 19 September 1994). What does the Venerable Sobhita say on this today?

16. The Buddha often argued that, among men, there are only two categories, free and enslaved. Thus the Buddha did not accept status ascribed by birth. But you divide human beings into categories like "Sinhala Buddhist" and "Tamil Eelamist." Are you venerable monks not violating the conceptions of your Founder?

This questionnaire, which has so far not been responded to, brings out not only the general moral state of the Sangha but also its more specific hypocrisy in its enjoyment of the full advantages of devolution while denying the same to the lay society. The questionnaire needs no elucidation, but in summing up, it is worthwhile to restate some of Kurukulasuriya's contentions: that Sinhala Buddhist hegemonism is class-based, implying its recent origin, in contrast to attempts by Sinhala Buddhist middle-class theorists to claim an ancient origin; that Anagarika Dharmapala accepted what we today call the theory of Tamil homelands; and that Anagarika Dharmapala also accepted the status of the Tamils as the original inhabitants of the island. Most perceptively, Kurukulasuriya makes a cultural argument that explains his distinction between "Buddhism" and "Sinhala Buddhism," namely that "Buddhism" is a cultural artifact that was implanted in a preexisting cultural environment whose intrinsic sociological characteristics were inhospitable for the nourishment of the ethics of the cultural artifact of Buddhism; and that resulted in the growth of a particular syncretism in which indigenous pre-Buddhist ethical characteristics held sway and those of "Buddhism" were made subservient. He supports this argument with the example of Russia, where the humane principles of the cultural artifact of socialism were made subservient to the overarching indigenous culture of Russian authoritarianism. This is a bold statement, which challenges the monumental edifice of the theory of Sinhala civilization subscribed to by practically all scholars of all the major social science and humanities disciplines that have ever studied Sinhala culture and civilization. But Kurukulasuriya is obviously not challenging the idea of the civilizing mission of Buddhism in most of the spheres normally accepted as having been subjected to that mission, like art, architecture, literacy, writing, technology, and so forth. What he is challenging is the generally accepted idea of the extent to which the ethical content of the new artifact of Buddhism permeated the culture. According to his dichotomy of "Buddhism" and "Sinhala Buddhism," that permeation was inadequate, contrary to the accepted view of a "Buddhist stamp" on Sinhala culture. Buddhism did not adequately stamp the Sinhala culture ethically, and it is the Sangha that weakened this stamp, because the Sangha was the institution in charge of the job of stamping. In the process of stamping, the Sangha placed its economic, status, and parochial group interests before the interests of the ethical life of the society.

Kurukulasuriya's critique of the Sangha takes a reverse form when he approvingly discusses the work of the handful monks who have attempted to articulate an ethical critique within the Sangha. The best examples he presents are Batapola Anomadassi and Udakandavala Saranamkara.[43] Other examples can be cited, such as Vallavatte Gnanabhivamsa. This appears to contradict my contention that the Sangha has failed to articulate an ethical critique within itself. These monks and others, for example those of the Lanka Pavidi Samvidhanaya who support the government's package of devolution, seem to indicate that there indeed exists such an internally generated critique.

My response to this is that the internality of critique of the monks is more an appearance than the reality, or that these humanistically based self-critical monks provide the exception that prove the rule. For, upon close examination of the life histories of these monks, it is clear that their humanism is derived not from Buddhism but from the social and intellectual relations of their involvement with Marxism and the socialist movement. This is of great interest because it dovetails with Kurukulasuriya's distinction between "Buddhism" and "Sinhala Buddhism," and his view that the cultural artifact of Bud-

43. Uvindu Kurukulasuriya, "Anomadassi maha na himiyangen vartamana sangha samajayata," *Ravaya*, 5 November 1995.

dhism lost its ethical content in the process of its institutionalization in the Sinhala culture. Stated differently, the social concern of these monks does not constitute a Lutheran-style questioning of the established "church," but is derived from extraneous sources. Therefore, it does not constitute a true inner questioning or a "revolt in the temple." This does not in any way detract from the validity of the social concern of these monks. But the point to note is that this social concern is individual or confined to a very small group of monks, and it has not been generalized to the monastic culture as a whole, the best explanation of which is its alienness to and incompatibility with the culture of "Sinhala Buddhism." The numerical negligibility of this group needs to be emphasized. It is also relevant here to remind ourselves of the demise of the MHBS, the only Buddhist humanist organization to emerge internally within the Sangha,[44] for which the only explanation is the inhospitability of the culture and ideology of the Sangha to such humanism.

The reactive and reactionary nature of the social concern evident in the mainstream monkhood today is of special relevance to this point. Their concern is reactive because, as clearly brought out in field interviews and often explicitly mentioned by these monks, their charitable activities are conceived as countermeasures to combat the alleged materially induced conversions of the poor by Christian evangelical groups. Thus ethical or humanitarian considerations, if any, are not overriding. The evangelical groups are mistakenly understood as "Catholics" and their missionaries as "fathers." Since the evangelicals are much better funded than these monks, the monks are envious, and it is this pervasive "father envy" and not any compassion or humanism that is the driving force behind their social concern. Their concern is reactionary because, as we often learn from the media, the other source of their "humanitarianism," besides beating the evangelicals at their game, is ethnicity: they collect funds and goods for the *Sinhala* poor or *Sinhala* victims of misfortune. They visit or shelter only *Sinhala* refugees. This "humanitarianism" is an integral part of a complex of parochial activities that include visits of the hierarchical and other prominent monks to the bunkers and to injured soldiers; and their conducting all night pirit ceremonies and bodhipujas to strengthen the army and magically enhance its success.

There is one other group of monks that needs to be mentioned here. These are what Sarath Amunugama calls "peripheral monks"[45] who inhabit the interstitial areas between the Sinhala and Tamil settlements and who

44. Indeed, even the MHBS had socialist connections but less obviously than in the case of the monks mentioned above.

45. Sarath Amunugama, Member of Parliament, in private conversations.

often have social relations with members of both communities. Sometimes these are village communities, like the one the Vidyodaya monk and Dharmapalite hero-giant Hendiyagala visited, (see chap. 3), whose members have been unclear and unconcerned as to their identity, at least until recently, when middle-class conceptions of ethnicity and identity were disseminated to these communities by propagandists of both the Sinhala and Tamil ethnic groups and by their respective chauvinist media. Even when such identities are clear, resident monks have, through long social interaction, established relations between themselves and the people with complete blindness to their ethnicity. This humanism may be not devoid of some ancestry in "Buddhism" in Kurukulasuriya's sense, but it is more related to the material realities on the ground that reflect the flexibility and adaptability of peoples as opposed to the rigidity of ideologues.

We must contrast this naturalized monk with the intrusive monk, the carrier of conscious Sinhala Buddhist expansionism to the periphery. These are monks who have their own mission of taking back for the Sinhalas the land they claim is primordially Sinhala but now appropriated by the Tamils. The hero and paradigm of this monk is Kitalagama Silalamkara, whose mission was to reclaim for the Sinhalas the forest hermitage of the medieval Buddhist saint Dimbulagala Kasyapa, which had become a settlement of the aboriginal Veddahs and the Tamils. According to the chief monk of the Amarapura sect and prominent Sinhala Buddhist champion Madihe Pannasiha, there were thirteen villages around Dimbulagala in the mid 1950s when Kitalagama started his efforts. Sinhalas lived only in one of these villages and they had only one school. They had only one representative in the local body, the gamsabhava. Madihe proudly states that Kitalagama increased the Sinhala villages to thirty, "expelled" the "Tamil gentleman" who was the president of the local body for thirty-six years, and made "a Sinhala gentleman" the president, "like crowning a Sinhala lord of men in a Tamil realm" *(Dravida rajadhaniyaka Sinhala narapatiyekuta otunu palndavannak meni).*[46] Madihe's vicarious pleasure in this act of king-making is inescapable. It is also pathetic because the king is Lilliputian. In addition to the explicit regal imagery, the Sinhala term *nerapa dama* for "expelled" is also remarkable for its conventional usage for the dethronement of kings. Hemasara,[47] another monk writ-

---

46. All quotations are from the Foreword (Prakasanaya) by Madihe Pannasiha in Gangodagama Pannavedha, *Dimbulagala Puvata* (Kuliyapitys: Sastrodaya, 1976).

47. The full name of this monk is Kitalagama Hemasara. I deviate from the usage adopted here and call him "Hemasara" in order to differentiate him from Kitalagama Silalamkara, whom I call "Kitalagama." The quotations here are from the second Preface to *Dimbulagala Puvata,* written by Hemasara.

ing in the same volume, continues the language and imagery of aggression and victory. Hemasara describes Kitalagama's acts of changing back to Sinhala "the Tamil names like Selliah, Kannaraja, and Kannaachchi the villagers had given themselves in place of their Sinhala names like Mudalihamy, Banda, Bandara, Silva, Sinno, etc.,"[48] and appointing Sinhala registrars and teachers to the area as "eternal monuments of this great national struggle." He also proclaims victoriously, hardly realizing that the Sinhala governments have repeatedly denied the fact, that Kitalagama Silalankara "took thousands of Sinhalas living in the Polonnaruva district and settled them in areas like Maduva, Punani, Nelugala, Vadamune, Uttusena, and Kallachchiya in the Batticaloa district." The author of the book from which I quote the above, Gangodagama Pannavedha, reiterates the Tamilization of the Sinhalas of the area: when Kitalagama first arrived at Dimbulagala, "he noticed that everybody in that village spoke Tamil,"[49] as if that needed urgent rectification.

The regalization of the acts of petty village-level political operatives, the use of the imagery of war and conquest, the depiction of the settlement of Sinhala villagers in conventionally Tamil territory as a movement and installation of vast multitudes in different and unknown lands, are of great anthropological interest for their multivocality and their divergent ethical configurations. At one level of meaning and ethics, these pronouncements indicate a worldview that goes back to the days of the national chronicle, the *Mahavamsa,* and indeed to still older pan-Indian conceptions of kingship in which rulers of petty principalities and postage-stamp realms proclaimed themselves, like Ozymandias, kings of kings, or like the Buddhist kings, styled themselves wheel-rolling emperors of the universe with meanings of magical potency and embodiment of the power of all the universe on the one hand, and more down to earth and functional propagandist boasting on the other. At another level we are undoubtedly witnessing characteristic monastic hyperbole and frenzied hagiographic embellishment that is the hallmark of Sinhala Buddhist monastic culture, but that is also familiar to us from premodern hierarchical and imperial systems. These two levels of meaning are

48. These "Sinhala" names deserve comment. Mudalihamy, Banda, and Bandara are Tamil. Silva and Sinno are Portuguese. To the credit of the ordinary Sinhala people, they have accepted them as Sinhala. When Hemasara calls these Sinhala, he accepts them too. But the Sinhala middle-class ideology that he has recently imbibed blinds him to his inconsistency. For the Sinhala man who calls himself "Kannaraja,"that name is Sinhala, as much as the Portuguese name "Silva" is Sinhala to Hemasara. More accurately, the Sinhala man who calls himself Kannaraja cares much less for the ethnicity and etymology of his name than for where his next meal comes from. Who is a Sinhala and who is a Tamil anyway, except in the imagination?

49. Gangodagama Pannavedha, *Dimbulagala Puvata,* 22.

ethically more or less neutral and can be anthropologically grasped more or less value neutrally. In contrast, we have a third level of meaning whose reference is to ethnic identity and hegemony, to the civilizing mission that drives a wedge in the structure of realistic and meaningful social relations that had evolved through the centuries between peoples different in language and "ethnicity" as a means of squeezing out an existence from the harsh natural conditions which these poverty-stricken people have had to contend with; in which bourgeois conceptions of nationalism and ethnicity are unknown and "identities" are ephemeral and, like the Buddhist notion of the self, devoid of a continuing essence; and in which such identities merge and become indistinguishable from one another as when Sinhalas become Tamil and vice versa. At this third level of meaning, the deliberate movement of people and their settlement in new territories becomes a disguised form of imperialism in which the newcomers and the original settlers are unwarrantedly and unnecessarily brought into confrontation with each other, establishing identities where none existed or sharpening them until friends are made into foes and ploughshares into swords. Whereas the first two instances of meaning and ethical configuration can be elucidated, as mentioned above, in a more or less value neutral way, employing technical vocabularies and jargons and generating statements of varying degrees of sense, the third demands that the responsible anthropologist introduce the element of value and make judgment and make his own contribution to the ethical critique articulated by members of a significant subculture of the culture he is studying. In more generalized form, this means there are some problems with the anthropological idea of culture. A society, however small scale, is not a cultural unity, and there are always individuals and groups who question it. A society is rather a cultural diversity warring within itself, and the anthropologist has no right to pretend that he has no interest in joining in.

Kitalagama was assassinated in 1996, by the LTTE it is believed, and the Sinhala Buddhist dimension of his work became evident, if any more than these activities themselves were needed for that, in the manner in which the Sinhala extremist elements tried to use his assassination to drum up support for their hegemonist cause and at the same time to discredit the government's attempt at a peaceful solution by means of a package of devolution. They organized a "memorial procession" that traversed much of the country, carrying a life-sized statue of Kitalagama, making sure that it got extensive media coverage, a fact acknowledged by the award of "memorial certificates" *(upahara sahatika)* to media personnel and organizations that helped broadcast the event.[50] The procession started from the village of Kitalagama, the

---

50. *Divayina,* 28 July 1996.

birthplace of Kitalagama, near the southern town of Matara, and traveled via Galle, Colombo, Kelaniya, Gampaha, Kandy, Dambulla, Anuradhapura, and Polonnaruva to its destination at Dimbulagala, taking sixteen days. A public meeting was held in Colombo subsequently, ostensibly to thank those who supported the procession, but along with the procession itself, such meetings and the later call to appoint a commission to investigate the assassination share the subtext of furthering Sinhala Buddhist propaganda in general and of discrediting the devolution proposals in particular as "dividing the country" and "selling out to the Tamils." Some of the speakers mentioned Kitalagama's "multi-religious" interests and his desire to see Sinhalas, Tamils, and Muslims coexist peacefully, and also that among the eight hundred young monks he ordained were some Tamils. One other speaker, however, Madihe Pannasiha, alluded to Kitalagama's plans to settle 35,000 Sinhala people in the Eastern province and attributed the failure of the plan to "sabotage" by some unnamed party, citing this failure as the reason for the "situation we face today," whatever that may be.

WHERE ARE THE RADICAL MONKS?
The Sangha and the One-way Flow of Goods

Regi Siriwardena, one of Sri Lanka's leading western-educated intellectuals,[51] articulates a specific and pointed ethical critique of the Sangha in the form of a question: why is there no movement of radical social concern in Buddhism?[52] The question was raised, after Siriwardena, by another western-educated intellectual, Dayan Jayatilleke.[53] The following discussion attempts to use Siriwardena's thoughtful question as a point of departure for further exploring the nature and etiology of the moral crisis of the Sangha.

Siriwardena's answer is built around the fact that the Buddha, as a prince, was separated from day-to-day toil, while Christ coming from the artisan class, was more aware of the mundane difficulties of ordinary people. The divergent paths of Buddhism and Christianity in relation to mundane societal

---

51. The term "western educated" is generally used in social science writings on Sri Lanka to refer to those who have received their education in the medium of the English language, as opposed to the indigenous literati educated in the national languages. This distinction, once profoundly indicative of completely different world views, is now (after the nationalist restoration of 1956) less sharp, as each group becomes more acquainted with the medium of instruction and the type of knowledge of the other group. Nevertheless, there is still a difference between the two types, the "western educated" being in the advantageous position of having access, through English, to a much wider world of knowledge than that available to the group educated in the indigenous languages.

52. Regi Siriwardena, "Where are the radical Buddhists?" *Lanka Guardian,* 15 March 15, 1979.

53. Dayan Jayatilleke, *Sri Lanka: The Travails of a Democracy* (see chap. 5, n. 21).

action spring from this basic difference in the social knowledge of the two founders. This is a perceptive answer, but more important is the fact that the question has been raised. It is striking, and suggestive of the directions in which we should look further for an answer, that the question had never been raised before.

It was an article on the Asian Theological Conference and its comments on the socially radical character of contemporary Christian movements that prompted Regi Siriwardena to raise the question. Siriwardena here represents the new social and intellectual awareness of the lack of a tradition of radical social concern in Buddhism, an awareness brought about by Christian activity going back to the nineteenth century and by the contemporary Christian movements of radical social concern, beginning with Liberation Theology. As observed above, the activities of the new evangelical groups in Sri Lanka, though hardly radical, are at present provoking a reactive social concern among Buddhist monks, most of which is parochial and defensive of "Buddhist interests." This reactive response is lacking in method, organization, vision, or genuine concern. As I have repeatedly emphasized, the rural development activities of the monks discussed earlier (chap. 3) are also of Christian inspiration, through the mediation of Dharmapala.

Clearly, it is in the comparative context of the post-colonial changes in Sri Lanka, in particular the advent of Christianity, that it has been possible to raise Regi Siriwardena's question. It was culturally unnecessary in the long history of Buddhism in Sri Lanka to raise it before advent of this social context. Stated differently, it was part of the complex of the basic and unquestionable cultural assumptions of Sinhala Buddhism that the monks, despite their vast properties, should not be a source of economic benefit to the laity. Conversely, the assumption was that economic goods and services flowed only in one direction, to the monks from the laity. The return gift to the laity was *non*-material: it consisted of ritual services in the form of bana preaching, pirit chanting, merit-making ceremonies, and spiritual guidance for the facilitation of the next world and ultimately liberation. The historical evidence for this process of mundane goods and services flowing in one direction and ritual/spiritual services in the other is ample. Never was this course changed or challenged. Far from any such, there were taboos backed by mystical sanctions against trespassing monastic properties or the use of its produce. There was a strong cultural sentiment to the effect that monastic property was of a certain ritual quality, which made it taboo for the laity and inauspicious for mundane purposes.

The springs of this were two fold. First was the *vibhavagami* or perfectly renunciatory nature of early Buddhism. Textualists as well as anthropologists

have cast doubt about this position, but it is difficult to see why, in its logically perfect form, Buddhism is anything less than this. The ultramundaneity of Buddhism became associated with inauspiciousness in the
context of broad Indian ritual ideas, despite Buddhism's very different conceptions of what and what was not auspicious, defining auspiciousness as it
did in ethical terms. Hence the beliefs held among rural Sinhala Buddhists,
despite the Buddhist textual position, that it is inauspicious to see a Buddhist
monk first thing in the morning; that the Buddhist monk should be kept
separate from marriage, the auspicious ceremony par excellence; and that
boys with horoscopes inauspicious for lay life should be selected for admission to the monkhood. This attitude to the monk expresses a radical separation in Buddhism between sacred and profane lives. In Hinduism, though
the renouncer is separated from the world, the sacred from the profane, the
ultimate goal is release from the cycle of rebirth into a divine and eternal
existence. In Buddhism, that goal is the bliss that derives from the annihila-
tion of the cause of rebirth, i.e., ignorance, thirst, and delusion. Thus in
Hinduism, unlike in Buddhism, despite the presence of renunciation, loop-
holes exist through which connections can be established between the mundane and the divine worlds: here the separation between the divine macro-
cosm and the human microcosm is, logically, not unbridgeable. The
commonest ritual expression of this connection is *puja,* in which food offerings made to the deities are returned to the devotees for consumption as
auspicious food. This contrasts with the practice in Buddhism where food
offered to the Buddha images is not consumed but thrown away to be eaten
by dogs and crows, evoking the ancient mystical sanctions against trespassing
monastic property and consuming its produce that proclaim that such tres-
passers will be born as dogs and crows.

The second source of the strong cultural idea that monastic property is
taboo and therefore that the laity cannot receive any economic goods or
services from the monks is the marked success of the monk's own propaganda. Most of the nearly exclusively religious literature in Sinhala, starting
about the twelfth century, along with the rituals designed by the monks,
constitute a chorus in praise of giving, i.e., of the one-way flow of economic
goods and services. This is perfectly consonant with early Buddhism's encouragement of wealth, which became one reason for its appeal for the urban mercantile classes (see chap. 7), whose wealth in turn made them exemplary donors and benefactors of Buddhism. Early Buddhist literature is
markedly populated with such patron figures, the model of whom is the
banker Anthapindika.

The effect of these two factors was to transform the monks, who were

Chapter Six

renouncers seeking their own salvation, into a priesthood which gradually receded from the goal of liberation and became practitioners of a ritual designed to meet what Max Weber called "plebeian religious needs." It is true that the monastery became the school as well, but the education imparted was primarily religious, and any mundane knowledge imparted was not practical or substantial but theoretical and minimal. The differentiation between the forest and village dwelling monks, despite the latter's greater interaction with the laity, did nothing to free the mind of the laity from the idea that the monk, forest or village dwelling, was a social category completely separate from mundaneity. The stamp of asceticism that the public imagination placed on the monk was so indelible, and the monastic propaganda about the unidirectional flow of material goods and services so successful, that the potential the differentiation into forest and village dwelling had for the evolution of a monastic concern for the material welfare of its flock withered away. From the laity's point of view, that differentiation was an internal problem of the monkhood, which in no way affected the ritual status of the monk in relation to them. Thus village dwelling continued to be imbued with the same ultramundaneity as the monkhood as a whole did prior to this differentiation. This meant that the taboos and interdictions that hedged the general monk/lay relation continued unabated. Any monk/lay association that went beyond the traditional was an abuse (kula dusanaya) that polluted the monk's morality or monkness.

It was not only in the conceptual world of the monk that the flow of material goods and services remained a one-way process. It was unthinkable for the laity, as well, that they would be any other than givers to the monks. Has giving after all not been elevated by monastic machinations as the first and foremost step, as well as the most potent, in the generation of merit, and has it not been connected to liberation through the mechanism of interpreting giving as a means of "thinning out" greed and the notion of the self? Thus both the average person interested in merit and the special person with a serious interest in diligently treading the path of liberation were neutralized as to any possibility of accepting the idea that monks could be givers.

In addition, there were broader factors that prevented the monkhood from developing an interest in the mundane welfare of the laity. The ideal radical separation of the renouncer from the world, which meant indifference to economic activity, ensured his total dependence on the laity for his subsistence. Though ideally a regimen designed for individual liberation and therefore "selfish," the monk's state was a sacred one and this, combined with his dependence on the laity, made the support given to monks highly meritorious. The monks were "fields of merit" that the laity, devoid of the strength to renounce, found to be ideal objects of cultivation for merit making. It would then be in the interest of the laity to give to the monks and foolish to receive from them: it would be a source of demerit to deplete the resources of a category who were so preeminently and sacrally deserving as recipients. These ideas contributed to the evolution of a worldview that was utterly inhospitable for the growth of the idea of monks working for the material welfare of the laity. Not without the model and challenge of Christianity was it possible for the monks to begin to modify this view, and that under the guidance of a persuasive and charismatic semi-monk, Anagarika Dharmapala.

The factors discussed above did not stop at merely preventing the growth of an ethic of lay economic welfare in the history of the monkhood. Aided by the lay greed for merit, the cultural idea that the flow of material goods and services is ideally unidirectional led to the formation of a specific monastic attitude akin to the spoilt child syndrome. The monks became a pampered group who gradually came to think of lay donations as their right far in excess of that allowed them, namely, requisites meant to maintain a state of physical health adequate for mental regimen. This, along with the deference paid to them by all including kings and nobles, bred in the monastic psyche a self-importance grossly at variance with the conceptions of monkhood as reflected in the vinaya literature. This is the origin of the renowned "king-size egos" and narcissism rampant in the monkhood, a phenomenon reflected in their love of long titles that mean nothing and their penchant for prefixing their names with "Sri," which Dharmapala saw through and ridiculed.[54]

The effect of these cultural notions also contributed to an isolation of the monk from any realistic and felt idea of the economic hardships of the ordinary people. Comfortably and bountifully ensconced, some of them became little kings and princes of their localities, their "power" arising not from their religious authority or "monkness" but their wealth. While rural monks, like their fellow villagers, were and are poor, they are still on the average better off than the villagers. The culture of the monks, especially that of the elite monkhood from whom alone overarching ideas applicable to the order as a whole could emerge, was nonconducive to the growth of an awareness of the sweat and toil that the productive process demanded. It was not possible for even ordinary social concern, far less radical concern, to arise in such a group.

The social factors discussed above also contribute to an explanation of

54. Guruge, ed., *Dharmapala Lipi*, 114.

the paradox of an allegedly infinitely compassionate order's appalling insensitivity to large-scale human suffering as reflected in its defense of war and bloodshed and, in the often quoted instance in the *Mahavamsa,* its denigration of the nonbeliever into an object fit for murder. Thus the ideal universalism of Buddhism has been transformed into the parochialism of elevating the Sinhala ethnic group to the status of true owner and citizen of Sri Lanka. The related parochial identification of Buddhism with the Sinhala ethnicity explains the monkhood's ignorance of its own history, an ignorance that has enabled it to isolate itself from the Tamil contribution to Buddhism. It also explains the failure, surprising for a missionary religion, to explore the proselytizing possibilities of neighboring non-Buddhist populations, in particular the low-caste Tamils subjected to religious discrimination by the upper-caste Jaffna Hindu Tamil establishment. This is the more glaring when we consider the work of the Indian Buddhist leader Ambedkar in spreading Buddhism among the untouchable groups in India. It is more than likely that even the elite monkhood, with the exception of a fraction of a percentage, did not and do not know of Ambedkar, their knowledge of India being confined to the legends about Buddhism and its migrations, which are taken literally. The ignorance of Ambedkar's work is a commentary on the limited geographical and intellectual horizons of the monkhood. In both its failure to make an effort to understand the Tamil contribution to Buddhism and to carry the message of Buddhism among low-caste Tamils, the monkhood has failed to use the opportunities genuinely available to it to work for "country, nation and religion."

Related to the monkhood's lack of broad social and human concern is the warmongering propaganda of the elite monks and the theory that a military victory alone would solve Sri Lanka's ethnic problem when it is perfectly clear that, had the monkhood taken a firm stand for peace, the question would have been easily solved. The warlike stand and its obverse, the opposition to devolution, in addition to illustrating the lack of humanism and compassion, is telling of the ignorance of the monkhood of its own social organization, which is one of the most extreme decentralization imaginable. Throughout its history monastic groups have had the privilege and freedom to break away from the hegemony of the majority and establish a consensual community of their own. The nineteenth and twentieth century history of Sri Lankan monasticism is one of splintering,[55] the most prolific example being the Amarapura Nikaya, which has over thirty such groups. The orthodox Siyam Nikaya, which already had three independent units prior to the

---

55. On splintering, see K. Malalgoda, *Buddhism in Sinhalese Society, 1750–1900.*

1970s, now has two more, one in the south and the other established, as discussed above (in chap. 5), in the early 1990s by Inamaluve Sumangala, who broke away from Asgiriya in an attempt to control the extensive economic resources of the Dambulla Vihara. Contrary to general belief, the nikayas are nominal entities, completely devoid of any organization. Not even the smallest social unit, the village monastery, is under any but its own control. The monkhood is ideally the epitome of devolution. This profuse self-determination the monks themselves enjoy stands in sharp contrast to their denial of that right to others, which further illustrates the unreasonableness, intolerance, and the spoilt child syndrome of the monkhood.

In a response to Siriwardene, Kumari Jayawardena has pointed out the example of rebel monks as constituting evidence of social concern.[56] However, this response fails to distinguish between the economic/pragmatic and the political/ideological, which was also the problem with the entire Dharmapalite project. The rebel monks no doubt, especially under imperialism, represented a certain subalternism, but its context was political. What Regi Siriwardena is raising is a question of economics. Far from questioning Siriwardena's position, the theory of the rebel monks, properly understood, is a confirmation of that position. For it is the preoccupation with the political/ideological that has prevented the monkhood from developing an interest in the economic/pragmatic. Concern for society is, in that preoccupation, politicized and sloganized, and denuded of possibilities of actualization. Even worse, such politicized concern, as the history of the monkhood shows, quickly degenerates into a championing of the Sinhala Buddhist cause and the oppression of the minorities. The monkhood's preoccupation historically has been political and even that has been an interest ultimately reducible to maintaining its wealth, influence, and privileges. The monkhood's only radical stand has been an anti-imperialism, but this was an anti-imperialism so narrow that it was little more than an attempt to safeguard and maintain elite monastic interests with no concern for even the non-elite monks and far less the lay society.

We have an excellent examples of interfering with the democratic process by the SLFP government in 1970 and the UNP government in 1977. The former postponed elections by two years, and the latter abolished the election altogether for an entire term of six years by means of a referendum. Each wore a constitutional fig leaf, but the truth in both cases was that the government was holding on to power illegally and undemocratically. Had

56. Kumari Jayawardena, "Bhikkhus in revolt," *Lanka Guardian,* 15 July 1979, continued in the next issue.

the Sangha had a true social concern, it could have staged a protest and demanded the restoration of the democratic process, but it did not. This contrasts with the large-scale protest by the monks at the signing of the 1987
Indo-Lanka Accord and more recently in their opposition to the devolution
proposals of the government and in their enraged reaction to the statement
made by a cabinet minister, Mangala Samaraweera, that the report of the
"Sinhala Commission" should go into the dustbin of history.[57] This silence in
the former case and protests in the latter cases reflects the parochialism of
the monks and their identification of their own sectional interest with the
national interest. Yet these and similar exercises of the monks are proclaimed to be "preserving" Buddhism and "protecting country, nation, and
religion."

PRECEPT AND PRACTICE
The Failure of Inner-worldly Asceticism

The lack of social concern on the part of the monkhood is intimately bound
up with its structural position as recipient in relation to the laity, and with
the cultural evaluation of renunciation which more or less prohibits the renouncer from making any material return gifts. The historic role of the
monk in Sri Lanka was religious and cultural, and not economic, despite the
attempts of Buddhist modernists to portray that role as a mundane one. I
have argued that this attempt, originating in the work of Anagarika Dharmapala and given a boost by Walpola Rahula's *The Heritage,* is a response to
the social changes that have taken place in the island as a result of contact
with the West, in particular British colonialism, and an adaptation to the
socially involved role of the Christian clergy. The fact that the monk historically played no role in providing mundane economic benefit to the people

---

57. The "Sinhala Commission" is a body appointed to investigate the "injustices" done to the majority Sinhalas. It is backed by Sinhala extremist mercantile interests, which will profit by eliminating
Tamil and Muslim business activities, particularly the retail trade. If the ethnic question were peacefully
resolved, they will face stiff competition from Tamil and Muslim businesses, which are generally more
efficient and more customer oriented. It is in their business interest therefore to oppose the government's proposals to peacefully solve the ethnic problem by means of devolution of power to the minorities. The Sinhala Commission is part of the Sinhala extremist campaign to derail the government's
proposals to solve the ethnic question peacefully by devolving power to the minorities. It represents an
attempt to evoke and identify itself with the "Buddhist Commission," which played a role in the victory
of the nationalist forces in 1956. Minister Mangala Samaraweera's assessment of the report evoked a
Sangha response of seething rage. They issued on the minister the *patta nikujjana kamma,* "the act of
turning over the bowl," which amounts to a Buddhist fatwa.

does not mean that Buddhism is devoid of a worldly economic ethic, or that the monks did not preach any such ethic to the laity. As I try to demonstrate in chapter 7, early Buddhism had precisely such an ethic. This ethic was also an integral part of the Buddhist revival in late-nineteenth and early-twentieth century Sri Lanka, which suggests that Buddhist "reformations" are accompanied by strong impulses for economic action. The activation of this ethic, however, was restricted to urban Buddhism, both in ancient India and in modern Sri Lanka. The problem is therefore not the absence of an economic ethic per se but of mechanisms for its generalization to the larger social order. It was such a mechanism that Dharmapala and his hero-giants tried to forge. This failed, yielding to the recurrent tendency in Sri Lankan Buddhism to keep precept and practice separate, as paradigmatically expressed in the second-century "victory" of the dhammakathikas over the pamsukulikas, theorists over practitioners. To put it in a nutshell, there is plenty of moral talk in Sri Lanka, but little of moral action.

From the point of view of social and economic development or of its broader expression, which is the rationalization of social life in Sri Lanka, there cannot be a more significant question than (1) the absence of socio-cultural mechanisms to yoke together precept and practice, and (2) the fact that this absence is not superficial but woven intricately and pervasively into the social fabric.

Dharmapala and his followers, in particular Kalukondayave, came up with the idea, revolutionary in the context of existing Theravada though less so in terms of "ancient Buddhism," that the best way to ensure a good rebirth and eventual liberation is to live a morally based, methodical, and successful life in this world. That moral base consisted of living according to the precepts and the concept of Right Livelihood of the Noble Eightfold Path. It is a theory that laid great emphasis on success in this world, in particular successfully taking care of one's family, and it also emphasized practicing a generosity that supported those in need, which preeminently included the monks. It banished magic from its world, in which merit-making and other forms of ritualism had no place either, as is well attested in the writings of Dharmapala, Kalukondayave, Rahula, and some other Buddhist modernists, and in ancient Buddhism's rebellion against Hindu ritualism. The other aspect of this moral base is what Dharmapala termed "non-sensuousness." As we have repeatedly noted, this mode of conduct, though serene and happy, was abnegating. It abhorred any kind of pleasure in the gratification of the senses—music, theater, alcohol, poetry, sex, and so forth. Nor was there in it a place for mystical pleasures and immersions derived from semi-sexual orgies, cultic unions with the divine, ritual feasts and intoxications, or any

other form of superexcitation of the physical and psychic life. One of Dharmapala's favorite exhortations was not to have big families, which in the
absence of contraception, meant only one thing, abstention. Instead, Dharmapala exhorted his followers not to waste time, not to be slothful, to be
clean and orderly, and to engage in relentless productive work. The parallels
with Max Weber's "this-worldly asceticism" are striking.

Despite Dharmapala's charisma and stirring speeches and the astonishing
energy that his hero-giants and soldiers put into the work of rural development, the message of hard work and abnegation did not take root. On all
fronts—hard work, moral behavior, and abandonment of ritualism—not
only did the message not take root, but the situation has degenerated since
the time of these reformers, the last of whom (Hendiyagala) worked well
into the 1940s. Clearly, a crucial link that would have translated precept into
practice was missing. The idea of rural development failed to connect in an
effective and lasting manner with society to generate the hoped-for dynamism. On the contrary, since the 1940s the workplace has become more
like a leisure place, ritualism has taken over social and political life, invading
even the national legislature and the presidency, and moral behavior has fled
the social order. Why?

For an answer, it is useful to look at the Calvinism from which Dharmapala derived his ideas about honesty, hard work, and thrift. As mentioned at
the beginning of this study, Weber established, convincingly to many, a series
of functional relations where certain religious doctrines led to certain work
habits culminating in a culture of work in the process of which the world
was ridden of magic and all institutions of society were rationalized.[58] The
crucial link is "inner-worldly asceticism," which enabled relentless work without enjoying its fruits. Both variables—work and nonenjoyment—had to be
present for the successful rationalization that according to Weber took place
in the case of ascetic Puritanism. This combination was made possible because of the Calvinistic idea of predestination. In the Sri Lankan case as advocated by Dharmapala everything else is present except a doctrinal mechanism to build into the individual psyche the impulse for action, with the
potential of this becoming a social fact autonomous of individual psyches.

According to Weber, it was the threat of eternal damnation that acted as
the activating mechanism of a life committed to do nothing but work with
no enjoyment whatsoever of its fruits. It is this variable that is missing in
Buddhist eschatology. The theory of samsara precludes eternal damnation,
for however lengthy and cruel the sufferings are of the multiplicity of hells,

58. See Max Weber, *The Protestant Ethic and the Spirit of Capitalism*. This thesis is also elaborated
elsewhere in Weber's work.

these are not eternal, and after paying for one's crimes one returns to a more acceptable birth in the samsaric journey. Since there is rebirth, it is possible to forever postpone to another existence the deep and methodical commitment necessary for liberation. The Buddhist theory does portray samsaric existence as suffering, sorrow, and recurring death. The problem in Buddhism is in fact not satiety with life but with death, as Weber pointed out. The literary descriptions of hell and their depictions in temple murals do portray samsara as an ocean of suffering. In addition, the Buddhist theory of the rarity of the factors that must combine for one to be able to liberate oneself—birth as an intellectually and physically capable human being at a time when the doctrine of liberation is available—does emphasize the urgency of toil. This attitude is also reflected in the Buddha's last advice to his disciples to be islands unto themselves and to strive with diligence. Yet it appears that nothing short of an everlasting cannon aimed at the head can act as an effective deterrent against human sloth. As against such a cannon, which the Calvinistic doctrine of predestination provided, the horrors of the Buddhist hells turn out to be minor inconveniences. The idea of rebirth effectively acted as a purging mechanism by means of which a bad rebirth functioned to expiate one's sins, making one ready to start the next round of sins, as in Catholic confession.

There were, besides, two further factors, the first ideal and the second material, that prevented the growth of an inner-worldly asceticism as envisaged in the theory of Dharmapala and his followers. First, the cultural practices of ritualism and merit in rural Buddhism were too powerful for it to successfully combat. As Buddhism became ruralized, the gap between the layman and the ideal monk, the slow and fast paths to liberation, grew wider. Conversely, the real monk became closer to the layman as a co-participant in a religious world of magic and ritualism. This led to an otiosization of the ideal monk, who was reduced to a mere ghost of an idea, or at best a few intermittent forest dwellers, the official "forest dwellers" themselves having been routinized and ruralized into garden variety monasticism. Stated differently, the ascetic ideal was fetishized, which prevented it from animating the workaday life of this world. Instead, workaday life and asceticism were radically estranged from each other.

This, coupled with the value placed on giving *(dana)*, made it much more appealing to stay with the traditional system according to which, instead of the difficult practice of renunciation, one took the easy way out by seeking liberation vicariously and through merit. This indeed was doctrinally sanctioned in the sense that the Buddhist search ideally called for a total commitment, i.e., treading the fast path, with the laity on the slow path aiding those on the fast path. This was done by supporting those who renounced, which effectively meant any robed person. That is, the culture of rural Buddhism or Sinhala Buddhism was so deeply rooted that the Dharmapalite idea, despite its forceful articulation by him and his able followers, was not strong enough to divert the majority away from the traditional system of magical practices and merit-oriented ritualism.

Second, and perhaps more important in the failure of the Dharmapalite idea in encouraging a culture of work, was the absence of institutional and infrastructural support. For, in the absence of strong cultural or individual imperatives or motivating forces, such a support system would have had the potential, through employment and other forms of incentive, to lay the foundation of activity equal to its advocacy. The rural development program, though admirable, was limited in its economic scope and remained so, gaining the support neither of capital nor the expert personnel needed to expand it to embrace the large-scale productive activity and industrialism dreamed of by Dharmapala. Neither his hero-giants nor any others succeeded in taking up the industry aspect of the Dharmapalite project, all remaining with its rural and small agriculture aspect. This was a function of the internal contradictions of the Dharmapalite project itself. While talking about industrialism, the project had no coherent plan to put it into action and instead placed an undue emphasis on the romantic and idyllic rural community, a notion derived from western romanticizers of sylvan villages. Where such support existed, including education, groups of people took to methodical work, giving rise to pockets of economic and other forms of systematic productive activity and the rationalization of individual and group life. These groups were the core of the middle classes who exorcised folk ritualism from their lives but who embraced, along with Buddhist morality, a renewed "Buddhist" ritualism. This preference for "Buddhist ritual," however, remained fragile: under strain, these classes accepted a ritualism more bizarre than any the folk system had ever invented.[59] At the same time, their economic, organizational, and other forms of rationalization of the mundane life, having come into being, have remained intact. In sum, the novelty of the Dharmapalite doctrine, its noncompetitive position in relation to the entrenched and powerful beliefs in magic, and the absence of institutional and infrastructural sources of support militated against its efforts and tipped the balance in favor of traditionalism. Any serious attempt at placing the society on a rational and systematic foundation must take adequate account of these factors.

59. See Richard Gombrich and G. Obeyesekere, *Buddhism Transformed.*

Appendix

DEVOLUTION PACKAGE AND MAHA SANGHA

"Only a plebiscite can decide Sangha opinion on ethnic issue"

by D. Amarasiri Weeraratne

It was with dismay that I read of the Maha Sangha meeting held at the BMICH on March 5 to denounce the Devolution Package offered by the Government. Very discreetly the Mahanayake Theras of the three Nikayas have kept away. The convenors of the meeting were the well-known Sinhala Only hardliners who oppose any form of devolution of powers to the minorities in areas where they predominate. These hardliners see any form of devolution as a stepping stone to separatism and the division of the country. They have gone paranoid with an Eelam phobia and they see the proposals as the writing on the wall for separatism.

It is well known that all attempts in the past to resolve the ethnic problem by the B-C pact, Dudley-Chelvanayakam pact, and the All-Party Conference convened by President Jayewardene were scuttled by hardliners in the Maha Sangha who spearheaded the Sinhala Only chauvinists. Thus Ven. Baddegama Wimalawansa led [the] Phalanx

that forced Premier S. W. R. D. Bandaranike to abrogate the B-C pact. Ven. Madihe Pannasiha spearheaded the chauvinists who scuttled the D-C pact. This fact is admitted on page 140 of the history of the Amarapura Dharmarakshita sect. The book is titled *"Dam Reki Naka."*

The attempts to settle the ethnic problem by the All-Party Conference convened by President Jayawardene was wrecked by Ven. Palipane Chandrananda in league with the Sinhala Only hardliners. The result of all these wreckings by the Sangha led to continued agitation and protests by the democratic Tamil parties.

When all attempts to settle the problem by democratic methods failed, the Tamils were driven into the arms of the terrorists who posed as the saviours of the Tamil people. They said the only method of reducing their aspirations was by military means. From this point the LTTE terrorists took over the leadership of the Tamil agitation for autonomy in their regions. Hence, the present war which is ruining our economy and taking a heavy toll of our military forces. Now the war has come to Colombo and the whole world has seen the carnage at the Central Bank through TV coverage of the incidents.

No ethnic problem

The Sangha leadership who spoke at the recent BMICH meeting have stated that there is no ethnic problem in Sri Lanka. Therefore, there is no need to ask for a solution to a non-existent problem. And also there is no need for the Government to evolve a plan to meet the aspirations of the Tamils for regional autonomy. The Sangha spokesmen saw only a terrorist problem and they called for the subjugation of the LTTE by military means. Then according to them, in the absence of an ethnic problem or dispute there will be peace, law and order in the country.

But the fact remains that before the LTTE took to arms, there was agitation by the Tamil democratic parties that believed in a negotiated settlement by peaceful means. They found that the Maha Sangha spearheaded the agitation against all three agreements and wrecked them. So to deny the existence of any ethnic problem and say there is only a terrorist problem is a failure to understand the background and the cause for the resort to arms. No terrorist war will be possible unless people sympathize and support them.

Chauvinists

The spokesmen who claimed to voice the opinion of the Maha Sangha are inveterate chauvinists who are not prepared for any form of devolution. They are not experts in political science and their knowledge of international political problems and constitutions is poor. Their opinions on the ethnic problem and democratic ways and means of settling it cannot be taken seriously. Only a plebiscite among the Sangha can indicate what is the opinion of the Maha Sangha on this issue. This probably is the last chance we have to settle this problem by peaceful means. If the government gives in to the arm-twisting tactics of the jingoist Sangha our nation will be doomed to unending war, economic ruin, and a strangulation of our efforts to rise above third world poverty status, and general ruin.

The Government has to be run by the elected Members of Parliament. There is no room in the constitution to give in to pressure tactics of reactionary monks. We have to respect the Sangha only when they teach us the Dhamma in which they are experts and authorities. Their advice can be sought by the rulers only on matters concerning how to rule in accordance with the Dhamma. Beyond this they have no right or scope. In the whole Buddhist world it is the Sinhala Sangha who says that "politics is the bhikkus' heritage." It is a heritage of apostasies coming down from the Anuradhapura period, and should be disallowed as recommended by the Buddhist Commission report which the first Bandaranaike Government undertook to implement. Before it could be done the Premier was assassinated by a power-hungry Buddhist monk. And with that, Sasana reforms recommended have gone underground.

If the Sangha is properly organized and controlled by the Maha Nayakes as is done in the other Theravada countries such as Burma and Thailand they will not resort to the present corruptions and apostasies such as politics, business ventures, renting out temple rooms to laymen including LTTE agents, running garages, printing presses, tuition classes, karate classes, parking vehicles for a fee, etc, etc. Therefore, the first duty of the Sangha is to set their house in order instead of trying to dictate to Parliament what it should do and not do.

—FROM THE *OBSERVER,* 17 MARCH 1996

FROM REGENERATION TO DEGENERATION

In these concluding remarks, I will first recapitulate the general argument of this study while appending to it a brief comment on the fate of Dharmapala's overseas missionary project. Next, I will revisit Max Weber's paradigm of Buddhism, with which I began this exploration, and both articulate a critique and suggest an archeology of Buddhist ethics especially relating to economic activity.

In the preceding chapters we have, as the primary theme of the present work, dealt with the contemporary Sangha's belated attempt to come to terms with the complex and bewildering new society brought about by the powerful forces arising from contact with the West in the form of colonial domination. This was essentially an attempt on the part of the Sangha to regain the status and influence it allegedly enjoyed in the precolonial society going back to two millennia. It is likely that this bid for status would have come about anyway, but it was hastened and given a particular stamp by the reformer Anagarika Dharmapala. The social empowerment of the monk in Dharmapala's imagination was legitimized by the monk's exemplary dedication, knowledge, and morality. Largely as a result of the Dharmapalite project, the Sangha has now made certain status gains, but these have been made at the expense of the morality that was central to the Dharmapalite project. To that extent the reformation that Dharmapala so earnestly intended to bring about has failed. To a large extent this moral failure is an intellectual failure that has prevented the Sangha from comprehending the nature of the modern state as an entity that consists of a diversity of ethnic groups, languages, religions, and cultures. But that moral failure has other aspects. In the preceding pages I have documented some of these in some detail.

The effective role of the monk in Sri Lankan society is the religious one, understood in the broad syncretistic sense. Some folk ritualist elements of this syncretistic religion have lost the wide currency they enjoyed even about half a century ago, and some, like the Pattini rituals, have more or less disappeared.[1] The elites have given up only the folk ritualism, or, more correctly, some parts of it. They remain engulfed in deity and planet worship, astrology, and the "Buddhist" ritualism developed by the "village dwelling" (gramavasi) monks through the centuries. The "Buddhist" part of this sociological whole consists of offering alms, preaching, and chanting of pirit texts (bana, dana and pirit) in ritualized form. Monks also ritually participate in funerals. The rural monk is bound to the village by bonds of reciprocity because he provides ritual service in return for material support the laity gives him. This "return gift" is nonmaterial. Rahula's *The Heritage* relegates this ritual service of dana, bana and pirit to the illiterate rural monks. This was part of an attempt to define the monk's role not as ritual (as it truly is) but as "social service." In Dharmapala's definition, the monk's role benefits society by means of its leadership in national regeneration. Rahula's definition of that role as "social service," instead, benefits the players themselves rather than the society. While Rahula pays lip service to asceticism as part of his conception of the monk, there is no systemic room for any such in the scheme he develops in which the monk's role is a completely secular one.

The task of the anthropologist is not to question and even less to denounce the monk's claim that his role is social service but rather to examine the social formations such a claim brings about. Part of that exercise is an assessment of the extent to which the claims become socially effective. In this case, has the monk become an effective social worker in the sense that

1. Gananath Obeyesekere's classic work, *The Cult of the Goddess Pattini* (Chicago: University of Chicago Press, 1984) is both the most comprehensive documentation and the most imaginative interpretation of this fascinating complex of rituals. This work provides one of the many examples of the ignorance of the nationalist intellectuals of the work in the area of national culture done by scholars they consider "western." Gananath Obeyesekere's contribution to the study of the society and culture of Sri Lanka, going back to his brilliant undergraduate days when he, along with some other young scholars, founded *Samskriti,* a journal that became one of the most significant cultural events of the island's recent history and was part of the golden age of the Peradeniya University, is virtually unknown in Sri Lanka and is a closed book for even the few people there who read "western" books. The work on the goddess Pattini is particularly timely today when extremists of both the Sinhala and Tamil ethnic groups are trying to separate the two groups. The Pattini rituals constitute one more demonstration of the cultural affinity between the Sinhala and Tamil peoples and of their synthesizing genius as opposed to the separating frenzies of demagogues of both groups. Obeyesekere's work is also a commentary on historiography in Sri Lanka, which has failed come up with a genuine national history that attempts to understand the objective reality of Sri Lanka as part of the rich tapestry of the south Indian complex of cultures that constitutes a distinct regional cultural whole. The obviously close affinities between the Sinhala and Kerala cultures, for which Obeyesekere's study provides evocative leads, are unexplored in Sri Lankan historiography. On the rituals of the goddess Pattini see also, Nur Yalman, "Dual Organization in Central Ceylon? or, The Goddess in the Tree-top," *Journal of Asian Studies* 24, no. 3: 441–47.

his goal of meaningful social work is achieved? Or has the definition of the monk as social worker instead led to developments other than social work? In short, what are the behavioral consequences of the contemporary definition of the monastic role? What kind of social monk has the definition produced?

There is no doubt that this definition produced some genuine social workers, but only a handful. We have discussed in detail the work of the three most important of these—Kalukondayave, Hinatiyana and Hendiyagala. The work of these pioneers, whatever their achievements—and they did achieve impressive results—failed to produce the vital spark necessary for a self-regeneration of the morality and productivity they and their leader Dharmapala envisaged. Their's was only a first ignition. When the flame of their movement blew out, there was no rekindling. The society failed to absorb their zeal. They remain isolated figures who made no lasting impact except a memory, and that only for a few devotees. In this their fate parallels that of the movement for rural regeneration in India inspired by Gandhi. Why this was so is the basic problem that besets the culture. It is the problem observed by the French priest who allowed Hinatiyana to "push" the members of the former's parish: namely, that the Sinhalas need to be constantly pushed to work for their own benefit (see p. 95). It is the problem Dharmapala saw with such clarity and denounced wrathfully as the Sinhala sloth. It is the problem unconsciously expressed in the Sinhala national anthem, reminding us of Dharmapala's recurring lush imagery of the Sinhala as eternally asleep: *nava jivana demine nitina apa avadi karan mata* (giving us new energy, O mother, keep waking us up forever; see p. 171n).

The definition of a new role for the monk did have a social consequence of a different kind. It produced a new monk. He was the monk of Rahula's, not Dharmapala's, definition. Rahula's monk is not the sober economic figure exemplified in the Dharmapalite monks Kalukondayave, Hinatiyana, and Hendiyagala, but the political monk of *The Heritage*. This dichotomy between Dharmapalite and Rahulite is not absolute. The Rahulite was implicit in the Dharmapala's conception of the monk. However, the realization of the Rahulite conception of the monk need not have necessarily occurred. The Rahulite conception could have remained dormant, as the case of the Vidyodaya monks shows. Monks could have entertained their own feelings about language, culture, ethnicity, and patriotism—and combined them with a broader vision of a harmonious, multi-ethnic, humane society, as the Vidyodaya monks did. That is, they could have been pragmatic nationalists whose social priorities were economic rather than ideological. In the end that pragmatism and the sober preoccupation with the economic were dethroned. Ideology was enthroned, holding the scepter of Sinhala Buddhist hegemonism.

The role advocated by Rahula ostensibly to benefit the society worked in the end to benefit the individual monks who, rather than doing any "social service," used their liberation from traditional duties and the education and travel opportunities in foreign lands that their new "social service" role enabled to engage in various employment and enterprising activities that brought benefit to themselves in the form of wealth, status, and sometimes power and influence. This gave rise to a monastic middle class with a small subclass of super rich monks, most of whom used their foreign connections to tap sources of wealth.

It will be recalled that it was Dharmapala's idea to spread Buddhism to a world waiting to receive it, and that the first missionaries were monks who worked on shoestring budgets. A generation later we come across the phenomenon of monks, many of them pupils or in some other way connected to these pioneers, going overseas and establishing themselves in foreign lands, facilitated by both philanthropists of those lands and by expatriate communities of Buddhists. A few of these monks control vast revenues and live the life of busy executives, replete with symbols like Mercedes Benzes, BMWs, and cellular phones. These monks have a foothold both in the country of their adoption and in Sri Lanka, and some hold immigrant status in several countries. At the lower end of this financially comfortable class are the salary-earning monks, mostly graduates, who, especially if they also have support from the laity as well as productive land, are able to invest money in businesses like repair shops, taxi services, rental properties, and tuition classes. A small minority also commercially practice astrology, medicine, and various occultisms, the "beastly arts" that are taboo for monks. Throughout history there were monks who practiced these, but now they do so with a new sense of legitimacy and commercialism.[2] These come from the new definition of the monk's role as social service. I have argued that once this definition was accepted, monks were liberated from their traditional role, and the floodgates were opened for them to do anything they pleased. Many monks who say their work is "social service" may not be engaging in this kind of activity for lack or resources, enterprise, or any other reason. Still, at the very least, the definition of the monk's work as social service has led to a greater secularization of the monks. Field evidence for this is unambiguous. In contrast, in other Theravada countries, in particular Thailand, the monk has been enlisted in "social service," for example in the Thammathuth (Dharmaduta) program, but its meaning, though not necessarily religious, is nevertheless strictly defined, leaving him no room for open and unlimited

---

2. In advertisements in national newspapers monks offer magical help in all spheres of activity—employment, examinations, court cases, family problems, love, interviews, and so forth. See for example the advertisement of the monk Telleke Dhammapala, *Divayina,* 7 January, 1996.

interpretation of that role. For the Thai monk, his social service work is an assignment from above, not an exercise in free enterprise.

Dharmapala's dream was a society with adequate economic resources, but not an excess of wealth. Economic success to him did not warrant a life of "sensuousness." Economic resources were only important insofar as they freed the people of day-to-day worries, enabling them to pursue the spiritual life. Though prosperous, Dharmapala's ideal society is an abnegating one. With the monk as philosopher and guide, society would engage itself in *ubhayalokartha,* "the gaining of both worlds," as Kalukondayave put it, a happy and contented life in this world and happy rebirths enabling eventual liberation from samsaric existence. Though contented, the life envisaged is a disciplined one. The parallel with the post-Calvinistic puritan society is striking. People would be living according to the five precepts, working hard so that the society has resources for an adequate standard of living and no more. The microcosmic model for this society Dharmapala had in mind is clearly the ideal monastery with its adequate yet not excessive resources, contented but not indulging. All activities would be purposive, orderly, and methodical, with no wasting of time in idle matters such as gossip and socializing. Literature, poetry, drama, theater, luxurious living, and exotic foods will have no place. The workaday life is the theater for liberation, for the gaining of both worlds. Thus in this scheme, the entire world would become the monastery. Instead, the monastery has become the world.

In precolonial society differences of wealth existed between monasteries. The poorer monasteries subsisted on the support of the villagers. But in its worldview the Sangha was one, although it was never anything like the politically powerful and unified class that it is assumed to be today by the media, the middle class, and politicians. The opening up of modern secular education has brought into being a class of modern secular-educated monks whose worldview is drastically different from that of the rural monk unexposed to that education. Modern secular education, however, has not imparted to them any of the broadening of vision that would have paved the way for a modernity of mind. Their secular education has in fact worked the other way: it has led them to the newly brewed Sinhala Buddhist nationalism that the less educated rural monks are spared. Due to the policy of teaching in Sinhala, the opportunity a modern secular education would have given them to broaden their vision has in fact been denied to them. (This obviously applies to lay students as well.) This is not to romanticize the rural monks. They are simply not caught in the primarily urban or urban-generated ideologies. Their activities are more localized, although the new attitudes and ideologies are steadily trickling down to the rural monks through the mass media.

The main reason why these new monks, who claim their work is social service, have failed to live up to the standards of service envisaged for them by Dharmapala is that they never intended any such in the first place. What they meant by social service was a license for them to have greater involvement with secular society beginning with politics. That license was given to them by *The Heritage*. Serious social service is a disciplined commitment, as Dharmapala rightly understood. It requires training, competence, and professionalism, which Dharmapala advocated and sought to provide. Had these monks been truly motivated to serve society, they would have sought the training to perform that service. It is because social service did not mean a serious commitment that they did not seek any. Further, social service, as Dharmapala envisaged it, was voluntary and honorary. It carried no emoluments and it left no room for business enterprise.

It is perhaps appropriate to speculate as to why for these monks social service did not become a commitment. I think it is because monkhood itself is not a commitment to most members of the Sangha. Sinhala Theravada monasticism as a cultural practice does not allow the individual to play a part in the choice of monasticism as a vocation. As perceptive members of the culture point out in their critique of the Sangha, these monks are typically admitted to monkhood when they are too young and immature to understand the nature of the commitment involved. Their recruitment is institutionalized and is often the result of a decision made by parents and other elders, including sometimes the village monk. From the point of view of sustaining a specific monastic establishment, there are good sociological reasons why this is a successful measure, but the success is limited to molding ("making," as the monks put it) the young new recruit into a typical member of the monastic establishment. The socialization process ensures efficient reproduction of the existing monastic culture replete with its prejudices, worldliness, and moral poverty. In the precolonial system there was at least a tradition of monastic learning that for all its traditionalism was a clearly discernible intellectual activity. This tradition, weakened during the nineteenth century, was revived in the latter half of that century, leading to a new flowering in the colleges of Vidyodaya and Vidyalankara. When these two colleges were conferred university status, the hope and dream of its sincerest supporters was that they would journey into a golden era. Instead they journeyed into death, bringing to an end a two-millennia-old tradition of scholasticism.[3]

3. During the debate in Parliament at the second reading of the bill to confer university status on Vidyodaya and Vidyalankara, N. M. Perera, Leader of the Opposition, made an incisive and lengthy

The most frequent label these monks now give themselves is that they are the "guardian deities" *(muradevatavo)* of the nation, a self-description reminiscent of the Brahmanic attempt to call themselves gods on earth. However, no one except a religious purist can quarrel with monks for determining what they want to do with themselves. If that task is playing "guardian deity" to the nation, the monks are entitled to do so, but the nation in turn is entitled expect that they are properly equipped to do so. For this they must acquire a minimum of basic knowledge in the areas of government, the economy, planning, nationhood, urbanism, public health, the arts, the sciences, ethnicity, human rights, rule of law, procedural justice, to name a few areas. And they must be generally knowledgeable about world affairs and the nature and functioning of world bodies and the key ideas underlying these bodies. In sum, if they want to function in an advisory capacity to the nation, they must have the qualifications to do so. It is one of the stark facts of the contemporary elite monastic scene in Sri Lanka that we do not have a single monk who would fit the basic requirements to qualify as an urbane, cosmopolitan, modern intellectual who alone would be qualified to play the role of "guardian deity." This is not to deny the presence of some thoughtful, broad-minded monks in the Sangha as a whole. But they are a tiny minority in a population of thirty thousand. At one stage in the present research, I was under the impression that a group of monks, those associated with the Manava Hitavadi Bhikshu Sangamaya (MHBS), which came into being in the 1980s, was an emerging force which would eventually transform the monkhood, especially the young monks, into a liberal, cosmopolitan, responsible social group. It is perhaps no accident that this group withered away, either by its members derobing, being killed off, or being compelled to seek foreign asylum. What happened is not clear, but what is clear is that the movement was nipped in the bud. The culture could not sustain it.

In fact, the problem is that "guardian deities" is a cliché. While it confers no status or power on the Sangha, it constitutes one manifestation of the

---

criticism. He made the central point that the bill was a carbon copy ("just paste, not even cut and paste") of the Ceylon University Ordinance that created the existing University of Ceylon. He argued that the bill duplicated the defects of that ordinance, and that the minister of Education, who tabled the bill, was simply "transplanting entirely western institutional forms on absolutely different institutions built purely upon oriental culture." He urged the minister to come up with a bill that would transform these two institutions into universities "on the basis of their own valuable traditions," and "without slavishly imitating what we had from abroad." These sentiments also express N. M. Perera's cosmopolitan patriotism and feel for national institutions, and contradict the theories of his cultural alienation spinned by the Lake House Group of newspapers. He prophetically said that the bill, instead of improving them, was doing a disservice to these institutions. As we now know, that was to put it mildly. See *Hansard,* 16 September 1958, columns 34–42.

specific kind of place the Sangha occupies in society today. That place is symbolic, which in fact is what it generally was historically. Stated differently, the term "guardian deity" is an aspect of the restoration of the Sangha to a place of ceremonial prominence in the post-independence era, more specifically and vociferously after the victory of the Sinhala Buddhist forces in 1956. In this ceremonial position, the Sangha is given public respect by the politicians by visits to the hierarchical monks and by giving them a place of honor and visibility on public occasions.[4] This is quite harmless, and, in fact, if both the Sangha and the politicians were to go about this with intelligence and a sense of social responsibility, both parties could benefit. The Sangha in particular would acquire for itself a certain degree of public esteem somewhat like that in which a constitutional monarch is held. With civility, intelligence, and good taste, the Sangha can achieve a place of esteem in the hearts of even non-Buddhist members of the society, as Kalukondayave did. However, no such exists at present either in the politician or the monk. In fact, the reality is worse. Politicians try to get any and everything out of dealings with the monks, and monks, yearning for status and "reflected glory," delight in hobnobbing with politicians, high bureaucrats, and other dominant figures, failing to distinguish between reality and symbolism. Politicians pretend that they are really asking the monks for "advice" when they are only flattering them, and the monks, taking literally what is only symbolic, expect the politicians to take their "advice." Thus both parties have cultivated an elaborate deception, the politicians deceiving the monks, and the monks deceiving themselves, with dire consequences to the nation the two parties claim to "guard" in their own ways.

THE FATE OF DHARMADUTA
Dharmapala's Overseas Mission

It will be recalled that the Dharmapalite project was an integrated whole consisting of national regeneration on the basis of Buddhist principles and also of the propagation of Buddhism overseas. Dharmapala considered the

4. The Sangha chiefs are also given certain perquisites, such as a Colombo residence and official vehicles. The following, however, is illuminating. According to informants and news reports, in 1997 the Mahanayaka of Asgiriya asked the government for a Mercedes Benz. The government complied but refused to give the title of ownership to the Mahanayaka personally, arguing that the vehicle was the property of the office, not the incumbent. The Mahanayaka insisted on personal ownership. The government agreed but informed the Mahanayaka that personal ownership meant that he had to pay customs duties, like any private citizen, whereupon the Mahanayaka refused the vehicle.

western industrial world as being particularly ready to accept the humane message of the Buddha. The first step in this project was the reestablishment of Buddhism in India, the land of its birth, and the reclamation for the Buddhists of control over the sacred sites at Buddha Gaya from the hold of the Hindu priest *(mahant)*. As with all other activities, the overseas missionary project was conceived of as a methodical venture that needed trained missionaries. For this purpose Dharmapala established a modest training program for the first missionaries who would gain further training in India. The fascinating details of this project are not our concern here. Our concern is merely to point out the same pattern of degeneration or goal displacement in this project as in the case of the definition of the role of the monk as social service. The foreign missions in fact are only the foreign arm of the same social service project, manned by products of the same monastic culture and subject to the same broad social forces. It is thus not surprising that it met with the same fate as the local project: the altruistic ideal was replaced by the desire of individual monks to gain status, influence, wealth, and, where possible, power.

An interesting development is the establishment of chiefships in various countries, paralleling those of the hierarchies of Malvatta and Asgiriya. Such hierarchies and titles were not anywhere within the scheme of planned by Dharmapala, and in fact they were mocked by him. Besides, these chiefships, like their prototypes in Sri Lanka, have absolutely no meaning beyond providing some purely vain psychological satisfaction to the bearer and to his and his domestic and local group's status pretensions at home in Sri Lanka. There are chief Sanghanayakas for England, India, Japan, Korea, Malaysia, and the U.S.A., and these are rapidly proliferating in all countries where there are missions. In this imaginary world conquest, there is a most peculiarly ironical consummation of Dharmapala's foreign missionary project.

These missionaries either stay on in foreign lands and establish themselves or have two establishments, one in the foreign country and the other at home. Going abroad even on short visits itself is prestigious and is consciously understood as potently convertible to mobility locally. The phenomenon of foreign travel as a means of mobility has three meanings: (1) purely symbolic, (2) part of status-striving in a pressure group, and (3) functional in economic/business advancement. In their own cultural analysis of the phenomenon of foreign travel in its role as facilitator of mobility and status, perceptive Sangha members call it "enforeignization" *(videsa-gatavima)*. This is explicitly understood as a swift mechanism of mobility. As in the local version of the total project, it is not the case that there were or are no committed individual monks. It is rather that the project as a whole succumbed to the same cultural forces that enabled goal displacement on the domestic front.

Two developments have taken place in the foreign missions. First and in keeping with the original purposes, the missions have targeted the nationals of the foreign country in which they are located. The monks concerned have found, not surprisingly that in most western countries subjected to modernism, there are people with a serious interest in what Buddhism has to offer. Often such clients, especially nuns, have had the salutary effect of elevating the moral life of these monks, for example, by being a force in inducing conformity to orthopraxy like vegetarianism, and in creating an atmosphere of seriousness in the broad program of the mission as well as in day-to-day activity. The second development is the gradual adaptation of the missionary establishment to the religio-cultural demands of Buddhist expatriates from Sri Lanka and sometimes other Theravada countries such as Burma, Vietnam, Cambodia, and Thailand. This development is not peculiar to the Sri Lankan missions but common to those from other Buddhist countries and also to other religions, including Hinduism. In this development, the missionary establishment caters to the "plebeian religious needs" of the expatriate communities, most conspicuously, the facilitation of merit making. Buddhist festivals like Vesak are celebrated along with more secular occasions of the cultural calendar, such as New Year. Resident monks are often offered alms commemorative of the dead in the home country. Thus the establishment functions as a duplicator of the ritual life the expatriates left behind when they left home. It is obvious that the two projects, missionary activity among foreigners and ritual activity for the expatriates, are widely divergent, and the majority of the establishments succumb to the lure of catering to expatriate needs, which provides for community activity the missionaries themselves seem to welcome. The tension between the two projects, ritualism for expatriates and Buddhism for the natives, sometimes leads to a schism or "revolt in the temple," with the champion of the cause of Buddhism for the natives leaving the original establishment and founding a haven of his own. To do so is not only to take a step in the direction of conforming to the original purpose of the mission but also to part company with a fractious parish so reminiscent of home.

RELIGION AND ECONOMIC ACTION
An Archeology of Buddhist Ethics

Throughout this work we have seen, in the resurgent Buddhism of the twentieth century, a connection between religion and economics, ethics and enterprise, often made not just explicit but the predominant theme of the exhortations and activities of the leaders, in particular Dharmapala and the soldiers and hero-giants of his immediate army, a connection well expressed in the conception ubhayalokartha, "the gaining of both worlds." As illustrated briefly in the introduction to this work, we also saw the same connection expressed as the affinity between urban wealth and reformist religion in resurgent Hinduism.

The most comprehensive sociological articulation of this relation is in Max Weber. In Weber's work we see it expressed in two forms. First, there is the well-known thesis that capitalism arose, via a series of functional links, from Calvinism's practical impulses for action. Second, in Weber's general sociology, a connection is made between wealth and its justification. As Weber puts it, people who are fortunate are not emotionally satisfied unless they feel their good fortune is deserved. Thus good fortune wants to be legitimate fortune, and religion provides a "theodicy of good fortune" for the fortunate.[5] Upon close observation, these two are only two different expressions of the same idea. Wealth is a sign of grace, thus the relentless work that produces wealth is also a relentless search for an inner feeling of a state of grace, which automatically justifies wealth. Though not the same as in the Protestant case, the Hindu-Buddhist karma theory does have some similarity to this in so far as it is, among other things, an explanation of good fortune.

In his determination of the practical impulses for action that religious ideas generate, Weber singled out Buddhism as the typological nemesis of the post-Lutheran reformed sects that he considered to represent "inner-worldly asceticism," labeling Buddhism an "other-worldly mysticism." Thus in his classification of the crucial carrier strata for the world religions, he identified Buddhism with "contemplative, mendicant monks, who rejected the world and, having no homes, migrated."[6] In Weber's model these "intellectually schooled mendicant monks" pursued the goal of salvation with absolute single-mindedness, "abolishing without consideration all holy means which had nothing to with it."[7] All their time and efforts were directed at "this and only this goal."[8] I have argued above that this picture of Buddhism is an idealization that represents more the needs of Weber's typology than a typification of the reality of early Buddhism.

5. Max Weber, "The Social Psychology of World Religions," in *Max Weber: Essays in Sociology*, ed. Gerth and Mills, 271.

6. Ibid., 269.

7. Weber, *Sociology of Religion*, 206.

8. Ibid.

Weber was well aware of Buddhism's urban affinity. In contrast to the rural surroundings of cattle and pasture that characterized the environment of Brahmanical teachers and schools, Weber associated early Buddhism with urban palaces and elephant-riding kings.[9] Thus it is curious that Weber placed so little emphasis on Buddhism's urban lay clientele, which he knew was commercially based and affluent. Whereas in terms of the Weberian scheme, we can expect such a stratum to be conspicuously associated with ethical conduct and largely uninterested or distrustful of ritual and cultic activity, Weber considered it logically impossible that "an ethic of active workaday life"[10] could emerge in Buddhism, and he considered the Buddhists' own attempt to theoretically reconcile morality with active life in the world to be "spiritual sophistry."[11] Instead, his conclusion was that the laity's Buddhism would be a "sacramental, hagiolatrous, idolatrous, or logolatrous ritualistic religion."[12] The distinction was absolute: Buddhism represented a duality that consisted, on the one hand, of the monkhood on which was concentrated all rationality, morality, ethical stature, and perfect goal-orientation, and, on the other, of an irrational, amoral laity immersed in a world of magic and mundaneity, and living a life of loose or diffuse goal orientations. This devaluation of the laity, I contend, is more an extension of Weber's typological needs than a reasonable typification of the reality. When we descend from this typological world to the real world of religion and economic action, we are able to look at these phenomena from different perspectives. Empirically, both in "ancient Buddhism" and in its historical evolution, the distinction between a rational, deritualized, ethical Buddhism and an irrational, ritualistic, amoral Buddhism corresponds less with monk and layman respectively than with various other possible typifiable variables, for example, urban/rural, commercial/agricultural, and merchant-banker-artisan/peasant, and so forth.

The historian Romila Thapar has posited an entirely different explanation of early Buddhism's relation to wealth and economic activity.[13] In her analysis, basic to Indian religions is the distinction between the householder and the renouncer. In Brahmanism, two categories of people, Srotriya Brahman and the guest, were always expected to be able to draw on the support of the householder, who is thus accorded an important place in this "prestation economy." Buddhism gives even greater importance to the householder than

9. Ibid., 205.

10. Ibid., 217.

11. Ibid.

12. Ibid., 218.

13. Romila Thapar, "The Householder and the Renouncer," *Contributions to Indian Sociology* 15, nos. 1 and 2 (Jan-Dec 1981): 283–84.

this scheme does. Monk and householder are more sharply contrasted in the two categories, bhikkhu and upasaka. We already have here an inclusion of the layman that is absent in Weber's formulation. The householder is the source of dana, the gift-giving that maintains the Sangha, the community of bhikkhus, which, as an institutionalized body of renouncers, is more dependent on the laity than is the amorphous and haphazard collection of individual renouncers in the Brahmanic religion. The categories bhikkhu and upasaka, which are thus more clear-cut than the renouncer and householder in Brahmanism, both complement and are a counterweight to each other. The householder (upasaka) provides not only dana but also recruits to the celibate Sangha. Thus, in this interpretation, the fact of the monk's renunciation of economic and other forms of worldly activity, rather than making a spiritual outcast of the layman as Weber imagines, elevates him to partnership with the monk in a common existential ecology, biology, and spiritual culture.

Since the Sangha's existence, as just mentioned, is dependent on the householder, supporting the Sangha becomes his most important religious role, which makes it his prime duty to ensure that he had access to wealth at all times. In the "prestation economy" of Brahmanism, wealth was destroyed in sacrificial rituals,[14] but since the support of the monks required surpluses, the Buddhists needed a system that multiplied rather than destroyed wealth. The most rational way to ensure a surplus was sustained economic activity through hard work coupled with minimal consumption.[15]

14. Later, in medieval Hinduism, under Buddhist influence, the sacrifice was replaced by donations (*mahadana*) especially by the royalty and the aristocracy. See Ronald Inden, "The Ceremony of the Great Gift (Mahadana): Structure and Historical Context in Indian Ritual and Society," *Asie du Sud, Traditions et changements* (Paris: Centre nationale de la recherche scientifique, 1979), 131–36.

15. While there are the well known sutras *Sigalovada, Mangala, Parabhava, Vyaghrapadya, Vasala,* and *Veludvara,* and the conception of Sevenfold Noble Wealth (*Saptarya dhanaya*) that have a bearing on this, the best example for advocating minimal consumption is the *Aryavamsa sutra.* This sutra was extremely popular in early and medieval Sri Lanka and was the focus of an elaborate festival. The *Aryavamsa sutra's* advocacy of minimal consumption fits in perfectly with the ancient Indian Buddhist scene. The association between minimal consumption and Buddhist devotion may well have continued throughout the ancient and medieval periods in Sri Lanka. But the elaborateness of the Aryavamsa festival and the extent of its patronage seems also to suggest more or less an opposite meaning: the possibility that the festival represents a routinization where popular belief transformed it into a high potency merit-making ceremony like the rainy season observance (*vassa*) with which it sometimes seems to have been associated. See Walpola Rahula, *History,* 268–73; and idem, "The Significance of 'Aryavamsa,'" *University of Ceylon Review* 1, no. 1 (1953): 59–67. It is no accident that the *Aryavamsa sutra,* nearly forgotten for centuries, was published in Colombo along with its Pali commentary and an old Sinhala gloss (*sanne*) in 1898, at the dawn of the "Buddhist reformation" we are concerned with, when other sutras that might be considered consonant with economic enterprise, such as the *Vyaghrapadya,* were also reprinted and became popular. It is interesting to note that these were published not only in Pali and Sinhala but also English; see, for example, the translation of the *Sigalovada* and *Vyaghrapadya* sutras by D. J. Subasingha in 1908 (Madras: Minerva Press). This work was prefaced by three laudatory "opinions," by Tibbotuvave Siddhatta, the Mahanayaka of Malvatta, Hikkaduve Sumangala, Founder and Principal of Vidyo-

This can be reached only by means of a code of strict conduct conducive to productivity and austerity. Stated differently, we have here an unmistakable prescription for an ethic that has remarkable resemblances to the Puritanism that Weber derived from the Calvinism. Thus, contrary to Weber's understanding, ancient Buddhism is well equipped with imperatives for action, and indeed compendia for behavior (*Sigalovada, Vyaghrapdya,* and other sutras) that are more the outcome than causation of these imperatives.

Further, this allows us to look at the prescriptions for the laity in ancient Buddhism in a different light from that of Weber, to whom it is an "insufficiency ethic of the weak." The problem here is that Weber looked at the householder from the religious/spiritual point of view that was demanded by his paradigm. We must instead, if we are interested in the empirical variables as they intertwined in reality, look at the laity not from a religious/spiritual point of view but as the mundane aspect of the Sangha. When viewed in this perspective, the ethic of the "weak" (i.e., laity) is actually quite sufficient, and constitutes a comprehensive ethical guide to productive social and economic conduct, yet within a style of life that is strictly limited and even abnegating, like the lifestyle that Dharmapala envisaged in his utopia and that Kalukondayave characterized as ubhayalokartha, the gaining of both worlds. It is a style of life that complements that of the Sangha, thus making the Sangha and laity—a twofold division made into a fourfold one with the introduction of gender—an integrated social, economic, moral, and spiritual whole.

Among the textual guides to this code of conduct are the *Mangala, Parabhava, Sigalovada* and *Vyaghrapadya* sutras. That they were invented in the first place is a clear indication of the integral nature of the laity to Buddhism, and their existence provides us with a further elucidation of the conception of Buddhism as consisting not just of the monks and nuns but also of laymen and laywomen—that is, of bhikkhu and bhikkhuni, upasaka and upasika.

---

daya, and D. B. Jayatilaka, Buddhist leader and premier politician. Both the Principal and the Mahanayaka referred to the use of the translation in the development of "moral culture."

The ethic of minimal consumption was given new meaning by the well-known Vajirarama preacher Narada, pupil of Palane Vajiragnana, the first "hero-giant" of Dharmapala, when he used it to admonish the Colombo elites. Characteristically he dwells on wasting money on elaborate apparel, pointing out that for girls, the best dress is the "half sari," of which the detachable collar, considered "Aryan Sinhala," is of Portuguese origin. Narada called minimal consumption the "Aryavamsa pratipadava." While "Arya" here refers to "distinguished" or "premodern," its racist "Aryan" associations, especially in early twentieth century Sri Lanka, are inescapable. Narada considered the ethic of the *Aryavamsa* the only true path of social reform. See Narada, "Aryavamsa pratipadava: Samaja sodhanayata ekama margaya," *Bauddha Rajyaya* 5, no. 4 (Oct.-Dec. 1958): 3, 18. For a descriptive anthology of the primary sutras that constitute the Buddhist lay ethic, see Valigepola Vimalasara, *Bauddha Samajaya* (Colombo: Gunasena, 1967).

That certain strata under certain conditions find these sutras attractive and suitable bases for social and economic action is illustrated in their popularity in early twentieth century Sri Lanka, as we saw above in chapter 1. At that time in the Sri Lankan scene, urban Buddhist groups were groping for a guide to social and economic conduct that was rewarding to them in terms not only of profit but of rationality, respectability, and legitimacy in the dominant and critical presence of a colonial regime and a powerful reformed Christianity, both of which they were trying to impress. For these enterprising groups, the icing on the cake of such a guide was the possibility of a guarantee for a good other world, this world being well taken care of already by an ethic of production coupled with nonconsumption. The concept of ubhayalokartha provided that icing. This is a strong social-psychological reason for the growth of a code of ethics that would apply to both their personal and business lives.

Under these ethical and rational circumstances, this Buddhist class, while valuing Buddhism for many reasons including its conferment on them of an ethically and rationally based identity, nurtured an inner discipline that held in check the impulse for narrow ethno-religious hegemony and exclusivism, by placing priority on the economic. Among the pillars of this class were the heroes of Buddhist capitalism in the late nineteenth and early twentieth centuries. A narrow Sinhala-Buddhist exclusivist ideology could not have arisen in the bosom of this class. But this class did not exist in a vacuum: it had to confront and reckon with the rising tide of a nationalist ideology much narrower than its own and championed by the indigenous literati. It was Dharmapala who bridged the gap between these two classes, the Buddhist capitalist aristocracy and the economically unmusical and plebeian literati. In that process of confrontation and reckoning with the nationalist ideology of the literati, the ethical base of the Buddhist capitalist class suffered dilution, which jeopardized the priority it accorded the economic over the ideological. With its ethical base thus weakened, this class eventually allowed itself to be largely conquered by the ideologies of ethno-religious hegemony.

Considering the parallels I have drawn between Protestantism and early Buddhism, I must raise the question, was it this early Buddhism that Dharmapala wanted to revive, as he claimed, or was he trying to invent a rational modern Buddhism on the basis of the Protestant influences that molded his early life, as I have by and large suggested in the pages above and as is generally accepted by most sociologists and anthropologists? I think the answer is both. As we know, Dharmapala himself says that he learned to do everything the Reformed Church way, and certainly some of the rules of conduct he promulgated for his ideal society as "Buddhist" clearly illustrate this, as do

many other facets of his life and work. But in the work of his soldiers, especially Kalukondayave and Hendiyagala, we see a more successful attempt to
relate the advocated behavior patterns to textual Buddhism. The influences
of Dharmapalite Buddhism and of "ancient Buddhism" on Dharmapala's soldiers are variable. For our central concern, however, namely, the definition
of a new role for the monk and its consequences, it is immaterial whether
Dharmapala's Buddhism and the patterns he envisaged as the ingredients of
his utopia were derived from "ancient Buddhism" or some newly constructed "Protestant" Buddhism.

The more important issue is the question of generalization. Whereas in the
case of Protestant Christianity the rationalization of life was generalized to the
social order, in the Buddhist case it did not. I have suggested an explanation of
why it did not: the absence in Buddhism of the equivalent of eternal damnation, which in the post-Lutheran sects apparently acted as the engine of motivation to relentless work and austerity. It appears that wherever there is some
leniency, as there is in the theory of samsara in which the sufferings of hell however tortuous are finite, humans are willing to enjoy sloth and the pleasures of
the flesh, commit deadly sins, and take the chance that paying for these could
be postponed by means of merit generating acts, and perhaps cancelled by
the latter, as it seems to be increasingly believed in Sri Lanka, especially in
the post-1977, post-"open economy" era. It is then no surprise that merit
making rituals enjoy a supreme place in Sri Lankan Buddhism, and monks
are still most valued for their ritual role rather than for any social service
they allegedly render, or as some divinized force that guards and guides the
nation as suggested in their self-representation as "guardian deities."

I have criticized Weber's formulation of ancient Buddhism, but in fairness
to Weber, we must remind ourselves of the fact that, while his ideal typical
Sangha was rational in an otherworldly way, he was well aware that the real
Sangha was a worldly institution and that the Buddhist monasteries were far
from steeped in poverty, as he makes clear in his account of the transformation of Buddhism.[16] In particular, he was aware of the potential the monastery had for accumulating wealth, which in some cultures such as Sri Lanka,
led to what he calls "monastic landlordism." In fact, Buddhist monastic
wealth could well be the first instance of the empirical paradox that sparked
his imagination in the investigations that ultimately led him to posit the hy-
pothesis for which his sociology is most widely known.[17]

16. Weber, *Religion of India,* chap. 7, 233–56.
17. As much was suggested to me by one of the best-known Weberian scholars, Reinhardt Bendix,
in a conversation in Chicago in 1972. Weber had certainly noticed, along with their architectural
achievements, the wealth of the Tibetan monasteries. See Bendix, *Max Weber: An Intellectual Portrait*
(New York: Anchor Books, 1960; rpt. 1962), 316.

INDEX